COURTS WITHOUT BORDERS

Courts without Borders is the first book to examine the politics of judicial extraterritoriality, with a focus on the world's chief practitioner: the United States. For much of the post-World War II era, the United States has been a frequent yet selective regulator of activities outside its territory, and U.S. federal courts are often on the front line in deciding the extraterritorial reach of U.S. law. At stake in these jurisdiction battles is the ability to bring the regulatory power of the United States to bear on transnational disputes in ways that other states frequently dislike both in principle and in practice. This volume proposes a general theory of domestic court behavior to explain variation in extraterritorial enforcement of U.S. law, emphasizing how the strategic behavior of private actors is important to mobilizing courts and in directing their activities.

Tonya L. Putnam is Associate Professor of Political Science at Columbia University, a lawyer with experience in international public law litigation, and a member of the California State Bar.

COURTS WITHOUT BORDERS

Law, Politics, and U.S. Extraterritoriality

TONYA L. PUTNAM
Columbia University

CAMBRIDGE
UNIVERSITY PRESS

CAMBRIDGE
UNIVERSITY PRESS

One Liberty Plaza, 20th Floor, New York NY 10006, USA

Cambridge University Press is part of the University of Cambridge.

It furthers the University's mission by disseminating knowledge in the pursuit of education, learning and research at the highest international levels of excellence.

www.cambridge.org
Information on this title: www.cambridge.org/9781107137097

First published 2016

A catalogue record for this publication is available from the British Library

Library of Congress Cataloging-in-Publication Data
Putnam, Tonya L. (Tonya Lee), author.
Courts without borders : law, politics, and U.S. extraterritoriality / Tonya L. Putnam.
New York : Cambridge University Press, 2016.
LCCN 2016017596 | ISBN 9781107137097 (hardback)
LCSH: Conflict of laws – Jurisdiction – United States. | Exterritoriality. | Courts – United States. | Effectiveness and validity of law – United States. | United States – Foreign relations – Law and legislation. | BISAC: LAW / International.
LCC KF413.J87 P88 2016 | DDC 347.73/012–dc23
LC record available at https://lccn.loc.gov/2016017596

ISBN 978-1-107-13709-7 Hardback

CONTENTS

FIGURES

TABLES

ACKNOWLEDGMENTS

In March 1999, Namibia's legal team in the Kasikili/Sedudu Island Dispute, of which I was extremely privileged to have been a member, had just concluded three weeks of Oral Arguments before the International Court of Justice in The Hague. Over celebratory drinks the team's leader, Abram Chayes – an amazing international lawyer, Harvard Law Professor, and mentor – posed the question of what I should choose as my Ph.D. dissertation topic to the Namibian official overseeing our efforts, Dr. Albert Kawana (who would soon thereafter become Namibia's Minister of Justice). Without much hesitation, Dr. Kawana responded that it would be useful for the governments of small states to understand better when the United States is likely to insist that others follow its laws, and when it was unlikely to do so. This prompted a lively discussion. Two hours and two (or maybe three) manhattans later, I was convinced that extraterritoriality was an area rich with international political as well as legal questions, and I have never looked back.

Sadly, Abe Chayes passed away a little more than a year after that conversation. As a result, I was not able to draw nearly as much as I would have liked to from his deep knowledge and experience of U.S. political and legal practice specifically in these matters. Even so, this project owes an immense debt to Abe and his scholarship. Abe's work on international legal process were what first drew me to international law as an area of research interest. And helped to cinch my decision to go to law school. His work with Antonia Handler Chayes on the politics of legal compliance remains a key touchstone for most of my research and teaching. My experiences working with Abe and Toni on projects related to international conflict resolution, and later as a participant in international public law litigation, provided me with a priceless education in how contestation over law and legal rules helps to structure international politics and political interactions. For this I will remain forever grateful.

This project has taken many years to complete, and, consequently, I owe thanks to many institutions and individuals for helping me to bring it to fruition.

Parts of the book have been supported by funding and sponsorship from the Department of Political Science at Stanford University, the Center for International Security and Cooperation at Stanford, the Niehaus Center for Globalization and Governance at Princeton University, and the Department of Political Science at Columbia University. The book has likewise benefitted immensely from feedback provided by seminar audiences at each of these institutions.

For additional invitations to present work related to this book, I thank Duke University; University of California, Berkeley; University of California, Los Angeles; University of Chicago; University of Pennsylvania; University of Wisconsin–Madison; and the Beasley School of Law at Temple University. I also want to thank the American Political Science Association, the American Society of International Law, the International Studies Association, and the Law and Society Association for the intermediate deadlines and opportunities for feedback they have provided over the years.

Several colleagues in the Department of Political Science at Columbia University have offered invaluable inputs at many points in this volume's development. Jack Snyder and Jeffrey Lax have been especially generous with their time and encouragement. Jeff also has been nothing short of princely with his liquor cabinet, and with his willingness to play backgammon at odd hours. (Both proved exceptionally helpful to my "process.") Also deserving of special thanks are Robert Jervis, Tanisha Fazal, Turkuler Isiksel, and Pablo Pinto. Kate Cronin Furman and Jacob Kopas have likewise been fabulous sounding boards for ideas, as well as occasional editors and code testers.

Numerous other individuals have provided helpful guidance and feedback along the way. They include Karen Alter, Mark Axelrod, Dan Bodansky, Anu Bradford, Dana Burde, Tim Buthe, Harlan Cohen, Marc Copelovitch, Mariano Florentino Cuellar, Christina Davis, Alexander Downes, Erik Gartzke, Judith Goldstein, Emilie Hafner Burton, Raymond Hicks, Duncan Hollis, Suzanne Katzenstein, Robert Keohane, Moonhawk Kim, Stephan Krasner, Helen Kinsella, Edward Mansfield, Lisa Martin, Ralf Michaels, Helen Milner, Abe Newman, Austin Parrish, Jon Pevehouse, Katharina Pistor, Netihorn Pradisarn, Kal Raustiala, Thania Sanchez, Todd Sechser, Kim Lane Sheppele, David

A. Singer, Paul Stephan, Michael Tomz, Leslie Vinjamuri, Erik Voeten, Allen Weiner, and Chris Whytock.

I owe special thanks to Susan Sell and Beth Simmons for their timely and extremely useful comments on late drafts of selected chapters; to my anonymous reviewers at Cambridge University Press; and to Teresa Lawson for her outside editorial contributions. I also want to extend particular thanks to Lynn Eden, Page Fortna, and Kelly Greenhill for being consistent friends, cheerleaders, and hard-nosed but constructive critics. I look up to each of you as models of scholars who are deeply engaged in your own work, but able to remain intellectually omnivorous, and unfailingly generous to others.

And finally, thanks to my family: Mor, Elai, and Kai. In part because of you, this book took a while. But, it's also in part because of you that it was worth doing.

1

Courts without borders

Many foreign governments and transnational actors consider the United States a "judicial bully."[1] Time and again on issues ranging from international cartel activity to torture, U.S. courts have asserted the primacy of U.S. law over the legal authority of foreign states within their own territories and in areas of shared sovereignty, such as the high seas and outer space. This book is about the politics and law of judicial extraterritoriality – the practice of domestic courts unilaterally applying domestic laws to conduct and persons outside a state's borders – and how it influences processes of international rulemaking and enforcement. Its focus is the world's foremost practitioner of judicial extraterritoriality: the United States.

For much of the post-World War II era, the United States has been a frequent though selective regulator of activities outside its territory. Among U.S. institutions, the federal courts often have been on the front line in battles over the extraterritorial reach of U.S. law – enabling it in some instances and restricting it in others.

It may strike some readers as odd to consider domestic courts as consequential actors in international politics. However, when a U.S. court decides to apply U.S. law to disputes with an extraterritorial dimension – for example, to protect the rights of U.S. trademark holders or to thwart a conspiracy to defraud U.S investors – it is, in effect, bringing the regulatory power of the United States to bear in ways that determine who gets what, when, and how.[2] It follows that domestic judicial actions in the transnational sphere have political importance as well as legal importance. Accordingly, we need to understand better how and why U.S. courts behave as they do when presented with matters involving extraterritorial applications of U.S. law.

1 Wai (2001:248).

2 Lasswell (1936). See, for example, *Levi Strauss & Co. v. Sunrise International Trading Company* 51 F.3d 982 (11th Cir. 1995) and *Alfadda v. Fenn* 935 F.2d 475 (2d Cir. 1995).

The authority that allows courts to hear and decide legal claims is called adjudicatory jurisdiction. In liberal democracies, jurisdiction to adjudicate is typically delegated to domestic courts by domestic political bodies through constitution-making powers, or indirectly by legislation.[3]

Jurisdiction claiming among states in the international system is generally governed by customary international law.[4] Under the post-Westphalian international law of jurisdiction, the default is to assume that jurisdiction to make and apply law within territorially defined states belongs exclusively to the territorial sovereign. In transnational legal disputes, however, this default may not apply straightforwardly since, almost by definition, more than one sovereign's territory is implicated. Another common basis by which states may assert jurisdiction over disputes relies on the nationality of alleged perpetrators of legal wrongs or that of victims.[5] It takes little imagination to see that in the context of transnational activity, nationality-based claims of jurisdiction can conflict with territory-based claims.

A further complication is that the territorial principle itself embodies two potentially contradictory faces. The first ("subjective") face is the more mundane. It confers jurisdiction on sovereigns to make and enforce law to govern acts undertaken inside their own territories. The second ("objective") face allows for jurisdiction over acts that originate outside a state's borders but generate effects inside its territory.[6] It is this second "effects-based" face of territorial jurisdiction that has been at the center of the more controversial aspects of U.S. extraterritorial practice.[7]

[3] See Chapter 2 for more detailed discussion of the types of jurisdiction at issue in extraterritorial claims.

[4] Ryngaert (2008). European states have codified these rules among themselves in the 1968 Brussels Convention on Jurisdiction and the Enforcement of Judgments in Civil and Commercial Matters (now the Brussels I Regulation) and the 1988 Lugano Convention.

[5] This area of the law is most fully developed with respect to criminal jurisdiction, but the same categories are used to describe the bases of jurisdiction in transnational civil claims.

[6] Wharton (1905:71–72). Whether a state's regulation of the external conduct on the basis of effects inside its territory qualifies as "territorial" or "extraterritorial" is thus at times a matter of definitional debate. See, for example, Taylor (1979).

[7] A third and considerably less common principle of jurisdiction, known as the "protective principle," allows states to assert jurisdiction over internationally recognized criminal acts that directly threaten its security or governmental operations such as treason. A fourth principle of jurisdiction that is more frequently discussed, but rarely used, is the universality principle, which allows any sovereign to assert jurisdiction over violations of international peremptory norms – known as *jus cogens* or "compelling law," such as prohibition of genocide, slavery, or torture – regardless of where such violations occur.

The argument in brief

The research presented here is structured around two inquiries: first, what drives U.S. courts to claim jurisdiction over extraterritorial conduct, and why have they done so in some situations but not in others? Second, how has variability in U.S. judicial extraterritoriality influenced broader processes of international and transnational rulemaking and rule diffusion? The answers to these questions are important to explaining how law and international legal processes mediate political interactions among sovereign states.

The analysis mainly concerns extraterritorial applications of domestic law in the civil realm. U.S. courts have considered a wide variety of civil (non-criminal) claims involving extraterritorial conduct.[8] The willingness of U.S. courts to find and exercise jurisdiction extraterritorially has varied both over time and across issues. For example, for more than half a century, U.S. courts have been willing to enforce domestic statutes extraterritorially to disrupt international trading cartels and to protect U.S. trademarks. Likewise, for decades, U.S. courts used U.S. law to counter transnational securities fraud, to award compensation to victims of torture ordered by foreign officials, to restrict re-exports of sensitive materials and technologies, and to protect migratory bird and animal species. At the same time, U.S. courts have generally declined to exercise extraterritorial jurisdiction over product liability claims, over alleged patent violations, to secure compensation for U.S. citizens killed in foreign plane crashes, or to require extraterritorial compliance with U.S. labor and anti-pollution laws.

In most instances, the texts of the underlying U.S. laws offer no justification for these differences. Nor has U.S. extraterritoriality varied neatly by legal issue area (as indicated, for example, by different trends within intellectual property law and across different areas of environmental law). This variation also cannot be explained by looking to the presence or absence of international treaties. In short, the extraterritorial regulatory behavior of U.S. courts exhibits a puzzling empirical pattern from a legal perspective.

Adopting a more political lens, one might expect extraterritorial applications of U.S. law to be directed toward promoting U.S. legal ideals in

[8] Civil and criminal laws often differ regarding who (or what) has the legal capacity to initiate proceedings to enforce them. In the United States, only government prosecutors may bring criminal charges, although many U.S. laws allow private entities to initiate civil claims.

foreign settings, toward improving U.S. economic competitiveness, or toward safeguarding the interests of Americans abroad. Alternatively, one might expect that U.S. courts would apply U.S. law extraterritorially in response to growth in cross-border judicial communication and cooperation. As I demonstrate, however, each of these expectations is wrong.

I find, instead, that U.S. federal court behavior is more generally consistent with judges seeking to apply U.S. law to decide the disputes before them in ways that support (or at least do not undermine) the integrity or operation of U.S. law. At times this requires U.S. judges to interpret geographically ambiguous laws as having extraterritorial reach – though often it does not.

More specifically, I argue that U.S. courts have applied U.S. law extraterritorially in two types of situations. The first is when extraterritorial conduct poses a threat to the functioning of U.S. law inside U.S. territory. Threats of this type exist where limiting the reach of U.S. law to conduct inside the United States would push the regulated behavior outside U.S. borders but would not simultaneously exclude its unwanted effects. Thus, for example, a U.S. law barring companies with U.S. ties from conspiring inside U.S. territory to fix prices on commodities but not elsewhere will not shield U.S. purchasers from price distortions if those commodities are traded internationally. The foreseeable result of a decision not to apply U.S. law extraterritorially in such circumstances would be to highlight loopholes for circumventing that law, thereby undercutting the public policy the law is intended to serve. Throughout this volume, I refer to this basis of judicial extraterritoriality as the "domestic rule integrity logic."

The second situation in which U.S. courts are likely to find extraterritorial jurisdiction appropriate is when U.S. citizens and others with close U.S. ties are accused of violating a short list of rights at the core of American political identity. This list includes the rights not to be subjected to torture, extrajudicial killing and other crimes against humanity, or forced labor. In rights-based disputes, unlike those in the regulatory sphere, there is often far less international disagreement about what the law requires. Instead, the governance challenge involves finding states that are willing and able to enforce those rules transnationally. Animating this logic of U.S. extraterritoriality, therefore, is the idea that if members of the U.S. polity, or others who benefit from close associations to the United States, are permitted to violate these fundamental rights with impunity anywhere, it undermines their status as American values everywhere. I call this second basis of judicial extraterritoriality the "rights-based logic."

This argument breaks new ground in political science as well as in international law scholarship. It advances international relations theory by demonstrating how the actions and inactions of domestic courts influence whether and how U.S. legal and policy preferences are projected internationally. It also advances legal understandings of U.S. extraterritoriality by providing an empirically vetted account of why some types of domestic effects matter more than others in accounting for patterns of U.S. extraterritorial practice. My analysis also seeks throughout to explain the politics of U.S. judicial extraterritoriality without losing sight of the fact that courts and judges are first and foremost interpreters of legal rules.

Elaborating and testing a novel theory of U.S. judicial behavior to explain patterns of U.S. extraterritorial practice is only part of the task of this book, however. Equally important are my efforts to embed this theory in a broader set of claims about the international political consequences of U.S. judicial extraterritoriality.

Although the international system lacks a central lawgiver, the behavior of transnational actors is rarely subject to wild unpredictability. Instead, consistencies emerge from the self-interested, strategic behavior of transnational private actors among themselves and when interacting with the governments of states touched by their conduct.[9] Strategic maneuvering around legal obligations, along with the bets that individual transnational actors place on the likelihood that one state or another will seek to enforce its legal preferences, help to shape, from the bottom up, the transnational "rules of the game" as they are experienced by transnational actors.

U.S. court decisions on the extraterritorial applicability of U.S. law matter to several categories of actors, including most immediately to the litigating parties. Foreign governments too often have an interest in decisions that purport to expand or contract U.S. extraterritorial jurisdiction – whether the government in question welcomes extraterritorial assertions of U.S. legal authority, or whether it views them as an illegitimate, or even internationally unlawful, form of overreaching. However, the impact of U.S. court decisions on the reach of U.S. law and adjudicatory authority does not stop there.

[9] For private actors "strategic behavior" entails efforts to make oneself as well off as possible, given known features of the decision environment and what one anticipates others will do.

Wider audiences of transnational actors likewise observe U.S. courts applying U.S. law extraterritorially or opting not to do so. Where U.S. courts decide to exercise jurisdiction extraterritorially, and their decisions have costly results for those found to be violating U.S. law, this catches the attention of others engaged in similar conduct – particularly when U.S. laws are more restrictive than those of foreign states. Evidence that U.S. courts are willing to apply specific statutory or constitutional rules extraterritorially can encourage additional plaintiffs to initiate similar claims.[10] This, in turn, creates incentives for prospective defendants to adjust their behavior so as to minimize this threat.

Patterns of domestic rule following (or rule evasion) among regulated actors also shape U.S. government incentives to engage with the governments of other states on transnational issues. Where U.S. extraterritoriality has been proven effective in safeguarding the transnational interests of U.S. entities, there is often little urgency for the U.S. government to bargain with others over coordinated rules. This has long been the case, for example, with regard to antitrust policy.[11] Where, by contrast, U.S. federal courts have shown themselves unwilling or unable to protect the interests of those seeking extraterritorial application of U.S. law, the U.S. government has come under considerably more domestic pressure to reach formal agreements with other states. For example, the failure of holders of U.S.-granted patent rights and copyrights failed to convince U.S. courts in the 1960s and 1970s that those rights should be interpreted as extending extraterritorially. This helped to fuel U.S. engagement in efforts to remake international intellectual property rules during the Uruguay Round of negotiations under the General Agreement on Tariffs and Trade.[12]

In the remainder of this chapter, I first situate my argument within theories of international relations and transnational politics. Next, I briefly describe how judicial extraterritoriality relates to older forms of extraterritorial practice, some of which still persist. Thereafter, I provide a short clarification of the scope of my inquiry and an overview of the remaining chapters.

[10] U.S. ties matter here because of constitutional due process restrictions on the ability of U.S. courts to force defendants to appear before them. See Chapter 2 for additional discussion.

[11] See Chapter 4 for development of this example.

[12] See Chapter 5 for development of this example.

Judicial extraterritoriality and international relations theory

Regulating transnational activities in an international system in which legal authority is formally apportioned among territorial states is complicated. Governments often disagree over how much (or how little) to regulate. As a result, efforts among states to forge shared laws and policies at the international level frequently fail or are never attempted in the first place. Even when agreements are reached, they invariably contain ambiguities that require elaboration. Different states' officials and institutions may implement shared rules differently, or they may prefer clashing modes of enforcement. New gaps and ambiguities also may emerge as underlying circumstances change, as regulated actors engage with and attempt to alter the laws in question, and as other laws are adopted or discarded. Under these conditions, states that are able and willing to apply legal rules extraterritorially can more effectively project their preferences onto others outside their borders.

As a means of creating or maintaining transnational rules, extraterritorial applications of domestic law and jurisdiction differ markedly from top-down, government-to-government modes of bargaining.[13] Standard approaches to international rulemaking involve the representatives of governments, or specialized agencies within them, sitting down to hammer out mutually acceptable solutions to shared problems, which domestic agencies are then presumed to implement. Judicial extraterritoriality, by contrast, is characterized by direct assertions of domestic legal authority over conduct and persons outside the state, often without the prior consent or cooperation of foreign governments. These contrasting approaches meet where extraterritorial regulation (or its credible threat) starts to influence the type, content, or timing of international bargaining.

Another distinguishing feature of judicial extraterritoriality is that its utility is not limited to any particular stage of international rulemaking and rule implementation. Indeed, disputes over extraterritorial jurisdiction in U.S. courts can arise in the absence of international treaties, while states are attempting to negotiate international agreements, or as part of efforts to interpret and apply international treaties and customary law *ex post*.[14]

[13] Slaughter (2009), Newman (2008), Raustiala (2002).

[14] The case study chapters that follow explore U.S. judicial extraterritoriality in each of these contexts.

The theory and analysis in this book draw upon several foundational ideas in contemporary international relations theory. Chief among them are the importance of state power in determining winners and losers in international political and regulatory contests,[15] and the influence of mobilized domestic actors in setting government policies and preferences for international bargaining.[16] The analysis also incorporates some less common actors and themes – beginning with domestic courts and judges. Also important is the strategic behavior of actual and prospective litigants, since without active, formalized disputes U.S. courts have no opportunity to act – extraterritorially or otherwise.

The power to compel compliance with domestic law

State power matters immensely for how legal jurisdiction is defined and exercised in the international system. The aspect of "power" I am most concerned with here is the ability of a state to compel transnational actors – whether its own citizens or those of other states – to behave in ways that are consistent with the state's domestic laws and policies.[17] In general, this entails leveraging ties to private and public institutions and citizens inside the state in order to extract compliance extraterritorially.

In its position as the economic hegemon of the capitalist world in the decades following World War II, the United States has had an uncommon degree of this type of leverage. Many transnational entities have, or desire to have, ties to the United States – for access to U.S. consumer and industrial markets, investment capital, financial services, or to benefit from its technological, educational, and organizational resources. The global allure of access to the United States has resulted in the presence of large amounts of foreign-owed assets inside U.S. territory. These assets have provided U.S. courts with a domestic constitutional basis for asserting jurisdiction over foreign entities and also with a ready capacity to enforce legal judgments against unsuccessful defendants without the assistance of foreign governments.

To be sure, the power of U.S. courts to enforce U.S. law extraterritorially has never been absolute. And, even when U.S. courts have had the

[15] Krasner (1976), Keohane and Nye (1977), Drezner (2007).

[16] Milner (1997), Moravcsik (1998), Hafner-Burton (2008), Simmons (2009).

[17] Simmons (2001). Switzerland, for example, is not a powerful state under standard indices. However, it has considerable leverage to shape international banking rules because of the sizeable proportion of global private wealth served by its banking institutions.

capacity to enforce U.S. laws extraterritorially, they have not always used it or used it to the fullest extent possible. Nor is this type of power unique to the United States. Most countries' legal systems contemplate applying some domestic law to conduct outside the state's borders, particularly where doing so is unlikely to interfere with the laws of other states. For example, when a government taxes the foreign income of its residents or threatens to prosecute foreign acts of treason by its citizens, this constitutes extraterritorial regulation.[18] A few other relatively powerful states, among them Germany, the United Kingdom, France, Spain, Australia, Canada, Japan, South Korea, have also enacted domestic laws that expressly contemplate extraterritorial application in competition policy and banking.[19] The Court of Justice of the European Union likewise has issued several decisions applying EU competition law extraterritorially, and has begun doing so with growing frequency.[20]

Still, the United States has been by far the most assertive practitioner of judicial extraterritoriality in the contemporary era, particularly when it comes to claims involving the conduct of non-citizens. It is therefore essential to understand how and why U.S. courts came to have this role, how that role might now be changing, and why it matters for international politics and for international law.

Private litigants as strategic agents

Regulated actors are rarely passive recipients of attempts to limit their behavior using legal rules. This is so whether the focus is on private entities or on governmental officials. To the contrary, regulated actors can be counted upon to champion rules and procedures that they expect to benefit them and to try to circumvent or reshape those that impose unwanted costs or constraints.

Domestic legal systems vary according to how they allocate responsibility for the enforcement of regulatory and rights-based laws. The United States is unique among its economic peers in the degree to

18 Jennings (1957:150).

19 Tamura *et al.* (2005), Harding and Joshua (2003), Ahn and Kim (2005), Griffin (1999), Gerber (1983), Taylor (1979).

20 Judgment of the European Court of Justice (now CJEU) of September 27, 1988, in *A. Ahlström Osakeyhtiö and others v. Commission of the European Communities (Wood Pulp Case)*, joining cases 89, 104, 114, 116, 117 and 125 to 129/85. See also "European Court Confirms Extraterritorial Jurisdiction of EU in Antitrust Cases" *Global Investigations Review* July 13, 2015, http://globalinvestigationsreview.com/article/3440/european-court-confirms-extraterritorial-jurisdiction-eu-antitrust-cases.

which litigation functions as a mechanism of regulatory enforcement.[21] It is also unusual in the degree to which the ability to bring civil suits for alleged legal violations – including for violations of many public (regulatory) laws – is shared between private actors and public officials.[22] Many other countries rely far more on government regulators to police compliance with laws governing the economic and social policy spheres.[23] Not only may U.S. officials initiate legal proceedings against private entities (including foreign nationals), under many U.S. statutes, private plaintiffs too may file suits against other private entities and also at times against government bodies, including foreign governments or their officials. As a result, U.S. law can be projected internationally into situations that have not been previously vetted by U.S. government officials outside the judiciary.

This research thus complements and extends several recent studies that examine how non-state actors affect international governance. The means by which non-state actors can influence national and international rulemaking examined in this literature are several: Private groups lobby legislatures to pass preferred laws (or block undesirable ones). Likewise they may ask executive officials to adopt international bargaining positions that favor their interests, to join desired agreements, and to avoid others.[24] Advocacy groups gather and disseminate information and organize public support to pressure elected officials.[25] Corporations and industry associations create institutions for informal self-regulation in order to preempt creation of formally binding laws.[26] Government agencies delegate the task of defining standards to private

[21] Smith (2000), Krisch (2005), Michaels (2005).

[22] Farhang (2008), Mattei and Lena (2001). Many federal statutes expressly give private entities a right to sue, and U.S. courts also have been willing to imply private rights of action in cases of government under-enforcement of statutory rules. However, not every situation where U.S. courts have acted extraterritorially involves private rights of action, and not every area where there are private rights of action involves extraterritoriality. For example, in the U.S. legal system only the government may bring criminal charges. And, in the civil realm, some statutes with clear extraterritorial applicability, for example, the 1977 Foreign Corrupt Practices Act (15 U.S.C. §§ 78dd–1, *et seq.*), restrict initiation of claims to government agents.

[23] Greve (1989). Legal systems in European states have long allowed private suits to address nominally "private" harms associated with violations of public law. Examples include compensatory claims for specific damages or for unjust enrichment related to violations of competition rules. In general, however, these suits are narrowly circumscribed and thus not readily comparable to U.S.-style private rights of action.

[24] See Singer (2007), Sell (2003), Milner (1997), Moravcsik (1998), and Legro (1996).

[25] Keck and Sikkink (1998).

[26] See Culter *et al.* (2001).

bodies (e.g. international best practices or product specifications) or adopt standards that have been developed and tested in the private sphere.[27] Notable in each of these examples, however, is that private-sector inputs are distinct from public acts.

Judicial extraterritoriality is, by contrast, a thoroughly hybrid means of enacting law and policy in that it fuses elements of public and private.[28] What makes it "hybrid" is worth spelling out carefully. Domestic courts are state institutions. Once a court is formally seized of a legal dispute involving the conduct of private actors, the court's involvement transforms the dispute and its outcome into a public matter. This is so even if the public policy at issue is uncontroversial – for example, underscoring the need to guarantee the enforceability of private contracts. Moreover, unlike Congress and executive agencies, which have discretion to ignore individual complaints, lower courts in the United States must respond when asked to do so by litigants – even if only to dismiss claims on grounds of legal or procedural flaws. U.S. courts are thus not only sporadic international actors but also simultaneously sites of strategic activity for litigants.

The extraterritorial assertiveness of U.S. courts is further enabled by what is, from a comparative perspective, an exceptionally unilateralist approach to assessing the prescriptive reach of U.S. laws.[29] The U.S. approach to deciding whether a U.S. statute applies extraterritorially begins from the premise that Congress, as the supreme legislative authority for the United States, can make laws that apply extraterritorially if it chooses, even if those laws conflict with international law or the laws of other countries. As institutions tasked with interpreting and applying U.S. statutory and constitutional law to decide disputes, U.S. courts thus have authority to apply U.S. laws extraterritorially when doing so is consistent with the law's intent. But, because most U.S. statutes are silent as to their geographic reach, U.S. judges often have some interpretative leeway in making these determinations – albeit limited by the U.S. constitutional framework of checks and balances among branches along with any accumulated legal doctrine. Notably, the prospect that other states may also want to exercise jurisdiction over the dispute need not enter into the analysis.

[27] See Mattli and Büthe (2005), Büthe and Mattli (2010), and Drezner (2007).
[28] Putnam (2009).
[29] Michaels (2005).

How transnational actors that fear being caught within the net of U.S. jurisdiction respond – with attempts to comply with U.S. laws, to undercut or avoid them, or to expand their applicability to others – is thus integral to understanding the broader effects of judicial extraterritoriality. Indeed, the self-interested choices of individual actors about which states' rules to use when calibrating their own transnational behavior, viewed in aggregate, help to structure the legal environments in which they and other transnational actors operate. These choices also shape the strategic environments in which governments bargain with others over new legal rules, or to improve enforcement of existing rules.

Judicial extraterritoriality as a source of international friction

Foreign governments often find U.S. judicial extraterritoriality, like other forms of U.S. unilateralism, upsetting in principle and in practice. This is especially so where U.S. law conflicts with the foreign laws being superseded.[30] In countries where the enforcement of public law is largely a task of public regulators, issues of overlapping jurisdiction in transnational disputes are generally resolved through consultation among officials who share an interest in avoiding international legal and political clashes. There is far less scope for this type of cooperation when private entities are the initiators of regulatory enforcement. Not surprisingly, therefore, U.S. extraterritoriality has at times proven to be a source of international friction.

Ambiguity about which countries' laws will be applied to transnational conduct can be quite vexing for regulated actors, and for their governments, particularly when the alternatives come with very different expected costs. For example, U.S. antitrust law prohibits corporate tying arrangements that link the purchase of one product (e.g. a computer) to an obligation to purchase another (e.g. an operating system). Other countries' laws and policies sometimes permit these arrangements as a component in a broader set of economic and industrial policies. If U.S. consumer prices are negatively affected by foreign tying activities, and the companies involved have U.S. connections, the potential exists for a lawsuit to arise. Because U.S. courts almost never apply foreign competition laws, and foreign courts rarely if ever apply U.S. antitrust laws, the determination

[30] Maier (1983).

of which forum (or forums) claim jurisdiction is thus critical to the likely outcome.[31]

Foreign governments may choose to express their ire over U.S. judicial extraterritoriality in a number of ways. Direct means for doing so include diplomatic channels or intervening in U.S. suits as *amici curiae* ("friends of the court").[32] Foreign governments may also try indirect means to thwart unwanted exercises of U.S. extraterritorial jurisdiction. They may, for example, allow or even encourage parallel litigation in their own courts to create conflicting rulings. Or they may refuse to cooperate in the enforcement of U.S. court awards involving extraterritorial claims. Several foreign governments in the 1980s, among them those of the United Kingdom and Australia, went so far as to adopt legislation prohibiting "voluntary" domestic compliance with extraterritorial discovery orders (orders to produce evidence pursuant to U.S. judicial proceedings). They also budgeted funds to pay resulting contempt fines levied by U.S. courts.[33]

Foreign government efforts to dissuade U.S. courts from exercising jurisdiction extraterritorially have often failed to produce the desired results. This is because U.S. courts have no formal obligation to take the opinions of foreign governments into account when interpreting U.S. law. Even in situations where the U.S. State Department or other executive agency has openly concurred with a protesting government, this is no guarantee that a U.S. court will not decide that extraterritorial jurisdiction exists and that it should be exercised.

This is not to imply, however, that U.S. courts are unconcerned with the foreign affairs implications of U.S. judicial extraterritoriality or that such considerations never affect their decisions on jurisdictional questions. To the contrary, domestic constitutional imperatives, international legal obligations, and considerations of judicial economy each at times prompt U.S. courts to forego the exercise of extraterritorial jurisdiction.

Concern with the foreign affairs implications of U.S. judicial extraterritoriality is, not surprisingly, at its greatest when it comes to respecting the separation of powers under the U.S. Constitution. Where exercising jurisdiction over a legal claim with an extraterritorial dimension, for example, threatens to compromise U.S. national security or to undercut ongoing political initiatives with foreign governments,

31 Ponsoldt and David (2006).

32 See Small (1987) for an overview.

33 Pettit and Styles (1982).

U.S. courts will sometimes decline to exercise jurisdiction on grounds that a dispute turns on a "political" question.[34] As hinted above, U.S. federal courts have not in every instance agreed with other branches of the U.S. government as to when circumstances requiring this type of deference are present.[35]

To avoid clashes with foreign governments on jurisdictional matters, U.S. federal judges have developed several doctrinal tools that allow them to abstain from deciding extraterritorial claims. These tools include doctrines of international comity (voluntary deference to foreign sovereigns), "acts of state" (abstention based on an unwillingness to pass legal judgment on the act of a foreign government on a matter within its own territory), and determinations that the dispute would be more properly decided in another national forum (*forum non conveniens*).

My argument expects that *forum non conveniens* will be used mainly in situations where neither the domestic integrity of U.S. law nor an alleged violation of a basic right is at issue. Conversely, doctrines of deference to foreign sovereigns will be most relevant when the integrity of domestic law or a basic right is at issue, precisely because the expectation in these situations is that a U.S. court otherwise would choose to exercise jurisdiction.

Scope of the inquiry

Judicial extraterritoriality is distinguishable in important respects from other, more generally familiar tools by which the U.S. government attempts to impose its preferences abroad, such as decisions to use military force or to impose economic sanctions.[36] While military force and economic statecraft obviously have extraterritorial consequences and are established and administered (in liberal democracies at least) using laws passed at the domestic level, their primary purpose is to influence

[34] See, for example, *Greenham Women Against Cruise Missiles v. Reagan* 591 F.Supp. 1332 (S.D.N.Y. 1982) (dismissing suit to prevent deployment of U.S. cruise missiles near London on political question grounds), and *Belk v. United States* 858 F.2d 706 (Fed Cir. 1988) (declining to exercise jurisdiction over claim against the U.S. government that it acted unconstitutionally in making an agreement with Iran to extinguish legal claims by former American hostages).

[35] Franck (1992). See Chapter 2 for further discussion and examples.

[36] U.S. courts indirectly oversee the U.S. Treasury Department's use of civil and criminal penalties to enforce foreign sanctions (Clark 1999:65, Ortblad 2008).

the political actions of other governments.[37] The effects of sanctions on private actors and non-targeted foreign governments acting in commercial (non-sovereign)[38] capacities, although often non-trivial, are incidental to the main policy goal.[39] This inquiry, by contrast, is primarily concerned with domestic laws and policies that are directed, first and foremost, at regulating the transnational behavior of private actors in their interactions with the United States and its citizens. Although the tools of military and economic statecraft can operate in parallel with the modes of judicial extraterritoriality examined here, the two are not the same, and at times they can be in tension.

Second, with the forms of extraterritorial regulation that are the subject of this study, entities may be called to account for conduct undertaken wholly or partially outside the United States on the basis of harm to the integrity or operation of U.S. laws inside the United States. This differs markedly from non-directed forms of domestic legal spillover. For example, denial of entry at the border is a common penalty for failing to adhere to a state's rules in trade, finance, or immigration. While information that a denial of entry is likely may prompt outside actors to alter their upstream behavior to take a target state's rules in account (as with the so-called California effect for automobile emissions), this, strictly speaking, involves territorial regulation, since it is only the attempt to gain access that triggers a penalty.[40]

Third, this is not a study of non-judicial arbitration. A great deal of formalized private dispute resolution occurs outside of courts in alternative institutions such as the International Center for the Settlement of Investment Disputes (ICSID), the International Chamber of Commerce (ICC), and the Mediation Centre at the World Intellectual Property Organization (WIPO). These activities undoubtedly also help to structure private interactions in the transnational sphere. However, the largely contractual arrangements that provide the bulk of the disputes handled by these institutions are crafted against the backdrop of state- or treaty-

[37] Baldwin (1985). Examples include the 1996 Cuban Liberty and Democratic Solidarity (Helms-Burton) Act prohibiting U.S. and foreign entities from trading with Cuba and state sanctions against Libya, Iran, Syria, and North Korea. During the Cold War, the United States also restricted trade with Soviet-aligned states (Rodman 2001).

[38] Fox (1941).

[39] U.S. government decisions to impose sanctions or declare armed hostilities have important effects on the permissible scope of private activities. Often such restrictions are enforceable using criminal fines administered by executive agencies such as the U.S. Office of Foreign Assets Control.

[40] Vogel (1997).

based public law, often expressly so in that they frequently contain provisions for choice of law and choice of venue. Consequently, this type of private enforcement takes place in the shadow of traditional state remedies. Arbitral institutions thus are likewise observers and consumers of the substantive and jurisdictional legal rules maintained by states capable of intervening in, and providing more traditional court venues for, dispute resolution among private actors.[41]

Finally, this book seeks to identify and account for a central tendency in U.S. court behavior across a broad spectrum of legal issue areas. It does not explain every twist and turn in the development of judicial doctrine around extraterritoriality. The extraterritorial jurisdictional contests at the heart of this research frequently involve highly technical issues of prescriptive (legislative) authority, adjudicatory competence, constitutional due process, choice of law, and statutory interpretation. I identify these features when they arise and explain their influence on the behavior of courts and litigants. However, I make no attempt to treat these topics comprehensively in the style of a legal treatise.

The origins of judicial extraterritoriality

Contemporary judicial extraterritoriality is related to, but in important respects distinct from, earlier forms and practices of extraterritoriality. Among the practices to which the label "extraterritoriality" is applied are rights and privileges conventionally extended to embassy and consular grounds, those claimed as privilege of nineteenth-century colonial conquest, and those pertaining to military forces stationed in foreign countries. Likewise, the jurisdictional fictions that attach to ships in international waters and to airplanes in international airspace have an extraterritorial flavor. A brief description of each of these types of extraterritoriality is useful for tracing the origins of judicial extraterritoriality as practiced by domestic courts, and for further defining the focus of this study.

Extraterritoriality as a legal fiction

The concept of extraterritoriality makes sense only in reference to "territoriality" – an idea traceable in its broad usage to the emergence of the

[41] Cutler (2003:167–168), Mnookin and Kornhauser (1979).

nation-state as a dominant form of political organization in fifteenth-century Europe. Territoriality transformed legal jurisdiction from an attribute primarily associated with personal loyalty to sovereigns and religious authorities into a spatially contingent concept.[42] Although challenged from many directions, territoriality functions even today as the baseline from which states claim jurisdiction over conduct under international law. At the same time, jurisdictional conflicts are an inevitable feature of an international system with multiple territorial sovereigns, in which entities interact across international borders.[43] The legal history of the international state system has been, in important respects, defined by efforts to manage, or minimize, such conflicts.

For nearly four centuries, strict territorial limitations on national law were the norm in international legal doctrines shared by European powers. So entrenched was the notion of territorially limited jurisdiction in medieval and early modern England that when making exceptions to this principle, courts were more free to bend the rules of geography than the rules of jurisdiction. Thus, in order to bring suit on an issue involving conduct "outside the realm," a plaintiff would include as part of his pleadings a declaration that the foreign locus of the dispute was actually in England. For example, the city of Hamburg might be declared to be a section of London – "to-wit, in London in the parish of St. Mary-le-Bow in the Ward of Cheap" – or Harfleur in France would be discussed as if it were in the English county of Kent. Courts actively encouraged use of these legal fictions in order to provide legal remedies in transnational disputes without formally encroaching upon the authority of foreign sovereigns.[44]

The term "extraterritoriality" (sometimes also called "exterritoriality") was coined by Hugo Grotius in the seventeenth century to describe the treatment of ambassadors as *quasi extra territorium* (as if outside the territory). However, the concept of immunity for ambassadors and envoys located temporarily in another sovereign's territory predated Grotius by many centuries.[45] The link between ambassadorial immunity and territorial exception was forged only after it became common for states to establish permanent embassies in foreign lands, thereby

[42] Zimmerman (1992:162), Raustiala (2009).

[43] Goldsmith (1998:1199–2000). Practical questions about the limits of territorial sovereigns' laws arose as early as the late Middle Ages in relations among Italian city-states (Juenger 1992:12).

[44] Miller (1910:629), Holdsworth (1914:552).

[45] Frey and Frey (1999:186).

necessitating the extension of privileges and immunities to supporting staff. Because diplomatic privileges and immunities generally vary by rank and official duty, assessing what exceptions were due in specific instances could be quite complicated. To simplify matters, host governments began to treat embassy grounds as fictive sites of foreign administration.[46]

The still more robust notion of embassy inviolability – the idea that host government authorities have no right to enter foreign embassy grounds except by invitation – has its roots in the post-Protestant Reformation right of chapel. At a time when the clash of religious ideologies was a central issue in European political affairs, embassy inviolability allowed those on embassy grounds to practice a religion not endorsed by the territorial sovereign.[47] In the contemporary era, these extraterritoriality fictions persist and are considered fundamental to the practice of formal (juridical) equality between sovereigns.

It has also long been the convention for conduct on board ships to be governed by the law of the state of registration (the "law of the flag") irrespective of location. In the twentieth century, the practice was also extended to airplanes and other transport vessels. Although ships and planes are in a sense "places" from a passenger's perspective, the underlying basis of this jurisdictional convention is nationality. The purpose of this fictive rule is to avoid the confusion and arbitrariness that might follow if a vessel and its crew had to adhere to a different set of laws each time it crossed an international boundary. Neither in the case of the embassy inviolability, nor the "law of the flag," is the concept of extraterritoriality to be taken literally to mean, for example, that U.S. embassy buildings in Tehran, or an American jet flying over Italian airspace, are actually claimed as state territory.[48]

Adherence to a strict principle of territoriality reached its zenith in the late nineteenth century and the early decades of the twentieth century in the race among European powers to acquire overseas possessions.[49] According to one commentator, "[o]verseas discoveries [...] revealed the advantages of using a territorial definition of power, because it allowed for exclusive and unambiguous claims to new possessions

[46] Extraterritorial courtesies, which attach to locations, are distinct from modern concepts of diplomatic immunity, which attach to persons.

[47] Frey and Frey (1999:160).

[48] For a widely criticized exception to this rule, see *U.S. v. Erdos*, 474 F.2d 157; see also Paust (1999:310–313).

[49] Born (1992:8–9).

without the need to know what exactly these entailed."[50] Where newly acquired territories and dependencies were acknowledged to have functioning structures of governance, imperial powers often imposed two-tiered legal arrangements, leaving members of the indigenous population to continue to use local rules and institutions to manage their dealings with one another. However, in all matters concerning its own nationals, the home law of the colonizing power was applied extraterritorially through consular courts.[51] The most extensive example of this type of extraterritoriality was imposed in China through the system of "Treaty Ports" and "Concessions" beginning in the 1840s and extending to roughly 1940.[52] Similar, though more restricted, consular court arrangements were also used in European relations with the Ottoman Empire and its dependencies in North Africa, as well as with Japan, Korea, Siam (Thailand), and Persia (Iran).[53] Most of these arrangements were terminated by the late 1940s. In 1956, the United States closed its last consular court in Morocco.[54]

Analogous arrangements can be observed in many contemporary foreign military basing agreements and status-of-forces agreements (SOFAs). These agreements exist to specify "rights and responsibilities" between states sending military forces and host governments. SOFAs negotiated by the United States generally contain robust provisions for U.S. jurisdiction over all criminal and civil matters tied to carrying out the official duties of U.S. military personnel.[55] Basing agreements are wholly distinct from SOFAs; each can operate without the other. As with the other arrangements discussed, however, basing agreements and SOFAs begin with the assumption that the territorial sovereign has

[50] Herb (1999:11) cited in Berman (2002:n.591); see also Anghie (2004).

[51] Fishel (1952:14–18).

[52] These arrangements were initially imposed by the Chinese Emperor to limit Chinese contact with foreigners, beginning with the first such treaty with Russia in 1689 (Fairbank 1953:208). At the apex of the foreign presence in China just before World War I, eighteen different European states had established such privileges.

[53] Scully (2001).

[54] The United States currently has extraterritorial-type judicial arrangements with several trust territories, including Puerto Rico, Guam, and the Northern Mariana Islands. Several European states have similar trust arrangements: France in French Polynesia, Wallis and Futuna; the Netherlands in Netherlands Antilles; and Great Britain in Bermuda, the Cayman Islands, and the Falkland Islands.

[55] The United States presently has permanent SOFAs with more than ninety countries, up from forty at the end of the Cold War. Global Security.org, http://198.65.138.161/military/facility/sofa.htm.

complete authority and then proceed to define the scope and content of the arrangement.

These bounded exceptions to the rule of absolute territorial sovereignty differ in important respects from the type of judicial or regulatory extraterritoriality that is the focus of this book. Whereas the former involves defining physical spaces for exceptional treatment, the latter seeks to apply domestic law *irrespective of location.* A second way in which extraterritorial diplomatic, military, and transport privileges are distinguishable from more recently formulated approaches to extraterritoriality is that they are maintained by means of a strict regime of reciprocity.[56] By contrast, a distinguishing characteristic of judicial extraterritoriality as practiced by U.S. courts is its unilateral character.[57]

U.S. hegemony and U.S. judicial extraterritoriality

Up until the early part of the twentieth century, the United States supported a strict view regarding the exclusive authority of territorial sovereigns inside their own states. It shared this position with European powers, including Great Britain, then the global hegemon. Throughout the late eighteenth century and the nineteenth century, U.S. courts had occasionally decided criminal cases with an extraterritorial dimension involving piracy on the high seas, slave trading, privateering, and liability for collisions at sea.[58] However, U.S. courts in this era uniformly refused to apply U.S. law to conduct that occurred in other states' territories.

In *American Banana v. The United Fruit Company* (1909), a widely known example, one U.S. company accused another U.S. company of attempting to monopolize the banana trade between Costa Rica and the United States in order to drive the plaintiff company out of business. The U.S. Supreme Court held that U.S. law did not apply since the relevant acts had all occurred outside the United States. Absent applicable law, the Supreme Court ruled, U.S. courts had no jurisdiction over the dispute. The decision, written by Justice Oliver Wendell Holmes, famously reiterated the doctrine of strict territoriality in regulatory

[56] Frey and Frey (1999:373).

[57] Maier (1982), Dodge (1996).

[58] Examples include *Church v. Hubbart* 6 U.S. 187 (1804) (upholding the right of a nation to seize a ship engaged in illicit trade); *The Antelope* 23 U.S. 66 (1825) (law against slave trading operates extraterritorially to permit seizure of a foreign ship on the high seas); *Cushing v. U.S.* (Spoliation Cases) 22 Ct.Cl. 1 (jurisdiction over prize claims exists under international law).

matters: "the general and almost universal rule is that the character of an act as lawful or unlawful must be determined wholly by the law of the country where the act is done."[59]

Shortly after *American Banana* was decided, however, U.S. courts began to take a more flexible approach to the principle of territorial exclusivity by occasionally agreeing to regulate the "foreign" aspects of disputes involving both U.S. and foreign conduct.[60] A key milestone in the development of U.S. extraterritorial practice came in 1945, when a court in the Second Circuit for the first time applied a federal statute, the Sherman Antitrust Act, to a dispute involving wholly extraterritorial conduct.[61] The claim alleged that the Aluminum Company of America (Alcoa) had attempted to monopolize trade in aluminum ingots in Europe in order to distort the international market to its benefit. The court held that Alcoa's actions violated §2 of the Sherman Act, despite their having taken place outside U.S. territory, because they directly harmed, and were intended to harm, aluminum producers and consumers inside the United States.[62] Other instances of U.S. extraterritoriality, in the antitrust sphere and beyond, have followed this general formula.

What explains this move and its timing? The rising power of the United States relative to European states in the interwar period is undoubtedly a factor. Although the rise in the relative power of the United States may have been necessary for American courts to begin to exercise jurisdiction extraterritorially on a large scale, hegemony alone fails to explain this change. Great Britain, for example, had supported the doctrine of strict territoriality of national laws in its relations with other great powers during its period of hegemony prior to World War I.[63]

Another plausible explanation for the change in the U.S. approach might look to growth in levels of international economic integration from the 1940s onward, at least within the spheres delineated by Cold War alliances. As others have observed, however, the international

[59] 213 U.S. 347, 356.

[60] See, for example, *U.S. v. Pacific and Arctic* Railway, 228 U.S. 87 (1913) (regulating monopolization of transport to and from the United States); *U.S. v. Twenty-Five Packages of Panama Hats*, 231 U.S. 358 (1913) (regulating false statements made on U.S. customs documents in a foreign country); *Thomsen v. Cayser* 243 U.S. 66 (1917); *U.S. v. Sisal Sales Corporation*, 274 U.S. 268 (1927) (regulating monopolization of international sisal market).

[61] *U.S. v. Aluminum Company of America (Alcoa)*, 148 F.2d 416.

[62] *U.S. v. Aluminum Company of America (Alcoa)*, 148 F.2d 416.

[63] Raustiala (2006).

economy was as integrated at the end of the nineteenth century as it was at the end of the twentieth century when measured in terms of capital flows and investment.[64] Furthermore, it was much less integrated during the interwar period when U.S. courts first began to experiment with exceptions to strict territoriality.[65]

A third hypothesis emphasizes the relatively free hand the United States had to order international economic affairs among Western states, particularly in the middle part of the twentieth century. Raustiala (2009) argues that the bipolar structure of the international system after 1945 allowed the U.S. government to disregard foreign discontent with its policies. This included foreign indignation over extraterritorial applications of domestic constitutional authority. However, while bipolarity may well have lowered the expected foreign affairs costs of U.S. extraterritoriality, more is needed to explain why U.S. courts chose to apply U.S. constitutional and statutory laws abroad when they could have invoked international law as a justification for non-action, or opted to apply foreign law, consistent with continental European practice.

A more convincing explanation, I argue, looks not only to shifts in U.S. power internationally but also to changes in the structure and character of the U.S. legal system, and, specifically, to the growing role of courts and litigation as tools for regulation and the vindication of private rights – both regulatory and personal – in the early decades of the twentieth century. Paralleling, and in some cases driving, these developments was the "rise of the regulatory state," which vastly expanded the range of issues within the ambit of judicial regulation.[66] Enforcement of regulatory rules then, as now, involved a mix of private suits and public administrative oversight.[67] Also relevant was the domestic experience with judicial extraterritoriality among the limitedly "sovereign" states of the United States, which likewise underwent a transformation in this era due to the growing impracticality of insisting on strict territorial limits to state laws.[68]

[64] Hirst and Thompson (2002).

[65] See *United States v. Sisal Sales Corporation*, 274 U.S. 268 (1927), in which the U.S. Supreme Court agreed to exercise jurisdiction over a conspiracy partially organized inside the United States between U.S. corporations and the Mexican government to fix prices for the importation and sale of foreign sisal in American markets.

[66] Skowronek (1982), Friedman (2002).

[67] Friedman (2002), Farhang (2008).

[68] *International Shoe Co. v. Washington* 326 U.S. 310 (1945) (holding a state can exercise personal jurisdiction over non-residents that have minimum contacts with the forum).

Once the effects of foreign conduct inside U.S. territory alone had been held to provide a sufficient basis for extraterritorial jurisdiction under the Sherman Act in the Alcoa case, the old legal-conceptual shackles were broken and the modern era of judicial extraterritoriality can be said to have begun.

Yet, this jurisdictional shift did not produce any sudden changes in U.S. judicial practice. Court decisions recognizing the extraterritorial applicability of new statutory rules accrued gradually through private and public experimentation, often characterized by more than a few unsuccessful litigation efforts. The extraterritorial application of U.S. laws geared toward social regulation and civil rights, in particular, lagged behind judicial extraterritoriality in the economic sphere, with dramatic changes occurring only in the 1980s and 1990s.

U.S. extraterritoriality under fire from within the U.S. legal system

The legal permissibility of extraterritorial regulation by U.S. courts remains an area of active contestation not only internationally but also inside the U.S. legal system. Much of the recent internal U.S. debate, both in the academy and in the courts, has centered on the use of a judicial canon of statutory construction known as the "presumption against extraterritoriality." This canon holds that U.S. laws should be presumed to apply only inside U.S. territory unless a contrary legislative intent is expressed.[69] Reasons commonly cited for applying the presumption range from international law and international comity to domestic constitutional and separation of powers arguments, including the claim that Congress legislates primarily with domestic affairs in mind.[70]

Use of the presumption against extraterritoriality – which was a key element in the *American Banana* holding discussed above – has been highly uneven in U.S. jurisprudence.[71] The presumption was pointedly ignored in the *Alcoa* decision, which involved international cartels, but was successfully invoked a short time later in a Supreme Court decision refusing to apply U.S. laws on worker pay to U.S. government contractors employing U.S. citizens outside U.S. territory.[72] Thereafter, the presumption against extraterritoriality fell into a long period of disuse at the

[69] Dodge (1998a), citing *EEOC v. Aramco* at 499.
[70] Dodge (1998a), Sloss (2013).
[71] Estey (1997), Ward (2001), Knox (2010–2011).
[72] *Foley Bros. v. Filardo* 336 U.S. 281 (1949).

Supreme Court level, where the favored approach involved case-by-case efforts to "balance" the interests of governments on jurisdictional questions.[73]

In 1991, however, the Supreme Court decided a case involving alleged employment discrimination by an American company against an American citizen in Saudi Arabia in violation of Title VII of the Civil Rights Act in which the presumption against extraterritoriality was a critical factor.[74] The majority in *Equal Employment Opportunity Commission v. Aramco* held it could not apply Title VII extraterritorially absent clear evidence of congressional intent allowing it to take this step. In the years immediately following, the Supreme Court invoked the presumption again several times in cases concerning the Endangered Species Act, the Federal Tort Claims Act, and the Immigration and Nationality Act.[75]

In 1993, the majority in another Supreme Court case, *Hartford Fire Insurance Co. v. California*, conspicuously ignored the presumption in asking whether §1 of the Sherman Act applied to an alleged conspiracy among foreign reinsurers to exclude U.S. entities from particular types of insurance, as did another extraterritorial antitrust case in 2004 involving an international vitamin cartel, *Empagran S.A. v. F. Hoffman LaRoche Ltd.*[76]

Individually and collectively, these decisions, and others since, have fueled an ongoing debate among legal scholars over the origins and legitimacy of the presumption against extraterritoriality.[77] I return to this topic in Chapter 7, where I discuss two recent U.S. Supreme Court decisions applying the presumption – one concerning securities fraud and the other egregious violations of human rights – in light of the theory and evidence presented in this book.[78]

[73] Ward (2001).

[74] *EEOC v. Aramco* 499 U.S. 244 (1991). Although originally a wholly private suit, after the claim was dismissed by a Court of Appeals, the Equal Employment Opportunity Commission intervened on behalf of the plaintiff and became a party.

[75] *Lujan v. Defenders of Wildlife*, 504 U.S. 555 (1992) (Stevens concurring opinion), *Smith v. U.S.*, 507 U.S. 197 (1993), and *Sale v. Haitian Centers Council, Inc.*, 509 U.S. 155 (1993).

[76] *Hartford Fire Insurance Co. v. California* 509 U.S. 764 (J. Souter), *F. Hoffmann-LaRoche Ltd. v. Empagran S.A.*, 542 U.S. 155 (2004). In both cases, Justice Scalia wrote dissenting opinions invoking the presumption.

[77] Sloss (2013), Parrish (2011), Dodge (1998a and 2011), Knox (2010), Ward (2001), Estey (1997), Kramer (1995), Born (1992), Turley (1990).

[78] *Morrison et al. v. National Australia Bank Ltd. et al.*, 561 U.S. 247 (2010).

Overview of the book

The purpose of this book is to explain when, how, and why domestic courts and private litigants bring U.S. law to bear on persons and conduct outside U.S. territory, and why such actions have affected U.S. foreign affairs and the development of international regulatory regimes. In Chapter 2, I elaborate the theory of U.S. court extraterritoriality sketched above. I then test this argument statistically using an original dataset of more than 600 U.S. federal court cases litigated between 1945 and 2011 in which the existence of extraterritorial jurisdiction, or the appropriateness of its exercise, was actively contested. These data encompass more than 100 foreign countries and a broad range of issue areas, from antitrust to environmental regulation, and from intellectual property rights to human rights. The results show that my theory of regulatory logic and basic rights logic accounts for a substantial proportion of the observable variation in court behavior around these questions.

Chapter 3 turns to theorizing the deeper causes of U.S. judicial extraterritoriality. I begin by discussing who benefits from a legally fragmented international order, and why legal harmonization frequently fails to occur. I next consider the conditions under which governments adjust their laws to those of other states, and how the strategic behavior of private actors influences such choices. I argue that when U.S. laws are more restrictive than those regulating foreign competitors, U.S.-based transnational actors will try to level the regulatory playing field. Where efforts to secure domestic legislative change fail or appear *ex ante* to be prohibitively costly, those disadvantaged by having to follow U.S. law may try to use litigation to extend U.S. rules extraterritorially to cover ever-wider categories of foreign actors and conduct. Private beneficiaries of U.S. legal rules inside the United States likewise have an interest in seeing U.S. rules applied as widely as possible in order to narrow options for U.S.-based actors to escape U.S. legal obligations simply by exiting U.S. territory.

To make this complex set of interactions more analytically tractable, I identify three conditions under which prospective litigants initiate claims in U.S. courts instead of, or in addition to, lobbying for legislative change, or seeking executive sponsorship (domestic or foreign) for their legal objectives. These conditions are the presence of: (a) ambiguity concerning the scope or applicability of legal rules, (b) agents capable of initiating disputes, and (c) litigant beliefs in the feasibility of enforcement of any judgments obtained in their favor. Subsequent chapters apply this framework in tracing the origins and effects of U.S. judicial extraterritoriality in international antitrust, intellectual property rights protections, and human rights.

Chapter 4 examines U.S. judicial extraterritoriality in the sphere of antitrust law and policy. International antitrust regulation is a thinly institutionalized area of international economic relations, and one in which U.S. judicial extraterritoriality has been especially robust. It is also an area in which there is a trend toward legal convergence around a core set of substantive principles, mainly as other states adjust to U.S. preferences. The chapter argues that U.S. judicial extraterritoriality, propelled initially by government suits, and later by private suits, undercuts U.S. government incentives to bargain internationally for greater legal harmonization. The chapter describes the mixed success of U.S. efforts to impose its anti-cartel ideas on the defeated European powers following World War II and traces how and why U.S.-style ideas have slowly taken hold over subsequent decades as European legal and regulatory integration has advanced.

Chapter 5 examines a contrasting issue area – intellectual property rights – in which U.S. courts have been generally unwilling to exercise jurisdiction extraterritorially, even though U.S.-based entities suffer large losses due to unauthorized foreign use of American patents, trademarks, and copyrighted materials. I explore why this is the case through the prism of the theory sketched above, with specific attention to how U.S. extraterritorial practice has varied over time and across types of intellectual property. I first trace key early developments in these areas, and the uneven record of U.S. engagement with early treaty regimes. I then show how the failure of private efforts to draw U.S. courts and judges into extraterritorial regulation in the post-World War II era, particularly in the patent and copyright spheres, ultimately prompted a strong domestic push for the United States to bargain internationally to create new, more robust treaties to address the extraterritorial challenges faced by owners of intellectual property.

Chapter 6 shifts the focus from the regulatory logic of the two preceding chapters to the basic rights logic in order to examine U.S. extraterritoriality in the sphere of international human rights. Human rights is an issue area defined by an international treaty regime that purports to formalize universal rights but is notoriously weak on enforcement. I describe how in the 1980s the U.S. Alien Tort Statute (ATS) was used to allow claims alleging extraterritorial violations of human rights to be litigated in U.S. courts, and how the range of allowable claims expanded incrementally to encompass additional offenses and categories of violators. I then examine evidence that actual and prospective violators of human rights may have taken strategic notice of U.S. judicial extraterritoriality – albeit not always in ways conducive to promoting human rights.

Chapter 7 provides a summary and discussion of key theoretical and empirical implications of the analysis and several pathways for further research. I draw attention to an increasingly unambiguous trend in recent U.S. Supreme Court jurisprudence toward reining in U.S. extraterritoriality in privately initiated claims, by reliance on the presumption against the extraterritorial applicability of statutes whose geographic reach is not clearly specified. I describe this trend in terms of the book's main argument with the help of two recent decisions in contrasting issue areas in which the extraterritorial reach of a U.S. statute was a core issue. I show that in both cases the Supreme Court's main holding delimits U.S. extraterritoriality in terms that resonate strongly with the claim that U.S. courts are concerned primarily with ensuring the integrity and operation of U.S. law inside U.S. territory.

Finally, I argue that the apparent waning of U.S. hegemony in economic and regulatory affairs, and the accompanying contraction of U.S. enforcement capacity, are narrowing the ability of U.S. courts to apply U.S. laws extraterritorially, except where clearly backed with support from the executive or legislative branches. I conclude that the turn toward judicial minimalism in determining jurisdiction in privately initiated extraterritorial claims is not a temporary aberration but is, instead, a phenomenon that is likely to continue and to gain force.

2

A theory of judicial extraterritoriality

On September 11, 2001, members of the militant Islamist organization al Qa'eda carried out a set of coordinated attacks in the United States. Operatives hijacked three commercial airplanes and crashed them into high-profile targets in New York City and Washington D.C. A fourth hijacked plane crashed over rural Pennsylvania after passengers overwhelmed the hijackers. Nearly 3,000 individuals perished in these attacks. Their direct costs alone have been estimated at tens of billions of U.S. dollars.[1] On October 7, 2001, the United States and a coalition of supporting governments launched military operations against Afghanistan with the objective of destroying terrorist assets and capturing the al Qa'eda leadership. Soon thereafter, U.S. soldiers in Afghanistan began sweeping up alleged Taliban and al Qa'eda fighters, many of whom were suspected to have information of use to U.S. military operations.

In January 2002, the U.S. military transferred the first of many detainees to the U.S. Naval Base at Guantánamo Bay, Cuba, for interrogation and confinement.[2] Among these early transferees were four British citizens, an Australian, and fourteen Kuwaitis, who immediately sought legal counsel and petitioned for U.S. court review of their detention on grounds including *habeas corpus*.[3]

Several aspects of the Guantánamo detainees' efforts to challenge their detention in U.S. federal courts highlight more general issues that arise when courts have to weigh the appropriateness of applying U.S. law extraterritorially. The first of these concerns the character of the location where U.S. law would be applied. The Guantánamo Bay Naval Base is

[1] See for example, www.iags.org/costof911.html.

[2] http://edition.cnn.com/2002/WORLD/asiapcf/central/01/11/ret.detainee.transfer/index.html.

[3] Petitions for *habeas corpus* may be submitted by incarcerated individuals to request judicial review of the legality of their detention, 28 U.S.C. §2241. These petitions were contained in Civil Actions No. 02-CV-0299 and No. 02-CV-1130.

located in Cuba – not the United States. Nonetheless, U.S. authorities just as obviously exercised exclusive legal and administrative control over the base under the terms of the 1903 treaty lease from Cuba and *de facto*. The detainees' petitions thus raised thorny questions about whether U.S. federal court authority to hear *habeas corpus* claims extends as a matter of U.S. statutory or constitutional law to non-U.S. settings in which the U.S. government exercises full detention powers.

A closely related question concerned whether the Guantánamo detainees had standing to invoke U.S. legal protections, given their status as foreign nationals located outside U.S. territory. The U.S. government's insistence that the individuals detained in the Guantánamo Bay facility were "enemy non-combatants," and not prisoners of war with Geneva Convention rights further compounded the political and legal difficulty of these cases, prompting the British government to accuse the United States of holding the Guantánamo detainees in legal limbo with protection from neither international law nor U.S. law.[4]

U.S. courts at both the district and appellate levels dismissed the cases for lack of jurisdiction, reasoning that neither the U.S. Constitution nor any of the statutes invoked by the detainees applied extraterritorially to allow foreign nationals to petition for *habeas corpus* review. In September 2003 the detainees petitioned for Supreme Court review of these holdings. The petition was accepted and the cases were consolidated since they each raised identical legal issues.

The following June the Supreme Court reversed the lower court holdings in a decision entitled *Rasul v. Bush*.[5] This was to many a surprising outcome, given that it involved the Court deciding against the U.S. government on an extraterritorial matter involving U.S. national security. Citing cases reaching as far back as the seventeenth century, a 6–3 majority of Justices found that *habeas corpus* petitions are intended to prevent the arbitrary exercise of sovereign power. Consequently, the rights at issue were neither contingent on the petitioner's physical presence inside U.S. territory, nor limited by their nationality. Instead, the critical factor is whether U.S. officials are acting in a "sovereign" capacity. In light of the "plenary and exclusive jurisdiction" exercised by the U.S. government at Guantánamo Bay, the majority held extraterritorial applicability of the statute was appropriate.

4 See, for example, "Britain, EU Set to Protest US Military Tribunals at Guantanamo," www.globalpolicy.org/component/content/article/157/26881.html.

5 542 U.S. 422 (2004).

This is not the end of this story, however. In response to the decision in *Rasul v. Bush* and a related case involving the treatment of a U.S. citizen at Guantánamo, the U.S. government created Combat Status Review Tribunals to provide a "one time administrative process" to determine whether individuals in U.S. detention met the definition of "enemy combatant."[6] The Tribunals provided few of the procedural protections available to *habeas corpus* petitioners in U.S. federal courts, and employed far looser standards of evidence. Federal courts in the D.C. Circuit were given authority to review Tribunal decisions, but this extended only to examining their consistency with the statute, which critics saw as deeply flawed.[7] Another Guantánamo detainee case was soon filed seeking federal *habeas corpus* review and challenging the adequacy of the Combat Status Review Tribunal procedures for determining detainees' status under the Geneva Conventions. The plaintiff, Salim Ahmed Hamdan, was a Yemeni citizen who had worked as a chauffeur for Osama bin Laden. Hamdan had been transferred to Guantánamo Bay in 2002 after being captured by Afghan military forces and handed over to the U.S. military.

The U.S. district court granted Hamdan's petition for *habeas corpus* review, and held that the United States could not subject Hamdan to a U.S. military commission without first establishing whether he was a prisoner of war and, therefore, due certain Geneva Convention rights. The government appealed this decision, and the D.C. Circuit Court of Appeals reversed. Its decision held that the Geneva Conventions, if applicable, conferred no individual rights on Hamdan, and that the tribunals set up to determine the status of detained individuals had been properly created by an act of Congress. Once again the U.S. Supreme Court accepted a petition for *certiorari*, and, once again, it decided against the U.S. government.[8] A 5–3 majority found that the Geneva Conventions were directly enforceable in U.S. federal courts, and that Congress and the Executive had exceeded their constitutional authority by creating tribunals that failed to comply with minimum standards of due process under U.S. law and international humanitarian law.

In 2006 Congress passed the Military Commissions Act in an effort to override the Supreme Court's decisions in *Rasul* and in *Hamdan* by addressing some of the procedural inadequacies on which those

[6] *Hamdi v. Rumsfeld* 542 U.S. 507 (2004).

[7] Sec. 1005 C and D.

[8] *Hamdan v. Rumsfeld* 548 U.S. 557, 415 F. 3d 33 (D.C. Cir. 2005), and Civil Action No. 04–1519 (JR) (D.D.C.).

outcomes rested. This statute sought yet again to strip U.S. federal courts of jurisdiction over *habeas corpus* petitions from alien enemy combatants held outside U.S. territory.[9] Three more Guantánamo detainees who had been denied *habeas* review then asked the Supreme Court to decide the constitutionality of this aspect of the Military Commissions Act. In *Boumediene v. Bush* a bare 5–4 majority held that the right to *habeas corpus* review was guaranteed by the Suspension Clause of the U.S. Constitution.[10] Thus, due to absence of the conditions specified in that clause, Congress could not enact laws to strip the federal courts of jurisdiction, even where those laws concerned the rights of aliens held outside U.S. territory.[11] After this defeat, Congress amended the Military Commissions Act to bring it into line with the U.S. Supreme Court's interpretation of U.S. and international law.[12]

These cases are dramatic examples of U.S. federal courts asserting their authority to safeguard individual rights under the U.S. Constitution, even in the face of direct and repeated resistance from other branches of the government. Admittedly, direct inter-branch challenges of this type are rare. Nonetheless, the outcomes are in line with an established propensity of U.S. federal courts to apply U.S. law extraterritorially when behavior violating a short list of basic rights is at issue and U.S. citizens or others with close ties to the United States are alleged violators.

In addition to situations invoking this "basic rights logic," there is another far more common class of situations in which U.S. courts have been asked to weigh in on the extraterritorial applicability of U.S. law: where conduct outside the United States is alleged to cause negative effects inside U.S. territory. The resulting patterns of U.S. jurisdictional practice reflect a parallel "regulatory logic."

Most law is not about establishing rights, but is, instead, concerned with incentivizing individuals and institutions to behave in socially and politically desirable ways. Examples range from setting speed limits to enacting prohibitions against torture. Because authority to create and enforce law is politically bounded, and political authority in the modern

9 Pub. L. 109–366, §7(a), October 17, 2006.

10 553 U.S. 723 (2008).

11 Article 1, §9 (Suspension Clause) reads: "The Privilege of the Writ of Habeas Corpus shall not be suspended, unless when in Cases of Rebellion or Invasion the public Safety may require it." The four dissenting justices insisted that denying Guantánamo detainees access to U.S. federal courts for *habeas corpus* review was not an unconstitutional "suspension" of the writ, and that the review procedures in the Detainee Treatment Act of 2005 were an adequate substitute.

12 Added *Pub. L. 111–84*, title XVIII, §1802, October 28, 2009.

international system generally attaches to territory, geography is often important when identifying applicable law – and also its limits. A key idea here is that strategic actors sometimes have incentives to exploit the geographic limits of legal rules for their own ends. Often this entails seeking out more permissive legal environments in order to undertake prohibited actions. However, if actions outside a state dilute incentives for private actors to follow legal rules inside the prohibiting state in systematic ways, this undercuts the more restrictive state's law and policy – not just in an immediate sense but more corrosively by demonstrating to other private actors inside the more restrictive state how to circumvent its regulations.

One option for dealing with this situation is for the more restrictive state to ask more permissive states to bring their laws into line with its preferred rules. Where international bargaining over legal rules fails to yield mutually acceptable results, actors and institutions inside the state with the more restrictive rules may seek other means to safeguard its domestic laws. For relatively powerful states, the menu of "other means" may include efforts to apply those laws directly to conduct outside the state's territory.

In this chapter, I elaborate my theory of when U.S. courts are likely to find and exercise jurisdiction over extraterritorial claims. After defining relevant legal terms and specifying the behavioral assumptions that undergird the theory, I contrast my account with those of other scholars to derive testable alternative hypotheses. The next section describes the data and models used to test these hypotheses and presents the results of the analysis. The results show that although U.S. courts are primarily inward-looking institutions, the need to safeguard the integrity of U.S. laws inside U.S. territory at times prompts U.S. courts to interpret those laws as having extraterritorial reach.

The theoretical argument

The primary task of federal courts in the U.S. legal system is to decide disputes that "arise under" the Constitution and laws of the United States.[13] I define U.S. judicial extraterritoriality as any exercise of jurisdiction on the part of a U.S. court, using U.S. law (or its foreign analog), to resolve disputes involving conduct occurring wholly or partially outside U.S. territory. Since roughly the middle of the twentieth century, this

[13] U.S. Constitution, Article III, §2(1).

charge has increasingly encompassed requests for U.S. courts to decide disputes involving persons or conduct outside U.S. territory. Before a U.S. court may assert authority over legal disputes encompassing extraterritorial conduct, it must first affirmatively establish its jurisdiction to do so under U.S. law.

As described in Chapter 1, U.S. judicial extraterritoriality has exhibited a puzzling degree of variation over time and across issue areas. Accounting for this pattern requires attention to law and politics at both the domestic and the international level. I argue that U.S. courts can be expected to find and exercise jurisdiction extraterritorially in two types of situations. The first is where conduct outside U.S. borders threatens the future integrity or operation of a domestic regulatory law or regime. Second, I expect U.S. courts to find extraterritorial jurisdiction appropriate where outside acts by, or against, a U.S. citizen or another entity with close U.S. ties, are plausibly alleged to violate a short list of staunchly protected "basic rights" at the core of American political and legal identity. I refer to these two possibilities as a "regulatory logic" and a "rights-based logic" of U.S. court behavior.

The regulatory logic operates where extraterritorial conduct satisfies the following conditions. First, the conduct must be prohibited if undertaken inside the United States. Second, it must produce harmful effects inside the United States. Without identifiable harm, there is no basis for legal complaint.[14] Allegations of harm from extraterritorial acts not proscribed if undertaken inside U.S. territory would not, by definition, threaten the integrity of any domestic law or policy. A third condition is that actors engaging in contested conduct anticipate net benefits from their behavior. Although outside the bounds of formal jurisdictional analysis, this element addresses underlying incentives to violate U.S. law. Thus it is directly relevant to judicial efforts to ensure the protection of legislative purpose.

Under these conditions, if a court does not find and exercise jurisdiction over extraterritorial conduct producing the harmful effects inside the United States, this essentially gives other actors a "green light" to also engage in that conduct. Where potential gains to be captured from exploiting the territorial limits of U.S. law are large or widespread, a decision not to apply U.S. law extraterritorially may, therefore,

[14] This requirement functions as an outer bound (or limiting condition) on jurisdiction that, in turn, prompts litigable questions about what constitutes "legally cognizable harm." Note that in extraordinary circumstances plaintiffs can sue to prevent "imminent harm" where the harm, were it to occur, would be exceedingly costly or irreversible.

undercut both the domestic operation of the law in question, and the public policy that law is meant to serve. Where, by contrast, a legal dispute concerns conduct that creates few opportunities for this type of regulatory arbitrage, a court may forego extraterritorial regulation without risking harm to the domestic legal order – even where extraterritorial conduct results in some demonstrable costs to U.S. actors or interests.[15]

The regulatory objective underlying the rights-based logic, by contrast, involves reinforcing core norms of the American political community. Here a defendant's association with the U.S. polity through citizenship, residence, or transactional ties is the primary basis for judicial assertions of extraterritorial jurisdiction to protect a short list of "basic rights." It follows that the requirement of a territorial nexus (in the form of demonstrable "effects") is correspondingly weaker, in that every violation of a core norm is considered harmful *per se*.[16] Substantively, this category includes rights not to be deprived of life, liberty, or property without due process of law, rights to free speech, and freedom from discrimination on the basis of nationality or membership in a traditionally disadvantaged group, and also the right not to be subjected to torture or other "crimes against humanity."[17]

These logics together imply that U.S. judges instinctively take a quasi-functionalist approach to contestation over the extraterritorial applicability of U.S. law, allowing it where necessary to ensure that the domestic object and purpose of legal rules is fulfilled, and rejecting it otherwise. Reinforcing this approach is the separation of powers structure of the U.S. Constitution, under which courts are tasked with resolving disputes in line with legislative purpose, and foreign affairs powers are shared between the executive and legislative branches. These incentives are further buttressed by the rules and norms of the judicial profession.

U.S. economic hegemony was undoubtedly important to enabling U.S. court assertiveness in applying U.S. law extraterritorially. Following the post-World War II recovery of Europe and Japan, the dominance of

[15] In short, the likelihood of U.S. court action is affected by the presence or absence of specific private incentives, not just the presence or absence of domestic "effects." In short, although domestic effects are necessary for U.S. courts to exercise jurisdiction extraterritorially in regulatory matters, they are not sufficient.

[16] Born (1996).

[17] Gunther and Sullivan (1997:663–664), Bassiouni (1996). Although many of these rights are recognized bases of "universal jurisdiction" under international criminal law, the U.S. approach draws a clear distinction between extraterritoriality and universality, as reflected in the insistence that, for jurisdiction to apply, defendants must have a territorial or transactional nexus with the United States.

U.S. producers and service providers began to be challenged more frequently. Perhaps counterintuitively, the rise of foreign economic competitors actually increased the capacity of U.S. courts to compel extraterritorial adherence to U.S. law. This is because, for many large foreign-based corporations, access to U.S. territory, markets, and services was very important. The more widespread this need to ensure U.S. access, the greater the power of U.S. courts, and other domestic agencies and institutions operating in the shadow of judicial oversight, to demand that transnational entities respect U.S. laws even in their non-U.S. conduct. This combination of competitive tension and regulatory power, coupled with a relative ease of private access to U.S. courts, laid the basis for decades of contestation over the prescriptive reach of particular U.S. laws.

Without question, individual courts and even entire judicial circuits have at times ventured beyond these hypothesized thresholds for extraterritorial action in the service of other political, economic, or moral principles. Perhaps the foremost example of this involves U.S. extraterritoriality in the realm of securities regulation.[18]

In 1968, a U.S. Second Circuit court held that U.S. Securities Exchange Act rules prohibiting fraudulent activities could apply to conduct in foreign countries where that conduct generates harmful effects to U.S. investors inside U.S. territory.[19] Within a few years, U.S. federal courts had extended the reach of U.S. anti-fraud rules to cover situations involving minimal U.S. conduct and negligible U.S. harm, on the argument that "Congress did not mean the United States to be used as a base for fraudulent securities schemes even when the victims are foreigners."[20] Because this was an era in which the United States was viewed as the guarantor of global capitalism, expansive use of U.S. jurisdiction to grease its wheels was tolerated – though generally not welcomed – by many foreign governments.

U.S. economic hegemony has eroded further in the post-Cold War era as the European Union has consolidated, and the economies of China, Brazil, India, South Korea, and other states have gained strength. Simultaneously, the willingness of U.S. domestic courts to interpret the extraterritorial reach of U.S. laws expansively has in many instances also gradually declined – in the sphere of securities regulation and elsewhere.

[18] See Chapter 7 for discussion of the recent judicial constriction of U.S. extraterritoriality in the securities realm.

[19] *Schoenbaum v. Firstbrook*, 405 F.2d 200, 2d Cir. (1968).

[20] *Bersch v. Drexel Firestone, Inc.*, 519 F.2d 974, 987 (2nd Cir. 1975).

My theory expects that even as U.S. hegemony wanes, we will continue to see U.S. courts applying U.S. law extraterritorially where necessary to ensure the domestic integrity and operation of U.S. law, and to ensure that fundamental U.S. constitutional rights and principles are respected by those with close ties to U.S. territory and institutions – but rarely otherwise.[21]

Constructing jurisdictional thresholds

Before a U.S. federal court may consider a dispute, it must first confirm its authority to do so under the U.S. Constitution and any relevant statutes. How federal judges approach challenges to extraterritorial jurisdiction is in many respects similar to jurisdictional challenges in wholly domestic claims.[22] However, the consequences for failing to find, or declining to exercise, jurisdiction over a legal claim differ considerably depending on whether the claim is domestic or transnational. When a federal court dismisses a valid domestic claim on jurisdictional grounds, the claim generally may be brought elsewhere in state court. However, for claims with an extraterritorial center of gravity, a federal court finding that jurisdiction is lacking (or should not be exercised on prudential grounds) is often tantamount to terminating the claim in the U.S. judicial system.[23] When deciding jurisdictional questions in the context of extraterritorial claims, therefore, federal courts are deciding the extent – in literal, spatial terms – of their own and other domestic actors' power to regulate persons and conduct outside U.S. borders.[24]

Throughout this book I refer to the extraterritorial reach of U.S. federal courts as shorthand for three different jurisdictional elements, each of which must be affirmatively established before a specific claim may be heard. The first element involves ensuring the existence of relevant law. This is known as "prescriptive jurisdiction." In the U.S. legal system, the

[21] Putnam (2009), Krasner (1999).

[22] It is not identical, however. Because the surrounding structural and political constraints are different in extraterritorial claims, the interpretative devices judges use also differ. See Chapter 7 for more extensive discussion of this point.

[23] Note, however, that sometimes transnational claims dismissed at the federal level can find a basis in state law such that a state court may exercise subject matter jurisdiction. For example, numerous U.S. human rights lawyers are, at the time of writing, activity probing bases for suing for extraterritorial human rights violations under state transitory tort laws.

[24] Occasionally courts must also determine the status of ambiguous spaces for jurisdictional purposes, for example, foreign military bases, foreign protectorates, embassies and consulates, airplanes, and ships at sea.

authority to prescribe legal rules, or to delegate that authority to others, rests with Congress. The U.S. Constitution contains no expressed limits on congressional power to create rules with extraterritorial application. Consequently, judicial assessments of extraterritorial prescription encompass assessments of legislative intent. Sometimes the intended reach of U.S. law is stated explicitly, but more often it is left to courts to interpret whether the operation of the law requires that it be given extraterritorial reach.

Finding the prescriptive limits of legal rules requires that judges look initially to the text of the law. Where this fails (as it often does) to provide clear guidance as to a statute's jurisdictional reach, judges next look to the law's legislative history to ascertain its intended purpose, along with any contemplated applications or exclusions.[25] The National Labor Relations Act (NLRA), for example, was passed to promote collective bargaining by safeguarding workers' rights to organize.[26] Whether this objective requires American companies to respect NLRA provisions when negotiating with American (or foreign) employees based outside the United States is the type of question on which prescriptive jurisdiction turns. In addition, courts also look to the law's prior record of application – in general, and with respect to closely related questions.[27]

This type of multi-step analysis is often necessary when novel extraterritorial claims arise, since Congress has been explicit regarding the extraterritorial reach of only a handful of statutes. All of these date from the 1970s or later. Examples include the Foreign Trade Antitrust Improvements Act (FTAIA) and the Foreign Corrupt Practices Act (FCPA).[28] Although extraterritorial claims based upon this type of statute get a free pass on the most basic hurdle to extraterritorial applicability, this does not mean that no further inquiry is needed. Courts must still ensure that the law plausibly encompasses the behavior alleged in specific claims.[29] Under the FCPA, for example, courts must decide whether the conduct at issue is "foreign," and whether it reasonably

[25] See Eskridge (1987).

[26] Government Printing Office, Legislative History of the National Labor Relations Act, 1935 (Vol. I).

[27] I assume here that a civil dispute that *exactly* replicates a previously decided case in a jurisdiction where the holding is controlling is highly unlikely to reach litigation.

[28] 15 U.S.C. § 6a, and 15 U.S.C. §§ 78dd–1, et seq.

[29] See, for example, *F. Hoffmann-La Roche Ltd. v. Empagran S.A.*, 123 S.Ct. 2359 (2004). Determining a claim's "fit" under a particular law invariably involves some consideration of the underlying facts. This, however, is formally distinct from weighing the "merits" of a claim in which the veracity and sufficiency of the "facts" are subject to scrutiny.

relates to the statute's definition of "corrupt practices."[30] A similar analysis is used when courts consider extensions (or elaborations) of jurisdiction for facially ambiguous statutes where prior decisions have established a basis for extraterritorial application. This is because prior extraterritorial applications of a statute are not necessarily determinative of subsequent applications where conduct, actors, or circumstances vary. Consequently, I consider both types of statutes in the empirical analysis that follows.[31]

The second element of the required jurisdictional package involves ensuring the court's jurisdiction to adjudicate the claims at issue. Satisfying this element requires identifying a *political* grant of court authority over the relevant category of legal dispute. The U.S. Constitution and several federal statutes specifically grant U.S. federal courts jurisdiction to adjudicate a wide range of disputes, from those involving ambassadors, to conduct on Indian Reservations, to injuries from conduct undertaken in violation of international law.[32] One extremely important U.S. statute, 28 U.S.C. §1331, grants federal courts broad jurisdiction over "all civil actions arising under the Constitution, laws, or treaties of the United States."[33] In most situations involving extraterritorial claims, therefore, a determination that U.S. law applies prescriptively is sufficient to ground adjudicatory jurisdiction.[34]

In a few situations the adjudicatory jurisdiction of U.S. federal courts can be established using slightly different means. For example, domestic courts are sometimes asked to apply another country's law in the course of resolving transnational disputes. This is especially common in disputes involving private contract claims, or in suits for personal injury. It is, however, rare for U.S. courts to apply the public (regulatory) laws of foreign countries. Where federal courts agree to apply foreign law, they must still affirmatively establish their own jurisdiction over the subject

30 *W.S. Kirkpatrick & Co., Inc. v. Environmental Tectonics Corp., Intern.*, 493 U.S. 400, 110 S. Ct. 701.

31 There are few FTAIA and FCPA claims in the data (described below). Their inclusion is based on a desire to be theoretically consistent. Excluding them has no notable effect on the statistical results.

32 See especially 28 U.S.C. §§1330–1364.

33 It is a statutory codification of Article 3(2)(1) of the U.S. Constitution. Chemerinsky (2007) observes that §1331 "makes many of the specific grants of jurisdiction superfluous."

34 Restatement (Third) of U.S. Foreign Affairs Law of the United States, §421 (Introduction), at 304–319. See Chapter 6 for discussion of an important exception to this general pattern as well as the complexities is creates.

matter by reference to U.S. federal law. Finally, plaintiffs in disputes with an extraterritorial dimension occasionally ask federal courts to resolve disputes concerning U.S. state law (only) using what is called "diversity" jurisdiction.[35] In these situations, plaintiffs must still also demonstrate that the law in question has extraterritorial applicability (here meaning outside the enacting U.S. state).

The third jurisdictional element requires establishing the existence of U.S. legal authority over the "persons" of prospective defendants ("personal jurisdiction").[36] This inquiry, unlike the others, is centered on due process protections granted to individuals under the U.S. Bill of Rights. (For these purposes, corporations are treated like individuals, though often with different rights and obligations.) Here the key query is whether it would violate principles of fairness to hold a defendant's extraterritorial conduct to U.S. legal standards – whatever those standards may be.[37] The answers turn on the relationship of the defendant to the United States.

There are two main categories of personal jurisdiction in the civil sphere.[38] The first involves "general" (or dispute-blind) jurisdiction. This type of jurisdiction applies to U.S. citizens, anyone found inside U.S. territory, however temporarily, as well as non-U.S. persons ("natural" or "corporate") who have very substantial U.S. ties.[39] Another, narrower means for U.S. courts to assert personal jurisdiction involves "specific" (or dispute-based) jurisdiction. As suggested by the label, where a foreigner's action gives rise to a legal claim, specific jurisdiction allows courts to reach entities whose U.S. presence is not sufficient to trigger general jurisdiction. This can occur though U.S. conduct, or by extraterritorial conduct that generates harmful effects either inside U.S. territory, or to U.S. interests elsewhere.

[35] Diversity jurisdiction (28 U.S.C. §1332) is an aspect of U.S. judicial federalism arising out of concerns among out-of-state litigants that state courts are biased in favor of their own citizens. It provides for U.S. federal court jurisdiction in cases involving citizens of different U.S. states, or U.S. states and foreign countries, where the stakes are above a set monetary threshold (currently $75,000).

[36] An alternative framing is that courts must establish jurisdiction over the *actions* ("subject matter jurisdiction"), and the *actors* ("personal jurisdiction"); see Michaels (2005).

[37] This too has a prescriptive element, since it entails asking whether the defendants fall within the class of actors Congress intended to regulate.

[38] In criminal cases, U.S. law requires physical custody of defendants.

[39] See *International Shoe v. Washington*, 326 U.S. 310 (1945), *Daimler AG v. Bauman* 517 U.S. (2014) (No. 11-965), and also Borchers (2001), and Twitchell (1988).

In deciding the break point for sufficiency of contacts for personal jurisdiction, U.S. judges must square broad principles of due process with the regulatory objectives of particular rules.[40] Although overtly constitutional in its framing, personal jurisdiction also has a pragmatic aspect tied to the fact that the criteria courts use to determine its presence for individual defendants – that is, the presence of interests and assets in U.S. territory – often also affects the prospective enforceability of any judgment against those defendants.[41] Strategic private actors, therefore, may attempt to insulate themselves from the reach of U.S. regulators – for example, by creating corporate subsidiaries in foreign countries, or by attempting to contract out of practices that are questionable under U.S. law. Defensive actions of this type help to generate the disputes examined here: claims challenging extraterritorial reach of legal rules, to whom or what they apply, and even what constitutes an "actor" under particular legal rules.[42]

Behavioral assumptions

I begin with the assumption that judges and litigants are self-interestedly rational actors with Bayesian instincts, but that their information about the environments in which they operate is incomplete. This incompleteness is due to the private nature of others' preferences, time horizons, and levels of risk aversion, and also to the fact that complex causal processes generally embody contingencies that can be, at best, estimated only probabilistically. In addition, I assume that the ability of actors to gather and process even observable information is limited by cognitive, institutional, and resource-based capacities. In short, their rationality is bounded.[43] One characteristic of boundedly rational actors that is of particular relevance to the theory elaborated here is a tendency to give disproportionate weight to information about readily observable, high-consequence events.[44]

40 Berman (2002:432).

41 Michaels (2005), Whytock and Robertson (2011).

42 Hornbeck (1995). Indeed, disputes over jurisdiction reach litigation precisely when defendants believe one (or more) of these elements is open to challenge.

43 March and Simon (1958).

44 The cognitive heuristics in play here are "availability," "representativeness," and "adjustment and anchoring." Bar-Hillel (1973), Kahneman and Tversky (1972), Tversky and Kahneman (1973) and (1974), Saks and Kidd (1980).

When determining the geographic reach of U.S. rules, judges are constrained by factors inside and outside the judiciary. From within, judicial behavior is constrained by the prospect of higher court review, and by formal and informal professional norms.[45] Outside the judiciary, the separation of powers framework articulated in the U.S. Constitution imposes robust legal and institutional checks on judicial behavior.[46] In carrying out their constitutionally mandated tasks, federal courts interact with other branches of government. These branches may have preferences over whether courts exercise jurisdiction extraterritorially, which they can express using institution-specific tools.

Congress, for example, has the power to override court decisions through legislative or constitutional amendments, and to use its appointment and budgetary powers as a source of indirect pressure.[47] On the executive side, an unambiguous signal of an affirmative preference for the extraterritorial application of U.S. laws may be given, as for example when an agency like the Securities and Exchange Commission initiates a court proceeding, or when the Equal Employment Opportunity Commission opts to intervene on one side of an ongoing extraterritorial dispute.[48] More commonly, the U.S. Solicitor General, the U.S. Attorney General, or the heads of other departments and specialized agencies issue formal statements of interest in specific cases or submit briefs as *amici curiae*. Presidents can attempt to clip the wings of unwelcome judicial decisions using executive orders and treaty-making powers. Less directly, both branches can also signal dissatisfaction with judicial behavior through the exercise of appointment and budgetary powers.[49]

At the same time, the constitutional separation of powers gives each branch incentives to exercise restraint in interactions with the others.[50] For example, the "shadow" of prospective judicial review encourages Congress to make laws, and executive branch members to carry them out, within the limits of what the U.S. Constitution and prior court rulings allow. Likewise, U.S. judges may weigh the foreign affairs implications of their extraterritorial decisions, particularly where those

45 Baum (2006:31).
46 Kozlowski (2003), Segal (1997), Ferejohn and Weingast (1992).
47 Ferejohn and Kramer (2002).
48 See, for example, *SEC v. United Financial Group, Inc.*, 474 F.2d 354 (9th Cir. 1973) and *EEOC v. Arabian American Oil Co.*, 499 U.S. 244 (1991).
49 Cross and Nelson (2001:1457).
50 Ferejohn and Kramer (2002).

decisions may affect the agendas of other branches.[51] Although domestic courts are largely insulated from the actions of foreign governments, their impact may be felt indirectly through executive pressure to exercise, or to refrain from exercising, extraterritorial jurisdiction in particular cases, or in efforts to interfere with the post-judgment enforceability of extraterritorial regulatory decisions.[52]

In sum, U.S. courts are structurally and constitutionally constrained actors. Even so, they often exercise a measure of genuine agency in carrying out their function as authoritative interpreters of legal rules.[53]

Competing accounts of U.S. court behavior

Although regulatory extraterritoriality has long been of theoretical and practical interest to international lawyers, it has received little explicit consideration in political science.[54] Moreover, with few exceptions, the accounts of U.S. extraterritoriality in legal scholarship are heavily doctrinal – that is, they are focused on illuminating pathways to particular judicial outcomes within the law with reference to interpretative tests, canons of construction, precedential rules, and other factors judges cite to justify their rulings.[55] While doctrinal treatments can be quite rich in terms of describing changes in the law, and identifying normative and practical tensions created or resolved by those changes, they seldom interrogate the causal origins or non-doctrinal effects of those changes.

Over roughly seven decades of post-1945 U.S. judicial extraterritoriality, two such tests have been especially important, both in judicial opinions concerning contentious claims of extraterritorial jurisdiction and in the legal commentaries on those opinions. The first test directs judges to evaluate the degree of harmful effects inside U.S. territory generated by extraterritorial conduct ("effects" test).[56] The second test requires assessing how much of the conduct underlying a claim took place in U.S. territory, along with its materiality to the legal complaint

51 Court actions (or inactions) may influence foreign affairs but this does not necessarily indicate improper interference (Franck 1992:5–6).

52 Zimmerman (1992:174).

53 Ferejohn and Weingast (1992:263), Segal (1997:31).

54 Jennings (1957), Falk (1958), Verzijl (1961), Maier (1982), Born (1992), Dodge (1996), Meessen (1996), Parrish (2008), Colangelo (2011). But see also Putnam (2009) and Kaczmarek and Newman (2011).

55 Posner (1981:1113–1114).

56 Dodge (1996).

("conduct" test).[57] Although arguably useful for substantiating doctrinal shifts *ex post*, effects and conduct tests are less helpful for explaining outcomes on novel jurisdictional questions.[58] This is because these tests contain no external metric by which thresholds for the types or amounts of U.S. conduct and effects needed to trigger jurisdiction can be identified *ex ante*.[59] The fact that these thresholds vary observably over time and across statutes, and may even vary contemporaneously across different judicial circuits, also cannot be explained using purely doctrinal tools.[60]

In recognition of these limitations, a few international law scholars have sought more general explanations for what drives U.S. courts to exercise, or to refrain from exercising, jurisdiction over extraterritorial claims. I now turn to two such accounts that provide alternatives to the logics of ensuring the integrity and operation of U.S. law domestically and safeguarding basic rights.

Protecting U.S. economic interests

One general account of U.S. judicial extraterritoriality developed by Jonathan Turley posits that U.S. court behavior is "biased" toward protecting U.S. economic interests, which he equates with rules that favor

[57] Some debate exists among scholars and judges over whether domestic conduct renders regulation "territorial" for jurisdictional purposes, even if it has extraterritorial aspects. My test turns on whether a valid cause of action would exist absent the foreign conduct. Where it would not, the "extraterritorial" label is necessary. That said, judges have strong incentives to base jurisdiction in territorial grants of power whenever possible to avoid controversy. At times this produces what others describe as moves to "localize" legal rules by redefining elements of transnational conduct to give it a domestic nexus (Dinwoodie 2009:727).

[58] Turley (1990), Choi and Guzman (1998), Willison (2000). Note, in addition, Justice Scalia's criticism of conduct and effects tests as aids to jurisdictional analysis in *Morrison v. National Australia Bank* 561 U.S. 247.

[59] Dodge distills three approaches. Under the "Holmes rule," courts should assert jurisdiction over extraterritorial conduct that is closely tied to U.S.-based conduct. Under the "Bork rule," extraterritorial jurisdiction is appropriate only where some effect is felt in U.S. territory. Under the "Mikva rule" either "conduct" or "effects" in U.S. territory are sufficient to trigger jurisdiction. See Dodge (1996: 104–110) for case citations.

[60] For example, prior to the U.S. Supreme Court decision in *Morrison v. National Australia Bank* 561 U.S. 247 (2010), there was a three-way split over the extraterritorial applicability of Rule 10b-5 in securities fraud claims. The D.C. Circuit required a defendant's alleged U.S. conduct to directly violate 10b-5 for jurisdiction to vest. *Zoelsch v. Arthur Andersen & Co.*, 824 F.2d 27, 32 (1987). The Fifth Circuit applied a much lower standard requiring only that some activity pursuant to fraud occur in U.S. territory. *SEC v. Kasser*, 548 F.2d 109 (1997). The Third Circuit fell in between, requiring U.S. conduct to be "more than merely preparatory." *Robinson v. TCI/US West Communications* 117 F.3d 900 (1997).

commercial fairness and market openness. Specifically, Turley expects U.S. courts to exercise jurisdiction extraterritorially far more often in economic ("market") disputes, like antitrust and securities regulation, than in social policy ("non-market") disputes – for example, those involving environmental protection and labor regulation.[61]

To assess this claim, Turley focuses on the character of the tests judges use for each category of case. He observes that when deciding close jurisdictional questions, judges can manipulate conduct and effects tests to achieve outcomes that favor or disfavor extraterritorial jurisdiction. In contrast to the doctrinal approach discussed above, Turley does not emphasize the details of these tests, but rather seeks to gauge their relative ease or difficulty.[62] In deciding whether to exercise jurisdiction over market disputes, Turley argues, federal judges generally apply easy tests requiring little beyond a *de minimus* showing of U.S. conduct or effects. In non-market claims, he argues that judges generally require, in addition, a showing of positive congressional intent for a U.S. statute to apply extraterritorially.[63]

The cases Turley examines support his claim that outcomes in disputes over extraterritorial jurisdiction tilt toward protecting U.S. economic competitiveness. Moreover, they fail to support the alternative hypothesis that U.S. judges are hesitant to interfere with the domestic sovereignty of other states. Yet the broader validity of Turley's findings is less than certain.[64]

First, without the use of appropriate sampling of contested cases of U.S. extraterritoriality, it is unclear whether and to what degree Turley's cases are representative of the broader universe of claims. One aspect of Turley's analysis that suggests strongly that his pool of cases may be biased is that it does not encompass any intellectual property disputes. These disputes account for a non-trivial share of new extraterritoriality claims from the 1970s onward. Second, Turley offers little guidance on the criteria he uses to distinguish different types of disputes. For example, is a claim in which an American labor union colludes with a sister union abroad to engineer a secondary boycott in order to secure foreign collective bargaining rights properly categorized as a "market" or a "non-market" dispute? Finally, even if Turley's arguments hold for the period

[61] Turley (1990:601).
[62] Turley (1990:644–645).
[63] Turley (1990:644) observes that the presumption against extraterritoriality is "an unevenly applied, highly chauvinistic canon of construction."
[64] Turley (1990:645).

prior to 1990, many things in the transnational legal and regulatory environment have changed. It may be, therefore, that drivers of U.S. court decision-making on extraterritorial questions also have changed.

Regime affinity

Anne-Marie Slaughter's work on judicial globalization likewise suggests a set of testable propositions about the conditions under which U.S. judges can be expected to exercise jurisdiction extraterritorially. As part of a broader account of transnational judicial cooperation and conflict, Slaughter describes a growing tendency among U.S. judges to assess the "fitness" of their counterparts in alternative forums when deciding whether to resolve transnational claims.[65] Specifically, Slaughter argues that where alternative judicial forums share a high degree of procedural similarity (or "affinity"), judges are *less* likely to dismiss claims on the basis of deference to foreign states. This is because such courts share a common set of values and a shared interest in resolving disputes in an orderly manner. In such situations, resolving transnational claims according to "local" rules and procedures is unlikely to produce serious friction, and may even generate harmonizing forms of conflict over identified variations in underlying rules.[66] Slaughter illustrates this argument using case examples involving the United States and other economically advanced countries.

A different set of interactions prevails in situations involving alternative forums that are not part of the emerging "global community of courts." Where alternative forums do not share basic affinities, Slaughter's argument is that U.S. judges will be *more* likely to defer to foreign courts, citing traditional notions of international comity.[67] Under these conditions, factors such as foreign citizenship and the locus of disputed conduct are expected to carry greater weight in judicial decision-making. Exceptions exist, however, where alternative forums are experiencing internal political violence, or when they are found to be systematically biased or corrupt.[68] In these situations, Slaughter expects U.S. courts to retain control over extraterritorial claims. If this argument is correct, we would expect U.S. courts to be more likely, after controlling

[65] Slaughter (2003 at 210).
[66] Slaughter (2004:322–323).
[67] See Restatement (Third) of Foreign Relations Law of the United States, §421.
[68] Slaughter (2003 at 213).

for cases in which there is no *ex ante* expectation of foreign justice, to exercise jurisdiction over transnational disputes involving other states with similar procedural standards.[69]

Slaughter's analysis of judicial decision-making on questions of contested extraterritorial jurisdiction invites concerns about generalizability and bias arising from non-random case selection. As with Turley's argument, Slaughter presents several supporting cases, but with no indication of whether they are representative of the relevant universe of claims. Consequently, Slaughter's conclusions about general patterns of judicial behavior may be broader than her evidence can reasonably support. At the same time, her claims are also precise enough to enable statistical testing using a larger randomly sampled selection of litigated claims.

Testing the arguments

To test the hypotheses just elaborated, I use multivariate logistic regression techniques and data from an original sample of 659 civil cases decided in U.S. federal courts between 1945 and 2010 in which the question of the court's extraterritorial jurisdiction was a factor.[70] The data encompass disputes involving roughly 120 countries and more than 20 distinct topics, which I group into 11 issue areas.

The dependent variable is whether a U.S. federal court finds and exercises jurisdiction extraterritorially.[71] Three different outcomes are possible. First, a court may determine jurisdiction is present and decide to exercise it. Second, the court may find it has no jurisdiction to decide the dispute on any one of several grounds. Third, even when a court determines that jurisdiction exists, judges may nevertheless decline to

69 Slaughter (2003:213).

70 My search used Westlaw, a simple query string ~extraterritorial*** & countr***!, and sequenced date restrictions. The "countr***" limitation was included for manageability, since purely domestic "interstate" claims containing jurisdictional questions use identical language. Including "country" helped to more effectively sample for international claims, but without correlating with terms of theoretical interest. The initial return of several thousand cases was narrowed by excluding purely domestic claims, cases involving border issues in which conduct is punishable only if it occurs inside U.S. territory, and several second-order issues – that is, suits to compel arbitration, forum selection clauses, and enforcement, and claims that fail to meet basic threshold requirements for bringing suit, such as standing and ripeness.

71 Note, the analysis here assumes the claim has satisfied all Article III procedural hurdles that precede jurisdictional analysis (e.g. standing, ripeness, statement of a case in controversy).

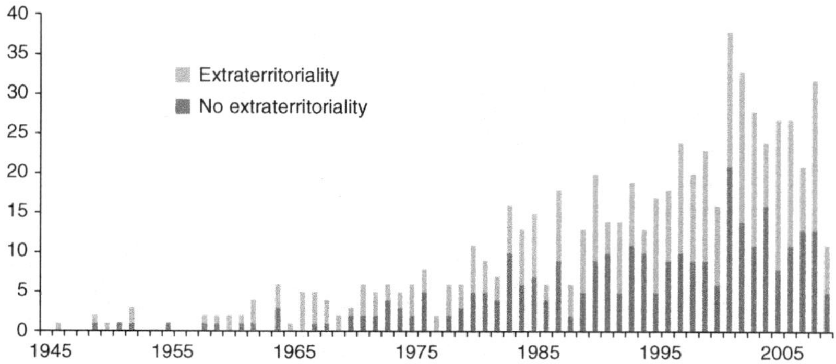

Figure 2.1 Contentious extraterritorial jurisdictional claims over time, by outcome

hear case by invoking a prudential (or discretionary) doctrine.[72] I group findings of "no jurisdiction" and discretionary decisions not to exercise jurisdiction together in the regression analysis, since they produce the same behavioral result: no extraterritorial action on the part of the U.S. court. In 54.6 percent of the cases in the sample, U.S. federal courts decided in favor of exercising jurisdiction.[73] When analyzing how well the theory predicts outcomes in my case sample for and against extraterritorial jurisdiction, I examine various discretionary and non-discretionary bases for dismissal.

Figure 2.1 shows the distribution of contentious extraterritorial claims over time, along with their outcome with respect to the courts decision as to whether to find and exercise jurisdiction. There is a clear upward trend in the number of cases brought, particularly after the mid 1970s. At the same time, there is a roughly equal distribution of positive and negative outcomes on the dependent variable across the board. The latter phenomenon is almost certainly an artifact of the close character of many legal questions that reach the litigation stage.

Figure 2.2 shows the distribution of claims across ten issue groupings. Some categories – like securities regulation and bankruptcy – are self-explanatory. Others are less so. For example, included in the commercial transactions category are contract, insurance, and racketeering claims. Economic regulation encompasses antitrust and tax claims. Human/civil rights covers race and gender discrimination, torture, forced labor, and

[72] These include international comity, international *forum non conveniens*, and deference to other branches of government.

[73] The cases were last systematically updated in August 2012.

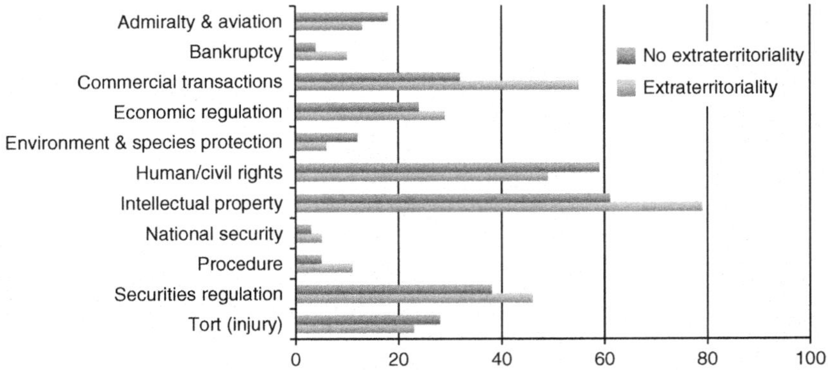

Figure 2.2 Contested extraterritorial claims in sample by issue area ($N = 609$)

other egregious rights violations, as well as labor and collective bargaining cases. Intellectual property rights include copyright, patent, and trademark claims.

One thing to note here is the large number (<50) of claims in the categories of commercial transactions, economic regulation, human/civil rights, intellectual property, securities regulation, and tort. By comparison, there are far fewer claims in the remaining categories, especially in environmental and species protection, and in national security. This likely reflects higher prospects for individual-level injury in the first set of issues. It may also reflect the expectations of potential litigants in light of the observed unwillingness of U.S. courts to exercise jurisdiction over claims in prior cases. Fewer instances of extraterritorial action not only discourage strategic plaintiffs, but also create less of a need to probe the limits of judicial actions expanding the extraterritorial reach of U.S. law.

Figure 2.2 also indicates that U.S. courts have exercised jurisdiction extraterritorially in fewer than half the claims considered in only three issue areas: admiralty, human rights, and tort. In admiralty, customary legal rules and international treaties govern much of what is, in general, a quintessentially "transnational" set of issues. Lawsuits that challenge this framework on the basis of U.S. law – and especially effects-based theories of liability – thus face steep challenges. In tort law there is widespread international agreement that jurisdiction normally lies in the place of injury. Here too, therefore, identifying legal principles that would justify deviating from this practice is difficult. Finally, the differential outcome in the human/civil rights totals is driven at least in part by the fact that many victims of foreign human rights violations have few options for taking legal action against their abusers other than to sue in U.S. courts.

Three considerations underlie the use of statistical methods to test the hypotheses laid out above. First, I am interested in how U.S. federal courts *in general* decide contentious questions of extraterritorial jurisdiction. Thus, even cases that add little to the jurisprudential corpus in terms of original reasoning or precedential weight are important. Second, the exclusive reliance on lead cases that is characteristic of legal analysis obscures theoretically relevant aspects of rule development within and across legal issue areas. In particular, it gives insufficient attention to false starts and failed efforts on the part of litigants to push the legal-doctrinal envelope. Analyzing a representative sample of claims addresses both concerns.[74] Third, statistical methods are useful when seeking to identify and quantify the marginal effect of specific variables across a large number of cases. They are, therefore, well suited to the task at hand: assessing the determinants of outcomes in contentious claims over U.S. extraterritorial jurisdiction.

One possible criticism of this approach is that it implicitly gives all reported legal opinions equal weight, regardless of the level at which they were issued, thereby discounting the greater precedential value of certain cases over others.[75] However, the task here is to track efforts to redefine the outer limits of U.S. extraterritorial jurisdiction given a decision to litigate. Although the strength and cohesiveness of underlying precedent may affect when and why plaintiffs emerge, it is rarely wholly determinative of what happens in actual extraterritorial claims.[76] Indeed, if we assume that plaintiffs and defendants are strategic about selecting claims for litigation, and that they (or their lawyers) have basic knowledge of the legal landscape at the relevant point in

[74] As discussed in Chapter 2, fully reasoned judicial opinions are themselves a *non*-representative subset of claims decided by courts (Coyle 2003).

[75] My thanks to Paul Stephan for raising this issue.

[76] Note, I have no general theoretical priors regarding what the effect of precedent is on the stream of litigated claims. For example, we might expect that a strong precedent on a legal matter would, almost by definition, incentivize settlement (or, where the stakes are highly asymmetric, a preference among at least one party to pursue non-judicial means for changing the law). Chapter 3 contains additional consideration of this topic. However, strategic litigants might still bring claims at the margin of a strong precedent to test whether the rule might be stretched further, to clarify its boundaries, and the like.

time, it follows that *legal claims that make it to litigation should be precisely those that cannot be easily decided by reference to precedent.*[77]

Another related issue that requires consideration is the unavoidability of observational biases tied to the writing and reporting of judicial opinions.[78] Only a subset of litigated cases ever results in the type of formal written opinions that constitute the universe of cases from which my sample is drawn. Judges are encouraged to report opinions formally for publication only when they "rule on an issue of first impression, modify a previously announced rule, reverse a published decision of an agency or district court, or create a conflict with another circuit."[79] Consequently, the disputes analyzed here, like those drawn from any pool of reported opinions, are not routine examples of judicial decision-making. In short, although my sample is drawn randomly from the universe of reported decisions on contested issues of extraterritorial jurisdiction, this universe is a non-random subset of litigated claims.[80]

These characteristics render judicial opinions appropriate data for answering some types of questions, but not others. By selecting out disputes in which the court's jurisdiction either is not challenged, or where such challenges are resolvable with a relatively straightforward application of existing law, reported decisions systematically understate the incidence of legal disputes involving extraterritorial conduct. Accordingly, this approach is poorly suited to observing overall patterns of regulatory enforcement. These factors, however, combine to make this approach well suited to observing areas of flux in the extraterritorial reach of U.S. law, and to testing hypotheses about U.S. court behavior under those circumstances.

With these clarifications and caveats in mind, I turn now to a description of the variables and models used to test the competing causal hypotheses about what drives patterns of U.S. court behavior in contests over extraterritorial jurisdiction.

[77] Priest and Klein (1984). And, if any such cases occur, their chances of being reported are slight.

[78] Only "reported" cases are formally part of the corpus that judges and litigants may draw upon for legal precedents.

[79] Coyle (2003:2472).

[80] Reported judicial opinions may encompass multiple issues, any of which may be the basis for a judge's decision to report. My sample undoubtedly contains at least a few such cases. See Kastellec and Lax (2008).

Explanatory variables

For the domestic rule integrity argument, the key explanatory variable is whether opting *not* to exercise U.S. jurisdiction extraterritorially is likely to prompt other actors to undertake similar conduct on a scale that could undermine U.S. domestic policy objectives.[81] Such incentives are foreseeable where the private benefits of circumventing a geographically limited application of the rule would be expected to outweigh the operational costs of taking the offending conduct offshore. Where the court's written summary of the facts indicates that these conditions hold, and the conduct allegedly produces harm inside the United States, the variable is coded as "1." An example of an "easy" coding decision of this type involves efforts to circumvent a U.S. trademark holder's rights by setting up a factory to produce counterfeit goods just outside U.S. borders with the intent to sell the goods in U.S. markets. If a U.S. court refused to exercise jurisdiction over the claim on grounds that U.S. law does not operate extraterritorially, the result would be to incentivize others to set up similar "offshore" operations to the detriment of the domestic trademark regime. Legal issue areas where easy cases frequently arise include antitrust, bankruptcy, securities regulation, RICO claims, and copyright claims after 1992 (when the World Wide Web first enabled low-cost digital transfer of copyrighted materials).

By contrast, where private incentives to engage in allegedly harmful behavior are already weighted in favor of compliance with U.S. laws, no comparable threat to U.S. rules exists, and the variable is coded as "0." For example, whether or not a U.S. court decides a legal claim arising out of a car accident in Mexico will have no effect on incentives for safe driving inside the United States. The underlying behavior is thus easily classifiable as "non-threatening" to U.S. law, even if U.S. citizens or their property were harmed in the accident. Claims involving foreign labor practices or violations of human rights by foreign state officials are additional examples.

[81] This is a back-of-the-envelope type calculation of the private costs and benefits of circumvention of the type a "reasonable judge" with a short time horizon and few external resources might make. The variable was coded "blindly" (*i.e.* with the outcome of the claim concealed) by the author. Two independent coders with legal training also coded the variable for sixty randomly selected cases (9 percent of the data). In only 12 percent of those cases did the independent coders disagree with the author, and in all but one instance (involving a complex Internet domain name case) the author updated the coding to reflect the majority's assessment.

Issues like extraterritorial age discrimination involve more difficult coding decisions. For example, suppose a U.S. company transfers a sixty-two-year-old employee to its London office and then fires her in circumstances that, had they occurred in the United States, would support an Age Discrimination in Employment Act (ADEA) claim. If the court were to hold that the ADEA does not apply extraterritorially, the question then arises whether this would incentivize a cascade of foreign transfers of older employees to exploit the geographic limitation on the statute's protection. Although quite close, this case would be coded as "0" under the regulatory logic, since similar opportunities to evade the ADEA are relatively rare and come with their own costs in the form of the price tag of the transfer, severance arrangements, and possible negative effects on company morale. Still more relevant to the coding decision is the fact that once the limits of the U.S. law become known, employees who might be caught in this loophole will quickly learn to contract around it *ex ante*. Because age discrimination does not receive heightened scrutiny in U.S. constitutional review, it would be coded as "0" under the "rights" logic also.

Finally, recall that a threshold condition for the regulatory logic to apply is that extraterritorial conduct must produce, or be intended to produce, some effect inside the United States. For this reason, I code as "0" what experts in American extraterritorial practice call "foreign cubed" cases – those involving foreign plaintiffs, foreign defendants, and foreign conduct.

A threat to domestic rule integrity is coded as featuring in 376 of 647 U.S. federal court cases in the sample (58 percent).

To construct variables to test the rights-based logic, the ability to distinguish between "basic" and "non-basic" rights is key. I code basic rights as those that receive strict scrutiny in federal constitutional review, and also rights considered *jus cogens* or "compelling law" under international law, such as prohibitions on genocide, slavery, or torture. Where a violation of any right in these categories is alleged in an extraterritorial claim, the case is coded as "1" and otherwise as "0."[82] Basic rights are at issue in 55 cases in the sample (9 percent).

Cross tabulations of the dependent variable and the domestic rule integrity and basic rights variables show that, jointly, they correctly predict 65 percent of the outcomes before controlling for other factors.

[82] I use "heightened scrutiny" only to delineate a discrete set of issues where regulation is likely, while recognizing that many cases in the sample would not satisfy the "state action requirement" for actual heightened scrutiny.

Turley's competing economic openness argument expects U.S. courts to find jurisdiction over extraterritorial claims involving market (commercial) disputes at higher rates than disputes involving social policy. Drawing conceptual lines between "market" and "non-market" disputes is not always simple, however. For the claims in my sample I differentiate between disputes where the crux involves a business transaction or a question of private compensation, and questions involving public burdens or benefits, or processes by which distributive questions of this type are resolved. For example, a labor dispute between a union and an employer where the central issue is enforcement of collective bargaining rights would be coded as a "social policy" dispute ("1"), but a dispute between the same parties over contract payment would be coded as "commercial" ("0").

Testing Slaughter's regime affinity argument requires distinguishing between judicial systems that share basic "affinities" with the U.S. system, and those that do not. Slaughter underlines that such affinities are present not only between highly economically developed countries, but also between the United States and some less developed states.[83] Beyond this, however, she offers little guidance about how to make these distinctions. As a proxy for such affinities, I use membership in the Organisation for Economic Co-operation and Development (OECD) at the time each dispute commenced in U.S. federal courts. The OECD is an organization of (currently) thirty-four member states that share several economic and political governance goals – albeit with observable variance in the degree to which they have been able to achieve those goals.[84]

Using OECD membership as a filter for grouping states according to those likely, and unlikely, to share basic judicial-procedural affinities, I construct two dichotomous variables. The first tracks whether any of the conduct at issue in a claim occurred in an OECD country, and the second whether any citizens of an OECD country were among the defendants to a suit filed in U.S. federal court. Where the answer to the query is affirmative, the coding is "1," and otherwise "0."

Slaughter also expects U.S. courts to exercise jurisdiction where alternative foreign jurisdictions are experiencing political violence, or their judicial systems are otherwise incapable of providing unbiased

83 Slaughter (2003:212).

84 OECD members include, for example, Mexico, the Slovak Republic, Poland, the Czech Republic, and Turkey. OECD website: www.oecd.org/pages/0,3417,en_36734052_36734103_1_1_1_1_1,00.html.

proceedings. If a legal dispute concerns conduct in a country that appears on PRIO's Main Conflict Table in the year the suit was commenced in U.S. federal court, I code it as "1."[85] The absence of fair and independent judiciary is a defining feature of autocracy. I therefore looked to state scores on the Polity IV scale in the year each suit commenced as a proxy for procedural inadequacy. If a foreign state where the bulk of the non-U.S. conduct occurred scored below a "−5" on that scale, I coded it as "1."[86] Together these exclusions capture all cases in the sample with a conduct nexus in Burma, China, Cuba, Haiti, Iran, Iraq, Libya, or Uzbekistan. It also affects the coding of some cases (but not others) involving conduct in states that have experienced regime volatility, such as Honduras, Lebanon, Liberia, Mexico, Nigeria, Panama, and Philippines. In total this protocol affected the coding of 116 cases.

The models also include additional control variables coded from written judicial opinions for the cases in the sample as accessed through the Westlaw Database. Some of these control variables are intended to capture the separation of powers dynamics described above, and the potential for U.S. courts to be swayed by the interventions of foreign governments. Others reflect concerns common in the legal literature. Those factors expected to increase the likelihood that a U.S. court will find and exercise jurisdiction extraterritorially are whether the claim involved any act inside U.S. territory,[87] and whether any U.S. citizens are plaintiffs or defendants.[88] I also control for whether the executive branch expressed an opinion supporting or objecting to jurisdiction, either as party to the claim or as an *amicus*

[85] PRIO codes a state as experiencing "armed conflict" if more than twenty-five battle deaths are recorded in a calendar year. www.prio.org/Global/upload/ … /Main%20Conflict%20Table.xls.

[86] Forty-two cases in the case sample had a non-U.S. nexus not included in the Polity IV dataset. These are primarily small island states (e.g. Bahamas, St. Kitts, Vanuatu) and quasi-autonomous protectorates (e.g. Hong Kong, Guam). I likewise exclude cases where the conduct at issue occurred in international waters, in outer space, or in Antarctica – all of which lack governments to which to defer.

[87] This is coded "1" if there is U.S. conduct mentioned in the decision's summary of facts, and "0" otherwise. Controlling for this factor is distinguishable from a "conduct test" insofar as U.S. conduct is not hypothesized as a *necessary* element; nor is there any express or implied threshold for how specific amounts of U.S. conduct influence jurisdictional determinations.

[88] "American plaintiff" is coded "1" if there is an American on the plaintiff side of a lawsuit, and "0" otherwise. "American defendant" is coded similarly.

curiae.[89] Likewise, I track whether any foreign government expressed an opinion for or against U.S. jurisdiction using these mechanisms.[90] Finally, given the focus on ideology by scholars of judicial behavior, particularly the attitudinalists, I control for the "liberalness" of the highest court issuing a written opinion on the jurisdictional aspect of each dispute.[91]

Regression results and discussion

To test the hypotheses discussed above, I ran numerous logistic regression models. The main results, summarized in Table 2.1, provide strong support for both my domestic rule integrity argument and my basic rights argument. However, the sparseness of the data underlying the basic rights results means they should be treated with greater caution. The analysis generates support neither for Turley's economic openness argument as a stand-alone explanation, nor for Slaughter's regime affinity argument.

Models 1 and 2 (base and full models) feature domestic rule integrity and basic rights as variables. In line with what the theory predicts, each of the resulting coefficients is substantively large and significant with at least a 95 percent level of statistical confidence. Model 6 contains the same variables as the full model (Model 2), but it restricts the sample to cases that received appellate-level consideration. Here too the domestic rule integrity coefficient retains its size and significance at the appellate level, but the basic rights coefficient does not. As noted above, however, the relative sparseness of cases involving alleged rights violations in the sample make this more suggestive than definitive.[92] The results for

[89] This is coded "1" if the U.S. Solicitor General or any agency from the executive branch officially intervened in the case, and "0" otherwise. In cases involving multiple written opinions, I searched each for *amicus curiae* submissions and "statements of interest," since these may occur at any time in a proceeding.

[90] This is coded as for U.S. government preferences. Note, this variable was not tested in Putnam (2009).

[91] See, for example, Segal and Spaeth (2002), Kastellec (2010). As a proxy for ideology, I start by coding for the party of each judge's appointing president (0 if Republican, 1 if Democrat). Where the highest decision was issued by an appellate panel or by the Supreme Court, the scores are divided by the number of deciding judges, yielding a number between "0" and "1."

[92] In only 51 of the 598 observations on the dependent variable in the base model is a "basic rights" violation alleged. In 29 of those cases, a U.S. court agreed to exercise jurisdiction extraterritorially, and in 22 it did not. In the model restricted to appellate cases, the numbers are 9 and 14, respectively, on 265 observations.

Table 2.1 *Probability that a U.S. federal court exercises jurisdiction over a claim with contentious extraterritoriality*

	Model 1 (base)	Model 2 (full)	Model 3 (controls)	Model 4 (economic openness)	Model 5 (regime affinity)	Model 6 (appellate only)
Key variables						
Threat to integrity of domestic rule	1.46***	1.41***				1.34***
	(.2)	(.21)				(0.34)
Basic rights violation	.9**	.88**				.63
	(.35)	(.39)				(.57)
Additional hypotheses						
Non-commercial dispute		.04		−.31		−.02
		(.26)		(.21)		(.4)
Conduct in OECD state + exclusions		−.14			−.17	.2
		(.23)			(.22)	(.36)
Defendant from OECD		−.31			−.36	−.85**
		(.22)			(.21)	(.36)
Controls						
Conduct in the United States	.57***	.74***	.64***	.56***	.8***	1.09**
	(.19)	(.2)	(.17)	(.18)	(.31)	(.32)

American plaintiff(s)	.23	.3	.49**	.46**	.56***	.22
	(.21)	(.21)	(.19)	(.19)	(.2)	(.33)
American defendant(s)	−01	−.02	0	−.01	−.06	−.58
	(.19)	(.21)	(.01)	(.18)	(.2)	(.36)
U.S. executive in favor	.8***	.76**	.85***	.92***	.81***	.68
	(.31)	(.33)	(.3)	(.3)	(.32)	(.44)
U.S. executive opposed	−11	0.6	−.16	−.01	−.12	.23
	(.32)	(.37)	(.3)	(.32)	(.35)	(.51)
Foreign government opposed	.68	.63	.7	.75	.63	.65
	(.4)	(.41)	(.38)	(.39)	(.39)	(.55)
Year suit commenced	−.01	−.01	0	0	0	−.03
	(.01)	(.01)	(.01)	(.01)	(.01)	(.01)
Judicial liberalness	.1	.24	.22	.07	.22	.11
	(.22)	(.21)	(.2)	(.21)	(.2)	(.49)
Constant	25.56	21.13	2.45	1.73	8.78	58.97
	(15.62)	(14.77)	(13.39)	(13.41)	(14.42)	(23.49)
Summary statistics						
Observations	598	550	598	598	550	240
Percent correctly predicted	68.7	68.2	61.7	59.4	62.2	68.8
Reduction in error	.28	.26	.13	.08	.10	.32

Note: Standard errors are in parentheses. *** indicates significance with 99% confidence; ** with 95% confidence using two-tailed t-tests.

Model 3, which contains only control variables, are roughly consistent with those in Model 1, indicating appropriate non-collinearity among these variables and the main variables of interest.

A common technique for understanding how much individual variables add to a statistical account is a first difference test. For models in which key explanatory variables are dichotomous, this involves estimating how much more (or less) likely an outcome is as those values change from "0" to "1," holding all other variables at their means.[93] Analysis of the marginal differences for the main explanatory variables in Model 1 indicates that where extraterritorial conduct poses no threat to the domestic operation of a U.S. legal rule, the probability that a U.S. federal court will exercise jurisdiction over a claim is roughly 40 percent. By contrast, where such a threat exists, this probability is 74 percent, a 34-point increase. Similarly, in situations where extraterritorial claims involve no basic rights issues, the probability that a U.S. federal court will exercise jurisdiction is 55 percent, but it rises to 75 percent when such issues are present, a 20-point increase. Substantively, these are large effects considering that in general only close cases are litigated.[94]

By contrast, the regression results indicate little consistent support for the economic openness hypothesis (Model 4). Table 2.1 shows that the coefficient for non-commercial dispute is moderately large with the expected negative sign, indicating that U.S. federal courts are less likely to exercise jurisdiction in these cases. The accompanying standard error does not, however, allow for much confidence that the result is distinguishable from a non-effect. I also investigate how much the time window matters, using different windows as robustness checks. Restricting the model to only the cases prior to 1990 produces substantially similar results. However, incrementally adding data past 1990 produces different results, with the negative coefficient for non-commercial dispute getting increasingly negative up to 1998, when it is twice the size of the coefficient

93 This analysis uses "Clarify," a statistical tool that uses Monte Carlo simulation to draw 1,000 values for each parameter of a multivariate normal distribution, and sets a mean equal to the point estimates of the model's coefficients, and variance given by a covariance matrix of the point estimates (Tomz *et al.* 2005).

94 Priest and Klein (1984). But Shavell (1996: 499–500) argues that differences in information available to litigants can call the assumption of equal likelihood of prevailing into question. However, transnational litigation in U.S. federal courts generally involves only highly sophisticated litigants. Consequently, the potential for large informational asymmetries that are not endogenously tied to features of the theory is lower in this pool of cases.

reported in Model 4 in Table 2.1, with a 95 percent level of confidence.[95] This suggests the possibility of changes either in the profile of disputes involving contentious questions of U.S. extraterritoriality that reach U.S. courts in the post-Cold War era, or in how courts handle those disputes, or both.

The regime affinity account (Model 5) receives no support in this analysis. When tested on the unrestricted sample, the coefficients for the variables intended to capture regime affinity are small with changing signs and large standard errors. This holds whether they are tested jointly (as reported) or separately. Sensitivity testing of Model 5 using incremental time restrictions produced no exceptions. Interestingly, however, the results for Model 6 indicate that having a defendant from an OECD country in an appellate case is strongly negatively correlated with U.S. judicial extraterritoriality with 95 percent confidence.[96] That is to say, where ties to an OECD country have a visible effect, they *reduce* the likelihood that U.S. federal courts will exercise jurisdiction extraterritorially. This is the opposite of what Slaughter's regime affinity account expects.[97]

Table 2.1 likewise confirms the importance of several control variables – but also provides a few surprises. As expected, where some part of the conduct from a transnational transaction occurs in U.S. territory, this increases the probability that a U.S. court will find and exercise jurisdiction with a high degree of statistical confidence.[98] This effect is present across the board in all models. This is intuitive, particularly with respect to the regulatory logic: conduct with a physical connection to U.S. territory is, all else equal, more likely to affect the domestic operation of U.S. laws. However, the ability to point to some conduct

[95] Restricting the model to 1998 and earlier, the coefficient for non-commercial dispute is –.89 (.29) (N = 323). Constraining the sample to cases prior to 2004 yields a coefficient of –.66 (.24) with a 95 percent level of confidence (N = 471). This is consistent with the results reported in Putnam (2009).

[96] This finding is robust to different thresholds for exclusions due to foreign regime inadequacy. For example, running the model using exclusion thresholds of less than "–3" and less than "0" on the Polity IV scale yields substantively similar results.

[97] Running the full model (Model 2) constrained to cases where no conduct occurred in U.S. territory, and to cases where some U.S. conduct occurred, also does not change the substantive performance of the OECD variables. Both coefficients remain negative with high standard errors.

[98] For Model 2, the marginal difference in the likelihood a U.S. court will exercise jurisdiction if some conduct occurred in U.S. territory is an increase of 14 percent with 99 percent confidence.

in U.S. territory is not always necessary to trigger the extraterritorial reach of U.S. law. Nor it is always sufficient

With regard to the nationality of litigants, the evidence is mixed. Looking first at Models 3, 4, and 5, the coefficients for American plaintiff and American defendant indicate that having an American entity on the plaintiff side of a lawsuit increases the likelihood of a U.S. court applying U.S. law extraterritorially by a non-trivial degree, but having an American defendant does not. However, in the models with the domestic rule integrity and basic rights variables included (Models 1, 2, and 6), the coefficients for both of these variables are small and statistically insignificant. Looking only at the results for Models 3–5, one might be tempted to conclude that U.S. courts are simply biased in favor of American plaintiffs' efforts to trigger extraterritorial jurisdiction. To the extent there is bias at work, however, it is unclear why it would not also operate when Americans are on the defendant side. Alternatively, it could be that American plaintiffs are systematically better at identifying extraterritorial claims that are likely to succeed in U.S. courts than are foreigners – or at least at hiring lawyers capable of doing so.

Parsing the data further sheds some insight on this question. First, removing suits by Americans against Americans from the sample and re-running Models 1, 3 and 4 (the base model and those testing the alternative hypotheses) decreases both the size and statistical significance of the American plaintiff coefficients. It likewise increases the negative size of the American defendant coefficients, but without bringing them anywhere near standard thresholds of significance. Cross-tabulations of U.S.–foreign dispute dyads and the dependent variable show that U.S. courts exercised jurisdiction in 61 percent of cases in the sample when Americans sued other Americans, or when Americans sued wholly foreign defendants, and 60 percent of the time when there was a mix of American and foreign litigants on the same side of a litigated dispute. By way of comparison, U.S. courts exercised jurisdiction just 41 percent of the time when foreign plaintiffs sued Americans, and 39 percent of cases when foreigners sued foreigners.

These figures are consistent both with there being an anti-foreigner bias in U.S. courts, and with the idea that U.S.-based litigants may be better at identifying plausible arguments to support more expansive interpretations of extraterritorial jurisdiction. However, examining in addition how disputes brought by each dyad type map onto threats to basic rights and domestic rule integrity suggests American plaintiffs may be better at identifying litigable claims involving novel extraterritorial jurisdictional questions. Only 45 percent of the cases initiated by non-Americans involved a "threat" of either type, versus 62 percent of cases initiated by Americans against foreign defendants, and 61 percent of cases involving only American litigants.

The results concerning expressed U.S. executive preferences for, and against, judicial extraterritoriality also warrant discussion. Table 2.1 indicates that where the U.S. executive branch favors extraterritoriality, this correlates strongly, though not determinatively, with court actions, except when the sample is restricted to the appellate level (Model 6).[99] Nevertheless, executive preferences cannot provide a general explanation for U.S. court behavior. First, expressions of preference are infrequent in the data sample. In 471 of 598 cases in the base model, or 79 percent, the U.S. executive expressed no preference, structural or otherwise, for or against extraterritorial jurisdiction. Second, U.S. court decisions are more often than not consistent with known U.S. executive preferences, but this does not mean that U.S. court actions are driven by those preferences.[100] Indeed, 77 percent of the cases where the U.S. executive articulated a preference for extraterritorial jurisdiction also involved a threat either to domestic rule integrity or to basic rights.[101] In short, the outcomes in most if not all of these cases were over-determined.

The coefficients tracking foreign government interventions to oppose U.S. exercises of extraterritorial jurisdiction also have substantive weight and statistical significance across all of the unrestricted models – albeit in the opposite direction from what one might expect. That is to say, foreign government opposition to extraterritorial U.S. jurisdiction actually correlates with its exercise.[102] This is not perverse behavior on the part of U.S. federal courts, however. Instead, foreign governments

[99] The marginal difference of having an expressed executive branch preference favoring extraterritorial jurisdiction is 18 percent with 99 percent confidence in Model 1.

[100] In the sample data the U.S. executive expressed a preference for judicial extraterritoriality in 71 cases, and the court exercised jurisdiction in 53 of those. The U.S. executive expressed a preference against judicial extraterritoriality in 56 cases. In 29 of the 56 cases the court declined to exercise jurisdiction.

[101] Where the executive favored jurisdiction, U.S. federal courts obliged 75 percent of the time. By contrast, U.S. federal courts declined regulatory extraterritorially only 52 percent of the time when the U.S. executive expressly opposed it – a low result driven in part by the series of Guantánamo *habeas corpus* claims discussed at the beginning of this chapter.

[102] Here the marginal difference of a foreign government opposing extraterritoriality is to *increase* that likelihood by 18 percent with 95 percent confidence in Model 1.

are likely to undertake *amicus* interventions into the domestic judicial proceedings of foreign states only in cases that appear especially likely to go against their preferences. This is supported by the fact that twenty-six of the thirty-eight cases in which at least one foreign government intervened encompassed either a threat to domestic rule integrity or to basic rights.

The "year suit commenced" coefficient is small and insignificant across all of the models using the unrestricted sample. As discussed above, because cases selected into litigation are, by definition, highly contentious, the rate of plaintiff success in suits initiated by private actors (which encompasses the vast majority of claims in the sample) should tend toward a .5 success rate irrespective of an upward trend in the number of new claims per year.[103] In the model restricted to appellate cases, however, the year coefficient, though still small, is negative and significant at 90 percent, possibly hinting at a trend away from U.S. courts exercising jurisdiction extraterritorially in highly contentious claims.[104] Finally, the judicial ideology coefficient, as expected, has no discernible effect in these models, including at the appellate level.

As an overall robustness check to ensure that the reported results are not being driven by activity in one specific period of time, I also tested the base and full models in R, rescaling the time variable and adding random effects by year. I then constructed a vector to show the effect of each key explanatory variable by year.[105] These results indicate relatively little internal variability over time, which, in turn, suggests that the model is appropriately specified, and that explanatory variables are of continuous relevance. In sum, the statistical analysis supports the conclusion that the domestic rule integrity and basic rights hypotheses offer a highly plausible account of federal court behavior on contentious questions of extraterritorial jurisdictional during the period between 1945 and 2010 that is superior to known alternatives.

[103] Priest and Klein (1984). See also Shavell (1996) on the effects of different litigant stakes on success rates.

[104] Note, controlling for *habeas corpus* claims, of which there were several in the 2000s surrounding the U.S. military's detention center in Guantánamo Bay, Cuba, reduces the time coefficient slightly, though the variable is dropped from the restricted model, since it predicts appellate review perfectly.

[105] My thanks to Jeffrey Lax for guidance on this part of the testing.

Judicial line-drawing and litigant convenience

These results bring into focus several questions about what additional factors might operate in the minority of cases in which the theory fails to predict the outcome of U.S. court behavior. Although some proportion of the incorrectly predicted outcomes likely result from measurement error, coupled with idiosyncrasies ("noise") in the underlying data, others may have more systematic causes not captured in the model.

Figure 2.3 shows correctly predicted cases by issue area, along with "false positives" (where the theory predicts that U.S. courts will not exercise jurisdiction, but they do) and "false negatives" (where U.S. courts decline to exercise jurisdiction where the theory predicts that they would exercise it). The first point to note is that the number of outcomes correctly predicted by the main variables of interest exceeds those not correctly predicted in all issue areas, except national security. In 16.5 percent of the cases on which Model 1 is based, however, U.S. courts exercised jurisdiction where the theory predicts they would not. The two categories with the highest proportion of "false positives" are admiralty and tort, each with 35 percent of the case sample.

Tort and contract disputes are paradigmatically "private law" – meaning that the existence of a legal obligation arises out of the direct interaction of two (or more) private parties. These types of claims are typically decided by the law of the place where harm occurs. However, where an injury occurs in a setting where the litigants are not normally present, courts in a more convenient forum will often agree to decide claims, though they may still apply the law of the *situs* of harm.[106] An informal examination of judicial opinions in admiralty reveals that many of these are actually contract disputes or tort claims for injuries sustained on board vessels, which is to say they do not trigger the extraterritorial regulatory logic as described above. Instead, the same types of private law considerations are key to the relative concentration of false positives in admiralty as with torts. A close third in the false positive tally is the category of securities regulation, which is unambiguously an issue of public law, where 25 percent of the claims in the sample produced false positives. Explaining why the path-

[106] See, for example, *Bushnell v. Wackenhut International Inc.*, 731 S.Supp. 1534 (S.D. Fla. 1990) in which a U.S. federal court agreed to exercise jurisdiction over an extraterritorial workers' compensation claim brought by a U.K. employee of a Florida company, but applied the law of Saudi Arabia, where the injury occurred.

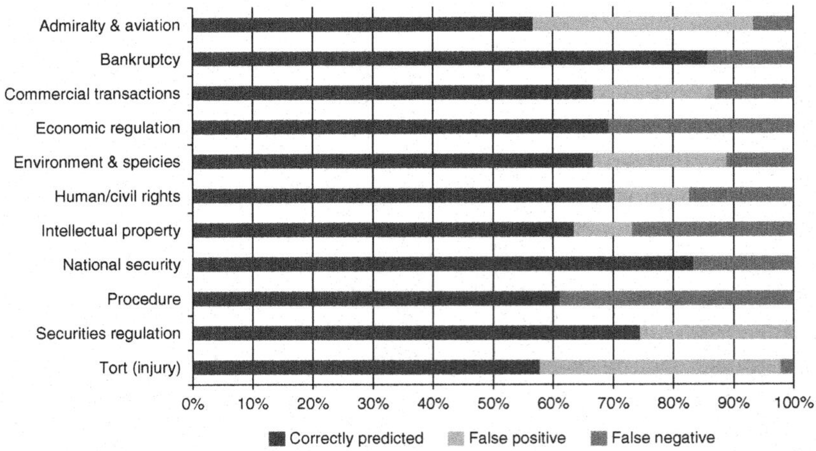

Figure 2.3 Predicted outcomes by issue area

dependent legal trajectory captured here emerged, and why it has recently been cut off and forced back to the modal decision rule, is addressed in Chapter 7.

In another 19 percent of the cases in Figure 2.3, the threat variables predict an exercise of jurisdiction where none occurred. These "false negatives" are concentrated in economic regulation, human/civil rights, intellectual property, procedure, and national security. Among the factors that might explain this result, two stand out. The first, and more mundane, is litigant-driven boundary testing of legal rules. The logic is that where an observable change in the scope or applicability of a rule occurs by either judicial or legislative means, plaintiffs frequently emerge to test the extent of the change, and they continue to bring claims until courts draw a line by issuing a negative holding, indicating its limits.[107] A second set of factors more specific to extraterritoriality involves judicial use of so-called prudential (or "discretionary") doctrines of dismissal. Judges use these doctrines in situations where sufficient grounds likely exist for a court to exercise jurisdiction extraterritorially, but they opt not to do so for reasons such as deference to foreign courts or governments, or to another branch of the U.S. government.[108] Consideration of this type

[107] See for example, *Atlantic Richfield Co. v. Arco Globus International Co., Inc.*, 150 F.3d 189 (2d Cir. 1998) following *Reebok International v. Sebelen*, 930 F.Supp. 720.

[108] Note, however, that U.S. federal judges do not always go to the effort to make formal findings of jurisdiction before invoking prudential doctrines. See Michaels (2005).

of dismissal, thus, comes into play in situations where international relations, U.S. separation-of-powers politics, and concerns about appropriate uses of domestic judicial resources are most evident.

To test to what degree the false negatives in the sample turn on these factors, I coded a variable "basis of dismissal" for each observation in which a U.S. court did not exercise jurisdiction. The variable encompasses the following categories: dismissals on jurisdictional grounds, for "failure to state a claim," and on prudential grounds. The category for prudential dismissals contains four subcategories. The first involves a judicial determination that another state has a superior legal or political interest in deciding a dispute ("international comity"). Inconvenient forum dismissals (*forum non conveniens*) are used when a court finds that the United States lacks a strong connection with the alleged wrong, and that another available judicial forum would be more appropriate. For example, when many of the witnesses and much of the evidence needed to conduct a fair trial are located abroad, well-advised defendants may raise *forum non conveniens* as an issue. "Act of state" dismissals are a third type that may be used if deciding an extraterritorial claim under U.S. law would require a U.S. court to sit in judgment of a foreign sovereign act that was intended to have effect only inside the foreign state. A fourth type is when U.S. federal courts determine that a complaint centrally concerns an issue explicitly reserved to another branch of the U.S. government ("political question").

Distinguishing between dismissals on jurisdictional grounds and dismissals for failure to state a claim for coding purposes can be difficult.[109] Classification as a jurisdictional dismissal is appropriate where the law does not appear to reach the general type of conduct at issue. By contrast, where a law has some acknowledged extraterritorial reach on the dispute issue, but something in the details of the pleadings indicates a poor fit between the law and the facts alleged, a case

[109] For example, U.S. law is very conservative about recognizing "cruel, inhuman, and degrading treatment" in international human rights law. Thus, a plaintiff who alleges treatment that was "degrading" according to international treaties or foreign law in the context of an Alien Tort Statute claim might find herself with a "no jurisdiction" ruling in U.S. court. From the other side, U.S. law clearly prohibits torture, but there is often contestation about where the definitional boundary of torture lies (cf. *Sosa v. Alvarez-Machain* 542 U.S. 692, 2004). The first of these would be coded as a "jurisdictional dismissal" and the second as a "failure to state a claim."

is coded as a dismissal for "failure to state a claim."[110] Also grouped under this coding are dismissals for lack of personal jurisdiction over the defendants, since there too the determinative issue is not the reach of the law *per se*, but whether specific entities can be called to account under it.

Coding for comparison across cases is complicated by inconsistencies in how judges themselves label dismissals and also because judges may cite multiple grounds for dismissing a single case.[111] Where the most recent written opinion for a case states one ground or another, the coding follows the judicial classification. For opinions containing more than one reason for dismissal, a lack of jurisdiction is presumed to have priority.[112] In the handful of situations where judicial reasoning was wholly non-transparent, coding proceeded on the basis of the case description and coder awareness of whether the underlying law had been previously applied extraterritorially.[113]

In slightly more than one-third of the one-hundred dismissals for which my theory incorrectly predicts a U.S. court would exercise jurisdiction, the court's reason was lack of jurisdiction. This encompasses situations involving both the extraterritorial inapplicability of U.S. law and an absence of personal jurisdiction over the defendants. In forty cases, the court's reason was a failure to state a claim under prospectively applicable law. The remaining twenty-four false negatives turned on judicial use of prudential doctrines. By comparison, among the 163 dismissals that Model 1 correctly predicted, 61 percent were for lack of jurisdiction, and 24 percent for failure to state a claim. Only 15 percent (twenty-four in total) cited a prudential doctrine as the main basis for dismissal.[114]

110 For example, in an alleged conspiracy to restrain trade through a cartel (an issue where U.S. courts have been extraterritorially very assertive), if the conduct alleged in the claim did not meet the U.S. legal definition of a "cartel," the case would be coded as a dismissal for "failure to state a claim."

111 Wasserman (2011).

112 For example, a case dismissed on comity grounds, and for lack of jurisdiction, is coded as a "jurisdictional dismissal."

113 The same two independent coders referred to in footnote 81 also coded this variable for the same subsample of cases. In 67 percent of these cases, all three coders agreed on the basis for dismissal. At least one of the coders agreed with the author in 90 percent of the cases. In five cases where the independent coders together disagreed with the author's coding, that coding was changed to reflect the majority assessment.

114 Recall that judges at times dismiss on prudential grounds prior to a formal finding of jurisdiction if the reasons for doing so appear compelling at the outset. Thus,

Table 2.2 *Primary basis of dismissal*

	Correctly predicted	False negative
No jurisdiction	99	36
Failure to state a claim	40	40
Discretionary doctrine	24	24
N	163	100

Also noteworthy is that roughly 85 percent of the false negatives summarized in Table 2.2 are concentrated in four issue areas – intellectual property disputes, economic regulation, commercial transactions, and human/civil rights.[115] Why might this be so? First, these are all areas of public law in which U.S. courts have long had a larger domestic administrative role than, for example, in national security. Second, these are also areas in which extra-legal developments in the form of political, organizational, and technological changes have at times generated sizeable ambiguities about whether, how, and against whom U.S. laws apply. Finally, some degree of boundary testing with regard to what conduct a rule encompasses, or to whom it applies, also emerges endogenously from judicial or statutory changes in the underlying law. Such changes, in turn, are more likely in active areas of litigation.[116]

In addition, Table 2.3 shows that features of the political environment in which U.S. federal courts operate sometimes override other incentives to exercise jurisdiction extraterritorially. This happens most often in economic and commercial interactions, and with regard to the extraterritoriality of U.S. ideas about rights to free speech and assembly, which are not universally shared by other states. That said, U.S. courts claim to rely on discretionary doctrines far less often than the frequency of their invocation by litigants might suggest. Defendants raised at least one – and often more than one – prudential consideration in 222 (37 percent) of the 598 cases in Model 1. In all

a prudential dismissal does not necessarily imply anything trustworthy regarding jurisdiction.

115 These figures are 39 percent, 16 percent, 11 percent, and 18 percent, respectively.

116 These issues are explored in greater depth in Chapter 3.

Table 2.3 *Discretionary dismissals by subcategory*

	Threat to domestic rule	Alleged violation of basic right	No domestic rule threat or basic right violation	*N*
Act of state	4	0	1	5 (10%)
Comity	11	1	9	21 (44%)
Forum non conveniens	3	3	12	18 (38%)
Political question	0	2	2	4 (8%)
N	18 (38%)	6 (12%)	24 (50%)	48 (100%)

but forty-eight cases, U.S. federal courts rejected these doctrines as a basis for dismissal.

Comparing rates of prudential dismissals across all outcomes in Model 1 shows that half occurred when there was neither a threat to the domestic operation of a U.S. legal rule nor any allegation of violation of basic rights. This accords with the logic of judicial economy. In confirmation of this, the subcategory of discretionary dismissal with the highest number involving no such threat is *forum non conveniens*.[117] Similarly, dismissals on political question grounds – when the judiciary essentially defers to executive branch concerns on foreign policy – occur in the sample only when there are no threats to the domestic integrity of regulatory rules. By contrast, most act of state dismissals in the sample – four out of five – involved conduct coded as threatening a U.S. domestic rule, indicating that U.S. courts will at times bow to higher international legal principles, even when doing so entails costs. Finally, twelve of twenty-one comity dismissals involved some type of threat, with most implicating the domestic rule integrity logic.

[117] Indeed, in only seven of the nineteen cases in which *forum non conveniens* was the primary basis of dismissal were one of these threats at issue.

Finally, prudential dismissals do not appear to be heavily driven by executive preference or by foreign government protest. Of the forty-eight claims in which a prudential doctrine was cited as the primary basis for dismissal, an expressed (non-structural) executive preference against jurisdiction was a factor in only three, and only one case involved a preference for jurisdiction. Likewise, in only one case was there a foreign government intervention for the purpose of opposing jurisdiction.

Conclusion

The findings in this chapter support the claim that U.S. courts are significantly more likely to find that U.S. law applies outside U.S. borders in situations where a failure to regulate extraterritorial conduct would create opportunities, or incentives, for circumventing domestic regulatory rules. To restate this point in terms with slightly more doctrinal resonance, when U.S. courts draw jurisdictional lines in the absence of clear legislative guidance, some kinds of adverse domestic effects matter more than others – namely, those that, if unchecked, would frustrate the core purpose of an act of Congress. The analysis also indicates that conduct inside U.S territory alone is insufficient to support jurisdiction on regulatory matters where the harmful effects of contested behavior are concentrated outside the United States. More tentatively, the analysis also suggests that where extraterritorial violations of core rights are alleged to have been committed by entities with close U.S. ties, U.S. courts are also likely to exercise jurisdiction extraterritorially.

U.S. courts are inward-looking institutions that, nevertheless, by virtue of being a part of a very powerful country, have a non-trivial capacity to affect actors and processes in the transnational realm. Because the authority of U.S. courts to decide extraterritorial claims extends only as far as the laws they are asked to enforce, U.S. judges have been concerned with the world outside the United States to the extent that extraterritorial conduct creates negative externalities for the operational integrity of U.S. law inside U.S. territory, or where such conduct by, or against, U.S. entities is alleged to violate rights fundamental to U.S. political identity, but rarely beyond this.

The next chapter situates this understanding of U.S. court behavior within a wider account of international processes of law formation and diffusion. It argues that patterns of judicial decision-making on extraterritorial jurisdiction influence patterns of strategic rule-following among private entities in the transnational realm and, by extension, the preferences and options that the U.S. government and other governments have over bargaining at the international level.

3

Domestic courts and transnational governance

Regulatory order in the transnational sphere – defined liberally to encompass rule-governed activity characterized by predictability – is a product of the often uncoordinated, or incompletely coordinated, actions of governments, international organizations, and private actors. Whatever "rules" exist generally have their operational center of gravity in states, and, specifically, in states' capacities to compel private actors to follow rules that accord with the state's policies or preferences. States that are willing and able to impose their legal preferences on others, either unilaterally or through international bargaining, have a heightened ability to shape the "rules of the game" for the system as a whole. They determine not only which rules apply, and to whom, but also the scope and meaning of those rules.[1]

Extraterritorial regulation by judicial means is one way that powerful states may impose their regulatory preferences on transnational non-state actors and, indirectly, on foreign governments. Despite its relevance to a wide range of international economic, social, and political issues, extraterritoriality is not a common theme in international relations (IR) scholarship. In one respect this is unsurprising, since extraterritorial regulation involves actors and institutions not traditionally featured in IR theory: law, non-governmental (private) actors, and domestic courts. In other, more substantively relevant respects, however, the paucity of attention to the strategic behavior of transnational private actors in and around law and courts reflects overly narrow ideas about their role in shaping the transnational regulatory order, and with it the government-to-government interactions that are the main focus of IR theory.

Law is a key medium by which governments formalize state policy. Most domestic law directly or indirectly concerns private actors – specifying rights and obligations they owe to governments, that governments

[1] See, for example, Nollkaemper (2007), Benvenisti (2008), and Roberts (2011) on domestic court decisions as persuasive authority in international law.

owe to them, or setting limits on how private entities may behave toward one another. Even international law, which, since the sixteenth century, has been concerned primarily with rights and duties among states, is indirectly about carving out spheres of sovereign authority in defined territories. The fact that individuals, both "natural" and "corporate," frequently cross international boundaries in pursuit of commercial, social, and political objectives has long complicated this otherwise elegant arrangement. If we consider, further, that law often has distributional effects, and that transnational and non-transnational entities generally compete for resources, prestige, and other "private goods," it would be remarkable if they did not approach law strategically, seeking its application, or limitation, in ways calculated to serve their own interests.

In this chapter, I examine the micro-foundations of U.S. regulatory extraterritoriality and identify conditions for its influence on the creation and maintenance of regulatory order in the transnational sphere. I contend that empowering private actors to initiate extraterritorial applications of U.S. law using the U.S. court system affects the transnational reach of U.S. law and, therefore, helps to shape the regulatory structures within which transnational actors operate. The efforts of private actors to convince U.S. courts to apply U.S. law extraterritorially to new variants of conduct, new actors, and new settings shape the transnational regulatory landscape in at least two ways. The first is by structuring the expectations (or incentives) of broader categories of private transnational actors concerning the potential costs (or benefits) of failing to adhere to U.S. law. The second is by influencing the conditions under which the United States government will seek to bargain with others internationally for purposes of regulatory coordination, and by shaping its objectives in those interactions.

The focus on laws and courts in the United States is not incidental. No other country has engaged in extraterritorial regulation to a similar extent. This is due, I submit, to structural features of the U.S. domestic regulatory system – specifically, its heavy reliance on private enforcement of public law through domestic courts – along with the near-hegemonic dominance of the United States in international economic affairs during much of the period since World War II. For decades this dominance provided U.S. courts unparalleled (though far from unlimited, or invariant) extraterritorial enforcement capacity.[2] This has allowed private

[2] In several issue areas the European Union has arguably attained a comparable level of enforcement capacity. See the case study chapters for further detail and discussion.

entities with U.S. ties to view the potential for court-based extraterritorial enforcement of U.S. rules as a resource – or a threat. The fact that for decades no other state was able, or willing, to provide such a mechanism on a comparable scale has also contributed to the character and perceived efficacy of U.S. extraterritoriality.

U.S. court decisions regarding the extraterritorial reach of U.S. law obviously matter a great deal to litigants contesting U.S. jurisdiction. However, these decisions are also observed by non-litigants, for whom they are a source of information about which U.S. laws apply, when, and to whom. In this way, the jurisdictional decisions of U.S. courts cast an enforcement shadow over the behavior of much wider audiences of transnational actors contemplating conduct that is confirmedly, or prospectively, within the reach of U.S. courts.[3] This, in turn, can make it more difficult for foreign states where U.S.-regulated entities are active to maintain regulatory policies that are significantly at odds with U.S. rules.

The frequently hybrid character of regulatory enforcement in the U.S. context is, again, worth underscoring. U.S. extraterritoriality is undeniably state-based, since domestic courts are state institutions. It is also in important respects decoupled from the state to the extent that agency in targeting enforcement has been partially delegated to private plaintiffs. As a result, U.S. law in several issue areas almost certainly has been projected far more widely, geographically, and in terms of actors and issue areas, than would have occurred in the absence of private enforcement. This is corroborated, for example, by the relatively timid extraterritorial enforcement of the Foreign Corrupt Practices Act of 1977 (which does not allow for private rights of action) for the first twenty-five years of its existence. During this period, which was a highly active one for extraterritorial private enforcement efforts of many stripes, the FCPA enforcement was "sporadic at best,"[4] averaging fewer than one case per year.[5] In short, it is not only the enforcement power of the United States but also the role of private litigants in selecting when to bring that power to bear extraterritorially in the service of U.S. public law, that

3 Mnookin and Kornhauser (1979).

4 Mark (2012:420).

5 www.sec.gov/spotlight/fcpa/fcpa-cases.shtml, last accessed on July 9, 2015. The rate of FCPA enforcement increased dramatically after 2004, which the Attorney General at that time, John Ashcroft, attributes the use of the FCPA to gain leverage over the financial aspects of international terrorism, Ashcroft and Ratcliff (2012:28–29).

makes transnational litigation in domestic courts worthy of attention.[6]

The following section describes how the strategic behavior of private entities complicates the transnational regulatory efforts of states and governments. Next I lay out a three-part framework for analyzing when private entities should be expected to seek changes in the extraterritorial application of U.S. law, and when they are likely to turn to courts to do so. This involves identifying agents in the creation of extraterritorial legal disputes, describing the incentives that drive their behavior, together with the domestic institutional, and international systemic, opportunity structures that describe the regulatory environment. I then consider the dynamism inherent in the framework together with specific sources of instability in legal rules.

Subsequent chapters examine these dynamics in three issue areas with differing degrees of institutionalization at the international level. In the first two case studies, international antitrust and intellectual property rights, the applicable extraterritorial logic is "domestic rule integrity." The operative logic in the third case study, international human rights, is "basic rights protection."

U.S. extraterritoriality, foreign governments, and international rules

Who benefits from a fragmented legal order, and for whom is a multiplicity of legal rules relatively more costly? Answering this question requires looking at the processes of legal and regulatory competition among states in the international system, and also within them. More specifically, it involves examining the political and distributional reasons why legal harmonization, which would result in substantial transaction cost savings, often fails to occur.

Under a unilateralist approach to managing conflicts of law, courts exercise jurisdiction whenever domestic law requires it, irrespective of resistance from foreign courts and governments. Because this approach gives more powerful states greater leeway in enforcing their rules, it is, unsurprisingly, often preferred by the United States. Where U.S. enforcement capacity is observed to be robust, decentralized, and capable of

[6] Of course, U.S. courts have not been infinitely malleable on this account. As Chapter 2 argues, U.S. judges are reluctant transnational regulators, opting to exercise jurisdiction extraterritorially principally where outside conduct threatens the domestic integrity of a U.S. law, or where entities with U.S. ties are implicated in alleged violations of basic rights.

imposing real costs on those found to be violators, it incentivizes actors with actual, or anticipated, U.S. ties to take steps to avoid violating U.S. rules.[7] Individual court decisions, thus, add incrementally to the pool of information that public and private actors have for calculating whether, and from what sources, they are likely to be sanctioned for violating a U.S. rule. Conversely, outcomes that suggest U.S. regulators are unable, or unwilling, to enforce U.S. rules extraterritorially likewise impart useful information to transnational actors about the risks of deviating from U.S. rules and standards.[8]

The ability of individual states to set and maintain their own regulatory policies is thus affected by the micro-level decisions of transnational actors such as corporations, investors, banks, and labor unions. The choices that self-interested private actors make regarding which states' rules to follow in their transnational activities are part of what regularizes their behavior and renders it predictable to other private actors. Importantly, these choices are heavily mediated by preferences over the content of different states' domestic laws, and also by each state's capacity to enforce those laws. It follows that where domestic-level regulatory institutions display both the willingness and the capacity to extract penalties for legal non-compliance not only inside the state but also extraterritorially, this gives those institutions a heightened ability to shape the transnational "rules of the game" for private entities that may plausibly come within their enforcement reach.

Whether and how private actors respond to regulatory preferences and capabilities of extraterritorial regulators in turn influences the options that governments have for managing regulatory competition. Extraterritorial assertiveness on the part of U.S. courts, for example, may make it more costly for foreign governments whose domestically influential nationals are targeted by U.S. litigation to maintain regulatory rules or policies that are strongly at odds with U.S. preferences. How much leeway any government has in setting regulatory rules for the activities of private actors may vary depending on the state's political and military status, its economic attributes, and its dependencies on other states and markets.

7 Enforcement need not be perfect, however, in order to influence the strategic behavior of private actors. This is due to the "shadow" of the law (and its enforcement) discussed above.

8 Putnam (2009), Abbott and Snidal (2000).

When do states adjust?

A first step in theorizing how extraterritorial regulation on the part of U.S. courts influences international regulatory competition is to consider where it fits in to the menu of alternatives available to the U.S. government and those of other states. As a preliminary matter, it is important to underscore that the existence of legal differences alone may not generate internal or external pressure for adjustment. Not all states' rules are incompatible, and even where incompatibilities exist, not all governments are equally intent on harmonization.[9] Where conflicts involving private entities prompt questions about which state will regulate, often they are resolved with little difficulty. Factors that may come into play to make these situations political non-events include principles of international comity (deference), efforts to conserve judicial resources, or the simple lack of foreign government interest or capacity to protest.[10] By contrast, where legal incompatibilities become a source of domestic discontent in one or both states, this may translate into pressures for change through either internal adjustments or for weaker states to adapt their rules to the demands of more powerful ones.

Trivially, unilateral adjustments toward harmonization are likely when the expected costs of maintaining the *status quo* are higher than those from adopting changes. Figuring out to whom costs and benefits of domestic legal and regulatory arrangements accrue and how beneficiaries are positioned politically is the key to identifying likely thresholds for change. In liberal democracies, legislated rules generally reflect prior political bargains. Consequently, they can be difficult to alter in the absence of substantial changes in the underlying interests that led to their creation. Even where baseline circumstances change, intervening patterns of formal institutionalization, along with accumulated residues of individual-level choices made in reliance on the rules, may prompt former opponents and those who were previously indifferent to favor the *status quo* – or even a more stringent version of the existing rule. It follows that opportunities for legislative readjustment may require external "shocks" that either negatively affect the state as a whole, or

[9] For example, claims under the U.S. False Claims Act concerning extraterritorial fraud against the U.S. government often generate little foreign government resistance. Likewise states' efforts to enforce their tax laws with regard to extraterritorial assets raise no "red flags."

[10] Juenger (1988), Efrat and Newman (2015). Private entities may also preemptively seek to minimize uncertainties using "choice of law" and "choice of forum" provisions in contracts.

which alter the preferences of the law's core supporters. Because large, powerful states like the United States are generally less likely to experience external shocks than are weaker states, such opportunities can be far from frequent.

Where transnational actors inside powerful states who are disadvantaged by differential foreign laws are unable to get their own states to adjust, they may instead (or in addition) support efforts to get other states to bring their laws closer to the more powerful state's ideal. This may encompass efforts to coerce, cajole, or entice foreign private actors and governments. The U.S. government has a diverse menu of options for signaling the existence and strength of its preferences in regulatory matters. On the more coercive side of the spectrum are mechanisms like aid conditionality and threats of political and economic sanctions.[11] From the other direction, the U.S. government may provide foreign governments with expert advisors and various forms of U.S. technical assistance to nudge laws and policies in more preferred directions.[12] Tactics of this sort often affect private entities only indirectly. Others, such as private certifications or exclusionary lists, are specifically targeted at the behavior of transnational non-state actors. Programs of this type exist in issues as diverse as air travel, banking and finance, species protection, international shipping, and efforts to suppress international terrorism. Their existence indicates acknowledgement by the U.S. government that at least some transnational non-state actors are capable of harming U.S. territory or interests in ways that other states are unwilling – or unable – to curtail.

Although clearly extraterritorial in both their intent and effects, these mechanisms differ in important respects from the court- based extraterritoriality in focus here. One key difference concerns how, and by whom, the mechanisms are administered. Another is the character of penalties that attach to violations. Whereas certifications and blacklists are directed mainly by executive officials, extraterritorial jurisdiction may be established by Congress, or articulated in U.S. federal court decisions at the prompting of executive officials, or private entities. Furthermore, the penalties associated with decertification are limited to denying entities access to U.S. territory, institutions, or resources. Court-based extraterritorial enforcement, by contrast, may involve penalties far

[11] Drezner (2007).
[12] Simmons (2001), Bach and Newman (2007).

beyond mere denial of access and can be triggered in some instances whether or not U.S. entry (or contact) is sought.

When do states bargain?

Efforts to extract adjustments from others may take the form of international bargaining among governments. Here the strategy is often to secure concessions from other states in for adjustments to non-essential features of one's own domestic law. Under what conditions, then, should we expect powerful states to participate in international bargaining, and how should we expect less powerful states to respond?

Bargaining theory suggests that where influential constituents inside a state expect to gain little from formal cooperation, they are unlikely to press for international engagement – except where necessary to block other states from bringing a less advantageous legal order into being.[13] That is to say, willingness to bargain is endogenous to some expectation of increasing benefits, or reducing costs. Drezner (2007) argues that when powerful states have fundamentally different, and incompatible, preferences over regulatory rules, there is little reason to expect bargaining to result in anything resembling harmonization. Instead, the expected result is a regime characterized by "rival standards" and no international agreement.[14] Under these circumstances, regulatory competition involves getting third states to adopt one's own preferred rules – or at least to not adopt those preferred by the competitor.

Court-based extraterritoriality can turn up the temperature in such situations by providing a venue for clashes among private entities that claim to be following different sets of rules. Legal-regulatory clashes are especially likely under two sets of conditions. The first is where different states' rules involve a direct conflict of laws – that is, when one forbids what another requires.[15] These situations are quite rare, however. Swiss banking secrecy laws that prohibit disclosure of clients' identities, contrary to the transparency laws of several other states, are one example. The second and far more common type of legal-regulatory clash is less acute. It occurs when one state permits (but does not require) what

[13] Fearon (1998), Sell (2003).

[14] Drezner (2007). In rare cases where an agreement of some sort is struck under these circumstances (e.g. in response to coordinated demand by weaker states), Drezner expects its contents to be vague and unenforceable ("sham standards").

[15] *Hartford Fire Insurance Corp. v. California*, 113 S.Ct. 2891 (1993).

another forbids or requires. In these situations, the decision as to which state will decide the dispute thus determines which rules will apply – and, often, also which litigant will prevail. Problems of an inter-governmental character arise here most commonly when the territorial sovereign favors the more permissive rule, and regulators in each state have a strong preference for having their own rule control.

In situations where U.S. laws are more restrictive than – or simply different from – those of other states, compelling businesses and other transnational actors under U.S. jurisdiction to follow U.S. law in their transnational transactions imposes net costs not faced by outside competitors. Often such requirements are viewed as imposing a competitive disadvantage. One obvious means to avoid such costs is to seek other locations with less restrictive regulations. However, exit is not always feasible if it requires walking away from needed assets, resources, or markets. Alternatively, one might aim to segment one's operations to capitalize on legal differences – to behave one way inside the state with restrictive rules, and another way outside it. This is possible, however, only when segmentation would not itself introduce prohibitively large transaction costs.[16] Yet another option is to attempt to apply the more restrictive U.S. rule outside U.S. territory, at least to other transnational entities with operations or assets in the United States.

Where U.S. courts have a record of applying U.S. law extraterritorially, transnational actors that have, or anticipate having, ties to U.S. markets are well-advised to forgo conduct that could produce harmful U.S. effects, even in locations where it is permitted. By narrowing the field of activity that private actors can consider safely outside the reach of U.S. regulation, court-based extraterritoriality helps to shape the transnational rules of the game in accordance with U.S. domestic preferences.[17] With respect to basic rights, the jurisdictional irrelevance of location is largely embedded in the concept itself. Consequently, the main sources of actionable variation concern which rights are held to be "basic," together with questions about who, or what, has the ability to claim those rights using U.S. courts, and against whom? The answers can change – and have changed – over time with regard both to the content of rights and to political and legal understandings of who may claim them in which forums.

[16] Vogel (1997).

[17] For example, effects-based extraterritoriality undercuts "race to the bottom" logics of international regulatory competition by making geography largely irrelevant.

Conversely, the prospect of harmonization through international bargaining may hold greater attraction for the governments of powerful states like the United States in situations where there is no stark divide on core regulatory premises or objectives, or where unilateral processes have proven unsatisfactory to relevant domestic interest groups. How can agreement over substantive rules alone help? Getting other states to agree to adopt shared legal rules and standards can make it easier to exert administrative or diplomatic pressure on foreign governments to step up enforcement, either directly or using treaty-based mechanisms (where available). At the same time, I expect domestic interest groups to resist entering into treaty arrangements that would require giving up established options for targeted protection of claimed rights and entitlements.

U.S. domestic courts as "sites of action": an agency-based framework

Transnational transactions, by definition, bring the laws of two or more states into contact and, at times, into conflict. Segmenting transnational conduct into location-specific components for regulatory purposes is often impossible, however. Consequently, whether seeking to clarify, comply with, or avoid legal rules, transnational actors should be rationally concerned with whether, and under what conditions, their own and other states' laws may apply to their actions. Divining the existence of applicable legal rules in the transnational sphere involves conjectures about (1) the prescriptive reach of the rules potentially in play; (2) availability and access to enforcement triggers; and (3) expectations about the efficacy of seeking regulatory enforcement. These conjectures also inform decisions to initiate or contest extraterritorial claims. I discuss each of these elements separately below. As will be quickly evident, however, developments in one area often have implications in others.[18]

In law-based systems of governance, multiple actors interpret and apply law simultaneously. In the United States, this includes not only courts but also executive branch departments, agencies, commissions, task forces, and the like. Private entities likewise interpret the scope and meaning of legal rules in the context of their own activities and in formulating expectations regarding the likely behavior

[18] Endogeneity is clearly at play here. Although courts cannot act absent formal claims, plaintiffs will initiate claims only where they believe they have a shot at convincing a court to exercise jurisdiction, and, ultimately, to find in their favor.

of others.[19] Unlike many of these actors, however, courts have no basis to interpret or apply law in the absence of a live dispute – not domestically, and not transnationally.[20] Therefore, for U.S. judicial extraterritoriality to be a factor in structuring the transnational regulatory order, agents outside the judiciary must initiate legal claims. This, in turn, requires beliefs among prospective litigants on both sides of disputes that litigation, relative to other options (including doing nothing), is likely to yield net benefits. This can be the case only where a degree of plausible ambiguity exists concerning the law's applicability, scope, or content. It also requires some belief in the *ex post* enforcement capacity of U.S. courts – both for the parties to immediate dispute and where litigants are seeking to shape legal rules to govern future transnational interactions, also more broadly.

Attempts to disentangle agents from the opportunity structures that help to delineate their agency for analytical purposes can be difficult. Legal rules (or their absence) often shape, and in some cases directly constitute, legal agents and define the actions they may take. For example, legal rules that assign patent rights to inventors specify procedural criteria for establishing such rights and also create rights holders who are then allowed to take steps to protect those rights, which includes the ability to sue alleged infringers. Although patent rights generally extend only as far as the law that establishes them, it is also the case that the agency granted to individual rights holders to enforce their rights also can be used in efforts to change the reach of the underlying law.[21]

In light of these complexities, a logical place to start in describing the policy-relevant strategies of private litigants in the transnational sphere is with questions about which states seek to regulate what kinds of transnational conduct, and what kinds of ambiguities emerge from those efforts.

[19] To reprise from Chapter 2, I approach litigants as rule-bound, strategic actors who respond rationally to professional and institutional incentives, while operating with incomplete information. Of course, different actors may have different underlying utilities and preferences and operate with different environmental constraints.

[20] See Chapter 2 for a discussion of jurisdiction and its elements.

[21] Note, however, that it is not always in the interest (or within the capacity) of individual rights holders to pursue enforcement against alleged infringers. In short, agency alone does not dictate behavior.

U.S. Law and its extraterritorial reach

In the United States, domestic law comprises rules and standards of behavior that are enforceable by courts, or by administrative institutions whose actions are reviewable by courts. The U.S. Constitution contains no limits on the ability of Congress to make (or "prescribe") law with extraterritorial reach. Nor does it contain any direct limits on the ability of U.S. federal courts to resolve disputes that "arise under" U.S. laws. However, a default rule of customary international law holds that domestic law generally does not apply outside the boundaries of the enacting state. This idea is rooted in the principles of sovereign equality, which include the right of each state to order its internal affairs without interference from others.[22] When the United States, or another state, attempts to apply its own law in another's territory, or to its citizens in areas of shared jurisdiction (e.g. the high seas), the potential for foreign governments to take legal and political umbrage is, therefore, high.

Legal disputes arise when one party alleges that another has caused it harm through behavior inconsistent with an applicable law, and – critically – the accused contests that claim on the basis of a different interpretation of the same law, or by invoking a superseding rule. Ambiguity regarding the applicability or content of rules is thus a core feature of any legal dispute.[23] While disputes about legal substance may be important elements in transnational litigation, jurisdictional questions are logically and procedurally prior to these disagreements. This is because in the transnational realm, outcomes on jurisdictional questions largely determine not only the forum in which the dispute will be decided but also which state's laws will apply.[24]

From an American perspective, the legal universe is a patchwork of overlapping jurisdictions within and between countries. Consequently,

22 Shaw (2008). This idea is also reflected in an American canon of statutory construction known as the "presumption against extraterritoriality." For a catalogue of justifications underlying this presumption, see Bradley (1998).

23 Priest and Klein (1984). In common law systems, where a dispute is substantially similar to a prior dispute decided by a competent court, then that court's holding is considered controlling precedent until overridden by a higher court, or overturned legislatively. Where a dispute involves some variance with respect to conduct, parties, location, or other legally relevant factor, then the party that is disfavored by the prior holding will try to parlay those differences into arguments that the court should reach a different conclusion.

24 Where disputes concern issues of public law, forum generally determines both procedural and substantive rules. Consequently, litigants are rarely indifferent about jurisdictional questions.

states with the ability and desire to exercise jurisdiction in areas of overlap may do so whenever it would not be patently unfair to defendants. This approach contrasts sharply with the continental European (or multilateralist) view, which holds that jurisdiction properly lies in only one venue, as predetermined by a comprehensive framework that purports to give full respect to the sovereign authority of all concerned states and to provide for the recognition and enforcement of foreign judgments.[25] Thus, whereas the U.S. approach emphasizes unilateral action tempered by concerns about unfair exercises of power over individuals by states – a view that, not coincidentally, privileges its own regulatory power – the European approach is more centrally concerned with the allocation of regulatory authority among co-equal sovereigns.[26]

Contemporary forms of U.S. extraterritoriality are frequently grounded in a deeply unilateralist legal construct known as the "effects doctrine" of jurisdiction. This doctrine permits U.S. courts to exercise jurisdiction over conduct that takes place outside U.S. boundaries if it generates harmful effects inside the United States.[27] Jurisdictional claims based solely, or primarily, on whether a given threshold of domestic effect is satisfied are, not surprisingly, often in tension with the principles of territoriality and domestic sovereignty. They are wholly anathema to strict multilateralist approaches. Assertive use of domestic effects-based claims of jurisdiction likewise has a critically important implication for transnational entities: it sharply pares down options for geographic exit.[28] This is because escaping U.S. regulation requires foregoing not just prohibited conduct in U.S. territory but also U.S. markets and services, since these can be bases both for anchoring personal jurisdiction and for satisfying adverse judgments.

Where U.S. courts or equivalent regulatory institutions are, in principle, open to asserting jurisdiction extraterritorially on the basis of domestic effects, defining the magnitude and quality of the effects required to trigger the applicability of U.S. law, and with it the

[25] The key treaty instruments in this regard are the 1968 Brussels Convention, and the superseding 2002 Brussels I Regulation, Regulation (EC) No 44/2001.

[26] Michaels (2005).

[27] Early articulations of the U.S. effects doctrine required both harmful U.S. effects and an intention to cause them. In several issue areas, however, judicial emphasis on intentionality eroded, and the ability to demonstrate harmful effects of specific types or magnitudes became sufficient to ground jurisdiction (Knox 2010).

[28] Basedow (2000:1045).

jurisdiction of U.S. courts, is critically important. These thresholds can affect not only the incidence but also the outcomes of litigated disputes.[29]

The legal and regulatory uncertainties that jurisdictional overlaps generate are, thus, important drivers of strategic behavior involving U.S. law and its extraterritorial reach. For transnational actors, the stakes in these judicial determinations can be quite high, since decisions about whether U.S. law applies extraterritorially to a particular types of conduct or classes of entities generally mean the difference between having the benefit (or burden) of the enforcement power of the United States and its institutions – or not having it. Whether and how transnational actors try to extend U.S. law or to test its boundaries depends on the existence of permissive institutions and opportunity structures for this purpose, coupled with more specific incentives to galvanize those institutions to action.

Agents and incentives to litigate

The main task of courts is to decide legal disputes. In the United States, regulatory disputes are often framed as legal disputes. This is likewise the case for the protection of personal rights. For U.S. courts to be involved in transnational regulatory processes, however, requires not only the existence of applicable legal rules and jurisdiction to apply them but also agents to trigger their application. Two factors are especially important here. The first is identifying actors for whom litigation is an option. The second involves ascertaining when litigation is likely to be a rationally preferred option – either alone or in parallel with other tactics. Preliminary to both inquiries, however, is identifying whom, or what, in the transnational sphere benefits from variability in the existence, content, or enforcement of states' legal rules, and who has incentives to minimize, or eliminate it?

U.S. courts and private rights of action

In all economically advanced states, government agencies and courts have some role in regulatory enforcement. Wide variation exists, however, regarding modes (or sites) of enforcement, and in who is permitted to initiate claims. On the administrative side of the spectrum, specialized

[29] For disputes that are primarily factual in character, differences in procedural rules can be critically important. They may determine, for example, the standing of plaintiffs, time limitations on the claim, the ability to obtain evidence, the presence of a jury, and the type and magnitude of relief that can be granted.

government agencies enforce regulatory rules directly, and also determine what consequences should follow. This contrasts with more decentralized modes of regulation in which courts have a more central role, and entities that claim to be harmed by illegal behavior may serve as direct initiators of enforcement. European states tend to prefer the first approach, the U.S. system epitomizes the second.[30]

With roots in the British common law tradition, the U.S. legal system was forged institutionally by a long of history of contentious legal federalism.[31] The U.S. federal judiciary is organized into twelve geographically delineated "circuits" and (since 1982) a Federal Circuit with authority to hear appellate patent and customs claims.[32] Each is nominally independent from the others except at the level of U.S. congressional and Supreme Court oversight. On the executive side, the U.S. Department of Justice has a large central administration in Washington D.C., ten regional offices, and more than 250 general and specialized field offices.[33] A further dimension of regulatory decentralization of critical relevance to this analysis is the ability of private actors (both American and foreign) to initiate civil claims – including claims with an extraterritorial dimension – in many areas of statutory and constitutional law. The mechanism by which this occurs is known as a "private right of action."[34]

The overwhelming bulk of civil litigation in U.S. federal courts is instigated by private actors seeking to apply, or enforce, U.S. law.[35] Although many plaintiffs are pursuing nominally private ends (e.g. seeking compensation for past harms, or attempting to enjoin, or compel, the behavior of others), privately initiated litigation frequently has a public law dimension where it clarifies, or elaborates, the content or reach of legal rules that embody public policies. Private rights of action

[30] Several executive departments and agencies, such as the Antitrust Division of the U.S. Department of Justice and the Securities and Exchange Commission, are frequent plaintiffs in U.S. federal courts. The acts of U.S. administrative agencies and Article I courts are likewise subject to judicial review in Article III courts.

[31] Friedman (2002), Skowronek (1982).

[32] The Federal Circuit specializes in trade and patent issues, together with the commercial affairs of the U.S. government.

[33] www.justice.gov/careers/legal/field-offices.html. By state the number of field offices varies from 26 in Texas to one each in Delaware, Hawaii, Puerto Rico, Rhode Island, and Utah.

[34] A private right of action is distinct from, and procedurally prior to, questions about standing to bring suit.

[35] See, e.g., www.uscourts.gov/uscourts/Statistics/FederalJudicialCaseloadStatistics/2011/tables/C02Mar11.pdf.

are delegated expressly, or impliedly, from Congress as a means to correct for public under-enforcement of federal laws.[36] They are "express" where statutory rules clearly provide private rights of action in the text and "implied" where a court or other authoritative agency derives such rights functionally from the objective, or purpose, of the legal rule.[37] The constitutional rights of individuals have likewise been determined to imply private rights of action, except where Congress has provided specific statutory remedies.[38] Not all federal statutes embody private rights of action, however. For example, many of the laws authorizing U.S. sanctions against foreign governments allow only U.S. government regulators to bring enforcement claims.[39]

For the purposes of this project, it is worth underscoring that the U.S. tradition of regulatory self-help that undergirds civil private rights of action had taken shape long before anyone envisioned a need to consider applying U.S. law extraterritorially. And, as the history of foreign affairs friction around U.S. regulatory extraterritoriality attests,[40] the involvement of private entities in selecting litigation targets has arguably at times transported American law to locations and situations where U.S. officials would not otherwise have been expected to act.

Importantly, heavy reliance on private rights of action not only affects (for better or worse) the amount of extraterritorial litigation in the U.S. judicial system, it also shapes the development of underlying rules. This is due to the influence of legal precedent in the U.S. judicial system, coupled with trajectories of contestation over how far underlying alterations of the law extend. In other words, each judicial determination that a particular rule applies (or not) in a specific situation can trigger further efforts to clarify the extent of the application (or limitation) with slightly

[36] This mechanism discussed in legal literature as the "private attorney general." Farhang (2008) finds private rights of action more common in legislation enacted under "divided" governments, or when Congress is under Democratic control.

[37] *Cort v. Ash* 422 U.S. 66 (1975).

[38] *Bivens v. Six Unknown Named Agents*, 403 U.S. 388 (1971), *Schweiker v. Chilicky*, 487 U.S. 412 (1988).

[39] U.S. sanctions are enforced by the Treasury Department's Office of Foreign Assets Control. Title III of the Cuban Liberty and Democratic Solidarity (LIBERTAD) Act of 1996 (Helms-Burton Act) creates a private right of action for suits against entities found in possession of claimed assets. Since its creation, however, Presidents have routinely waived its application "in the national interest" under §306(c)(2) of the Act. See, e.g., http://groups.yahoo.com/group/CubaNews/message/103804.

[40] Meessen (1996 and 1989), Born (1992), Kramer (1991), Gerber (1984), (1983), Maier (1982 and 1983), and Dam (1983).

different facts. In this way, private litigants contribute to the elaboration of U.S. legal rules and standards, and in associated processes of embedding those rules and standards in broader expectations regarding transnational conduct.

Private rights of action have had this impact in part due to other plaintiff-friendly features of the U.S. judicial system, coupled with the relative economic strength of the United States in the international system during the time period under consideration. Whereas the first of these factors affects parties' assessments of the likelihood of legal victory, the second has important implications for litigants' expectations about the efficacy of legal victory.[41] As a comparative matter, the latitude of private actors (both U.S. and foreign) to initiate civil court claims outside the realm of contract and tort is exceptionally wide. Furthermore, the U.S. legal system gives plaintiffs considerable control over the scope, timing, and forum for their claims.[42] Importantly, plaintiffs (not government officials) generally also choose whether, and on what terms, to terminate valid legal disputes in advance of a final court decision.[43]

U.S.-based litigants also have at their disposal other legal forms and procedural tools that do not exist in many other legal systems. These include liberal provisions for notice (service of process), aggressive mechanisms for compelling the production (discovery) of evidence, and fee-shifting arrangements that incentivize risk-taking.[44] Another prototypically American legal form that also may be used for extraterritorial claims is the class action lawsuit. By allowing groups of poorly resourced or disparate individuals who, on their own, would have neither the incentive nor the capacity to pursue legal action to "have their day in court," class action suits vastly expand the universe of prospective plaintiffs, and, notably, the incentives of law firms to invest in developing these types of cases.[45] Finally, a handful of U.S. statutes, among them the Sherman Antitrust Act (discussed in Chapter 4), provide specific incentives for private plaintiffs to initiate regulatory enforcement claims by

41 See the following section for additional discussion of this point.

42 Limits on plaintiff autonomy include satisfying requirements for standing, ripeness, "mootness," venue, and immunities legitimately claimed by defendants. These restrictions are themselves frequently challenged, and occasionally adjusted by courts, and, more rarely, by Congress.

43 Exceptions include when the underlying law is modified, or superseded by treaty, so as to eliminate the claim, and class action suits, where a court is generally required to certify any settlements agreements among the parties.

44 Born (1996).

45 Garth *et al.* (1987), Buxbaum (2001).

allowing them to recover "treble damages" (i.e. compensation three times larger than the actual harm suffered from the legal malfeasance) if successful.

Why litigate?

In a world of overlapping jurisdictions and institutions, aggrieved parties often have choices about how to pursue their objectives. Where private entities are dissatisfied with how others interpret and apply (or fail to apply) legal rules, litigation may be one possible course of action. It may not be the only option, however. As described in Chapter 2, to bring a civil claim in a U.S. federal court, a prospective plaintiff must be able to allege an offense under an applicable federal law, and must have standing to bring the claim.[46] The defendant must be in the class of entities the law is designed to regulate, and the specific defendants must have a sufficiently strong connection to the United States to give the court jurisdiction over their person under rules of constitutional due process. Where these jurisdictional and procedural requirements are satisfied, litigants must still weigh the expected utility of litigation – both on its own terms and relative to other options.

Parties' individually held beliefs that they have a chance of prevailing in court, and of extracting benefit from a legal victory, drive litigation.[47] The first part of this formula, therefore, turns on the *ex ante* existence of relevant types of jurisdictional and legal ambiguity, as discussed above.[48] Absent ambiguity, rational defendants with a losing legal position will generally choose to settle the claim. Rational plaintiffs will drop the dispute, or never formalize it in the first place. The rest are settled, or simply dropped.[49]

Even where litigants believe they have a shot at winning, there are several reasons why net benefits may not be forthcoming. First, expectations of benefits from winning must be discounted by anticipated costs of litigation. U.S. federal litigation is expensive, time-consuming, and not guaranteed to yield the results desired by litigants. As a consequence,

[46] Standing refers to a legally cognizable interest in a given dispute, normally satisfied by demonstrating actual or prospective harm.

[47] Polinsky and Shavell (1998), Priest and Klein (1984).

[48] Ambiguity concerning the substantive requirements of particular rules may also factor into extraterritorial claims, but it is secondary; it matters only if the jurisdictional hurdle is first cleared.

[49] Priest and Klein (1984).

claims involving only trivial stakes for one or both sides are generally not litigated.[50]

Second, the likelihood that litigation will yield net benefits after factoring in expected costs also depends on the nature of actors' objectives. Where plaintiffs seek compensation for past harms, to enjoin or compel the conduct of others, or to build a reputation as an aggressive enforcer of legally protected rights and entitlements, litigation may be an effective tool. Defendants may seek to affirm the legal permissibility of contested forms of conduct, or may try to establish reputations as entities that fight frivolous or predatory claims. An accurate assessment of stakes involved in litigation at times may require looking beyond the dispute at hand.[51] Sophisticated actors may choose to litigate even in situations where the immediate stakes appear relatively small where the real goal is to shape legal rules for future interactions with wider audiences of similarly situated actors.[52] Each of these considerations may be in play, alone or in combination, in disputes over the extraterritorial reach of U.S. law.

Third, who, or what, is on the other side of a dispute also matters. Litigation is unlikely to be effective when known sources of harm are highly diffuse or lack assets to provide adequate compensation. For example, it makes little sense to try to sue individual purchasers of counterfeit goods or to target companies without judicially reachable assets. International legal rules grant various immunities to foreign diplomats and also generally preclude domestic courts from exercising jurisdiction over foreign states, or their top leaders. Although states were once considered strictly immune from proceedings in foreign domestic courts, during the twentieth century many states began to permit exceptions to their own, and others', sovereign immunity in specific, carefully defined areas such as those involving the commercial dealings of governments. In the United States, determining whether governments and other foreign defendants claiming immunities are, in fact, entitled to those immunities has been the

[50] Born (1996), Priest and Klein (1984).

[51] Stakes need not be symmetric between plaintiffs and defendants for litigation to occur. Where stakes are unequal, the side with more at risk may accept a lower probability of success. Similarly, a belief that one's likelihood of winning is very high may lower the threshold of expected benefits required to litigate. Also, where both jurisdictional and substantive aspects of an extraterritorial dispute are contested, this reduces the odds that the plaintiff will ultimately prevail. This may, therefore, affect the size of the stakes needed to incentivize litigation (Shavell 1996).

[52] Daynard (1972), Galanter (1974).

task of courts since 1976.[53] As in other areas, U.S. courts have had to grapple with litigant efforts to test, or adjust, the outer bounds of various stripes of immunity privileges.[54]

Also important to recall is that non-judicial options for pursuing legal and regulatory objectives likewise vary by issue and by combinations of actors. On the domestic side, aggrieved private entities can, in theory, lobby the executive for changes in the interpretation and administration of legal rules, including, where relevant, the imposition of economic and political sanctions. They might also ask members of Congress to pass legislation that creates technical barriers to trade. Examples include the adoption of formalized regulatory standards for commodity imports, or the creation of certification programs for transnational financial and accounting services. Viewed through the lens of international trade law and policy, such measures might be viewed as "disguised barriers to trade." In other respects, however, they are mechanisms for projecting U.S. legal and regulatory standards extraterritorially.

The key point for the purpose of this analysis, however, is that, as with litigation, these efforts can be expensive and time-consuming and are likewise not guaranteed to yield the results desired by their sponsors. Where rules governing transnational conduct have been crafted primarily for U.S. domestic purposes and are strongly favored by powerful domestic constituencies, efforts to seek legislative change may have little chance of success.[55] For non-U.S. entities, the challenges to lobbying successfully for U.S. executive action or legislative change through domestic institutions and channels are even greater.

At the international level, options for enacting preferred regulatory policies vary widely by issue depending on prior treaty-making and institutionalization. In international trade, for example, there are (in theory) forums available for formally evaluating transnational conduct. For U.S.-based entities, this might include the World Trade Organization, NAFTA, and UNCTAD, along with a large number of commodity-based trade organizations. However, as with domestic courts, international institutions are restricted regarding the issues on which they can act, and over what, and whom, they have authority. Critically, access to many international courts and other institutions is

[53] Foreign Sovereign Immunities Act of 1976, U.S.C. Title 28, §§ 1330, 1332, 1391(f), 1441(d), and 1602–1611.

[54] See, for example, *Samantar v. Yousef* 130 S.Ct. 2278 (2010).

[55] Lobbying is rarely one-sided. Efforts to lobby for executive enforcement or legislative change can trigger counter-lobbying efforts.

formally limited to states. For private actors to use international institutions to address complaints therefore requires the sponsorship of an appropriate body within a member government. How likely such sponsorship is in any given instance depends on the importance of the issue to policymakers and constituents, balanced against the political (or other) tradeoffs governments would need to make to pursue the issue internationally. In short, such determinations are highly political. Furthermore, when executive bodies agree to take up the cause of aggrieved private entities at the international level, those entities may retain little direct influence over when and how their issue is handled.

Relative to these options, litigation may be attractive in part due to the degree of control it allows plaintiffs over the scope and timing of dispute initiation, and the ability to target specific alleged violators. For many actors, the prospect of receiving restitution or damages (again, if successful) also may factor into choices of tactics.

Of course, private entities with sufficient resources need not pursue just one strategy. Large multinational corporations, for example, may lobby the U.S. and foreign governments regarding a desired legal or policy change, directly or through private industry associations, while also undertaking litigation-based efforts to alter or enforce the rules in question.[56] They may also seek to influence international-level processes by sending delegates to international meetings, or by participating in international standard-setting efforts.[57] For the most well-resourced private transnational actors, therefore, the key question is how to design a maximally effective mix of activities. Less well-resourced transnational actors often must choose among these options, or opt simply to free-ride on the efforts of others.

To summarize, the choice to litigate is at least partly endogenous to the existence and accessibility of other domestic- or international-level institutions, the resources available to individual actors, coupled with the degree of support, or resistance, their objectives elicit from others in the political and regulatory environment. Because assessing likely benefits, in turn, is in many instances closely tied to expectations about the *ex post* enforceability of U.S. court judgments; it is to this topic we now turn.

[56] Nye (1974), Levy and Prakash (2003).
[57] Büthe and Mattli (2011).

Enforcement capacity

The mere existence of law does not guarantee that those whom it is intended to affect will take notice of it. Where legal compliance demands behavior that is consistently, or even only occasionally, at odds with the preferences of regulated actors, a credible threat of enforcement may be needed to keep non-compliance within politically acceptable bounds. A final element in the analytic framework, therefore, concerns the relative capacity of states to enforce their domestic laws extraterritorially, and how this, in turn, affects litigant expectations regarding the efficacy of court-based extraterritorial claims.

Of what does this capacity consist, and how does it vary by claim? Viewed broadly, the extraterritorial enforcement capacity of U.S. federal courts derives from the relatively high density of market, financial, and other ties a state has within the universe of actors (citizens and noncitizens) engaged in a regulated issue area.[58] These points of contact provide U.S. courts with a basis for exercising personal jurisdiction over non-U.S.-based defendants at the commencement of litigation, and also the ability to seize assets, to enjoin or compel behavior by means of fines, to threaten territorial exclusion, or even to impose criminal penalties *ex post*. In other words, the enforcement capacity of U.S. courts on extraterritorial claims is solidly rooted in conventional instruments of territorial sovereignty: the ability to control persons and property inside the state's territory, to control flows across external borders, and to exclude unwanted entities.[59]

The size and importance of the U.S. economy throughout much of the post-World War II era has provided U.S. regulators and domestic courts considerable capacity to apply U.S. law extraterritorially in several issue areas.[60] This capacity fluctuates with U.S. economic and political fortunes relative to other states. In the current era, the centralization of European markets and institutions, coupled with the appearance of China, India, Brazil, and other regional powers on the global economic stage, are transforming the international

58 Simmons (2001).

59 See Krasner (1999), Goldsmith (1998).

60 Putnam (2009). Note that recent territorial expansion of the EU has brought its GDP into rough parity with that of the United States. A few observers have argued that this is allowing Europe to compete directly with the United States in some issue areas as a global source of regulatory rules and enforcement (Bach and Newman 2007, Bradford 2012).

environment in ways that give the United States a less pivotal role, thereby diminishing its extraterritorial enforcement capacity.[61]

Even in situations where the U.S. density of transactions remains high, actual patterns of extraterritoriality may not closely track enforcement capacity. One set of reasons stems from variation in U.S. courts' willingness to exercise jurisdiction, as examined in Chapter 2. A second arises from variation in agents' incentives to bring, or to defend, legal claims in certain issue areas – which is in part a function of expectations about the efficacy of doing so. The discussion above underscores that rational plaintiffs initiate claims in U.S. courts only where they expect to gain. For individual plaintiffs, this generally requires a positive probability that any remedy obtained in court will be practically satisfiable vis-à-vis the defendant(s). Where defendants have substantial ties to U.S. territory, extraterritorial enforcement differs little from purely domestic claims.[62] The situation is more complicated when defendants have fewer U.S. ties.[63] Under these conditions, a successful plaintiff may need to rely on foreign governments to enforce U.S. court judgments.[64] If such assistance seems *ex ante* unlikely – because foreign law differs from U.S. law, or foreign governments object to U.S. extraterritoriality – this reduces expected payoffs accordingly.[65]

Expected efficacy, as defined here, thus, encompasses both estimates of the willingness of U.S. courts to exercise jurisdiction extraterritorially and observable information about the capacity of U.S. domestic courts to compel losing defendants to satisfy court judgments. Analytically, the two are distinct, and neither is strictly necessary for the other to operate.[66] Practically, however, they are closely intertwined due to

[61] Quintanilla and Whytock (2011).

[62] These include the existence of attachable assets where compensation is the goal, and the capacity to alter behavior where injunctive relief is desired.

[63] For non-U.S. citizens, the presence or absence of these ties can affect the ability of U.S. courts to claim personal jurisdiction over their actions in the first place as a matter of constitutional law.

[64] Westin (1987), Yuan (2004), Wurmnest (2005).

[65] The link between likelihood of recovery in any specific case and incentives to sue can be overstated, however. Indeed, plaintiffs who litigate with the goal of reshaping their legal environment, or that of competitors, may prefer to litigate complaints most likely to yield the desire rule – not necessarily those with the greatest expected level of recovery. Van Schaak (2004).

[66] Where a state's extraterritorial enforcement capacity is low, opportunities for it to demonstrate willingness to regulate extraterritorially are likely to be rare, particularly where contingent upon initiation by self-interested private actors.

constitutional constraints that allow courts to act only when presented with a case or controversy.

Likewise, where the expected efficacy of extraterritorial private enforcement is not capable of offsetting the combined costs of harm generated by extraterritorial behavior and the resources required to pursue enforcement – for example, where harm is diffuse or differentiated enough that it impedes collective action – I expect private actors either to simply absorb the costs of the harm or to press governments to explore alternative unilateral, bilateral, or multilateral options. Finally, to the extent broader trends of U.S. political and economic engagement at the international level indirectly influence judicial line-drawing on the character or magnitude of U.S. effects needed to trigger extraterritorial jurisdiction, here too U.S. hegemonic decline should manifest itself in an increasingly cautious approach.

Sources of legal ambiguity and change

Legal ambiguity is a necessary feature of disputes that lead to litigation, and, by extension, to forms of strategic behavior involving domestic law and legal institutions. These disputes and their outcomes, in turn, may have implications for other transnational actors and processes. Among the numerous possible sources of legal ambiguity, many are sufficiently remote from the strategic behavior at issue here to permit an assumption of exogeneity. Others follow more directly from prior efforts to alter legal rules and the behavior governed by those rules.

Shifts in regulatory environments caused by political, social, and technological change are one common source of legal ambiguity. The legal effects of such changes may become evident gradually, or emerge in sudden bursts.[67] Although diverse in both origins and effects, their important shared element is that they force determinations about fit within existing frameworks of rules. The generality and brevity of most statutory and constitutional rules is another, related source of ambiguity that allows for contestation over how laws should be interpreted to apply to new developments not specifically envisioned or described by their enactors. A third is an artifact of decision-making in complex systems: rule variance arising from the interpretation (in good faith, or otherwise) of legal rules by horizontally equivalent institutions and actors.[68]

67 Pierson (2007).
68 Bardach and Kagan (2002), Farhang (2008).

Technological innovation, defined broadly to encompass advances in applied sciences, together with new organizational forms and practices, can have destabilizing legal effects. New technologies may give rise to new and unforeseen types of conduct, or enable existing activities to take place on a previously unimagined scale. They may also render prior technologies, practices, and even entire industries obsolete.

To the extent such changes threaten the vested rights and interests of U.S.-based actors, the latter may choose to challenge territorial limits on regulatory rules, or to expand the reach of rules already acknowledged to have some extraterritorial applicability. For example, the development of increasingly sophisticated finance and accounting tools such as markets for derivatives, futures, and hedges has transformed international investment and increased the global supply of credit. These innovations, however, also impose costs upon entities invested (or socialized) in older technical or organizational modes of behavior and create new opportunities for manipulation and fraud, in both domestic and transnational forms. Those harmed directly or indirectly by new developments may attempt to challenge their permissibility under existing rules, whereas those who benefit can be expected to defend their consistency with those rules.

Other changes at a macro-political level can further amplify the effects of technological change. The United States emerged from World War I with a dramatically enhanced position in the international system in terms of its relative economic and military power. Nevertheless, U.S. political engagement in international affairs lagged behind its power in the interwar period. Having escaped the additional destruction that World War II brought to many parts of Europe, the United States came out of that conflict the undisputed leader of the non-communist world.[69] The more heavily institutionalized, and purposefully interdependent, international economic and political order established in the aftermath of World War II ensured that the United States would play a major role in international affairs for decades to come. This new role created many new opportunities for entrepreneurs and corporations, both inside the United States and abroad. However, it also created new vulnerabilities and pressures on the U.S. domestic system, particularly after countries devastated by war began to recover, and their rebuilt industries began to compete with U.S.-based entities.

[69] Frieden (2006:254–270).

Beyond these exogenous sources of legal ambiguity are others with more endogenous roots. Of particular relevance are legislative, executive, and judicial modifications of domestic legal rules and standards. Court decisions purporting to interpret existing law occasionally also give rise to statutory changes. For example, the U.S. Supreme Court held in 1971 that U.S. patent law did not reach alleged infringements that involved shipping unassembled parts of patented machinery outside U.S. territory for the purpose of later assembly and sale to foreign users. Thirteen years and numerous lawsuits later, Congress amended the Patent Act to cover this type of conduct specifically.[70] Regardless of their source, changes to domestic law can give rise to legal disputes as actors probe the limits of those changes. For example, in 1999 the U.S. Congress passed the Anti-Cybersquatting Consumer Protection Act, which prohibits registration of Internet domain names in bad faith in order to extract an unreasonably high price from a legitimate trademark holder to acquire the name, or to unfairly capitalize on the goodwill of an existing trademark. This legislation prompted a string of cases seeking to establish the limits of the Act's extraterritorial enforceability.[71]

At the same time, when a court decides a law applies extraterritorially in a specific case, this does not imply that it applies extraterritorially in all subsequent cases that may be brought under the rule. To the contrary, the precedential ambit of U.S. court decisions is robust only to particular configurations of actors and actions, which must then be overtly analogized to variations of fact. Each new case thus provides attentive observers with additional data regarding to what, and to whom, U.S. law is likely to apply (or fail to apply) extraterritorially. Subsequent litigants may seek to test this, or to attempt incrementally to expand (or contract) the field of conduct that law covers, the range of entities to whom it applies, or both. Indeed, even statutes with an extensive history of extraterritorial application, such as the Sherman Antitrust Act, continue to undergo reinterpretation and modification as underlying circumstances change.

[70] 35 U.S.C. §271(f). Congress amended the Act further in 1988 to define infringers as anyone who sells, or offers to sell, something produced by a patent-protected invention in U.S. territory without authorization (§271(g)). A 1994 amendment excluded from the definition of "offer to sell" transactions that will occur after patent rights are set to expire (§271(i)) (Wasserman 2007:286).

[71] See, for example, *Cable News Network L.P., L.L.L.P. v. CNNews.com*, 177 F.Supp.2d 506 (E.D. Va. 2001), *Internet Billions Domain v. Venetian Casino Resort, LLC* No. 01CV5417 (E.D. Penn, 2002), and *Microsoft Corp v. AT&T Corp* 550 U.S. 437 (2007).

Similarly, changes to U.S. understandings of the scope, content, or importance of individual rights can lead to disputes over whether those rights end at the border, and, if not, who may seek their enforcement in U.S. courts. For example, over the course of the 1950s and early 1960s, U.S. courts found domestic acts of racial discrimination unconstitutional in a series of rulings covering a wide range of practices. These decisions were further elaborated and codified in the 1964 Civil Rights Act and other statutes. Where American corporations have subsequently engaged in discriminatory practices in their foreign operations, U.S. and foreign plaintiffs have duly sought extraterritorial application of these laws – albeit with varying success.

Conversely, a court's refusal to find and exercise extraterritorial jurisdiction at one time does not preclude a different conclusion later on. Plaintiffs can (and sometimes do) continue to bring new claims under rules that courts have previously refused to apply extraterritorially, citing changed circumstances. For example, the first reported suit alleging extraterritorial violations of the Copyright Act was brought, unsuccessfully, by a U.S. record company in 1964. A trickle of similar claims followed. It was not until 1986, however, that a U.S. federal court issued a judgment supporting the Copyright Act's extraterritorial applicability – and it too was overruled eight years later.[72] The global diffusion of the Internet and related technologies in the 1990s dramatically altered the ease of copying and sharing digitized materials. Not surprisingly, this has spurred a new generation of extraterritorial copyright claims.[73] Consistent with what my theoretical account would expect, some U.S. federal courts have responded by taking a less rigid approach to the Copyright Act, for example, by exercising jurisdiction over claims of unauthorized extraterritorial use where any act undertaken inside the United States facilitates unauthorized use outside U.S. territory.[74]

In short, once a court is seized of an issue, *anything it does alters the legal status quo*. It either reinforces prior understandings of what the law

[72] See *Peter Starr Production Co. v. Twin Continental Films, Inc.* 783 F.2d 1440 (9th Cir. 1986) and *Subafilms Ltd. v. MGM Pathe-Communications Co.* 24 F.3d 1088 (9th Cir. 1994). See also Chapter 5 for a detailed discussion of the latter case.

[73] These technologies give individuals the tools to easily circumvent mechanisms of domestic copyright regulation, e.g. production, sales, and broadcasting licensing inside U.S. territory, and customs controls to prevent large-scale importation of unlicensed copies.

[74] See, e.g., *Update Art, Inc. v. Modiin Publishing, Ltd.*, 843 F.2d 67, 73 (2d Cir. 1988) and *Shaw v. Rizzoli International Publications* 1999 U.S. Dist. LEXIS 3233 (S.D.N.Y. March 23, 1999).

requires, and expands their applicability to novel configurations of facts, or it alters earlier holdings by modifying their scope or content. In rare cases characterized by entirely "new" law, it can create such understandings.[75] This is as true for jurisdictional questions as for other areas of the law.

Conclusion

Transnational activity, by definition, brings different states' regulatory approaches into direct contact, and sometimes into conflict. This creates opportunities for regulatory arbitrage, forum shopping, and other practices calculated to maximize private welfare of self-interested transnational actors. Where conduct that aims to take advantage of regulatory fragmentation produces negative externalities inside U.S. territory, and those effects, moreover, are of the sort recognized by U.S. courts as justifying extraterritorial regulation, the threat of privately initiated enforcement of U.S. legal rules outside U.S. territory becomes part of the regulatory environment. Because the international system lacks a centralized interpreter and enforcer of legal rules, states are pivotal in transnational regulation, even in situations nominally governed by treaties or other formal agreements.

Most states lack the capacity to regulate extraterritorially on a wide scale. Even the United States does not have unlimited power in this regard. The limits of what U.S. law allows are, moreover, perpetually open to question as actors, technologies, norms, and politics change and evolve. How U.S. courts respond (or are expected by relevant parties to respond) to contested claims of extraterritorial jurisdiction is an important element in how the United States plays its hand in the game of international regulatory competition. Furthermore, because private litigants have been far more active than U.S. government regulators in initiating transnational regulatory litigation, it follows that U.S. regulatory behavior in the transnational sphere is driven in part by the agendas of private entities in quite direct ways.

To influence behavior, rules must have some non-trivial probability of being enforced. This, in turn, requires both the availability of mechanisms for this purpose and conditions conducive to their use by public officials, by private actors, or both. Awareness of who stands to benefit from the extraterritorial enforcement (or non-enforcement) of

[75] Sandholtz and Stone Sweet (2004).

U.S. rules, and of the opportunity structures that shape their choice, is key to any rationalist theory of agency. Understanding how legal disputes arise, and how, and by whom, they are selected for litigation, is, therefore, critically important to explaining how U.S. domestic courts factor into the creation, maintenance, and diffusion of transnational and international rules.

Taken together, these factors may restrict the set of treaty bargains the U.S. government will seek or conceivably support. From one direction, private actors that benefit from the existence of private rights of action can be expected to demand that those rights be preserved (or enhanced) in any international agreement. This makes robust forms of coordinated international enforcement less likely to receive support than might otherwise be the case. Court-based extraterritoriality also often improves the reserve bargaining position of the United States. Where domestic public and private actors have other ways to get at least part of what they are bargaining for, they are less likely to compromise on issues of importance in order to reach a deal.[76]

International legal harmonization is most desirable in situations where outside conduct produces negative externalities in U.S. territory, but the prescriptive reach of U.S. law is largely absent or unreliable – that is, where the domestic effects from behavior inconsistent with U.S. rules are not of the type or magnitude sufficient to trigger jurisdiction. It may also occur in settings where U.S. extraterritorial regulation is, in theory, possible, but where U.S. enforcement capacity is limited due to identity of the violators and their ties (or lack thereof) to the United States. Even where efforts to harmonize occur, however, I expect U.S. willingness to coordinate to be limited to measures that include substantive definitions and standards. Far more rare are situations where the United States will agree to procedures or to modes of enforcement that would undercut the ability of private entities to protect their own interests using existing private rights of action.

Among the core conjectures examined in the first two case study chapters that follow, therefore, is that the existence, use, and perceived efficacy of private rights of action in pushing the extraterritorial reach of U.S. law matters to whether the United States government seeks to bargain internationally over regulatory coordination. I expect, in

[76] Of course, litigation-based options for vindicating claimed rights are still often considered far from ideal; otherwise the actors in question would not agree to bargain in the first place.

addition, that where the U.S. government takes this step, it will tailor its formal commitments to measures that will enhance – or at least not undercut – the effectiveness of private extraterritorial enforcement mechanisms. More broadly, I anticipate that where U.S. courts are assertive in finding and exercising jurisdiction extraterritorially, transnational private actors will respond – whether by adjusting their behavior to hew more closely to U.S. legal preferences, or with attempts to circumvent or undermine U.S. law.

4

Extraterritoriality in the absence of agreement

International antitrust

> The greater our zeal in proceeding against cartel practices, the more careful such foreign groups will be in their efforts to remain beyond the reach of the authority of the American Government. If they succeed, present laws will be ineffective.
>
> Corwin D. Edwards, U.S Department of Justice (1944)

Between 2008 and 2011, twenty-one international airlines were fined more than US$1.7 billion by the U.S. Department of Justice (DOJ) for criminally conspiring to inflate international air cargo shipping rates through coordinated fuel, security ("war risk"), and insurance surcharges.[1] Several of these companies agreed to pay, in addition, a combined total of nearly US$450 million to an international class of private plaintiffs to settle a consolidated set of more than one hundred private civil actions filed in U.S. federal courts to recover damages from these same price-fixing activities.[2] The settlements called for payments of US$85 million by Lufthansa, US$87 million from Air France-KLM, and US$89.5 million from British Airways, to name only the largest.[3] Both the civil and criminal actions allege a "global conspiracy" to distort markets for international air cargo shipping services in violation of §1 of the U.S. Sherman Antitrust Act and §3 of the Clayton Act.[4] In 2010,

[1] In addition, the DOJ issued individual criminal charges against more than twenty U.S. and foreign airline executives, several of whom have served prison time (Hanney 2011).

[2] www.joc.com/cargo-airlines/eight-air-cargo-carriers-get-court-approval-price-fixing-settlement.

[3] Hanney (2011).

[4] Among the foreign defendants are: ABSA Cargo Airlines, Air Canada, Air China, Air France, Air India, Air New Zealand, Alitalia, All Nippon Airways, Asiana Airlines, British Airways, Cargolux, Cathay Pacific, China Airlines, El Al, Emirates, EVA Airways, Japan Airlines, KLM, Korean Air, Lan Chile, Lufthansa, Martinair, Nippon Cargo, Polar Air, Qantas, SAS, Saudi Arabian Airways, Singapore Airlines, South African Airways, Swiss International Air Lines, Thai Airways, and VARIG. Several executives of the defendant corporations are also named defendants.

European Commission regulators fined several carriers an additional US$1.1 billion for their participation in this scheme. However, private entities in Europe have not recovered on anything like the same scale as U.S. litigants for harms by these anti-competitive activities.

While the air cargo conspiracy is notable in terms of its scale and in the central involvement of the U.S. Justice Department in spearheading enforcement, the efforts by private civil plaintiffs to recover for private harms from extraterritorial anti-competitive conduct in U.S. courts is no way extraordinary.[5] Indeed, experts estimate that, in recent decades, for each antitrust enforcement action brought by U.S. government regulators, nine have been initiated by private entities.[6] This situation stands in sharp contrast to countries in Europe and elsewhere, where public regulators are overwhelmingly responsible for enforcing competition law.[7]

Despite the wide gulf between U.S. and European enforcement regimes, the underlying substantive rules and policy goals of the two systems appear, from a contemporary prospective, quite similar, particularly with regard to anti-cartel measures.[8] However, this was not always the case. Prior to World War II, and continuing for decades after World War II, European states permitted a range of practices that were expressly banned in the United States. Strikingly, the relative convergence in U.S. and European antitrust rules has come about with only a very thin veneer of formal treaty coordination. Indeed, despite the importance of antitrust law as measured in terms of the money value of the transactions it covers, and its close association with international trade rules, it is arguably among the least formally institutionalized areas of international economic relations. Why this is the case constitutes a puzzle.[9]

The objective of this chapter is to begin to explore in detail how U.S. judicial extraterritoriality has affected the origins, diffusion, and operation of transnational regulatory rules. I argue that allowing private

[5] Between 1990 and 2007, government regulators, mainly in Europe and the United States, together issued roughly US$25 billion in antitrust fines against international cartels. In this period, several billion dollars also changed hands in private settlements – virtually all of it in U.S. proceedings (Lande and Davis 2008).

[6] Woods (2004:435). Note, this figure is lower for international antitrust claims, and estimates of how much lower vary according to definitions of "international" and "foreign" (Zanettin 2002).

[7] Connor *et al.* (2010).

[8] Basedow (2000:1039), Stephan (2005), Bradford (2007), Leveque (2007), Kelemen (2011).

[9] Wood (1992), Guzman (1998).

entities to sue in U.S. courts to enforce U.S. antitrust rules extraterritorially has had an important, if often overlooked, influence on the form and content of transnational and international rule development in this area. Specifically, enforcement actions initiated by private firms seeking to safeguard their own interests have been important in projecting U.S. antitrust rules and policies into the transnational sphere – even as U.S. judicial interpretations of U.S. laws changed over time.[10]

I first situate my approach to this topic within the international political economy (IPE) literature on institutional bargaining and adapt the analytic framework developed in Chapter 3 to U.S. courts and private actors in international antitrust enforcement. I then use historical process tracing to examine how regulators on each side of the Atlantic have sought to shape transnational rules regulating competition, with particular attention to the incentives that each system established for private entities seeking to impose (or avoid) antitrust penalties. The chapter concludes with a discussion of the evidence, and the formulation of further hypotheses concerning when we might expect courts to be instrumental in projecting the shadow of domestic law extraterritorially.

Antitrust, international trade, and extraterritoriality

Antitrust (or "competition law" as it is often called outside the United States) is public regulatory law that limits how private enterprises behave toward market competitors. The animating goal of antitrust law and policy is avoidance of unfair competition (however defined) and unsanctioned monopolies, together with the higher prices, restricted output, and disincentives for innovation that are often assumed to accompany such practices.[11] It is a regulatory sphere in which the costs of the policy are borne by individual firms, which must forego certain private arrangements that could increase their own net profits, in order to generate a set of diffuse economic and social benefits. For this reason, ensuring

[10] For example, as discussed in greater detail below, in the 1970s, many U.S. federal judges began to favor Chicago School-style ideas involving consumer price theory, and efficiency-enhancing forms of market concentration. This was a sharp break from earlier approaches that viewed high levels of market concentration as *per se* violations of the Sherman Act.

[11] Hovencamp (2005). The definition of unfair competition is as much a normative and distributional issue as an economic or legal one. Since the late 1970s, U.S. regulators have championed maximizing consumer welfare (as opposed to competitor welfare) as the touchstone of antitrust law and policy, Brodley (1987), Hovencamp (2005).

adequate enforcement of domestic antitrust rules can be a challenge for governments.

Antitrust regulation encompasses two primary spheres. The first concerns cartels and related anti-competitive practices, such as horizontal price controls, agreements to allocate territories of operation, predatory pricing, tying arrangements, and refusals to deal. Its second focus is market concentrations – or, in extreme form, monopolies.[12] International antitrust thus concerns the operation of national competition rules across international borders.[13] The discussion here focuses mainly on efforts to regulate international cartels and cartel-like behavior, since this has been the primary site of transnational regulatory activity.

Classical international trade theory describes the aggregate positive benefits that can be expected from international trade openness.[14] Prominent qualifications of this theory highlight the fact that international trade openness often creates winners and losers. These inequities and the political cleavages they spawn, in turn, place pressure on governments to provide firms and interest groups made less well off by open competition with various types of protection or compensation.[15] In the contemporary era, international trade rules and institutions have all but eliminated once common responses like import tariffs. Consequently, governments under fire domestically now tinker at the margins of international trade rules with policies such as subsidies, export inducements, and regulatory impediments to foreign trade.

Although not often discussed as a component of international trade policy, private anticompetitive activities also can have trade-distorting

[12] The law in this area chiefly involves review of proposed mergers. In the United States, regulation of monopolies may also involve breaking up companies found to limit competition to an "unreasonable" degree, Hovencamp (2005). See *Standard Oil Co. of New Jersey v. United States*, 221 U.S. 1 (1911).

[13] Connor *et al.* (2010:202) observe "[t]he principal difference between a monopoly and a cartel is that a monopolist operates openly, usually under the direct scrutiny or regulation of the government, whereas a cartel general operates under the cover of secrecy."

[14] Heckscher and Ohlin (1933, reprinted in 1991), Stolper and Samuelson (1941), Bhagwati (2004). Several legal scholars argue for the desirability of an integrated system for international antitrust – to eliminate remaining divergences in substantive rules and to achieve greater efficiency in enforcement (Guzman 1998, Fox 2002–2003, Wood 2004). Others reject this as untenable for reasons rooted either in collective action theory and economic nationalism (Stephan 2005), or differences in domestic institutions and cultures (McGinnis 2003, Buxbaum 2005, Gerber 2005).

[15] Stigler (1971), Pelzman (1976), Hillman (1982), Rogowski (1987), Hiscox (2001), Grossman and Helpman (2002), Melitz and Ottaviano (2008).

effects. When governments turn a blind eye to private collusive practices intended to distort market pricing or to impede the ability of outsiders to compete, the line separating these behaviors from trade barriers can become blurred.[16] As markets for many goods and services become more international, private anticompetitive behavior in any geographic segment can have distorting effects elsewhere.[17]

Under a regime of antitrust regulation organized strictly along territorial lines, opportunities for international regulatory arbitrage – efforts to profitably exploit differences in states' laws and enforcement policies – would abound.[18] Firms based in states with more restrictive rules (like the United States) would accrue many of the costs of having to operate in an international environment riddled with privately segmented markets, but without being able to enjoy the benefits available to firms based in more permissive environments. This would increase pressure on elected officials to lower those standards or risk incentivizing private firms with viable exit options to seek greener regulatory pastures. It is, thus, not surprising that antitrust law and policy have been for decades at the forefront of U.S. extraterritorial practice.

Framing the discussion that follows against a backdrop of insights from the international political economy and public choice literatures helps to focus attention on two questions. First, under what conditions, and by what means, have private entities with U.S. ties most actively sought to shape U.S. and international antitrust rules? Second, what has been the impact of those efforts?

Chapter 3 argues that private transnational actors attempt to use law and institutions strategically to further their own objectives. Applied to international antitrust, this suggests U.S.-based entities harmed by foreign anticompetitive practices prohibited under U.S. law will, first, seek legislative changes to permit similar conduct on the part of U.S. entities, or lobby the U.S. government to pressure foreign governments to change their laws or patterns of enforcement. Where these options fail, or appear unlikely to succeed *ex ante*, those seeking relief have frequently looked to U.S. federal courts to apply U.S. law extraterritorially.

Before considering the historical development of antitrust law and policy in detail, I first direct attention to the three elements of the analytic framework elaborated in Chapter 3 – legal rules, the existence of agents

[16] Hudec (2003).
[17] Stephan (2005).
[18] Juenger (1988), Trachtman (1993), Lowenfeld (1997).

to contest the extraterritorial reach of U.S. law, and changes in the enforcement capacity of U.S. courts – and their interactions.

Rules and ambiguity

Antitrust law and policy has traditionally been a concern of relatively large liberal capitalist states, including many of those most concerned with achieving and maintaining trade openness. Currently, more than half the states in the international system, and virtually all states with domestic economies characterized by steady growth and productive levels of international engagement, have adopted antitrust laws in some form. This is a recent development. A mere twenty-five years ago, only a few economically advanced capitalist-oriented states, mainly in Europe and North America, had such laws. Some states (including several in the early group) acquired these laws through external pressure or even imposition. Others adopted domestic competition rules in an effort to emulate the institutions of more successful states, particularly at moments of transition to market economies. Still others were coaxed into adopting such laws by international technical assistance programs and peer evaluation mechanisms.[19]

The United States was among the first countries to attempt to regulate concentrations of economic power on a wide scale.[20] Although modeled in part on earlier British law, the form that U.S. legislation and regulatory practice ultimately assumed has deeply American roots.[21] U.S. antitrust laws have been, and continue to be, shaped primarily by domestic factors, even as the heightened importance of international trade to the U.S. economy added new actors and interests to the political and economic rationales for those rules. For firms with transnational activities or interests, the "competition among competition rules" and accompanying enforcement regimes is highly consequential.[22]

The theory elaborated in the previous chapter expects domestic U.S. firms harmed by extraterritorial conduct prohibited under U.S. law,

[19] Sokol (2009).

[20] Timberg (1953:446–447) argues that early significant efforts encompass protests against the abusive practices of guilds and other local monopolies in Europe. The British Statute of Monopolies of 1623 is the earliest known piece of national legislation to this effect, and it provided a model for the U.S. drafters of the 1890 Sherman Antitrust Act. In 1889, Canada also enacted an Act for the Prevention and Suppression of Combinations formed in Restraint of Trade.

[21] Harding and Joshua (2003:46–47).

[22] Noonan (2008:122), Townsend (1980:129–130), Haight (1960:256).

or that are disadvantaged in competitive terms by the existence of looser rules elsewhere, to seek to extend the reach of U.S. law in order to level the playing field whenever achieving domestic change is not feasible, or would be prohibitively costly. Often this involves efforts to expand the geographic reach of U.S. law, to lower the threshold of domestic effects required to trigger U.S. jurisdiction, or to shrink the amount of foreign defendant ties to U.S. territory required for judicial assertions of personal jurisdiction.[23] In line with the theory of U.S. judicial extraterritoriality laid out in Chapter 2, such efforts are far more likely to succeed when they are linked not just to addressing sources of private harm but also to identifying forms of extraterritorial conduct that, if left unchecked, could threaten the domestic integrity or operation of domestic antitrust laws.

During much of the post-World War II period, U.S. antitrust rules were considerably less permissive than the laws of many other states with respect to cartel formation and other types of horizontal firm coordination.[24] In the United States, private collusion to restrain markets, the costs of which are generally borne by consumers and small competitors, has historically been viewed, first as a moral transgression, and only secondarily as an economic one. In this vein, Harding and Joshua cite the provisions of the main U.S. antitrust statute, the 1890 Sherman Antitrust Act, which encompasses criminal penalties, including jail time, for persons found guilty of efforts to engage in private collusion, regardless of the results achieved.[25] The Act likewise allows individuals harmed by collusive activity to recover treble damages – penalties three times the amount of the harm actually caused.[26]

Although interpretations of the Act have evolved over the post-World War II period to incorporate more permissive approaches toward market-enhancing forms of concentration, U.S. law has been fairly categorical in its condemnation of horizontal restraints. In contrast, regulators in European states have traditionally held less negative attitudes toward cartels.[27] Also during this period, European regulators at the national level and at

[23] Scafuri (1965:565).

[24] Wells (2002), Harding and Joshua (2003), Fox (2009).

[25] Harding and Joshua (2003:50–51 and 57).

[26] Timberg (1957:404) locates this attitude in a pervasive cultural hostility to "all forms of concentrated power – political as well as economic."

[27] Note, U.S. authorities have been at times willing to allow some sectors to engage in price-fixing activity and market division, albeit where those arrangements have an overt statutory basis, as with the 1922 Capper-Volstead Act, which grants immunities from antitrust laws to qualifying agricultural cooperatives (see Varney 2010), and the 1982 Export Trading Act (see Jones 1999:17).

the supranational level have gradually adopted more American-style views regarding the harmful effects horizontal restraints can have on innovation and consumption. Even so, European regulators still put greater emphasis on assessing the consequences of private collusion of all types and are keen to prohibit only those that result in what they regard as harmful distortions.[28]

Overall, substantive differences between U.S. and European rules are less evident today than in prior decades. However, differences grounded in contrasting values and system structures remain – particularly on the procedural and enforcement side.[29] Even where the systems are nearly identical with respect to the types of conduct they seek to regulate, differences remain regarding who may access courts, the legal forms their complaints may take, the procedural tools they have to follow through on claims, the evidentiary rules brought to bear, and the penalties that may follow. For the purposes of this discussion, one very important aspect of divergence is the long-standing U.S. practice of allowing domestic courts to apply U.S. antitrust laws extraterritorially on the basis of harmful effects in the United States, and the comparative unwillingness, or inability, of European regulators to emulate this practice.[30] Consequently, for private transnational actors seeking to navigate these differences, knowing which system's rules are likely to apply in which circumstances can be vitally important.

Agents and triggers

Private firms and governments embody a range of preferences over the content and enforcement of their own, and other states' antitrust rules, and they should be expected to attempt to enact those preferences when institutional and political opportunities arise.[31] The local menu of antitrust enforcement options, however, differs greatly between Europe and the United States with regard to both the initiators of legal claims and the institutions in which those claims are handled.[32] These differences have deep legal-cultural roots that are reflected in, and reinforced by, earlier

[28] Harding and Joshua (2003:53) describe this as "*regulatory rather than confrontational, administrative rather than judicial, employing economic rather than moral evaluation*" [emphasis in original].

[29] Gerber (2010).

[30] Townsend (1980:124).

[31] Geradin (2009).

[32] Swaine (2001–2002), Kelemen (2011).

institutional choices and complementarities.[33] Attention to these differences is important to explaining who (or what) has agency to trigger enforcement, and also against whom and on what basis.

Corporate plaintiffs and defendants in private U.S. extraterritorial antitrust litigation are generally large firms with extensive transnational interests. If foreign, they are more often than not based in other economic highly advanced states. Commonly, these firms are in highly capital- or knowledge-intensive sectors. Examples include raw material production, heavy manufacturing, and transportation, as well as consumer electronics and computer software.

Since 1914, U.S. antitrust statutes have expressly permitted private entities harmed by alleged violations of U.S. law to initiate claims directly in civil courts ("private rights of action").[34] U.S. antitrust rules are, in addition, designed to encourage private enforcement through the availability of treble damage awards – compensation at three times demonstrated losses for successful enforcement claims.[35] In many European states, by contrast, competition law is enforced by specialized administrative bodies with little direct involvement by domestic courts.[36] In Germany, for example, when activities prohibited under German or EU law are brought to the attention of the Federal Cartel Office (FCO), an investigation is launched, and, if wrongdoing is found, the FCO has the authority to impose penalties and to order remedial actions. In France, antitrust cases are "launched and prosecuted" by an investigation service in the *Autorité (neé Conseil) de la concurrence.*[37] In Netherlands, state competition authorities rarely interfered with cartel arrangements at all until the 1990s, despite growing enforcement pressure from the EC beginning in the 1980s.[38]

At the European Community (EC) level, competition policy has been an important substantive focus of European integration, and a critical area for

[33] Thelen (1999), Pierson (2000), Hall and Soskice (2001).

[34] Only U.S. officials may initiate criminal antitrust proceedings.

[35] 15. U.S.C. §4 and 15 U.S.C. §16. This provision was modeled on a 1623 English Statute on Monopolies that had fallen into non-use by the time the Sherman Act was drafted, Jones (1999:35).

[36] In the United Kingdom and Ireland, courts have some role in competition regulation due to the common law roots of their legal systems (Furse 2008). Also, German competition law includes a highly circumscribed private right of action covering situations where harm is narrowly targeted and generates no systemic effects. Where broader effects are anticipated, complaints fall under the exclusive purview of the FCO (Buxbaum 2005).

[37] Lasserre (2009).

[38] Drahos (2001), Kelemen (2011).

building supranational-level institutions and capacities.[39] The European Court of Justice, which allows private entities to appeal national-level decisions alleged to be incompatible with European Union laws and policies, has been a key institution in this process and has also experimented cautiously with effects-type logics of grounding jurisdiction over extraterritorial conduct.

By contrast, the U.S. approach to international antitrust is often described as unilateralist and horizontalist. The "unilateralist" label encapsulates the U.S. preference for each state to enforce its own rules whenever its interests dictate, and for domestic institutions to manage conflicts over competing efforts to regulate as they arise.[40] "Horizontalist" refers to the U.S. practice of limiting efforts to coordinate policies and to minimize frictions that arise from unilateralism to independent government-to -government initiatives – notification, information-sharing, non-binding recommendations and statements of best practices, and the like.[41] U.S. policy preferences thus have stopped well short of measures to centralize authority over cross-border transactions, or to allocate jurisdiction over enforcement *ex ante*, whereas regulators in Europe have long pressed for multilateralist (or internationalist) approaches to smooth over differences in competition rules and procedures.[42]

A central claim in this analysis is that the availability and widespread use of private rights of action in U.S. antitrust enforcement, but not in Europe, has been an important, but largely overlooked, source of the far more assertive pattern of U.S. extraterritoriality in the antitrust sphere. To a non-trivial extent, the distribution of public and private enforcement activities in the United States reflects a tacit division of labor, with private entities taking on cases featuring relatively concentrated harms, and Justice Department and the Federal Trade Commission taking on claims involving more diffuse harms for which no natural group of plaintiffs is likely to emerge. To be sure, the court-sanctioned delegation of private agency to initiate extraterritorial claims occasionally generates situations that rankle Executive branch officials and foreign governments. In the antitrust sphere, however, very

39 Alter (1998), Büthe and Swank (2007), McGowan (2010).

40 Aside from a handful of bilateral agreements requiring governments to notify one another of impending antitrust actions, and a few non-binding multilateral mechanisms for coordinating enforcement, no formal agreements on international antitrust currently exist.

41 Dodge (1998b), Mehra (2004).

42 Alford (1992–1993), Dodge (1998b), Fioretos (2001), Fox (2002–2003).

little of this has spilled over into congressional action. Likewise, with a small number of modest exceptions, it has not prompted the initiation or support of international treaty-making initiatives. Consequently, use of this trigger has resulted in efforts to apply U.S. competition rules outside U.S. territory in a broader range of settings, and against a different profile of defendants, than likely would have been the case if U.S. regulators alone had the capacity to initiate enforcement.

The availability of court-based mechanisms for enforcing, and at times incrementally extending, U.S. laws extraterritorially also diminishes pressure for domestic legislative adjustments to changing international conditions. The transnational character of many markets for goods and services makes it difficult for states to maintain geographically segmented competition laws. Even so, in countries where competition laws are the result of extensive domestic battles over firm- and sector-level approaches to internal market entry and control, revamping domestic laws to improve the international competitiveness of an elite group of transnational firms is politically challenging. The theory elaborated in Chapter 3 expects that where the costs of achieving domestic legislative adjustment are prohibitively high, private entities disadvantaged by U.S.-specific legal requirements will instead press to have those requirements projected extraterritorially in order to level the playing field.

Enforcement capacity

The willingness and capacity of U.S. courts to exercise jurisdiction over extraterritorial conduct affects transnational actors beyond those directly involved in U.S. litigation. A transnational private entity's assessment of its own specific vulnerability to regulation by the states in which it operates turns on its beliefs about each state's capacity to enforce its preferred rules in various locations and circumstances, coupled with expectations about when that enforcement power may come into play. Thus, where a state's enforcement capacity is observed to be robust, decentralized, and costly to absorb, actors with actual or anticipated U.S. ties should rationally avoid violating U.S. rules. The behavioral regularities that these expectations generate in many instances endogenously reinforce the legal rules that underwrite those expectations.

A corollary proposition is that affirmative evidence that a state is unwilling or unable to enforce its regulatory rules transnationally is also informative. For example, if an anticompetitive practice (e.g. horizontal price coordination) is prohibited inside a state, but occurs outside its territory in a manner that harms the state or individuals within it, a decision not to apply the state's law extraterritorially signals to other private actors that gains can be captured simply by carrying out all or part of prohibited conduct outside the state's borders. When anticipated gains from such acts outweigh the costs of shifting activities outside the state, rational economic actors should be expected to seize such opportunities to the detriment of less geographically mobile private competitors and to the domestic regulatory regime as a whole.

The formal capacity to apply and enforce domestic laws extraterritorially, in turn, depends upon how courts and institutions operating in their shadow draw key definitional lines – on the boundaries of specific types of allowed (or prohibited behavior), on the nature of domestic effects capable of triggering U.S. prescriptive jurisdiction, and on the character and extent of ties needed to reasonably demand that transnational actors follow U.S. laws. In the commercial sphere, the recent trend toward vertical integration among firms in many sectors complicates this line-drawing further, necessitating highly fact-intensive inquiries into relationships among corporate parent companies, subsidiaries, and contacting firms.

Finally, it is worth underscoring that private incentives to initiate enforcement at times may deviate from those motivating public agencies and officials. Indeed, whereas public officials are supposed to act only when the public interest requires it, private litigants act only when their own interests are threatened. At times the self-interested actions of private entities may be less than optimal from a societal perspective – either because private entities act when public officials would prefer no action, or they fail to act where the domestic public interest would benefit from more robust private enforcement of domestic laws. It follows that where domestic courts are an integral part of private actors' efforts to compete internationally, understanding when and why U.S. courts might be expected to apply U.S. law extraterritorially is critical.

Applying the framework

I now apply this framework to an examination of key developments in international antitrust law and policy in the United States and Europe to illustrate how U.S. extraterritoriality has influenced regime development in this area, both through direct assertions of regulatory authority vis-à-vis transnational actors and by helping to shape U.S. preferences concerning the desirability of creating a formal treaty regime for international antitrust. Viewing this history through the framework elaborated above allows for clear elucidation of what those differences are, and also why U.S. and European preferences on competition law enforcement have begun to converge in recent decades.

The origins of modern antitrust

The Sherman Antitrust Act, enacted by the U.S. Congress in 1890, was the world's first modern antitrust statute.[43] It was passed to assuage U.S. public concern over the growing threat that large economic conglomerates in railroads, oil, and manufacturing posed to small entrepreneurs that had been, up until the 1880s, the backbone of the U.S. economy.[44] The Act itself is short and broadly drafted. Section 1 prohibits "[e]very contract, combination in the form of a trust or otherwise, or conspiracy, in the restraint of trade or commerce among the several states, or with foreign nations."[45] Section 2 establishes that monopolization, attempts to monopolize, or "conspiracies" to monopolize trade or commerce among U.S. states or with foreign countries are a felony offense. Sorting out which types of contracts and combinations qualified as impermissible restraints on trade was a task delegated by default to the courts.

Early domestic applications of the Sherman Act focused on rooting out private collusion among independent firms.[46] This triggered a turn-of-the-century frenzy of mergers in many sectors, which perversely further concentrated economic power.[47] In response, the Justice Department redirected enforcement toward monopolies and attempts to monopolize. Large firms pushed back, using both lobbying and litigation, arguing that the aggressive application of de-monopolization laws would undercut private property rights.[48] Eventually these arguments prevailed in U.S. courts, when on a single day in 1911 the U.S. Supreme Court issued two important decisions that jointly established what came to be known as the antitrust "rule of reason." In *Standard Oil Co. of New Jersey*

[43] 15 U.S.C. §§ 1–7. For older legal concepts of impermissible restraints of trade, see Furse (2008:3–6).
[44] Wells (2002), Cini and McGowan (1998).
[45] Section 1. Section 2 specifies that all persons who monopolize, attempt to monopolize, or engage in acts prohibited in Section 1 may be punished as felons.
[46] *Drystone Pipe and Steel Co. v. United States* 175 U.S. 211 (1899).
[47] Wells (2002).
[48] Peritz (1990:272).

v. United States, the Court determined that only contracts and combinations that "unreasonably" restrain trade are actionable under §1 of the Sherman Act. *United States v. American Tobacco Co.* held that §2 of the Sherman Act likewise applied only to "unreasonable" acquisition or use of monopoly power.[49]

In addition to formally carving out regulatory space for large firms to operate, the centrality of the inherently fuzzy standard at the heart of these holdings ensured U.S. courts would remain heavily enmeshed in the business of regulatory line-drawing in the antitrust sphere.[50]

In 1914, Congress passed two additional pieces of legislation intended to bring greater clarity and predictability to U.S. antitrust policy – in part by decreasing the range of discretion judges had assumed in the construction of the Sherman Act's prohibitions.[51] The Federal Trade Commission Act created a specialized agency to investigate and enjoin alleged anti-competitive practices. The Clayton Act took a preventative approach by providing for review of prospective acquisitions, and prohibiting those expected to "substantially lessen competition" or to increase the likelihood of harmful monopoly practices. The Act also specifies that private parties harmed by anti-competitive activity may bring civil claims, and provides for treble damages.[52] By the middle of the twentieth century, when U.S. courts began to entertain assertive forms of extraterritorial regulation, legislative withdrawal of this private right of action would have been politically impracticable.

These early U.S. developments had no parallel in Europe. To the contrary, European governments and publics had relatively tolerant attitudes toward cooperation among nominally competing firms.[53] During the economically volatile decades of the 1920s and 1930s, for example, Europeans considered cartel membership a responsible – even

49 221 U.S. 1 and 221 U.S. 106 (1911).

50 In subsequent litigation, U.S. courts identified a set of antitrust violations that are considered illegal *per se* (e.g. horizontal price fixing and territorial allocations) and which, therefore, do not prompt the close evaluation required to apply the rule of reason (Loevinger 1964).

51 Jones (1999:10), citing Letwin (1981:267), argues that in passing this legislation, Congress expressly sought (unsuccessfully) to "undo" the rule of reason established in the Supreme Court's 1913 decision in *Standard Oil*.

52 Jones (1999:8), 15 U.S.C. §12 et seq. Private rights of action were granted in §4 of the original act; today they are in 15 U.S.C. §26(a).

53 Gerber (1994:28), Freyer (2006:61). This is not to say European governments in this era found all private restraints unproblematic: Germany, Sweden, and Norway all passed national competition legislation in the 1920s, as did Denmark, Bulgaria, Romania, and Yugoslavia in the 1930s (Edwards 1967:4).

"civilized" – strategy for managing market and price uncertainties that "replaced the brutal ethos of competition with a system of cooperation."[54]

The 1920s in the United States were a period of strong economic growth during which antitrust officials and U.S. courts adopted a relatively "hands off" approach to business collusion short of blatant bids to fix prices or divide markets.[55] By the time Franklin D. Roosevelt assumed the U.S. Presidency in 1933, however, the United States was reeling from the depression that gripped the global economy in the decade between 1929 and 1939. The Roosevelt administration took an unprecedentedly interventionist approach to stabilizing the U.S. economy and curbing its rampant unemployment. Many of these "New Deal" policies, which encompassed government-administered production and price controls, wage controls, and banking restrictions, were deeply unpopular with American business leaders. Somewhat ironically, given what was to come later, enacting these measures actually necessitated the temporary suspension of U.S. antitrust laws.

Roosevelt sold the New Deal to Congress and American voters in part using populist charges that big business was threatening to undermine American free enterprise for selfish private gains.[56] American business leaders vigorously contested Roosevelt's accusations, cited the inconsistency of New Deal policies with market reliance, and sought to have the core of the New Deal legislation invalidated by U.S. federal courts. The litigation effort came to fruition in 1935 when the Supreme Court declared the National Recovery Act of 1933 unconstitutional.[57]

In the subsequent period Roosevelt succeeded in wresting acquiescence for more modest versions of his policies from U.S. federal courts in revised legislation. But, whereas in his first term as President Roosevelt had viewed U.S. antitrust law as an impediment to his recovery plan, a sharp recessionary downturn in 1937–1938 prompted Roosevelt to embrace antitrust enforcement "out of desperation" in order to salvage

[54] Wells (2002:9), Drahos (2001). Note, U.S. regulatory hostility to international cartel activity has never been absolute. Shortly after the passage of the Clayton Act in 1914, U.S. entry into World War I prompted legislative back-pedaling in the form of the 1918 Webb-Pomerene Act, which carves out antitrust exemptions for U.S. export trade where cartel participation does not affect U.S. markets. Due to its popularity, the Act was retained after the War, and still undergirds a policy of limited tolerance toward U.S. firm involvement in export cartels (Wells 2002:33).

[55] Kovacic and Shapiro 2000:47.

[56] Wells (2002:34), Freyer (2006).

[57] *A.L.A. Schechter Poultry Corp. v. United States*, 295 U.S. 495.

some political momentum for what remained of his recovery agenda during his second term.[58]

As a first step along this path, Roosevelt appointed a known antitrust zealot, Thurmond Arnold, to head the Justice Department's Antitrust Division. In Arnold's first two years, he nearly quadrupled the Division's staff from 58 to more than 200 lawyers and increased its output from 11 cases and 59 investigations in 1937 to 92 cases and 215 investigations in 1940.[59] In 1939 Roosevelt also created a joint executive-congressional body, the Temporary National Economic Committee (TNEC), to study and report on the extent and effects of monopolization and to make recommendations.[60] Although these efforts initially had a domestic focus, several influential members of Roosevelt's administration came to share the belief that cartels and the distortions of markets and trade they produced had been an important cause of the global economic malaise of the 1930s.[61]

As a consequence, the regulatory attention of TNEC and the Antitrust Division increasingly spilled over to transnational cartel activities. At the same time, these U.S. antitrust regulators were acutely aware that the United States lacked natural partners for combating international cartels, even among its close allies.[62] In short, if the Justice Department was going to address this problem, it had to do so unilaterally.

War, occupation, and the Western-liberal international order

Outside the United States, the Great Depression helped to underwrite a slide into domestic political extremism and international aggression in key European and Asian states. As the idea that Germany under Adolf Hitler posed a genuine threat to European peace was taking hold, TNEC and the U.S. Justice Department's Antitrust Division were finding many prominent American firms with cartel ties to German firms, among them Standard Oil, General Motors, and the U.S. chemical firm DuPont.[63]

[58] Wells (2002:38).
[59] Wells (2002:40), Freyer (2006:27).
[60] Note, these records are still under seal. National Archives, Guide to Federal Records, www.archives.gov/research/guide-fed-records/groups/144.html.
[61] Wells (2002:90–91).
[62] Edwards (1944).
[63] Kolko (1962:718) reports that as of 1937, twenty-six of the top one hundred American firms had cartel ties to German industry. He states further that "economic significance of the involved companies [was] much greater than their numbers," since those twenty-six accounted for 60 percent of the total assets of that elite group of American firms.

By the early 1940s, the belief that the high degree of cartelization among large German industrial firms had played an important role in the rise of the National Socialist (Nazi) Party in Germany had gained broad currency among U.S. policymakers.[64] The scale and ubiquity of the anticompetitive arrangements uncovered by TNEC and Justice Department investigations essentially ensured that antitrust policy would be an important element in Allied postwar planning.[65]

To avoid interfering with the war effort, the Justice Department suspended antitrust enforcement proceedings against U.S. and Allied firms in 1941. However, Antitrust Division lawyers continued to assemble charges against major U.S. and foreign firms in dozens of cases with the intent of pursuing them once the external threat had subsided. After the strategic tide had turned definitively against Germany and the Axis powers in Europe, Justice Department officials began acting on its backlog of cases.[66] Among the first was a major claim, filed in January 1944, against DuPont, and a British firm, Imperial Chemical Industries, alleging a "worldwide conspiracy" to fix chemical prices. After filing the case, then head of Antitrust Division, Wendell Berg, issued the following statement: "[U.S.] antitrust laws are going to be enforced whenever [cartel] arrangements restrict or affect American trade and commerce. I hope that the bringing of this case will serve as a warning to American and foreign monopolies."[67] Other suits targeting conspiracies in oil, rubber, alkali, steel, and other industries followed. This great push, which encompassed a total of 315 cases between 1941 and 1946, and many more investigations, sent a strong message to U.S. companies that restrictive practices in violation of U.S. antitrust rules would be tolerated neither at home nor abroad.[68]

Among the cases that had been suspended in 1941 was a claim against the Aluminum Company of America (Alcoa) involving an alleged conspiracy to monopolize international trade in aluminum ingot. A lower court had ruled in favor of the firm in 1937, and the Department of Justice decided to appeal. Wells notes that during 1939 and 1940, the case frequently made newspaper headlines and generated roughly 70,000

64 Bernstein (2003).

65 See, for example, Letter from the Secretary of State to the President, September 11, 1944, *Department of State Bulletin* at 292–293 (1944), cf. Haight (1960:240).

66 Freyer (2006:43).

67 Wells (2002:99–100).

68 Freyer (2006:43).

pages of documents and transcripts.[69] The final *Alcoa* decision, which was handed down by a U.S. federal appeals court in 1944, involved a landmark opinion by Judge Learned Hand announcing the effects doctrine – the idea that U.S. statutory rules should be interpreted as reaching (and, therefore, conferring U.S. federal court jurisdiction over) extraterritorial conduct having the intent and effect of causing harmful effects inside U.S. territory. The decision then applies the Sherman Act to numerous acts of Alcoa and one of its Canadian subsidiaries, all of which had taken place in Europe, and finds those acts violated U.S. law.[70] The era of U.S. regulatory extraterritoriality had arrived.[71]

Less celebrated but equally important for explaining the subsequent rise of private antitrust enforcement was a Supreme Court case, *International Shoe v. Washington*, decided the following year.[72] This decision allowed state-level judicial authorities to exercise personal jurisdiction over non-resident individuals and businesses not present in the regulatory forum at the time a civil suit is brought. The Court held that where private entities had established minimum contacts with a U.S. state (e.g. by transacting business inside its territory), they could be held accountable before its courts without offending "traditional notions of fair play and substantial justice." Applied internationally, this decision and subsequent refinements from later case law provide a framework for U.S. courts (federal and state) to secure jurisdiction over non-U.S. persons for the purpose of U.S. civil court proceedings.

Concern with cartels and monopolies also extended to international negotiations over postwar institutions. U.S. postwar planning, based in the State Department, featured an inter-agency Special Committee on Private Monopolies and Cartels to generate proposals for dealing with private economic collusion and its effects on the international economy. While influential members of the Committee stopped short of arguing that cartel policy had been a direct cause of World War II, there was a consensus that allowing the situation to revert to pre-war levels of private restriction on international exchange would be fundamentally

69 Wells (2002:59).

70 *U.S. v. Alcoa* 148 F.2d 416. Judge Hand's expansive formulation of the effects doctrine extended the Sherman Act to U.S. and foreign persons whose activities negatively affect U.S. markets and commerce.

71 There were a few earlier antitrust cases with mixed domestic and extraterritorial elements (and also mixed U.S. and foreign defendants) in which a U.S. federal court had agreed to exercise jurisdiction. See *U.S. v. American Tobacco Co.*, 221 U.S. 106 (1911), and *U.S. v. Sisal Sales Corp.*, 274 U.S. 268 (1927).

72 326 U.S. 310 (1945). Zanettin (2002).

incompatible with the goal of establishing a liberal international order.[73] To this end, a full chapter of the never-to-be-adopted 1948 Havana Charter of the International Trade Organization (ITO) focused on curtailing restrictive business practices, reflecting what Wells describes as the "minimum demands" of the U.S. Cartel Committee.[74] Ultimately, however, the ITO foundered and no bargain was reached.[75]

Another key front in U.S. efforts to transform European attitudes regarding restrictive business practices was the Military Occupation of Germany.[76] Following Germany's defeat in the spring of 1945, the country was divided into four administrative zones, one for each of the former Allied countries, the United States, Britain, France, and the USSR. Although all shared the objective of preventing the revival of aggressive right-wing fascism in Germany, they disagreed strongly on strategy and tactics. France wanted to see the German state permanently dismantled. The British and Americans preferred to reintegrate Germany into the postwar liberal international order, although they had different assessments regarding the institutional prerequisites for this integration. Roosevelt (and later Truman) insisted that Germany's economy would have to be fully "de-cartelized" and "de-concentrated."[77] Although generally in agreement with the Americans with respect to cartel policy, British authorities were less convinced of the need to break up large German industries. The USSR, for its part, rejected the Western-liberal agenda on principle and proceeded with policies that ultimately resulted in the establishment of a separate German state with a Soviet-style planned economy.[78]

With few exceptions, the new class of German leaders slated to assume political control after military occupation ended in the western zones did not embrace American views on the need for radical decartelization and

[73] Wells (2002:111).

[74] Wells (2002:116–119). Chapter 5 of the Havana Charter prohibited price fixing, territorial apportionment, discrimination, production quotas and limits, and agreements to restrain technological innovation.

[75] Wells (2002:125), Harding and Joshua (2003:90–91). Note, two other contemporaneous initiatives for the international regulation of cartels likewise failed to gather sufficient support. The first originated in the Council of Europe, and the second in the United Nations Economic and Social Council, see Harding and Joshua (2003:92–93).

[76] The United States had a similarly ambitious agenda with respect to postwar Japan (Wells 2002, Freyer 2006).

[77] McGowan (2010:70), citing Hofstadter (1964).

[78] Wells (2002:156).

decentralization.[79] This was so even though, as Harding and Joshua note, German attitudes had shifted quite far toward accepting a need for some legal regulation of cartels.[80] Of more immediate and overriding concern both to postwar German leaders and to the western Occupation authorities, however, was preventing the collapse of Germany's remaining domestic economy. Consequently, policies that would have interfered with any functioning industrial concerns encountered stark resistance. More broadly, American-style faith in market competition with minimal state involvement ran against the culturally and institutionally conditioned preferences of German policymakers who wanted instead to create a more closely managed and consultative social market economy.[81] In the end, diplomatic pragmatism and growing U.S. domestic political fatigue with postwar European reconstruction prompted American officials to settle for far less than their original goals for restructuring Germany's economy and economic practices.[82]

One area where U.S. preferences prevailed, in formal legal terms at least, was in Germany's adoption of laws against so-called hard-core cartel activities (e.g. market sharing, price, and quota agreements) and the establishment of a Federal Cartel Office (Bundeskartellamt). Both occurred within a few years of Western military occupation being terminated in 1955.[83] Also around this time, several other European states adopted national legislation to limit horizontal restraints. As one knowledgeable contemporary noted, competition policy in Europe had come to be viewed "as a middle course between extremes of collectivization and cartelization."[84] At the same time, the regulatory practices that accompanied these domestic legal changes in Europe "appear[ed] in comparative terms to be a soft form: cautious, discretionary, and in the administrative rather than the judicial sector." They produced a competition regime characterized by a "consensual culture

[79] Members of the Freiburg School of neo-liberalism actively promoted American-style free market competition, Jones (1999:24–25). See also Buxbaum (2005:486–490).

[80] Harding and Joshua 2003:86.

[81] Buxbaum (2005), Wells (2002).

[82] Wells (2002:156), Freyer (2006:247).

[83] Buxbaum (2005:478). Notably, Section 98(2) of the German Act Against Restraints on Competition includes an express articulation of the U.S. effects doctrine. It states in relevant part, "this act shall apply to all restrictions of competition occurring in the territory of the application of this Act, even if they result from restraints conducted outside this territory" (Zanettin 2002:16). This provision was not widely used until the 1970s (Gerber 1983).

[84] Edwards (1967:13).

of negotiated compliance, rather than one of contentious enforcement" in which regulatory decisions were largely non-reviewable.[85]

Achievements in the sphere of de-concentration were more modest. Although Occupation authorities succeeded in breaking up the chemical giant I.G. Farben, along with a few other conglomerates, a combination of economic necessity and political resistance resulted in others remaining largely untouched. Notably, American authorities abandoned efforts to de-monopolize the German steel industry in order to prevent its collapse, and instead gave strong political encouragement to the creation of a six-nation European Coal and Steel Community (ECSC). The ECSC was established in 1952 under an initiative devised by Jean Monnet and Robert Schuman. The high-minded rhetoric behind the ECSC encompassed making the prospect of war between France and Germany "materially impossible" by creating a common market for two key commodities required for future militarization. In less lofty terms, the ECSC simply created an internationalized public administration for what had previously been a large privately controlled cartel.[86]

Be that as it may, the ECSC served as a founding institution of what became a far more ambitious project for European integration under the European Economic Community (EEC), and later the European Union. Especially noteworthy, therefore, is that Article 65 of the ECSC Treaty (which was "drafted by [U.S. State Department official] Robert Bowie with meticulous care") embodies an "American-style prohibition" on cartel practices, backed by a threat of criminal sanction.[87]

From U.S. dominance to competitive rivalry

In the early 1950s, the post-World War II recovery effort wound down, and the U.S.–Soviet Cold War rivalry began to intensify. As in prior eras, twists and turns in the development of European and U.S. competition law can be traced to broader (and partially endogenous) changes in the international political and economic system, and the responses of domestic governments, private entities, and national publics to those changes.

[85] Harding and Joshua (2003:98 and 99), Kelemen (2011:191).

[86] Schuman (1950), Harding and Joshua (2003:94) *cit.* Friedmann and Verloren van Themaat (1956:512).

[87] Harding and Joshua (2003:95).

United States

The 1950s and early 1960s proved to be a period of fairly sustained economic growth and prosperity in the United States and elsewhere. Under the Eisenhower administration, the U.S. Justice Department began to deprioritize anti-cartel enforcement as the backlog of World War II-era cases dwindled. International enforcement capacity in the Antitrust Division was scaled back accordingly. At the same time, those extraterritorial antitrust cases that were pursued by the Justice Department began to elicit greater pushback from foreign governments, among them several close U.S. allies and economic partners.[88] These states claimed that extraterritorial enforcement of U.S. law on the basis of the effects doctrine violated international legal rules of jurisdiction along with widely accepted choice of law principles, and thus interfered impermissibly in other states' domestic sovereignty.[89] Not surprisingly, the sharpest foreign protests concerned situations in which U.S. extraterritoriality directly impaired the ability of foreign governments to make law for their own citizens inside their own territories.

One illustrative post-World War II case that was widely criticized for the breath of its claimed jurisdictional reach was *United States v. Watchmakers of Switzerland Information Center, Inc.*[90] At issue was whether the Swiss watch industry's practice of limiting the production and sale of spare parts, which was allowed under Swiss law, impermissibly interfered with U.S. markets in violation of the Sherman Act. The claim was initiated in 1963, and the decision, in which the plaintiffs prevailed, was delivered in 1967. In notably expansive terms, the U.S. court held that the Sherman Act prohibited all Swiss contracts (including those involving non-parties to the case) restricting the production or sale of watches and watch parts if those restrictions affected markets outside Switzerland. Following this judgment, the government of Switzerland protested vociferously, and even threatened to bring a case against the United States in the International Court of Justice.[91] In response, the U.S. State Department urged the Department of Justice to seek a modification of the court's order. The modified judgment preserved the outcome, but also added language stating that if the Swiss law in question had *required*

[88] Triggs (1979).
[89] Hacking (1979).
[90] *United States v. Watchmakers of Switzerland Information Center* 134 F.Supp. 710 (SDNY 1955) and 168 F.Supp. 904 (SDNY 1958).
[91] Rahl (ed.), *Common Market and American Antitrust: Overlap and Conflict* (1970:334), cited in Triggs (1979:251).

the limitations complained of by the plaintiffs, U.S. courts would have abstained from finding violations under the "act of state" doctrine.[92]

Although U.S. government enforcement of U.S. antitrust law in transnational claims fell in this period, this decline was accompanied by an increase in extraterritorial private civil enforcement.[93] This included, strikingly, the willingness of U.S. federal courts to enforce U.S. antitrust law even against the U.S. government – for example, in its efforts to coordinate with German, British, and Japanese companies to stabilize steel prices.[94] Indeed, during this era private antitrust suits began to eclipse public litigation domestically and internationally, even as federal courts tightened rules for evidentiary burdens, standing, and damage awards.[95]

Why did private firms begin filing extraterritorial antitrust suits in large numbers? Although direct evidence to answer this question is lacking, congressional hearings on private litigation and the extraterritorial application of U.S. antitrust laws in the early 1970s point to private firm concern that foreign competitors (particularly the Japanese and the Germans) had unfair advantages arising from their less restrictive policies on competition. Firms taking this view saw private antitrust claims as an important weapon in efforts to address those disparities, particularly given U.S. government passivity.[96] These records also suggest that the lure of securing treble damages was a valued incentive. In addition,

[92] Norton (1979:581–582). The act of state doctrine is an interpretative tool that prohibits U.S. courts from sitting in judgment of (i.e. invalidating) another sovereign's laws as they apply within their own territory.

[93] Waller (2002), Connor (2007).

[94] See, for example, *Consumer Union of U.S., Inc. v. Rogers* 352 F.Supp. 1319 (D.D.C. 1973) (declaring "the Executive has no authority under the Constitution or acts of Congress to exempt the Voluntary Restraint Arrangements on Steel from the antitrust laws and that such arrangements are not exempt" and, further, that the Executive "may enter into agreements or diplomatic arrangements with private foreign steel concerns so long as these undertakings do not violate legislation regulating foreign commerce, such as the Sherman Act [. . .]") cited in Timberg (1973:166).

[95] Posner (1970:371), Rill (1988), Connor (2007). Shughart (1990:54) reports that by the early 1980s, approximately twenty-five private antitrust suits were filed in U.S. federal courts for every government enforcement action. This ratio had been roughly 7:1 in the period spanning 1961 and 1977.

[96] See, for example, International Aspects of Antitrust Laws: Hearings before the Subcommittee on Antitrust and Monopoly of the Committee on the Judiciary, United States Senate, October 3, 1973; April 29, 30; May 1 and 2, 1974, pages 164, 177, 1418, and 1432. More than a dozen congressional hearings between 1970 and 1979 touched extensively on this issue.

the fact that U.S. federal courts were quite clearly open to extraterritorial antitrust claims almost certainly lent its own momentum to the trend.

Importantly, the shift toward private litigation in the transnational sphere meant a loss of executive branch control over the incidence, timing, and targets of extraterritorial claims. With private plaintiffs largely determining the extraterritorial dockets of U.S. courts, regulatory antagonisms between the U.S. courts and foreign governments increased, albeit with the U.S. government often acting a "disinterested spectator."[97]

On the surface, much of the friction involved the extraterritorial application of U.S. procedural rules, which are more plaintiff-friendly than those in most European jurisdictions. Examples include permissive rules for notifications of suit ("service of process"), and for requiring defendants, and even third parties, to produce requested documentation in evidence-gathering ("discovery").[98] At the same time, international discord over procedural issues has quite often been a preface to, or a means of trying to avoid, clashes over underlying substantive rules.[99] Foreign government reactions to extraterritorial assertions of U.S. law and judicial authority encompassed not only official complaints but also attempts to preempt U.S. regulation through parallel court proceedings, and even legislation intended specifically to block voluntary domestic compliance with the extraterritorial orders issued by federal courts in the United States.[100] According to one expert's count, twenty countries, among them Britain, France, Germany, Australia, and Japan, enacted some form of blocking statute in reaction to perceived U.S. court overzealousness.[101] Even so, many U.S. law firms advised transnational

[97] Feinberg (1980–1981:346).

[98] U.S. discovery rules permit court orders for documents at a considerably earlier stage of proceedings, and in greater breadth, than in most European courts and administrative proceedings, thereby prompting European critics to label their use "fishing expeditions."

[99] Maier (1982), Meessen (1996). A point of irritation here is that multilateral treaties standardizing approaches to these issues exist (the Hague Conventions on Service Abroad (1965) and Taking of Evidence Abroad (1970)) and have been adopted by most European states. The United States has refused to join either.

[100] Scafuri (1965:564), Meessen (1996), Waller (2002), Zanettin (2002). Zimmerman (1992:174) notes that U.S. extraterritoriality sometimes resulted in foreign retaliation against U.S. corporations, c.f. Douglas E. Rosenthal and William M. Knighton (1982: viii–ix).

[101] Meessen (1996:157). The first such statutes were enacted by Ontario and Quebec in the 1940s in response to U.S. court meddling in the organization of Canada's paper industry (Jones 2004:418). Few examples exist of these laws being used in transnational litigation. See, for example, "The French Supreme Court Applies the 1980 Blocking Statute for the

clients to simply "assume that American antitrust rules are always applicable."[102]

The late 1960s brought slowed economic growth and shrinking international and domestic market shares to many U.S. industries. For the first time since the Second World War, demand for protectionist trade measures began to surface.[103] In 1971, U.S. balance of payments problems prompted the United States to unilaterally suspend the convertibility of the U.S. dollar to gold, thereby ending the international exchange rate arrangements established at Bretton Woods in 1944. Politically engineered shocks to global oil markets, high domestic inflation, and growing rates of unemployment all combined to further exacerbate U.S. economic difficulties – and increasingly those of other states as well.

In this climate, some U.S. business leaders began to complain that the extraterritorial application of U.S. antitrust law impaired their ability to compete internationally and deprived the U.S. economy of foreign trade and investment.[104] Some U.S. officials feared that U.S. legal assertiveness would drive foreign governments to more actively orchestrate the restrictive conduct of enterprises in their territories in order to shield those enterprises from the reach of U.S. courts.[105] Others countered that broad enforcement of U.S. antitrust rules benefitted U.S. enterprises by forcing them to avoid arrangements that would restrict their ability to compete openly on international markets.[106]

The economic hard times of the 1970s also coincided with a revolution in U.S. antitrust law and policy that effectively shifted the balance of extraterritorial enforcement of U.S. antitrust rules still further toward private litigants. At the vanguard of the change was a group of neo-liberal economists with ties to the University of Chicago who challenged the economic desirability of judicially constructed *per se* condemnations of

First Time and Strengthens the Conditions Under Which Evidence To Be Used in Foreign Litigation Can Be Obtained in France," www.gibsondunn.com/publications/Pages/FrenchSupremeCourtApplies1980BlockingStatute.aspx (January 2008).

102 Rahl (1974:1).

103 Goldstein (1986), Milner (1988).

104 Timberg (1973:169 n.52), citing statement of Senator Hart in 113 Congressional Record 11494–97, reprinted in 575 *BNA Antitrust and Trade Regulation Report* A-16, Townsend (1980). The logic was that foreign actors avoided ties with U.S. enterprises, since they could be used as a basis for U.S. jurisdiction over a wide range of conduct, Wood (1995).

105 Waller (1989–1990:101), citing Letter from Assistant Attorney General Donald Baker to Senator Edward Kennedy (February 16, 1977), reprinted in Trade Reg. Rep. (CCH) No. 274, at 15–16 (March 29, 1977).

106 Rahl (1974:4–5).

market concentration and restrictive practices.[107] Chicago School theorists argued that antitrust policy needed a firmer grounding in empirical analysis of market effects. Key proponents advocated using long-term consumer price projections as a universal touchstone for defining "efficiency."[108] Underlying this approach was a strong faith in the efficiency-generating capacities of markets, which, in turn, engendered strong preferences for government deregulation.

By the late 1970s, Chicago School-influenced views on antitrust law and policy were finding some expression in U.S. federal court rulings, including at the Supreme Court level.[109] However, many U.S. officials remained proponents of the old approach, or advocated other ideas that had emerged from reassessments prompted by the Chicago School critique.[110] As a result, government-initiated enforcement in this era appeared to be driven by "sporadic and conflicting enforcement priorities."[111] Similarly, few federal court judges had sufficient economics training to competently undertake the anti-formalist, consequence-driven analysis advocated by the Chicago School, and many were disinclined to make the attempt in the absence of legislative direction.[112]

These factors combined to create tremendous ambiguity regarding how core precepts of U.S. antitrust law would be interpreted and applied in federal courts, including in claims with an extraterritorial dimension. As posited by the theory expounded in Chapter 3, this ambiguity incentivized a great deal of privately initiated litigation, some of which keenly aggravated foreign governments. In one such suit involving an alleged uranium cartel, the U.S. Justice Department went so far as to intervene on behalf of the foreign defendants to counter aggressive discovery efforts.[113]

107 Harris (2001:12), Posner (1979), Bork (1979). This period, for example, saw passage of the 1976 Hart-Scott Rodino Act, giving federal authorities a role in case-by-case pre-merger review.

108 Hovencamp (2005:31–35).

109 *Continental T.V. v. GTE Sylvania*, 433 U.S. 36 (1977).

110 Hovencamp (2005:35–39).

111 Waller (1989–1990:100–101).

112 Scheuerman (1999).

113 Testimony of Senator Albert Gore, Jr. before the House Committee on Interstate and Foreign Commerce, No. 96-214, 19, June 1980, referring to private litigation that followed a congressional investigation of a spike in global uranium prices in the late 1970s. In this litigation, Westinghouse Corporation sued twenty-nine U.S. and foreign entities alleging domestic harm from cartel restraints, *In re Uranium Antitrust Litigation* 617 F.2d 1248 (7th Cir. 1980). The defendants eventually settled the case for $400 million in damages.

In the face of widespread complaints that variability in U.S. government enforcement was itself becoming a problem for U.S. enterprises, the Antitrust Division of the U.S. Department of Justice sought to clarify its extraterritorial enforcement priorities. At first these efforts were merely informal – an example of what one contemporary commentator called "law-making by luncheon speech."[114] In 1977, however, the Division issued the first of three (to date) official *Guides for Antitrust Enforcement in International Operations.* Additional Guides were issued in 1988 and 1995. The 1977 *Guide* described in sweeping terms the Justice Department's understanding that "U.S. law in general, and U.S. antitrust laws in particular, are not limited to transactions that take place within our borders." Echoing *United States v. Alcoa*, it goes on to explain that when foreign transactions affect U.S. commerce in substantial and foreseeable ways, "they are subject to U.S. law regardless of where they take place." The insistence in the *Guide*'s introduction that U.S. policy is applied with an eye to international comity and "avoid[ing] unnecessary interference with the sovereign interests of foreign nations" did little to assure wary foreigners.[115]

In 1981, the Senate Judiciary Committee assessed a proposal to establish a Commission on the Foreign Application on the U.S. Antitrust Laws.[116] The accompanying hearings underscore divergent preferences among those seeking to expand the scope of antitrust regulation including extraterritorially (mainly medium and small enterprises), and those seeking its relaxation, or, failing that, additional exemptions for foreign and export-oriented activities (mainly large multinationals).[117] Also featured in these debates are conflicting assessments of the degree and acceptability of foreign affairs frictions brought about by U.S. judicial extraterritoriality.

In the end, these disagreements generated two observable responses – one judicial and the other legislative. The federal judicial response took the form a new interpretative canon requiring courts to balance the interests of the United States against those of foreign governments in deciding whether to exercise jurisdiction over extraterritorial claims.[118] Efforts to promote this "jurisdictional rule of reason" drew strong

[114] Unattributed comment cited in Rahl (1974:3).
[115] See, for example, Stanford (1979:197), Hacking (1979).
[116] HR 4661, USGPO 1981; S 432, HRG-1981-SJS-0068.
[117] Senate Judiciary Committee Hearings on International Aspects of Antitrust Laws, HRG-1973-SJS-0002, October 3, 1973, April 29–May 2, 1974.
[118] Lowenfeld (1979), Kestenbaum (1982).

criticism from many sources on grounds that judges in domestic courts are, in general, poorly equipped to assess the interests of foreign states in deciding the appropriateness of jurisdiction. Fears that balancing analysis would further undermine legal predictability in transnational litigation arguably proved accurate – not least due to lack of guidance concerning when and how judges should apply balancing criteria.[119] This led to procedural splits among U.S. judicial circuits, which, in turn, generated divergent thresholds for the exercise of extraterritorial jurisdiction over antitrust and other types of claims.[120]

In 1993, the U.S. Supreme Court weighed in on this issue in *Hartford Fire Insurance Co. v. California*, a case involving an alleged international conspiracy to restrict the availability of specific types of reinsurance contracts in U.S. markets.[121] The majority opinion reaffirmed the older unilateralist approach by upholding the applicability of the Sherman Act and finding that it prohibited conduct in the United Kingdom that was allowed (but not required) under British law. In a dissenting opinion, Justice Antonin Scalia countered that any analysis of the extraterritorial applicability of a U.S. statute must begin by asking whether the U.S. Congress intended for it to have extraterritorial reach. Although he found that the Sherman Act failed this test, Scalia acknowledged that its long pattern of prior extraterritorial application was a relevant factor. He then used balancing analysis and concluded that the United Kingdom – which had vigorously protested U.S. court jurisdiction – had the greater regulatory interest. Similar questions surrounding the proper boundaries of U.S. law and court jurisdiction have continued to be heavily litigated in U.S. federal courts and, increasingly, in the Supreme Court.[122]

On the legislative side, domestic pressure for looser antitrust regulation of transactions with minimal U.S. impact combined with rising

[119] Maier (1983), Dodge (1998b). The doctrinal criteria at issue were in the form of checklists devised by judges and scholars to highlight potentially overriding foreign interests. However, the checklists contain no guidance for how judges should assess individual elements, or how they should weigh them in relation to others.

[120] See *Timberlane Lumber Co. v. Bank of America* 549 F.2d 597 (9th 1976). This approach was adopted and formalized in the *Restatement (Third) of the Foreign Affairs Law of the United States*. However, Congress rejected legislation in 1985 that would have amended the FTAIA to codify the jurisdictional rule of reason, www.govtrack.us/congress/bills/99/s397.

[121] 509 U.S. 784 (1993).

[122] See *F. Hoffmann-La Roche Ltd. et al. v. Empagran S.A. et al.* 542 U.S. 155 (2004), *Morrison v. Australia National Bank, Ltd* 561 U.S. 247 (2010) No. 08–1191, and *Kiobel v. Royal Dutch Petroleum* 133 S.Ct. 1659 (2013). See Chapter 7 for additional discussion.

foreign ire over extraterritorial claims to prompt the U.S. Congress to enact a 1982 amendment to the Sherman Act entitled the Foreign Trade Antitrust Improvements Act (FTAIA).[123] By the late 1970s, courts in key U.S. circuits had all but abandoned the intent requirement of the effects doctrine articulated in *Alcoa*. Excising this element from the jurisdictional test radically widened the basis for bringing international antitrust claims in U.S. courts, to the annoyance of foreign governments and increasingly overburdened federal judges.[124] One objective of the FTAIA, therefore, was to establish a uniform threshold for what level of domestic effects were required to trigger U.S. extraterritorial jurisdiction under the Sherman Act. The Act specifies in relevant part that the Sherman Act shall not apply to foreign commerce except when imports are concerned, "unless such conduct has a *direct, substantial, and reasonably foreseeable effect* on the domestic or import commerce or on the export business of a domestic person." The FTAIA does not define these modifiers, however. For this reason, it has done little to divorce enforcement from the vagaries of existing case law.[125]

A second objective behind the FTAIA – to underscore the non-applicability of U.S. antitrust laws to commerce intended purely for U.S. export – was considerably less accommodating to foreign interests. Although the intent was to reduce the amount of antitrust litigation involving foreign enterprises in U.S. courts (which foreign governments, in principle, favored), the amendment sought to achieve that reduction by eliminating the cause of action most likely to be used by foreign plaintiffs to counter enforcement loopholes favoring U.S. enterprises. This change is consistent with theories of economic nationalism in regulatory terms cited above.[126] However, it is also consistent with the idea that the task of U.S. domestic courts is to apply U.S. antitrust rules extraterritorially only where failure to do so would harm U.S. markets and consumers.

More definitive of the U.S. government approach to antitrust policy in the 1980s than the FTAIA was the election, and re-election, of Ronald

[123] 15 U.S.C. §6. In 1979 the Committee on Governmental Affairs had established a Commission to study the international application of U.S. antitrust laws, S. 1010 UGPO 1980.

[124] Waller (2002), Cavanagh (2003), Huffman (2007).

[125] Cavanagh (2003:2159).

[126] Indeed, the legislative history indicates that numerous U.S. lawmakers were concerned that robust extraterritorial enforcement of U.S. antitrust laws by private actors was hurting U.S. exporters, and driving down an already unfavorable balance of trade (Waller 2002, Huffman 2007).

Reagan as President. Throughout this era proponents of deregulation and other neo-liberal policies were influential at the executive level and worked to support a range of policies friendly to big business. In this environment extraterritorial enforcement of antitrust rules by the U.S. government all but disappeared.[127] Notably, adjustments to the U.S. approach in this period also did not incline American officials to attempt to coordinate antitrust policy internationally on anything other than an *ad hoc* basis. Throughout this period, however, the U.S. federal courts remained accessible – and therefore important – sites for private entities seeking to clarify and enforce U.S. antitrust prohibitions extraterritorially, despite a palpable lack of executive support for many of those claims.[128]

In sum, private plaintiffs were instrumental in bringing extraterritorial antitrust suits during the 1970s and 1980s, thereby incrementally expanding the reach of U.S. law, and demonstrating the enforcement power of U.S. courts. Foreign litigants contested many of these efforts. Foreign governments also protested on many occasions, though often to little avail.

Europe

Soon after World War II, it would have been difficult to predict that political coordination around the enforcement of European competition law would become a lightning rod for broader regional integration. On March 25, 1957, six states – Belgium, France, Italy, Luxembourg, the Netherlands, and West Germany – signed the Treaties of Rome, thereby establishing the European Economic Community (EEC) as a platform for economic cooperation and free trade. In 1967, the EEC merged with the European Coal and Steel Community and a third organization, the European Atomic Energy Community, to form a single organization, though each retained its distinctive profile and competences.

Competition rules featured prominently in the EEC Treaty and in its early administration. The driving logic, according to at least one key observer, was

[127] Zanettin (2002:14) citing Klein (1999). The Justice Department brought no antitrust cases against foreign corporations or individuals from 1987 to 1990, and in 1991 and 1992, only 2 percent of its cases involved foreign persons and conduct (Zanettin 2002:14).

[128] Jones (1999:16) reports that in the late 1970s there were roughly 1,400 private antitrust claims filed in U.S. federal courts annually – roughly twice as many as in prior and subsequent periods. Although most did not have an extraterritorial dimension, the overall trend is striking.

to ensure that efforts to lower government barriers to trade within Europe were not immediately undercut by private arrangements.[129] The EEC encompasses four institutions – a Commission, a Parliament, a Council of Ministers, and a Court.[130] In a pair of landmark decisions in the early 1960s, the European Court of Justice (ECJ) established that the EEC could establish rights that were enforceable before the courts of its member states by natural and legal persons, and that in the event of a conflict, EC law had supremacy over national law.[131] Although neither case concerned competition law directly, the influence of the holdings on the subsequent development of European law and institutions around competition policy would prove to be immense.

The EC's competition rules were laid out in Articles 85 and 86 of the Treaty of Rome.[132] These articles roughly mirror §§1 and 2 of the Sherman Act, although they were nominally modeled on Germany's competition laws. The first prohibits private agreements that restrict or distort competition inside the European Community, and the second makes it illegal for any firm or group of firms to "abuse" a dominant position so as to negatively affect trade between member states. The Commission quickly established itself as the main elaborator of European competition law and policy after the Council of Ministers enacted a measure in 1962 giving it exclusive authority to declare specific "notified" arrangements as non-infringing, and, therefore, exempt from sanction.[133] This authority enabled the Commission to deal directly with firms, rather than going through national governments as required in other areas of EEC law.[134] In its very early years, EC competition authority was used to police back-sliding into prewar patterns of public and private restraints on trade. By the 1970s, however, competition law, and the ancillary competences its enactment had spawned had become a key driver of European integration.

Procedurally, the Commission is empowered to issue non-binding recommendations on the compatibility of state laws with EEC rules,

129 Cini and McGowan (1998:60) citing Agnew (1985).

130 In 1965, the ECSC merged with the EEC (and Euratom) under the Brussels Treaty.

131 Alter (1998), Zanettin (2002). See *Van Gend & Loos v. Netherlands Inland Revenue Administration* [1963] ECR 1 (26/62) (establishing the principle of "direct effect"), and *Flaminio Costa v ENEL* [1964] ECR 585 (6/64) (establishing the supremacy of EC law over national laws).

132 These later became Articles 81 and 82, TEU, and are now articles 101 and 102, TFEU (2009 Treaty of Lisbon).

133 Council Regulation 17 [1959–62] OJ Spec. Ed. 87.

134 Kelemen (2011:154).

directives requiring non-specific legislative action at the state level, or regulations which are considered binding legislative acts. Although in most areas the Commission has no direct power of enforcement, in practice EC member states have rarely challenged these issuances. In the competition realm, by contrast, the Commission was empowered to impose fines directly, and even to authorize "dawn raids" against the premises of suspected violators as a means to obtain evidence of wrongdoing.[135]

A key feature of the EC system's operation has been the ability of individuals to petition the Commission to review the laws and regulatory actions of member states to ensure their compatibility with EC law.[136] This right appears nowhere in the founding treaties, but is implied, instead, from the principles of direct effect and supremacy described above.[137] Numerous commentators describe this mechanism as a "shield" protecting defendants from national regulatory actions based upon incompatible national competition rules. At the same time, constraints on the ability to recover private damages, or to obtain direct injunctive relief for violations of public law (including competition rules) in many states' national courts, have rendered private suits claiming violation of EC/EU rules against restrictive agreements and abuse of dominant position "very rare."[138]

As global economic malaise spread during the 1970s and 1980s, several European countries followed the United States in taking a neo-liberal turn in their domestic economic policies. High unemployment and slowing rates of growth were placing strain on domestic social welfare commitments.[139] One consequence of these stresses was weakened resolve at the national level for vigorous anti-cartel enforcement, thereby increasing opportunities for supranational institutions to flex their

135 Articles 15 and 14 of Council Regulation 17/62. See also Kelemen (2011:154).

136 Stone Sweet and Brunell (1998), Jones (1999), Alter (2000), Wils (2003).

137 Jones (1999:33–34), citing *Firma Molkerei-Zentrale Westfalen/Lippe GmbH v. Hauptzollamt Paderborn* [1968] ECR 143, 153. The logic is as follows: creating an independent body of supranational law conferring rights on individuals would have no meaning absent mechanisms to secure those rights, and because national courts are obligated under the Treaty to safeguard Community rights, "individuals are entitled to enforce those rights in national courts."

138 Wils (2003:6), Buxbaum (2005:484). One feature of the system that favored defendants in private competition claims was their ability to petition the Commission for a ruling on national law, which had the effect of suspending the national level proceeding, and undercutting it altogether when the Commission found national law incompatible with EC law.

139 Hall (1999), Fligstein and Mara-Drita (1996).

muscle.[140] Many scholars have pointed to the prominence of European competition regulation in driving European market integration by eliminating barriers to exchange.[141] Not coincidentally, clashes over competition rules turned out to be an important site for the Commission and the ECJ to define, and incrementally increase, their legal and institutional authority (or "competence") over member state policies.[142] The Commission's power in this respect was greatly enhanced with the 1986 passage of the Single European Act (SEA), which laid the groundwork for establishing the Community as "an area without internal frontiers in which the free movement of goods, services, persons, and capital is ensured."[143] The Act's main sponsors put heightened emphasis on competition enforcement and merger review at the forefront of this effort in order to sweep away local forms of protectionism that threatened to repartition the common market.[144]

Despite formal similarities in the underlying law, European state practice has differed substantially from that of the United States with regard to extraterritoriality grounded in effects-based jurisdiction, with Europeans displaying far greater restrictions on its use.[145] Here too, Community-level regulators have been more assertive than those at the national level.[146] In an early line of cases, EC regulators asserted authority over conduct outside EC territory where harm was alleged to have

140 Cini and McGowan (1998:30–32), Gerber (1984), Swaine (2001–2002). Van Waarden and Drahos (2002) explain that the Commission has not sought to directly invalidate national competition rules in member states or to insist on their positive harmonization. Instead, the Commission, often with the backing of ECJ rulings, has sought to "superimpose" European rules where national practices negatively impact trade between members (Van Waarden and Drahos 2002:914).

141 Kelemen (2011), Büthe and Swank (2007), Wilks (2005), Van Waarden and Drahos (2002), Drahos (2001).

142 Moravcsik (1993), Alter (1998), Sandholtz and Stone Sweet (1998), Drahos (2001), Rosamond (2005), Kelemen (2011), Büthe (2011).

143 Moravcsik (1991:19–20), citing Article 8A of the 1985 EC Commission White Paper, as amended by the SEA.

144 *1985 Commission White Paper* at 39. See also Büthe and Swank (2007:183), Kelemen (2011:157–158).

145 Such differences are deeply rooted in the civil law approach to the allocation of jurisdiction and choice of law problems; see, for example, Michaels (2005).

146 The largest among the European state economies have had some capacity to apply their antitrust rules extraterritorially for much of the post-World War II era – although still considerably less than the United States. Buxbaum notes that the United States is not the only country to recognize effects-based jurisdiction in its competition law, citing §130(2) of Germany's law, which provides: "This Act shall apply to all restraints of competition [. . .], also if they were caused outside the area of application of this Act."

occurred inside the Community in violation of EC competition law. In the 1969 *Dyestuffs Case*, which involved an alleged price-fixing conspiracy among several producers of aniline dyes, the European Commission began to suggest openly that its anti-cartel decisions applied whether the conduct at issue occurred "within or outside the Common Market" – an approach that echoed the U.S. effects doctrine.[147] Not coincidentally, *Dyestuffs* also occasioned the first assertion of jurisdiction over entities based outside EEC member states – in this instance, British and Swiss companies.[148]

This nascent authority expanded in 1985 when the ECJ formally recognized a limited ("modified") effects-type jurisdiction in its handling of the *Wood Pulp I* case. The underlying complaint involved an alleged cartel of American, Canadian, and Scandinavian companies accused of conspiring to fix prices in European markets. The ECJ held that Article 85 applied to enterprises that engage in foreign anticompetitive activity if those practices affect markets inside the EEC, even if the enterprises have no registered presence in the European Community.[149] The ECJ insisted, however, that its holding was not extraterritorial regulation, but was, instead, an exercise of territorial jurisdiction based on where the anticompetitive agreements were implemented.[150] Be this as it may, it appears clear in retrospect that the ECJ had taken the leap into effects-based extraterritorial regulation.[151]

One final feature of the international antitrust regime in the 1970s worthy of note involves multilateral efforts to create soft law. For example, the United Nations Conference on Trade and Development (UNCTAD) drafted a set of non-binding Multilaterally Agreed Equitable Principles and Rules for the Control of Restrictive Business Practices which was adopted by the General Assembly on December 5, 1980.[152] In 1976, the Organisation for Economic Co-operation and Development (OECD) adopted its first set of Guidelines for Multinational Enterprises (MNEs), which included a section on competition. These guidelines, which have been revised

[147] Griffin (1999) citing *Aniline Dyes Cartel* 1969, O.J. (L. 195) 11 [1969] C.M.L.R. D23 D33.
[148] Harding and Joshua (2003:124).
[149] O.J. 1985 L 85/1.
[150] Jacquemin (1993).
[151] See, for example, Griffin (1993:356) (citing several then-recent EC cases regulating external conduct).
[152] A/RES/35/63.

several times, most recently in 2011, enumerate a core list of prohibited practices, and direct MNEs to refrain from "strengthening the restrictive effects of international or domestic cartels or restrictive agreements."[153]

It is difficult to gauge the impact (if any) of these efforts on government and private behavior. What is clear, however, is that these international soft-law initiatives have not paved the way to more "legalized" obligations.

Post-Cold War era

National and supranational developments

The end of the Cold War ushered in large changes in the structure and character of the international system and the global economy. Economic liberalization spread rapidly into Eastern Europe, to the newly independent states of the former Soviet Union, and to former Soviet client states. This prompted a new wave of states to adopt competition rules at the domestic level. It also proved to be a time of heightened demand for aggressive anti-cartel enforcement on both sides of the Atlantic. Perhaps sensing a need for a more proactive stance in the emerging "competition among competition laws," the Department of Justice under President George H.W. Bush once again embarked on a period of more active antitrust enforcement with an emphasis on large criminal cases, including many with an international dimension.[154] This approach was pursued even more vigorously under President Bill Clinton. According to one study, roughly 25 percent of the 625 criminal antitrust claims Justice Department regulators filed between 1990 and 1998 had an international dimension. Furthermore, a non-trivial proportion of defendants in government anti-cartel cases have been foreign-based.[155]

The resurgence in anti-cartel prosecutions also fed into increases in rates of private civil proceedings. Private plaintiffs and the law firms that serve them know that criminal cases, whether successful or not, often can

[153] Davidow (1977).

[154] Connor *et al.* (2010). The move toward stricter patterns of U.S. criminal enforcement was aided by a revamped leniency program whereby the first participants to come forward and expose anti-competitive schemes were granted reduced penalties, or even immunity from prosecution. Such bargains, however, have no effect on the ability of private entities to bring follow-on civil suits to recover for harms suffered, www.justice.gov/atr/public/criminal/leniency.html.

[155] Zanettin (2002:14).

be mined for lucrative civil damage claims. This generates an informal, and often mutually beneficial, division of labor, with the DOJ focusing its resources on high-profile criminal cases knowing that much of the remaining effort will be taken up by private civil enforcement.[156]

In Europe, political anxieties related to Germany's reunification in 1990 prompted European Community officials to further accelerate the integrationist agenda embodied in the 1986 Single European Act. Under the 1992 Treaty of Maastricht, European Community members established the European Union (EU), a three-pillar structure with the EEC and its key institutions as the first and most important pillar.[157] The transformation ushered in further consolidation of EU authority in a wide range of economic and social policy arenas, chief among them monetary affairs. Shortly after the EU's creation, and in response to demand from several former Eastern Bloc states, European authorities set out to expand the EU geographically. State accessions in the mid-1990s, 2004, and in 2007 created a much larger bloc of coordinated economic and market power than had existed previously. Indeed, 2013 World Bank figures indicate the EU's gross domestic product exceeded that of the United States by a small margin – a development that, if my theory is correct, could begin to erode traditional EU reluctance to enforce its competition rules extraterritorially.

In fact, since the early 1990s, patterns of EU enforcement in the competition realm have edged closer to those of the United States in both volume and approach. Changes in the world economy, which included the EU's creation and subsequent enlargements, prompted regulators in the Directorate General for Competition (DG-COMP) to step up enforcement significantly over prior levels.[158] Stricter enforcement on cartels followed a move in the late 1980s to tighten Community-level responses to claims of "abuse of dominant position" in merger reviews and in ongoing regulation.[159] During this period, the Commission undertook a larger number of significant investigations, both in traditional raw materials and manufacturing sectors and in several service sectors, among them banking, telecommunications, and the freight shipping area described in the opening paragraphs of this

[156] Connor *et al.* (2010), Ghosal (2008).

[157] The second pillar dealt with common foreign and security policy, and the third concerned criminal and juridical affairs, Shaw (1996).

[158] Wils (2010).

[159] Debate continues, however, both within the EU and between the EU and U.S. regulators, over what constitutes "abuse."

chapter.[160] More than a few involved an extraterritorial dimension.[161] The Commission also has imposed ever-larger fines on parties found in violation, with fines of tens of millions of euros now being routine.[162] In this respect, EU practice largely mirrored U.S. practice during this same period.

Underwriting this change is a noteworthy shift toward greater judicialization of supranational regulatory functions and, as a result, less complete reliance on regulator-managed oversight.[163] In their early stages, these developments were a response to discontent on the part of both regulated actors and national competition agencies with perceived inconsistencies with the Commission's decision-making on competition questions, fed by a lack of transparency in Brussels-based processes.[164] From the 1970s onward, numerous challenges to Commission decisions were referred to the ECJ, and after 1989 also to the Court of First Instance, focusing on factors ranging from elements of due process in the investigation of alleged offenders, to evidentiary standards for proving allegations of inappropriate collusion, to decisions on appropriate sanctions. This developing jurisprudence had the effect of expanding the Commission's oversight powers. Court-based oversight of Commission procedures also spilled over, perhaps unavoidably, into an ever greater judicialization of the standards by which the Commission interprets underlying substantive law.

A key move toward erecting an institutional framework for more U.S.-style enforcement occurred in 1999 when the European Commission issued a White Paper on the need to modernize EU competition rules and processes in response to anticipated EU enlargement.[165] This action culminated in a set of broad reforms formally adopted by the Council of Ministers in 2003. The general thrust of the reforms was to delegate administration of EU competition law to national institutions to a far greater degree than before.[166] One significant feature of the reform was the discarding of the Regulation 17 notification system, which had allowed the Commission to grant legal exemptions to individual firms

160 Harding and Joshua (2003:139–140).
161 Griffin (1999).
162 Forrester (2011:185).
163 Harding and Joshua (2003:170), Kelemen (2011).
164 Harding and Joshua (2003:177 and 232).
165 Gauer *et al.* (2003:3).
166 But see Alan Riley, *EC Antitrust Modernization: The Commission Does Very Nicely Thank You!*, 2003 EUR. COMP. L. REV. 604 (suggesting the Commission has effectively centralized enforcement around itself), cited in Fiebig (2005).

for competition-restricting arrangements that were claimed to promote economic or technical progress without unduly burdening consumers.[167] Going forward, national regulators and judges would make determinations both about the applicability of EU law and the status of particular entities under it. Another central feature of the reform gave EU competition rules "direct effect" in member states. Whereas previously national authorities had some discretion in recognizing individual rights under EU competition law, after the reform member states could "no longer rely on national law alone" in deciding questions within the scope of Articles 81 and 82 (formerly 85 and 86).[168]

The reform was prompted in part by the volume of competition issues implicating EU rules that were being referred to the Commission and Court of First Instance. These changes thus freed the Commission to focus more on complex multi-jurisdictional matters.[169] Questions have arisen about whether the 2003 reforms were a genuine effort to decentralize decision-making, or a plan to further co-opt national competition authorities and institutions into carrying out policies crafted in Brussels.[170] While the abolition of the Commission's notification system is evidence of the first stance, because actions taken in this realm at the national level are nominally subject to supranational review, this, in effect, drafts national institutions into the service of EU law.[171]

Key to predictions about how the reform ultimately will play out, both as a tool of further European integration and as a driver of regulatory diffusion, are expectations for the role of private enforcement. According to the theoretical framework articulated above, the availability of points of access for private enforcement in independent national courts leads to streams of litigation that would not be brought by government regulators, provided there is a reasonable expectation of compensation in terms of recovered damages or forms of injunctive relief beneficial to prospective plaintiffs. Where, in addition, the underlying conduct is transnational in character, it should generate pressure for courts to begin asserting jurisdiction extraterritorially. It follows that developments with regard to private enforcement may also have implications for the

167 http://eur-lex.europa.eu/legal-content/EN/TXT/?uri=URISERV:l26092.
168 Woods (2004:434) and Buxbaum (2005:488). Note, these articles have since been renumbered and are currently Articles 101 and 102 of the Lisbon Treaty.
169 Gauer *et al.* (2003:3).
170 See, for example, Kelemen (2011), Woods (2004), Harding and Joshua (2003).
171 See Article 7 of Council Regulation 1/2003, O.J. (L1).

character and frequency of clashes between the United States and Europe going forward.

Although Council Regulation 1/2003 mentions private damage awards as an example of how national courts should protect the substantive rights of individuals under Articles 81 and 82, it contains no measures to this effect.[172] A groundbreaking 1999 ECJ decision, *Courage v. Crehan*, however, had held that member states must allow remedies in the form of private damages for proven violations of Articles 81 and 82.[173] Considered together, these developments prompted a few member states to begin, haltingly, to revamp their procedural rules. Overall, however, the changes have been modest.[174] Ten years after the launch of the 2003 reforms, private enforcement in the competition realm, although on the rise in some jurisdictions, remained well below what many expected.[175]

To be clear, private rights of action in the competition realm exist in many European legal systems, albeit in forms that are highly circumscribed compared to those in the United States. In seeking to comprehend the differences, the first place to look is standing – the formal recognition of the right to bring a claim under a specific law. In Europe, private standing for damage claims is generally limited to losses tied to obligations existing between private parties.[176] By contrast, such claims are the backbone of the "private attorney general" system in the United States.[177] The European approach reflects a deep institutional and cultural preference for administrative forms of public regulation described above, in which the goal of public enforcement is to deter unwanted behavior, not to compensate injured parties. Many Europeans fear, with good reason, that giving private entities standing to bring private damage disputes will change the profile and character of enforcement proceedings.[178]

[172] Council Regulation 1/2003, Recital 7. Gauer *et al.* explain "[i]t was not the ambition of Regulation 1/2003 to tackle all issues which could remedy the limited [sic] private enforcement" but that suspension of Regulation 17 was "a first necessary step to improve the private enforcement of EC competition rules."

[173] *Courage Ltd. v. Bernard Crehan and Bernard Crehan v. Courage Ltd. and Others* Case C-453/99, 2001 E.C.R. 1 (Eng. C.A. 1999), *available at* 1999 WL 394609. Note, this holding was actually *obiter dictum*, since the ECJ ruled there had been no violation of EC rules.

[174] See, for example, Kelemen (2011:177–191).

[175] A related prediction was that variation in national rules for standing in private enforcement claims would prompt increased forum shopping, Woods (2004:442).

[176] Buxbaum (2005:493).

[177] Buxbaum (2001).

[178] See Wils (2003) for a survey of specific aspects of this fear.

In addition to narrow definitions of standing, several other features of national-level legal systems in Europe combine to undercut incentives for private enforcement. They include the absence of class actions, restrictive pretrial discovery rules, the non-availability of compound damages, and the fact that losing plaintiffs often must pay the defendant's legal fees.[179] Indeed, a comprehensive 2004 study on private damage claims for violations of competition rules found that since the 1970s, only sixty suits had been fully litigated in national courts – half of them in Germany.[180] Of these, twenty-eight resulted in damage awards for the plaintiff. Moreover, Wurmnest (2005) observes that only twelve of the sixty suits involved European law.[181] This is despite the fact that since the 1970s, the European Commission has encouraged (at least rhetorically) use of private claims to bring about broader enforcement of competition law.

Thereafter, the Commission issued a 2005 Green Paper that, to no one's surprise, located the root of the problem in the procedural rules found in member states' legal systems. The Paper also suggested that those problems would be "best addressed by a combination of measures at both Community and national levels."[182] This was followed in 2008 by a Commission White Paper containing specific suggestions for revamping national laws on questions of standing, access to evidence, fault requirements, damages, limitation periods, and assigning liability for litigation costs so as to encourage higher rates of competition-related damage claims. Kelemen observes that the White Paper sparked heated debate, with many in Europe's competition law community concluding that the EU was trying to "introduc[e] a series of exotic plants to European soil."[183]

179 Woods (2004:435–438), Buxbaum (2005:490), Wigger and Nolke (2007:495). Woods (2004:435, n.11) notes that in the United States there have been roughly nine private suits for every government antitrust proceeding since the 1970s. In contrast, in Europe (where, he explains, "[f]igures are harder to come by") one estimate covering 1989–1992 found among the (then) eleven EEC members, minus Ireland, where figures were unavailable, a ratio of one private suit to every twenty-one public actions.

180 This study, conducted by the Ashurst law firm, surveys substantive law, standing, available damages, standards of evidence, burdens of proof, and discovery rules among other issues in twenty-five European countries. See http://ec.europa.eu/competition/antitrust/actionsdamages/study.html.

181 Wurmnest (2005:1174, n.4). Of course, the figure of sixty fully litigated suits understates the total number of suits initiated by an unknown magnitude. Consequently, as the analysis in Chapter 2 suggests, one should be wary about drawing implications regarding the deterrent effect of private damage claims in Europe from these figures alone.

182 Commission White Paper on Damages Actions for the Breach of EC Antitrust Rules, COM (2008) 165:2.

183 Kelemen (2011:172–173).

In June 2013, the Commission released its proposal for a formal Directive on Antitrust Damage Actions.[184] True to standard EU legislative processes, the Proposed Directive incorporates many of the details from the 2008 White Paper, which, when they become binding, could bring about a noticeable shift in the rate of private damage claims – thus further enhancing the influence of EU competition law as a deterrent. The Commission's press release took care to contrast the Proposed Directive to aggressive U.S.-style enforcement, describing it as a "European way," in which private damage claims serve as a mechanism "to facilitate full and fair compensation for victims *once a public authority has found and sanctioned an infringement*" (emphasis added).[185] Thus, while the new rules do give private entities an important set of new tools for making private damage claims more feasible, the limitation that claims can only follow public sanctions keeps the selection of disputes firmly within the control of state and EU regulators.

International processes

On a still wider scale, the end of the Cold War, which occurred alongside the beginnings of a technological revolution in private electronic communications, prompted even greater internationalization of markets for many products and services. In an effort to minimize the frequency of direct legal clashes, U.S. and EC regulators attempted a few measured steps to formalize mutual assistance in antitrust enforcement – albeit exclusively in a horizontalist mode.

In 1991, for example, the United States and the EEC signed a Competition Cooperation Agreement featuring procedures by which competition authorities in each jurisdiction may notify other competition authorities of impending enforcement actions, and pledging each to consider the interests of the other when weighing enforcement options. This Agreement included a mechanism for "positive comity," allowing parties to request that their foreign counterparts initiate enforcement proceedings in their own territories on the requester's behalf.[186] In 1998, the parties clarified the procedures for making requests for assistance

[184] On December 2, 2013, the Council of the European Union (formerly the Council of Ministers) opted the proposed Directive. As of January 2014, it is awaiting action from the European Parliament's Economic and Social Committee.

[185] http://europa.eu/rapid/press-release_IP-13-525_en.htm.

[186] Competition Cooperation Agreement, Article V.

under an Enhanced Positive Comity Agreement. The reason, however, was not excessive use of this mechanism, but its near non-use. To date no formal request has been made under either the 1998 Agreement or a similar agreement that was signed with Canada in 2004. Federal Trade Commission (FTC) officials maintain, however, that the existence of these agreements has influenced several informal interactions over issues of transnational concern.[187]

In a similar vein, the U.S. Congress in 1994 passed the International Antitrust Enforcement Assistance Act (IAEAA) authorizing the FTC and the U.S. Department of Justice to negotiate mutual assistance agreements with parallel enforcement bodies in other countries. After a slow start, these initiatives have begun to generate some interest and activity. To date, the United States has concluded bilateral cooperation agreements, or exchanged memoranda of understanding on antitrust policy, with thirteen states, among them Canada (1995), Brazil (1999), Japan (1999), Russia (2009), China (2011), and India (2012).[188] The caution with which these bilateral cooperation efforts have been met by other countries is almost certainly tied to the fact that they may open the door to the types of assertive U.S. extraterritorial claims that many states have long protested – if not through U.S. government enforcement, then through private follow-on suits.[189]

Modest though these arrangements may appear, they represent the outer reaches achieved in treaty-based international antitrust cooperation. Unlike the failed Havana Charter of the ITO described above, the 1995 Marrakesh Agreement establishing the WTO, which was signed by the United States and more than 125 other countries, contains no measures expressly regulating private restraints on trade, despite the ability of cartels and other horizontal restraints to have international trade effects.[190] Subsequent proposals to bring competition policy more directly under the auspices of the WTO were rejected by the United States and have been largely shelved since 2004 due to political deadlock

[187] Tritell and Kraus (2015:4, n.6).

[188] www.justice.gov/atr/antitrust-cooperation-agreements.

[189] In addition, these agreements generally require foreign jurisdictions to allow the operation of U.S rules for pre-trial discovery and information sharing, which can be in tension with local laws, White (2010:273).

[190] Noonan (2008:407–409 and 445 *et seq.*), Basedow (2000:1038) notes, however, that TRIMs requires review of compatibility of investments with local competition laws.

at the Doha Round of tariff negotiations.[191] Although the OECD has continued to highlight competition policy as a topic of interest, and to advocate use of its enforcement and merger notification mechanisms, it shows no signs of ripening into a forum for more formal coordination on international competition law and policy.[192]

The newest and, by some estimates, most promising initiative to foster inter-governmental cooperation is the International Competition Network (ICN), which aspires to be a virtual community of agencies focused on antitrust enforcement.[193] Established in 2001, the ICN has 127 members from 111 jurisdictions, a total that includes almost all competition agencies currently in existence.[194] The ICN incorporates a multidimensional strategy to develop transnational regulatory structure in this area. Beyond promoting classic enforcement model notions of mutual assistance, the ICN provides governments with antitrust education, model codes, best practices, and local capacity-building.[195] Another aspect of the ICN's mission involves facilitating informal cooperation and information sharing on enforcement – an issue that has long been a particular challenge for U.S. antitrust authorities attempting to investigate and prosecute claims involving transnational (and thus extraterritorial) conduct. European governments in particular are limited in the formal cooperation they can provide by the 1968 Brussels and Lugano Conventions on Jurisdiction and the Enforcement of Judgments in Civil and Commercial Matters, and the 1970 Hague Convention on the Taking of Evidence Abroad.[196]

At the same time, foreign states have continued to look for ways to hem in what many still view as unacceptable jurisdictional overreach by U.S. courts. For example, in 2000 an attempt was made to include antitrust claims within a draft Hague Convention codifying rules for

[191] www.wto.org/english/tratop_e/comp_e/history_e.htm.

[192] Between 1979 and 2009, the OECD Council adopted six non-binding Recommendations, and two additional sets of Guidelines on specialized areas of competition policy. The standing Committee on Competition also occasionally issues "best practices," and in 1998 it began conducting Reviews of individual states' policies and practices. In 2001 the OECD initiated an annual Global Forum on Competition. www.oecd.org/document/59/0,3343,en_2649_34715_4599739_1_1_1_37463,00.html.

[193] Djelic (2011:83).

[194] Coppola (2014).

[195] Kovacic (2006).

[196] White (2010:276). European regulators created a similar institution, the European Competition Network (ECN), in the 2004 reform, which exists to facilitate coordination among national competition authorities and the Commission.

enforcement of foreign court judgments in international civil and commercial matters. Few of the sponsoring states had been previously willing to enforce U.S. antitrust judgments, and several had domestic laws explicitly blocking their enforcement. Key to this, at first glance, puzzling proposal were other draft provisions limiting when national courts may exercise personal jurisdiction over various types of defendants. Dodge explains, "[i]t takes no great insight to see that the reason Australia, Canada, most members of the European Union, and other[s] [. . .] sought to bring antitrust within the draft Convention was not primarily to provide for the enforcement of those judgments, but to limit the [extraterritorial] jurisdiction of U.S. courts in antitrust cases." In response, U.S. negotiators notified the Conference that the draft stood "no chance of being accepted in the United States" due to fierce opposition by the U.S. antitrust bar.[197]

Discussion

Throughout the post-World War II period, the United States has maintained a distinctive, though far from stagnant, approach to antitrust law and policy. Other states, particularly those in Europe, have incrementally brought their competition laws and practices more closely into agreement with those of the United States – notably, without the influence of an international treaty. The actions (and inactions) of U.S. domestic courts have been important in shaping the character and content of the U.S. approach to antitrust inside and outside U.S. territory, which, in turn, has shaped how the international legal regime has developed. Three elements are jointly necessary to explain how U.S. domestic courts, as distinct from those of other states, came to inhabit this role: the existence of ambiguity regarding the scope and applicability of U.S. law, the existence of agents willing and able to give U.S. courts opportunities to resolve such questions, and the observable strength of U.S. legal enforcement power.

Legal ambiguity, in particular, is necessary, but not always sufficient for the production of legal disputes – including disputes in which the extraterritorial applicability of U.S. law is a factor. A starting premise of

[197] Dodge (2001:364), citing a Letter of February 3, 2000, from Jeffrey D. Kovar, Assistant Legal Advisor for Private International Law, to J.H.A. van Loon, Secretary General of the Hague Conference on Private International Law. In 2005, a notably scaled-back draft was adopted, absent antitrust provisions, as the Hague Convention on Choice of Courts. The United States has signed the Convention, but has not ratified it.

this analysis is that strategic actors will exploit legal ambiguity, or use law and legal institutions to try to foreclose others from doing so, when expected benefits outweigh expected costs. For this condition to be triggered, several factors must align. Prospective litigants must have incentives to initiate, or defend, legal claims – that is, they must have something of importance at stake. In addition, they must believe that the deciding court has *ex post* enforcement power– otherwise a legal judgment will be of little consequence. Finally, prospective litigants must lack other, superior means by which to pursue their objectives.

Each of these elements operates with the others to create, reinforce, and, at times, redirect extraterritorial legal efforts. For example, legal ambiguity generates new legal claims, but the outcomes of specific disputes, while resolving some legal questions, may create others. This is perhaps most critical with regard to enforcement power: litigants must bring claims for this power to be visible, but they generally will do so only if they have some prior belief that U.S. court decisions can be enforced. Theorizing agency is also crucial, since it is the decisions of litigants and regulators that direct judicial enforcement toward certain actors and practices, but not others – which, in turn, feeds back into the production of legal ambiguity.

The arc of U.S. economic and political hegemony following World War II and its uneven decline are relevant to accounting for the timing of U.S. extraterritorial assertiveness. The foundational federal judicial move in *Alcoa* occurred at what turned out to be the height of relative U.S. economic and political influence. However, it was only later, when the crisis of worldwide economic depression and its associated forms of political extremism had been largely overcome that U.S. extraterritoriality in antitrust came to be more strongly defined, both indirectly and directly, by the interests of private actors. The relative strength of the U.S. economy during much of this era coupled with the growing integration of global markets increased the unilateral enforcement capacity of U.S. courts by increasing the number and proportion of transnational actors with U.S. ties.

The agency element of the theory focuses on actor stakes in the extraterritorial reach of U.S. law and the availability of options for pressing courts and other domestic institutions to expand, or contract, its reach. After nearly seventy years, no strong U.S. domestic constituency has emerged that favors scaling back effects-based jurisdiction in antitrust litigation,[198] although opinion concerning some aspects of

[198] Fox (2002–2003).

private enforcement, particularly the availability of treble damages and the use of undefined class actions, has been more varied. With legislative change to soften U.S. antitrust rules unlikely, and variably aggressive enforcement of U.S. laws against foreign competitors from the Justice Department, transnational private entities that found themselves unable to exit the regulatory reach of U.S. antitrust laws were incentivized to bring as many competitors and forms of conduct as possible within the grasp of U.S. rules. They did so despite its myriad uncertainties with regard to cost, duration, and outcomes, and despite the risk of complicating U.S. foreign affairs. As a consequence, private rights of action have for decades underwritten streams of U.S. extraterritorial antitrust litigation that projected American law far beyond U.S. borders – and far beyond what would have occurred had the ability to initiate claims been the sole purview of U.S. government regulators.

Also worth underscoring is that during much of the period under examination, the willingness of U.S. courts to exercise jurisdiction over extraterritorial antitrust claims arguably lagged behind U.S. enforcement capacity. The theory developed in this book explains this by reference to internal political and constitutional limits on how U.S. judges may interpret ambiguous statutory provisions. In general, U.S. courts have been most likely to find exercises of extraterritorial jurisdiction appropriate only when a failure to apply U.S. law extraterritorially is likely to harm the integrity or operation of U.S. law inside U.S. territory, or where it would permit the violation of a narrow, but important, set of basic rights.[199] These constraints prompt courts to be concerned primarily, if not exclusively, with safeguarding the integrity and operation of U.S. laws inside the United States – even where this creates foreign policy complications or undermines informal efforts at coordination.

In maintaining a legal and institutional capacity to apply U.S. law extraterritorially on the basis of U.S. effects, U.S. courts have prompted a broad spectrum of private entities – American and foreign – to give U.S. rules substantial weight in their transnational operations. Of course, foreign governments can block their own domestic institutions from enforcing unwelcome U.S. court judgments, which restricts the efficacy

[199] That is to say, many things that occur outside U.S. borders may produce harmful consequences in the United States, if "harm" is defined broadly to encompass, for example, accidents, broken contracts, and other events and transactions that are generally managed locally at the site where they occur. These types of harms, however, do not affect the ability of U.S. authorities to set rules on such matters inside U.S. territory. See Chapter 2 for a full discussion of this idea.

of U.S. courts to situations where the United States has independent enforcement power. Foreign governments also retain the option to engineer legal grounds for defendants in U.S. litigation to claim "sovereign compulsion" by enacting laws expressly requiring private entities inside their territories to take actions that violate U.S. law. In many instances, however, taking such steps would narrow options for private actors in foreign jurisdictions in ways that would have large commercial and economic downsides (as, for example, if the Swiss government had changed its laws to require, rather than merely to permit, domestic watchmakers to restrict the production and sale of watch parts). In sum, the ability and willingness of U.S. courts to apply U.S. antitrust laws extraterritorially has shaped not only the incentives of private entities but also the menu of domestic legal options available to foreign governments whose citizens have U.S. ties.

In contrast, the legal and administrative tools for effects-based extraterritoriality have existed in German, British, and EEC law since the 1950s and have been used at a modest but growing rate since the late 1960s. Over this period, European competition rules and practices, particularly with respect to anti-cartel policies, have increasingly come to resemble those of the United States.[200] Economic integration achieved through the EEC, and now the EU, correspondingly, has given European regulators and courts an enforcement capacity analogous to that of the United States. However, this equality of capacity has not yet translated into extraterritorial regulatory claim-making on a scale approaching that of the United States. A key reason why is that the power to initiate competition enforcement in Europe remains, in many practical respects, under the near-exclusive control of EU and member state regulators.

The hypothesis that U.S. extraterritoriality influences private strategic behavior in the antitrust realm is further confirmed by other empirical work that focuses on firm behavior. One study, by Julian Clarke and Simon Evenett (2003), examines the effects of international anti-cartel enforcement on the decisions of private entities about whether and on what level to engage in legally prohibited activities in particular settings. Their approach uses a gravity trade model and data from the World Trade Analyzer database to measure actual trade flows for a specific

[200] Swaine (2001–2002:632), Fiebig (2005). Some differences remain concerning where to draw the line at the margins of allowed behavior, particularly with regard to vertical restraints. See Fidler (1992) and Gerber (2010) for arguments that differences grounded in economic theory are more substantial and consequential than the majority view allows.

commodity (vitamins) for nine countries on three continents. They then compare those results with estimated benchmarks in the absence of a cartel constructed from OECD budget and enforcement records. Overall Clarke and Evenett find that robust enforcement of antitrust rules has deterrent effects on international cartel activity.

Another study by John M. Connor (2007) compares the effectiveness of U.S., Canadian, and EU anti-cartel enforcement in the period between 1990 and 2008 along two dimensions. The first is the likelihood of detecting illegal behavior. The second concerns the harshness of penalties. Connor finds the U.S. system both more likely to detect wrongdoing and more likely to produce a swift and harsh response when wrongdoing is identified, for example, by imposing large corporate fines or individual criminal penalties. Among the observable ways in which this affects private strategic behavior is in the selection of locations for cartel meetings. Connor finds that conspirators generally avoid U.S. territory, preferring instead to meet "in Switzerland, Mexico, Japan, Hong Kong, and several EU cities that were regarded as less risky."[201] Still more to the point, he finds that, although the U.S. and EU economies have become roughly equal in terms of GDP, 62 percent of the enterprises that were the target of criminal antitrust enforcement during his study were headquartered in Europe, and only 16 percent were headquartered in the United States. This implies a high degree of awareness among U.S. enterprises about the outer limits of U.S. antitrust rules and a healthy respect for U.S. enforcement power.

To summarize, U.S. government regulators and many key private constituencies inside the United States stand to gain little from a more internationally centralized approach to antitrust enforcement. As Europeans have edged ever closer to U.S.-style antitrust rules and practices, EU regulators and those in Europe's larger states have learned to wield the effects doctrine to their advantage. At the same time, the integration of European markets has given those regulators increasing leverage to use it effectively. European extraterritorial enforcement, however, has been, with few exceptions, limited in comparison to U.S. practice. If this were to change substantially in the future with the growth of private enforcement in Europe, the result could be an increase in clashes over the authority and appropriateness of extraterritorial regulation and the erosion of the long-standing U.S. preference for unilateralism in international antitrust enforcement.

201 Connor (2007:204).

Conclusion

Why have the United States and European states not sought a formal international agreement on antitrust policy since 1948, despite the acknowledged importance of competition policy to both systems? Scholars focused on this question have emphasized everything from clashes of economic theories to claims that governments use antitrust policy strategically in international economic competition. Most accounts conclude that key states simply have divergent substantive preferences. The more sophisticated among them highlight the role of institutional path dependencies and domestic politics, including the importance of courts in the elaboration and administration of antitrust policy. Few, however, take the additional step of systematically examining the mechanisms that governments and private actors use to muddle through in the absence of uniform rules. Still fewer have sought to generalize insights gleaned from international antitrust to a broader class of international regulatory issues.

To the extent one can refer to "international antitrust" as a coherent body of policies and practices, it involves relative convergence around a set of substantive rules prohibiting horizontal restraints on trade, and consumer welfare-sapping levels of market concentration. Though its modern origins are in the United States, these ideas and policies have been transmitted piecemeal on a global scale through a combination of imposition and emulation. In stark contrast to this rough consensus on substantive rules and objectives, there has been a notable absence of conformity on enforcement procedures and practices.[202] Since the EU's founding, Europe has increasingly come to resemble the United States in terms of its enforcement capacity.[203] In this period, the preferences of its regulators likewise shifted decisively toward U.S.-style rules. As several recent studies have emphasized, this shift may have far less to do with European efforts to compete effectively with the United States than with the revealed usefulness of U.S.-style rules and practices to EC regulators seeking to wrest control over competition policy from member states.[204]

For much of the post-World War II era, the United States has been both more able and more willing than other states to press its antitrust preferences on others. Nevertheless, U.S. influence has fallen far short of dictating cross-national uniformity of competition policies

[202] Zanettin (2002).
[203] Bradford (2012).
[204] Kelemen (2011).

or practices.[205] Up until recently, time has been on the side of U.S. regulators. The longer they resisted international cooperation, the closer the policies of the main U.S. rivals in this area approached. For the United States this has been a safe game to play, since in European enforcement practice the ability to use effects doctrine in transnational litigation remains in the hands of regulators who have been, for the most part, more concerned with ensuring EU and domestic-level economic and legal cohesion than with poking U.S. firms with a sharp stick. This has given U.S. rules and preferences freer play in transnational regulatory competition for influence over private actors than would have been the case if Americans and Europeans worked with the same set of enforcement triggers. U.S. federal courts and attitudes regarding regulatory extraterritoriality are a big part of this story.

While U.S. capacity to engage in assertive forms of extraterritorial regulation was an artifact of organic processes of economic growth and accompanying global political outreach, in Europe supranational authorities have constructed it painstakingly through the project of economic integration. Many actors in that system remain loath to open its use fully to private entities, however, out of a desire to avoid what are widely considered excessive levels of U.S. litigation.[206]

In the meantime, erosion of U.S. economic hegemony in the post-Cold War era has diminished U.S. enforcement power. Access to U.S. finance and consumer markets has become less critical to many international commercial endeavors as the European Union has consolidated as a single market, and a new, more diverse set of developing states, with China at the forefront, have emerged as important economic players. Likewise, private actors have become more sophisticated and corporate structures have become more fragmented. Because the prospect of commercial non-engagement with Europe as a means of evading regulation is increasingly a high-cost choice for transnational actors, EU has a growing capacity to throw its weight around in interactions involving smaller states, and private actors within them, including on issues where U.S. and European law continue to diverge.[207]

As private entities seek to adjust to this emerging transnational and international regulatory landscape, the trans-Atlantic regulatory situation may be entering a period of flux. This could begin to chip away at the

205 Wells (2002).
206 Kelemen (2011).
207 Newman (2008), Bradford (2012).

fixity of U.S. preferences for antitrust unilateralism. At the same time, this analysis suggests strongly that any future bargaining on this account will be constrained on the U.S. side by the need to include a role for private enforcement.

Finally, with regard to the conditions under which domestic courts may influence transnational regulatory rules and structures, this examination of antitrust law and practice highlights two propositions important to developing and testing a broader theory of transnational rulemaking. The first is that courts, and the rules that they apply, are more likely to be influential when private actors have access to direct mechanisms of enforcement. The second proposition is that domestic courts are more likely to be influential in situations where the regulatory advantages of geographic arbitrage are weak or non-existent. Whether or not they are weak, however, is endogenous to how domestic regulators interpret the rules, coupled with public and private expectations about the likely efficacy of enforcement. What determines how U.S. courts are likely to interpret the reach of underlying rules is the overarching subject of this volume.

5

Extraterritoriality's limits and U.S. bargaining over intellectual property protection

"Judicial enforcement is a profoundly political act," as one specialist in international intellectual property law observes.[1] Conversely, enforcement sought and denied by courts also has important implications for how private actors comprehend the legal constraints on their behavior. Although cloaked in law and legal procedure, judicial decisions in disputes over patents, trademarks, and copyrights determine who may access valuable resources and on what terms. Where contests over these issues have transnational features, who wins and who loses can have international impacts on individuals, the viability of economic sectors, and, where access to medicines and other public health-related innovations are concerned, even the development trajectories of entire states. As in other areas of the law, where the disputes that arise are decided, and even what arises as a dispute, matters tremendously.

In 1968, for example, the iconic animated Beatles film, *Yellow Submarine*, first hit the big screen around the world. Roughly twenty-five years later, a legal dispute over rights to distribute videocassette versions of the film made American copyright law history. In 1967, the film's British and American producers had negotiated a distribution deal with the United Artists Corporation. In the early 1980s United Artists declined to license *Yellow Submarine* for home video distribution due to uncertainty about whether the 1967 agreement granted it the necessary rights. Thereafter, United Artists merged with MGM to become MGM/UA Communications Co. This company took a less cautious approach, and in 1987 it unilaterally authorized one of its subsidiaries to begin video distribution of *Yellow Submarine* in the United States. It also authorized Warner Bros. Inc., which at the time handled all non-U.S. video distribution of MGM/UA films, to begin foreign video distribution. In response, the producers, operating as Subafilms, Inc., filed suit in U.S. federal court

[1] Dinwoodie (2004:906).

against MGM/UA, Warner Bros., and relevant subsidiaries alleging infringement of its copyright and violation of the 1967 agreement.[2]

The Special Master appointed to hear the case determined that the 1967 agreement gave MGM/UA no home video licensing and distribution rights. From there, he held that, by authorizing video distribution of *Yellow Submarine*, MGM/UA had infringed the plaintiffs' rights under §106 of the U.S. Copyright Act.[3] This decision was adopted by a U.S. district court, which awarded the producers more than US$2.2 million in damages, plus attorneys' fees. The court also permanently enjoined the company (now MGM-Pathe) and its subsidiaries from all future distribution of the film for home video. The decision was affirmed on appeal in 1993.[4] Although the domestic aspects of the case received no further scrutiny, the finding that MGM-Pathe violated U.S. copyright law in authorizing foreign video distribution proved more controversial. The reason was that copyrights in the United States (and elsewhere) are widely understood to have no extraterritorial applicability[5] – a principle called into question by this holding.

The legal thread on which the 1993 *Subafilms* decision hung was MGM/UA's admission that its authorization of foreign distribution had occurred inside the United States. This detail had opened the door to a judicially constructed exception to the territoriality of U.S. copyright law that allows U.S. law to reach extraterritorial losses directly caused by acts undertaken inside U.S. territory.[6] The 1993 appeals court decision thus could easily have been the end of the line for this dispute, but for one development: a nearly contemporaneous copyright decision (albeit without an extraterritorial dimension) in the same circuit had concluded that improper authorization alone does not constitute a violation if the authorized acts are not held to be infringing.[7] As a result of the conflict

2 *Subafilms Ltd. v. MGM-Pathe Communications Co.* 988 F.2d 122 (9th Cir., 1993).

3 17 U.S.C. § 101 *et seq.* (1988).

4 As summarized in *Subafilms Ltd. v. MGM-Pathe Communications Co.* 24 F.3d 1088 (9th Cir. 1994). Half of the US$2.2 million damage award was designated as compensation for foreign distribution of infringing videocassette copies.

5 Statements to this effect are ubiquitous in judicial opinions involving extraterritorial IP claims.

6 *Peter Starr Prod. Co. v. Twin Continental Films, Inc.* 783 F.2d 1440 (9th Cir. 1986).

7 *Lewis Galoob Toys, Inc. v. Nintendo of America, Inc.* 964 F.2d 965 (9th Cir. 1992), *cert.* denied 113 S.Ct. 1582 (1993). This dispute concerned whether plaintiffs (who were seeking a declaratory judgment of non-infringement) could market a device in the United States to override certain features of Nintendo game systems. The court held the device did not infringe Nintendo's copyright.

between these two decisions, the Ninth Circuit agreed to an *en banc* rehearing of *Subafilms*.

The judicial panel set itself the task of examining the "vexing question whether a claim for infringement [...] can be brought under the Copyright Act [...] when the assertedly infringing conduct consists solely of the authorization within the territorial boundaries of the United States of acts that occur entirely abroad." The functionalist logic behind the initial *Subafilms* holding was that U.S. copyright law, while generally having only territorial reach, should not be understood to allow exploitation of international boundaries to elude U.S. legal rules.

A competing view grounded in the legislative history of the U.S. Copyright Act argued that Congress added the authorization clause to §106 in 1976 merely to create a basis for reaching acts that facilitate infringement.[8] Under this view, however, contributory infringement requires a primary act of infringement. Because U.S. copyrights have no extraterritorial validity, unauthorized use of U.S.-protected works outside U.S. territory cannot, by definition, constitute infringement. In short, where the law creates no rights, there can be no violation. In its rehearing, the Circuit Court adopted the latter interpretation, thereby vacating the prior holding and depriving *Yellow Submarine*'s producers of any ability under U.S. law to recover foreign losses.[9]

Critics charged that the decision opened a prospectively costly loophole through which private actors could evade U.S. copyrights, and squandered an opportunity for U.S. courts to make up for lax foreign enforcement. Others saw it as a straightforward reaffirmation of the territoriality of intellectual property rights as specified in international treaty law.[10] Indeed, the opinion expresses concern that "international discord" could result from clashes with foreign law if the mere act of authorization inside U.S. territory was held to support extraterritorial application of the U.S. Copyright Act. Yet, the court also acknowledges that such clashes have been tolerated in other issue areas.[11] Also in a foreign policy vein, the opinion underscores the court's hesitation to

[8] Crowley (1996:151). The analysis also invokes a judicial canon of statutory interpretation known as the "presumption against extraterritoriality". This presumption is discussed extensively in Chapter 7.

[9] *Subafilms Ltd. v. MGM-Pathe Communications Co.* 24 F.3d 1088, 1090 (9th Cir. 1994). This holding thus overruled *Peter Starr*, the source of the exception initially relied upon in the earliest District Court decision, see fn 6 and the accompanying text.

[10] See, for example, Ballance (1994), Crowley (1996).

[11] 24 F.3d 1088, 1090, 1096.

interfere with (then) recent congressional efforts to "secure a more stable international intellectual property regime."[12]

Subafilms is but a single dispute among many concerning the extraterritorial reach of U.S. intellectual property law. Still, it imparts a sense of the domestic and international constraints on court action. It also illustrates that the authority delegated to courts to determine geographic reach of U.S. law is real and that their decisions can have important consequences for litigants, policymakers, and wider audiences of observers. In the intellectual property realm, the collective stakes are far from trivial. For example, when *Subafilms* was decided in the mid-1990s, annual U.S. losses from unauthorized foreign use of American-produced intellectual property, coupled with inadequate enforcement of foreign intellectual property law, were estimated in billions of dollars.[13]

Rapidly evolving technologies for the cheap and easy reproduction of U.S. copyrighted materials have further heightened the potential for losses and increased the stakes for U.S. intellectual property rights holders since *Subafilms* was decided. Still, the response of the U.S. federal courts has been mixed. While some lower courts outside the Ninth Circuit have adopted the *Subafilms* line,[14] others continue to insist that improper domestic authorization of foreign use does provide an independent cause of action under U.S. federal law.[15] Neither the U.S. Congress nor the Supreme Court has yet weighed in directly on this question, although both have addressed other aspects of copyright law involving new technologies. Consequently, whether and under what conditions the extraterritorial losses of U.S. copyright holders are (or should be) actionable under U.S. law remains a highly contested issue,

[12] 24 F.3d 1088, 1090, 1095. This refers to the U.S. accession to the 1886 Berne Convention for the Protection of Literary and Artistic Works in 1988, and accompanying amendments to U.S. copyright law.

[13] See, for example, Boyle (1997:90–91). Boyle and others point out that the methodologies behind estimates of piracy costs are hotly debated among experts. At the upper end of the estimate spectrum at the time were claims that annual U.S. losses totaled in the tens of billions. But see also Raustiala and Sprigman (2009) on creation of value through piracy in the fashion industry.

[14] The judicial precedent set in *Subafilms* is binding only in the 9th Circuit. See, for example, *Seals v. Compendia Media Group*, 2003 WL 731369 (N.D. Ill., 2003); *Illustro Systems Intern. LLC v. I.B.M. Corp.*, 2007 WL 1321825 (N.D. Tex. 2007).

[15] *Curb v. MCA Records* 898 F.Supp. 586 (M.D. Tenn. 1995); *Expediters Intern. of Washington, Inc. v. Direct Line Cargo Management Services, Inc.* 995 F.Supp. 468 (D.N.J. 1998); *National Football League v. PrimeTime 24 Joint Venture* 1999 WL 163181 (S.D.N.Y. 1999).

and one in which domestic courts have considerably sway. The situation with patents and trademarks is similar.

This chapter examines the fate of U.S. judicial extraterritoriality in the intellectual property sphere. In contrast to antitrust law, efforts on the part of U.S.-based plaintiffs to seek the extraterritorial application of U.S. intellectual property law failed as a strategy for achieving global protection of these rights. Why did this occur, and what role did domestic courts have in this failure? How has the absence of court-based solutions shaped subsequent American efforts to achieve the international protection of intellectual property rights? To tackle these questions, I first define key terms and describe the legal and political challenges to regulating intellectual property internationally, with specific emphasis on the territoriality of rights. I next trace the development of the U.S. position for each category of intellectual property rights through key structural and technological changes, highlighting the efforts of private litigants to secure extraterritorial protections. I then examine how U.S. judicial reluctance has helped to shape developments internationally by repeatedly forcing the United States to the bargaining table to remake the international intellectual property regime. I conclude by drawing out several implications of this case for theory building.

Territorial rights in a globalizing world

What is intellectual property?

Intellectual property law specifies rights and procedures for regulating the creation, distribution, and use of non-tangible property. At the core of the intellectual property regime are three categories of rights: copyrights, patents, and trademarks.[16] Copyrights today apply to a wide range of literary, artistic, and musical works, and also computer software. Patents are assigned to scientific discoveries and inventions. Trademarks and trade dress use distinctive words, symbols, or packaging to designate the source of products or services for commercial purposes.[17] Copyrights and patents give intellectual property owners exclusive rights to use or license their works for statutorily fixed terms. Trademarks likewise confer exclusive rights on use. However, trademarks and trade dress are

[16] Use of the term "intellectual property" to refer to legally protected copyrights, patents, and trademarks dates to the mid-seventeenth century. Individually, these concepts have much longer histories of use. See Hughes (2006).

[17] Baroncelli *et al.* (2005:765).

protectable indefinitely as long as they continued to be used by their owners.

Violations of intellectual property rights have many labels. Misappropriation of protected materials is known as "piracy." Unauthorized sale, reproduction, and use are forms of "infringement." Trademark infringements can involve efforts to "pass off" goods or services as those of the trademark owner using confusingly similar identifiers. This tactic also has recently extended to Internet domain names. Another common type of trademark infringement is counterfeiting, which involves attaching a known mark to goods without the holder's permission.[18] Under patent and copyright law, unauthorized use does not destroy the work itself; it simply deprives owners of value they might otherwise claim. Trademark rights are different. Here the essence of violations is subterfuge, which can generate market confusion and interfere with the capacity of a mark to reliably inform consumers about a product's origins or quality.[19]

Intellectual property is directly tradable domestically and internationally through sales and licensing, and it is an important component of many more tradable goods. Unlike with tangible commodities, use of intellectual property by one user does not diminish the quantity available to others – though with trademarks especially, the *quality* may suffer. For this reason, the commercial value of intellectual property is heavily dependent on legal on its acquisition and use. Political and legal contestation over what these restrictions are, and how they should be enforced, is common both within states and across international borders.

The main exporters of intellectual property are economically advanced states. These states (or more accurately, export-oriented sectors within them) also have been the main source of the demand for strengthening intellectual property protections internationally. By contrast, states that are net consumers of foreign intellectual property generally have few incentives to establish restrictive intellectual property rights, since doing so simply facilitates revenue transfers from poorer states to richer ones.

Those favoring restrictive intellectual property rights underscore that innovation is expensive. They argue that without robust intellectual property rights, innovation would decline in areas such as medicine, material sciences, engineering, and technology that generate broad social

18 www.inta.org/TrademarkBasics/FactSheets/Pages/Counterfeiting.aspx.

19 Whether such confusion always results in harm to the trademark holder is subject to some debate. See Raustiala and Sprigman (2009).

benefits. Similar arguments are used for the production of films, music, literature, computer programs, and other creative works enjoyed by millions of people around the world. Those in favor of looser intellectual property restrictions dispute these claims on normative and empirical grounds, particularly as applied on a global scale. According to this position, intellectual property exporting states already possess overwhelming advantages in the global economy. Furthermore, these states generally secured their advantaged positions in part by "borrowing" the scientific and technological innovations of others – a pathway they should not now deny to others, particularly when economic incentives to innovate can be easily maintained within rich states through domestic intellectual property rights.[20]

Institutionalizing territoriality

These sharp divisions of interest are reflected in, and reproduced by, the international intellectual property regime. The defining feature of this regime is its robustly territorial character. Then as now, a perfected trademark in the United States, for example, confers no rights in Sweden, or India, or Chile, and vice versa. There are no international trademarks (or patents, or copyrights).[21] Territoriality is the international systemic default. It is also the approach taken in a set of treaties initially concluded in the late nineteenth century which still shape the regime to a significant degree.[22] These treaties give member states exclusive rights to grant and enforce intellectual property rights within their boundaries ("independence of rights"). A rigidly territorial approach to intellectual property rights, in turn, strongly discourages recognition of extraterritorial claims.

So how, then, does this system handle alleged violations that have transnational elements? Absent international-level mechanisms for resolving many intellectual property-related disputes,[23] rights holders

[20] Pogge (2008), Leaffer (1991).

[21] Note the European Union is exploring options for creating EU-wide unitary patents enforceable by a specialized Patent Court. This effort is the third such attempt. Earlier efforts in 1975 and 1989 failed.

[22] The treaties are: the Paris Convention for the Protection of Industrial Property (1883) and the Berne Convention for the Protection of Literary and Artistic Works (1886).

[23] No specialized international courts exist for adjudicating such disputes, although the European Court of Justice has decided intellectual property-related claims. In addition, international private arbitration may be used, particularly for disputes that turn on contract issues. Private arbitration is not used for resolving disputes of a "public law"

who think they have been wronged must turn to national laws and institutions. Theories of forum-shopping expect legal claimants to select the forum that provides the greatest likelihood of prevailing with the largest expected payoff. In the intellectual property sphere, however, standard choice of law rules specify that the applicable law is that of the state where the alleged violation occurred. When combined with domestic court reluctance to apply foreign intellectual property laws, this reduces the choice in many cases to a single option. In remaining largely deaf to the cries of U.S. rights holders claiming foreign extraterritorial harm, U.S. courts have helped to maintain this regime.[24]

The non-responsiveness of U.S. courts to this costly drain on American-owned resources is puzzling at first glance, particularly since the most obvious place to seek explanations for U.S. court behavior – the text of U.S. law, and U.S. treaty obligations – provide few consistent clues.[25] Looking more broadly, an economic nationalist might expect U.S. federal courts to resolve ambiguities over U.S. law and jurisdiction permissively in extraterritorial claims involving U.S. intellectual property rights.[26] A juridical textualist concerned with countering perceived overreaching on the part of domestic courts would advocate the opposite. Those preoccupied with international judicial cooperation and its effects would offer a more mixed set of expectations based on legal affinities between affected states. Although each of these ideas has some plausibility, each ultimately fails to provide a convincing account of U.S. court behavior.[27] And, because U.S. courts have not been entirely deaf to U.S. rights holders' pleas, intellectual property rights continue to be an active area of litigation concerning the extraterritorial reach of U.S. law.[28]

The argument that U.S. courts tend to apply U.S. law extraterritorially only when necessary to ensure the integrity or operation of U.S. law inside the United States, however, provides a compelling explanation for this pattern. The nature of the harm claimed by plaintiffs is, therefore,

character. Up until 1983, for example, U.S. law prohibited arbitration of *any* patent claims on grounds that they involved issues of public law.

[24] Bradley (1997:525).

[25] Bradley (1997:536–537).

[26] U.S. courts tend to interpret even statutorily specified avenues for extraterritoriality narrowly. See, for example, *Transocean Offshore Deepwater Drilling v. Maersk Contractors USA, Inc.* 699 F.3d 1340 (Fed. Cir. 2012) (cert. denied) (regarding extraterritorial offers to sell).

[27] See Chapter 2 for evaluation of these arguments in the context of multiple issue areas, including intellectual property.

[28] See Figure 2.2 in Chapter 2.

critical. Because unrecovered private revenue from wholly extraterritorial use of American-produced intellectual property does not diminish the operability or value of U.S. rights inside U.S. territory, it would be out of character for U.S. courts to apply U.S. law extraterritorially where this is the only type of harm claimed.[29] Where, by contrast, foreign conduct threatens to interfere with the operation of valid intellectual property rights inside U.S. territory, U.S. courts are more willing to apply U.S. laws extraterritorially – though cautiously, and, as the *Subafilms* example illustrates, with sometimes inconsistent outcomes.

The need to demonstrate domestic legal interference with intellectual property rights has proven a far from trivial barrier to prospective plaintiffs in U.S. courts. A few plaintiffs have succeeded in convincing U.S. courts to carve out minor exceptions to the strict territoriality of U.S. trademark laws. Here where a reasonable claim could be made that extraterritorial conduct is directly linked to counterfeit goods entering U.S. commerce, U.S. trademark holders could also argue that this created confusion among U.S. consumers, and diluted the value of the marks in question inside the United States and U.S.-controlled territories, thereby justifying the extraterritorial application of U.S. law. These deviations are notable for their rarity, and for their narrowness.[30] For producers and owners of intellectual property facing the challenge of finding ways to safeguard those rights internationally, or outside entities seeking to benefit from foreign innovations, the contestability, and potential malleability, of these thresholds are an issue of concern.

Territoriality, extraterritoriality, and intellectual property

U.S. intellectual property rules, like antitrust rules,[31] have their origins in an era in which the United States occupied a very different position in the international hierarchy of states. Over the last two centuries many legal issue areas have been radically transformed by changes in the structure of the international political and economic system, together with technological and organizational innovations. Few have been as deeply affected as

[29] The difference, admittedly, is one of degree. Where private harm of this type occurs on a massive scale, it may eventually dissuade business entities in investing in high-quality brands.

[30] See, for example, *Steele v. Bulova Watch Co.*, 344 U.S. 280 (1952), and *The Scotch Whiskey Association v. Barton Distilling Co.*, 489 F.2d 809 (7th Cir. 1973). In both instances, the key defendant was a U.S. citizen acting extraterritorially, and U.S. conduct was involved in the infringement. But see American Rice, Inc. v Arkansas Rice Growers Cooperative Assn., 701 F.2d 408 (5th Cir. 1983).

[31] See Chapter 4.

intellectual property. This has made intellectual property law a site of considerable volatility, and also, increasingly, a subject of international importance.

From international pirates to producers to pariahs

Britain's relations with its American colonies in the late seventeenth and early eighteenth centuries were dictated by the then-dominant mercantilist strategies for economic growth and security. In practice, this meant industrial policies were set in London and geared toward maximizing the welfare of the metropole.[32] Early on, Britain's policies brought technology, equipment, and skilled workers to the American colonies – but only up to the point that the colonies became reliable suppliers of semi-finished raw materials (e.g. lumber, pig iron, ginned cotton, and wool) to feed industries in England.[33] Further development was strictly controlled. For example, at the beginning of the eighteenth century, British laws specifically forbade skilled workers in many areas of manufacturing from migrating to the New World.[34]

For much of the early colonial period, a large and vibrant shadow-economy involving smuggling and tax evasion operated in the American colonies.[35] These practices were tolerated until the 1760s due to a combination of administrative neglect and corruption on the part of British officials. At this point, however, two developments combined to prompt a sharp change in British attitudes. The first was a British revenue crunch due to debt incurred fighting the trans-continental Seven Years War (1754–1763), which made effective collection of taxes and duties in the colonies more urgent. The second development was the British discovery that many American colonists had enriched themselves by supplying both the British forces and their French enemies in that conflict.[36] The American colonists' resistance to the British crackdown that followed ultimately led to the war for U.S. independence.

Over the next century, the United States experienced a massive shift in its economic position – going from a colonial backwater of the British Empire to a major industrial power. The large-scale piracy of European

[32] Britain's 1651 Navigation Acts effectively prohibited commerce between its colonies and other European powers.

[33] Ben-Atar (2004:23–25).

[34] Ibid.

[35] McClellan (1912:xvii).

[36] Andreas (2013:22).

inventions throughout this period is an important part of this story.[37] Smuggling routes and supply lines that had been used for illicit commercial activity under British rule proved vital in provisioning the American Revolution. After independence, these practices, and the moral attitudes underpinning them, were partially redirected toward the wide-scale theft of foreign know-how – machines, equipment, and human expertise – in the service of American industrialization.

Early patent laws

U.S. laws and policies in the years immediately following U.S. independence created a permissive environment for intellectual property piracy. The U.S. Patent Act of 1793 contained no substantive provisions for ensuring the originality of claimed inventions, thus allowing importers of foreign inventions to secure U.S. patents with relative ease.[38] Massachusetts, for example, provided loans to defray the initial costs of acquiring and setting up industries based on new (as in previously not found in the Commonwealth) inventions, and Pennsylvania awarded cash prizes to pirates of European technologies.[39] Those who succeeded in securing and transporting especially valuable inventions were feted as national heroes.[40] At the same time, U.S. laws denied foreigners protection for their patents and copyrights in the United States. In this respect, however, U.S. patent law differed little from other states' laws at this time.[41]

Nor was the permissiveness of American rules confined to patents. Unauthorized appropriation of the works of foreign authors and artists was similarly encouraged under the U.S. Copyright Act of 1790. This Act also restricted awards of U.S. copyrights to citizens and permanent residents and gave no consideration to prior publication or registration elsewhere.[42]

[37] Andreas (2013).

[38] Andreas (2013:102). The 1793 Patent Act was amended significantly from the 1790 Act. The earlier act required applicants to provide proof of novelty to a standing committee – a procedure that proved slow and onerous. The 1793 Act eliminated this requirement, but for an oath. It was partially reinstated only in 1836 (Federico 2003:45).

[39] Ben-Atar (2004:128–129).

[40] Andreas (2013:104), Ben-Atar (2004:141).

[41] May and Sell (2006:111–113).

[42] Ben-Atar (2004:125–126), Johns (2009:295). Recognition of property rights in trademarks was granted in British courts only in 1838 and was not codified in U.S. law until 1870, Greely (1902:392).

The American strategy of taking as much as possible from European innovators helped to fuel American economic growth and territorial expansion – a fact that did not go unnoticed in Europe.[43] By the middle of the nineteenth century, however, the United States had shifted from being a net taker of others' innovations to a net maker. It was at this point that American attitudes toward international recognition of intellectual property rights began to shift. Also during this period, international economic relations among the European powers were becoming less mercantilist, and more trade-oriented. The widespread practice of denying foreign nationals intellectual property rights proved to be an unwelcome inhibitor of free trade.

By the 1870s, top-tier industrializing powers were keen to find a way around the growing piracy problem in industrial property (a term of French origin encompassing patents, aesthetic designs, and distinguishing marks and designations). Thus, when U.S. inventors and manufacturers threatened to skip the 1873 Vienna International Exhibition of Inventions unless the Austrian government changed its laws to ensure exhibitors' ideas could not be "stolen," this proved an occasion for action.[44] A meeting convened in Vienna with delegates from sixteen countries, including Brazil and India, at which a Permanent Committee to examine issues related to the international protection of intellectual property was established. Three official Conferences were held in Paris to draft what became the 1883 Paris Convention for the Protection of Industrial Property.[45] The United States joined the agreement in 1886.

The Paris Convention committed its members to measures that would have been individually foolish, but when adopted collectively on reciprocal terms resolved some of the most vexing international issues then plaguing states and intellectual property holders. Its foundation is the obligation to provide the nationals of all member states rights that are at

[43] See, for example, a speech by Henry Lord Brougham before the British Parliament urging British manufacturers to sell at a loss to the United States "in order, by the glut, to stifle in the cradle those rising manufactures [...] that [the War of 1812] had forced into existence, contrary to the natural course of things" (Brougham 1841:274). This speech was much discussed among prominent manufacturers in the United States (Johns 2009:204).

[44] Iselin (1898:294).

[45] Blakeney (2004). For the 1873 Vienna Exposition, the Austrian government passed a provisional law for the specific protection of inventions exhibited there. The British and French had created similar provisions for international expositions in London and in Paris on four prior occasions, the earliest in 1851, Blakeney (2004:2).

least as favorable as those granted to one's own citizens ("national treatment"). Discrimination against foreigners would no longer be tolerated.[46] Each state, however, retained the right to determine its own laws for granting such rights, with the consequence that no state's actions could be understood to have any formal effect on others ("independence of rights").[47] Whereas the first of these principles is compatible with internationalization, the second is at the core of the territoriality of patent rights.

Emergence of international copyright law

The Paris Convention was not the last intellectual property treaty to be based on the formula of national treatment and the independence of rights. The same year the Paris Convention was adopted, representatives from many of the same states formally convened in Berne, Switzerland, to draft a treaty for protection of rights in literature and the arts.[48] Although the United States initially sent delegates, it did not actively participate due to ongoing deliberations in Congress on related issues.[49] These efforts culminated in the 1886 Berne Convention for the Protection of Literary and Artistic Works and an accompanying Union of member states.

It would take more than one hundred years and a great deal of structural and technological change for the United States to accede to the Berne Convention. The Convention was (and to some extent remains) a difficult fit with American intellectual property ideals and practices. At the Berne Convention's core are distinctly continental notions of the "moral" and "natural" rights of authors in the use of artistic works. These notions dictate long periods of exclusivity, and high degrees of authorial control over use and alterations. By contrast, American law, then as now, was primarily oriented around copyrights – quite literally regulation of the right to make and sell copies of protected works. Consequently, the American approach was, like that of the

46 Another key feature established common standards for the priority of rights for registration in different countries, which prevented non-inventors from seeking patents on others' innovations for a specified period of months.

47 Note, the independence of rights, though implicit in the structure of the 1883 Convention, was not formally articulated until 1889 in the Protocol of Interpretation and Execution adopted at the Second Conference of Revision at Madrid. See Blakeney (2004:7), citing *Proces-Verbaux de la Conference de Madride de 1890* (1890:135–139).

48 Ringer (1968:1052).

49 Message of President Chester Arthur, December 1, 1884, cited in Solberg (1925:66).

British, shaped by commercial sensibilities – not aesthetic and philosophical ones.

At the time the Berne Union was created, U.S. federal law permitted "importing reprinting, publishing and selling [...] foreign authors' work" while also restricting copyrights to U.S. citizens and permanent residents.[50] Starting mid-century, pressure mounted from inside and outside America's borders for the United States to jettison these provisions, at least for states willing to grant reciprocal rights. Both France and Great Britain, the era's major copyright exporters, were rapidly concluding bilateral copyright treaties, and in 1852 France unilaterally granted copyright protections to foreign authors.[51] The United States came close to concluding a bilateral treaty with Great Britain in 1853 – a course of action heavily favored by American authors, high-end publishers, university professors, and others eager to eliminate institutionalized piracy as a foreign relations embarrassment. The effort was scuttled at the eleventh hour, however, when the Attorney General advised the Senate that the treaty would "supersede" domestic copyright legislation.[52]

During the 1870s and 1880s, multiple bills for the international recognition of copyrights failed in U.S. Senate and House Committees due to concerted opposition by private associations of publishers and typographers.[53] In December 1887, however, a bill was proposed that included a clause making U.S. copyrights for foreign works conditional on their manufacture inside the United States. This proved sufficient to crack the opposition. The final version of the bill provided no affirmative protection for foreign authors and, instead, merely dropped the clause in the extant law restricting foreigners from acquiring American copyrights. The law also contained a requirement that two U.S.-manufactured copies of any "book, photograph, chromo, or lithograph" be deposited at the Library of Congress. In 1891, the International Copyright Act was signed into law.

Insofar as the United States had used naked protectionism to combat its institutionalized piracy, international applause was understandably muted. Nor did the United States show signs of acceding to the Berne Convention once its domestic deliberations had concluded. As the United States dawdled on the sidelines, the ground was shifting toward

50 Section 5, Federal Copyright Act of 1790 and retained in revisions of 1831 and 1870. Cited in Solberg (1925:50–51).

51 May and Sell (2006:120), citing (Clark 1960:134).

52 Opinions of the Attorney General, 291 (1854), cited in Dubin (1954:97).

53 Solberg (1925:55–56).

ever greater internationalization. At the 1908 review conference in Berlin, the Berne Convention was revised to require all members to automatically recognize authors' rights in covered works immediately upon their completion – thus forcing members to eliminate the type of domestic notice and registration requirements recently adopted in the United States.[54]

These changes to the Berne Convention were made as Congress was concluding a major revision of the U.S. Copyright Act. Although the 1909 Act contained limited gestures toward international cooperation, the Act retained the filing formalities of the 1891 Act, together with the manufacturing clause.[55] Eliminating formalities was no simple matter, however, given the "duality" of the U.S. system, whereby unpublished works were protected only under state common law, and published works were protected exclusively by federal law.[56] These constraints notwithstanding, to many the 1909 revision smacked more of retrenchment than of efforts to meet developments at the international level.

Trailing with trademarks

U.S. law on trademarks likewise progressed out of step with international trends. Up to the middle of the twentieth century, trademarks in the United States were viewed as emerging solely from use and accumulated goodwill. Their purpose was to allow purchasers to distinguish among products in the marketplace. Distinctiveness was their hallmark, and violations in the form of unauthorized use, or passing off, were often described using the language of "unfair competition" – a concept of public law.[57] The idea, common in civil law systems, that trademarks could be created by "sudden invention" through registration was wholly antithetical to American ideas.[58]

Trademark law in the United States was exclusively state law until 1870 when Congress enacted the first federal trademark statute under the Copyright Clause.[59] This Act contained no substantive rights, since these were understood to originate in common law. But, the Act provided

[54] Dubin (1954:95).
[55] Solberg (1925:61).
[56] Nimmer (1967:502).
[57] Hopkins (1917:47).
[58] Hopkins (1917:17).
[59] Act of July 8, 1870, ch. 230, 16 Stat. 198. The immediate impetus for federal trademark legislation was the railroad boom of the 1860s, which rapidly broadened the circulation of what had previously been local marks.

for federal registration of marks along with some additional legal protections. Nine years later, however, the U.S. Supreme Court declared the law unconstitutional on grounds that Article 1, §8 gives Congress no power to regulate trademarks.[60] In 1881, Congress passed another Trademark Act, this time under authority of the Commerce Clause. This constitutional anchor expressly requires that regulated subject matter be *used in commerce* between states, foreign countries, and Indian tribes, thus further institutionalizing reliance on use-based rights.

The 1881 Trademark Act was passed as the Paris Convention negotiations were taking place. Consequently, the Act did not extend U.S. trademark rights to foreigners as ultimately required under the 1883 Paris Convention. These revisions to the U.S. Trademark Act did not occur until 1905.[61] This was not enough to bring the United States to the vanguard of international trademark protection, however. Here too the ground had shifted. At the Second Conference of Revision for the Paris Convention held in Madrid in 1889, delegates proposed a special agreement to create a centralized international mechanism for bundling national-level trademark registrations in order to simply acquire marks in multiple states simultaneously. In 1891, the Madrid Agreement Concerning the International Registration of Marks was enacted.[62]

Despite support for its objectives among many American businesses,[63] the United States has never joined the Madrid Agreement due to aspects of the treaty that roundly disfavor American rights holders. First, securing registration in use-based systems is much more onerous than under registration-based systems. Second, the scope of assigned rights is typically narrower in the United States than elsewhere and is subject to more formalities. For example, the so-called particularity requirement requires applicants to describe not only the mark (as is universally required) but also the particular goods to which it will be applied. Errors, misstatements, and failures to update are all grounds for invalidation. Third, under the Madrid Agreement, rights acquired through bundling are dependent upon maintaining a basic registration in one's country of citizenship. Stringent use and notice requirements in U.S. law make

60 *Trademark Cases* 100 U.S. 82 (1879).

61 U.S. Constitution Art 1 §8(3). Greely (1905:13–15). The 1905 Act also expanded private rights of action in federal courts, added the possibility of penalties to damage awards for successful infringement claims, and gave courts authority to impose nationwide injunctive relief.

62 Only Paris Convention members can join the Madrid Agreement; fifty-six have done so.

63 Dinwoodie *et al.* (2001:142).

invalidating a trademark registration much easier in the United States than in most other Paris Convention jurisdictions.[64]

Falling behind by standing still

World War I radically altered the preceding international political and economic order. The United States emerged from that conflict several pegs higher in the international economic pecking order, in part due to its avoidance of the physical destruction, population decline, and debt that afflicted European victors and vanquished alike. Nevertheless, the political isolationism that radiated from the American heartland following the War blocked U.S. legal engagement at the international level on a number of dimensions. This was amplified following the 1929 stock market crash, which heralded the beginning of a global economic depression.

In virtually all respects, the decades between the 1909 revision of the Copyright Act and the end of World War II are notable for the dearth of major U.S. intellectual property legislation, though U.S. courts were very active in this period.[65] With regard to patents in particular, developments in U.S. domestic law and politics combined to ensure that the interwar years would not be a period of legal expansion. The roots of this go back to the 1836 Patent Act.

In 1836, Congress began to require patent applicants to demonstrate the novelty of the inventions for which they were seeking U.S. rights and created a U.S. Patent Office to review the applications.[66] Although directed at undercutting piracy, these changes made the patent process more onerous and expensive for legitimate inventors. To facilitate the approval process, Congress passed a statute in 1871 requiring the Patent Office to disseminate printed information about all new patents to designated public libraries. However, the availability of this information also led many more court challenges to the validity of existing patents – thereby

64 Add to this deadlines and fee structures poorly suited to the U.S. system, and a requirement that applications be submitted in French, and it is easy to see why the United States remained outside this agreement.

65 Note, however, that in 1912, Congress passed the Townsend Amendment giving copyright protection to films, and in 1930 it passed the Plant Patent Act creating an important new category of patents. It also passed a revision the Trademark Act in 1920 that prohibited misrepresentation of source of trademarked goods.

66 Under the 1793 Act, patent approval had been a mere clerical duty assigned to the U.S. Secretary of State (Federico 1954:164).

adding to their cost.[67] Still more time and expense was required to police and respond to infringements, thus making patent holding increasingly a "sport for the rich."[68] Also reinforcing the trend away from small inventors was the growth of capital intensity required to produce patentable innovations. In many industries, patents were leveraged as business assets to attract capital, which further concentrated innovative activity in large companies.[69] Some even constructed what May and Sell describe as "patent-based cartels" that clustered these rights and used them to impose trade restrictions and price-fixing.[70]

As described in Chapter 4, the economic downturns of the 1880s triggered an American populist backlash against large corporations. The 1890 Sherman Antitrust Act and the 1914 Clayton Act heralded an era of court-stewarded trust busting and attacks on unfair competition. Predictably, corporate concentrations of the so-called monopoly rights in intellectual property did not escape enforcement scrutiny.[71] Numerous American manufacturers and producers of industrial materials were forced to defend antitrust lawsuits in which intellectual property holdings and licensing agreements featured centrally. In many instances, courts upheld the underlying rights, while also placing limits on their use.[72]

Thanks to its Paris Convention membership, the United States remained abreast of international patent developments during this period. Periodic revision conferences held in Brussels in 1900, Washington 1911, The Hague 1925, and London 1934 brought several changes to the treaty. They included extensions to the minimum period of protection, improved guidance on claiming priority, rules to prohibit patent

67 See (Khan 2005:81) (Figure 3.1).

68 May and Sell (2006:123). A further revision of federal patent laws occurred in 1870 pursuant to a larger effort to consolidate all U.S. laws (the Revised Statutes of 1874), though this had only minor consequences for U.S. patent rights (Federico 1954:165–166).

69 Lamoreaux and Sokoloff (2001).

70 May and Sell (2006:127–128).

71 Khan and Sokoloff (2001:243).

72 See, for example, *Bement v. National Harrow Co.*, 186 U.S. 70 (1902) (holding that monopoly rents from patents exist by design and thus do not violate antitrust laws); *United States v. General Elec. Co.*, 272 U.S. 476 (1926) (holding that patent holders may set pricing requirements for licensees); *Motion Picture Patents Co. v. Universal Film Mtg Co* 243 US 502 (1917) (holding that tying the sale of patented and non-patented good is prohibited, thus overruling *Henry v. A.B. Dick Co.* 224 US 1 (1912) which had held the opposite); and *Carbide Corp. v. Am. Patents Dev. Corp.*, 283 U.S. 27, 34 n.4 (1931) (holding that patents generate restraints on trade only where used to gain leverage beyond their original purpose).

invalidation for importation by patent holders, and clarification of legitimate grounds for invalidation and refusal to register.[73] The use of unanimity voting at these conferences ensured that U.S. concerns were taken into account at every step.[74]

By contrast, international developments in the copyright sphere placed U.S. copyright law still further behind the curve. At periodic review conferences of the Berne Convention in Rome in 1928 and in Brussels in 1948, members significantly broadened the subject matter covered by the agreement to more than two dozen different types of works,[75] including some that had no protection under U.S. law.[76]

Increasingly, the United States' refusal to join the Berne Union generated international ire. U.S. authors and artists were by this point adept at exploiting a loophole whereby prior, or simultaneous, first publication in a Berne Union country gave American works full Convention protections. Reciprocal access to the less generous package of protections under U.S. copyright law was, thus, cold comfort to European authors, especially as the United States emerged as a major exporter of copyrighted works.[77] Although adamant about its inability to join the Berne Union, in the late 1930s the U.S. government expressed openness to creating a multilateral copyright arrangement alongside the Berne Convention.[78] Little progress was made on this idea, however, before World War II intervened.

Efforts at (partial) reengagement

From the late 1930s to the late 1940s, intellectual property law developments were put on hold as Europe and much of the rest of the world focused on the demands of fighting World War II and on planning the postwar political and economic order. When the smoke cleared, the United States had emerged as an undisputed leader of the Western world, economically and politically. It assumed this mantle within the

[73] See Bodenhausen (1969) for a complete treatment.

[74] The Paris Convention was revised on six occasions between 1900 and 1967. It was also formally amended in 1979.

[75] The Rome revision also enumerated more than two dozen examples of covered "works," http://keionline.org/sites/default/files/1928_Rome_revisions_Berne.pdf.

[76] In 1802, the Copyright Act added prints as "protected works." In 1831 musical works were added, and in 1865 photographs and negatives were added. *Copyright Information Circular*, 1a, www.copyright.gov/circs/circ1a.html.

[77] Ringer (1968:1060).

[78] Goldstein and Hugenholtz (2012:44).

framework of international organizations it had helped to create – the United Nations and the international financial institutions agreed to at Bretton Woods.

After the War, the idea of a parallel international copyright treaty was resuscitated under the auspices of the United Nations Educational, Scientific and Cultural Organization (UNESCO).[79] In November 1952, a group of thirty-six states, including the United States, enacted the Universal Copyright Convention (UCC) and three separate Protocols.[80] The UCC, which entered into effect in 1955, followed a reciprocity model of national treatment but contained few substantive requirements.[81] This was not a coincidence. During the negotiations, the United States had extracted several concessions to ensure that it would join the agreement. Central among these were allowance for formalities of notice, registration and deposit.[82] The UCC's more permissive requirements also allowed the Soviet Union and numerous developing countries to join. Several Berne Convention members also joined as a means to engage with non-Berne members. For U.S. copyright claimants, the treaty offered "simple, direct protection" for works first published in a UCC member country, along with enhanced protections for unpublished works.[83] Unresolved issues remained, however, regarding the form and timing of formalities, incomplete coverage of substantive categories, variance in national periods of protection, and derivative (or "neighboring") rights.[84]

The period immediately following World War II also saw the modernization, and partial internationalization, of U.S. trademark law. In recognition of the increasing integration of the U.S. economy and the growing role of advertising in marketing, Congress passed the Lanham Trademark Act in 1946.[85] This Act, which was the product of roughly two decades of consultation with legal experts and industry groups, for the first time established federal trademark rights that applied

[79] *Copyright Bulletin*, UNESCO, No. 2, December 1948, 70, cited in Dubin (1954:89).

[80] Ringer (1968:1063). By this point the United States had reciprocal arrangements with fifty-three states, and bilateral treaties with three others.

[81] Colino (1962:231). The UCC contains minimum conditions regarding the duration of copyrights, the complexity of allowable formalities, and translation rights, although they are very permissive compared to Berne standards.

[82] For example, Subdivision 3 allows members to define, for the purposes of the treaty, any resident alien as a "national," for the purpose of which formalities are required of "citizens and nationals" (Dubin 1954:102–103).

[83] Colino (1962:232–235).

[84] Colino (1962:239–247).

[85] See, for example, House Report No. 219, February 26, 1945, and Ladas (1949:269).

uniformly throughout U.S. territory.[86] Among its objectives was to bring U.S. law into line with U.S. obligations under the Paris Convention and related treaties.[87] Specifically, the Act not only extends to foreigners all domestic rights under the national treatment principle but also provides certain convention rights that exceed the protections offered to U.S. citizens under U.S. law.[88]

Shortly thereafter, in 1952, Congress passed a revision of the Patent Act. In the preceding, "virulent[ly] anti-patent era," U.S. courts and regulators had regularly pitted the exclusivity of patent rights against principles of free competition and found that the domestic and international licensing practices of large corporations had crossed a line into cartel-type behavior.[89] Although World War II temporarily suspended direct legal pressure on U.S. corporations in critical industries, the immediate postwar era was defined by "aggressive antitrust enforcement and judicial attacks on [the scope and validity of] patents."[90] Surprisingly in this environment, a National Patent Planning Commission established by Executive Order in 1941 gave American patent law a "clean bill of health."[91] As a result, the 1952 Act focused on rationalizing and codifying existing rights in light of the many court decisions handed down since the last comprehensive revision in 1870. A key modification was the adoption of a statutory definition of "infringement" as a hedge against judicial overreaching in antitrust claims.[92]

As the codification projects for trademarks and patents were coming to fruition,[93] the post-World War II U.S. economy was in the early stages of a major boom, reflecting – and reinforcing – unprecedented levels of international political and commercial outreach tied to postwar reconstruction. Between 1950 and 1960, the U.S. gross national product nearly doubled, fueled by growth in industries such as automobiles, aviation, heavy agricultural machinery, chemicals, and military hardware. This

86 Fisher (1999). The Lanham Act achieved this with the doctrine of nationwide constructive use.

87 The Lanham Act contains a special section (Title 9) for International Conventions (Ladas 1949:270).

88 Ladas (1949:272–273).

89 May and Sell (2006:141) citing Merges (2000:2223).

90 May and Sell (2006:139).

91 Riesenfeld (1954:294).

92 Rich (1953:498).

93 Note, a parallel effort to revise U.S. copyright laws during this period failed due to deep divisions among private sector actors and members of Congress about what reforms were needed.

growth reflected changes in the volume of U.S. production, as well as in the content. Whereas only roughly 10 percent of U.S. exports in the immediate postwar period had a significant intellectual property component, this had doubled by 1970.[94] In this climate, U.S.-based entities increasingly felt the pinch of exclusion from international coordination around intellectual property rights.[95] This was especially palpable in the trademark arena, as U.S. brands and products gained international recognition and prestige.

By the late 1960s, the relatively successful accord achieved in international intellectual property circles since the creation of the UCC began to develop fissures. The reason was the large number of newly independent former colonies that had, through a mix of legal compulsion and incomplete understandings of their own interests, joined the Paris and Berne Unions.[96] Now locked into these arrangements, these states began demanding preferential access to protected works to further their economic development. Longtime members were reluctant to grant these demands. They feared that relaxing restrictions anywhere would cause the entire system to unravel to the deep detriment of powerful economic constituencies in their own domestic orders.

Developing countries, led by India, used the occasion of the 1967 Berne Convention diplomatic conference in Stockholm to mount a coordinated bid to force adoption of a Protocol to the Berne Convention. These efforts continued at the biennial meeting of the Intergovernmental Copyright Committee, a body of representatives from the UCC and the Berne Union's Permanent Committee, in Geneva.[97] At this meeting (where the United States was able to participate fully due to its UCC membership), the U.S. delegation took a strong stand against amending either agreement, and against the Stockholm Protocol. The Protocol formally entered into force in 1970, but its members included no core Berne or UCC states – a fact not missed by developing states.

In order to head off a revolt from within, a compromise was reached in 1971 in which the Protocol was replaced with an Appendix to the main Convention covering Special Provisions for Developing Countries. One key concession permitted self-declared developing-state members of the

94 Deere-Birkbeck (2010:39).

95 Goldman (1955:4).

96 Deere-Birkbeck (2010:30–31). Only three developing states were members of the Paris Union in 1958; this had grown to forty-four by 1973.

97 Ringer (1968:1075).

Berne Convention to switch to UCC membership without penalty.[98] Another allowed developing states to demand compulsory licenses for translation and reproduction of protected works for "teaching, scholarship, or research." This proved a pyrrhic victory, however, since the complexity of procedures for securing compulsory licenses prevented their widespread use.[99]

Another noteworthy development at the 1967 Stockholm conference was the adoption of Convention establishing a World Intellectual Property Organization (WIPO).[100] Based in Geneva, WIPO was created to coordinate the administration of the Paris and Berne Unions (which retained their separate existences, memberships, and secretariats) and to spearhead initiatives to strengthen intellectual property rights internationally. The United States supported the creation of WIPO and was an original signatory. The expectation was that it would give Americans a greater voice in international intellectual property debates, despite its non-membership in several key treaties.[101] WIPO became a specialized agency of the United Nations in 1974.

These hopes would prove short-lived, however, insofar as by the early 1970s, the United Nations had become a primary site for developing countries to agitate for preferential treatment from economically advanced states with regard to intellectual property rights. During this decade, initiatives were launched in UNTAD, ECOSOC, UNIDO, and WIPO to promote technology transfers to developing states through compulsory licensing and requirements to "work" patents.[102] From the perspective of intellectual property-producing states, many of these proposals would have essentially gutted established arrangements from which they benefitted. In 1975, developing states secured a General Assembly Resolution calling for the reform of the Paris Convention to address the needs of those states. A 1977 WIPO Declaration of Objectives for the next diplomatic conference, scheduled for 1980, emphasized similar principles.[103] These efforts, unsurprisingly, were staunchly opposed by the United States.

98 This was a substantial concession, since it allowed these states to circumvent the UCC's "Berne safety clause," which stipulates that Berne members who denounce their membership must be denied all UCC privileges. The clause exists specifically to prevent Berne Union members from defecting to the UCC's more permissive rules.

99 Deere-Birkbeck (2010:34).

100 The Convention came into force in 1970, and was amended slightly in 1979.

101 Ringer (1966–1967:420).

102 U.S. law does not require patent holders to use patents to retain their rights.

103 Deere-Birkbeck (2010:37–38).

It was against this evolving backdrop that private litigants in the United States first began to consider judicial extraterritoriality as a possible avenue to protect their intellectual property rights in transnational endeavors.

Experimenting with extraterritoriality

Throughout U.S. history, courts have had an important role in determining the scope and content of intellectual property rights.[104] By the middle of the twentieth century, the territorial limits of American intellectual property law, though never seriously contested prior to that time, began to appear less self-evidently "settled." To understand why, it helps to recall that law is generally reactive.[105] The expansion of U.S. political and economic activities in the post-World War II era, while creating new opportunities for Americans, also resulted in new threats to established rights. Attempts to address these threats placed unaccustomed demands on domestic institutions. One dimension of this concerned questions about whether U.S. intellectual property laws could – or should – reach persons and conduct outside U.S. territory.

The analytic framework elaborated in Chapter 3 discusses three elements that together determine the likelihood of U.S. court involvement in extraterritorial legal disputes. I now briefly review these elements with reference to intellectual property.

Legal ambiguity

Ambiguity regarding the law's scope, content, or applicability is fuel for litigation. But when and how do such ambiguities emerge? Changes in regulatory environments are a key factor. Technological and organizational innovations that alter legally defined relationships and processes can create ambiguity in the scope or meaning of existing rules. Macro-level changes in economic or political conditions can likewise alter the range and character of regulated behavior, introducing new actors and new settings.[106] Changes in law brought about by new legislation, executive orders, agency regulations, or decisions from higher courts also frequently require interpretation and elaboration. Each of these

104 Khan (2005:66).
105 McDougal (1956).
106 Sell (2003:37).

categories was majorly in play in the latter half of the twentieth century in the intellectual property universe.

Deciding disputes provides opportunities for judges to reconsider established interpretations and understandings of relevant laws in light of new developments.[107] One American expert on copyright law explains "[c]opyright owners have regularly expected the federal courts, particularly the Supreme Court, to protect them against the threats posed by new technologies. If Congress takes twenty years to bring a new technological use under copyright control, perhaps the Supreme Court could be convinced more quickly to interpret the existing copyright laws as encompassing the new use."[108] Questioning the geographic reach of domestic laws in U.S. courts is one site where such reconsideration might occur.

Agents of extraterritoriality

Which actors have authority and incentives to initiate the (re)interpretation of legal rules heavily influences patterns of disputing, and likewise prospects for change through court decisions. In the United States, protecting or contesting intellectual property rights is almost exclusively the task of private entities using civil lawsuits (or their credible threat). A key theoretical expectation is that private agents will seek to extend the geographic reach of domestic legal rules in two situations. The first is where domestic rules favor domestic actors in some way, and they, therefore, reasonably seek to have them applied as widely as possible. The second is when private entities are subject to domestic legal requirements that are more onerous than those that foreign competitors must follow. If they cannot alter the law or escape its application to their own conduct, they will seek to have the law applied as widely as possible in order to constrain others in the same way. In the intellectual property context, both logics have some resonance, though the first is clearly dominant.

Expectations about U.S. court openness (or lack of openness) to particular types of legal claims thus help to create agents for the elaboration and enforcement of legal rules. Where foreign mechanisms for perfecting, vindicating, and enforcing claimed intellectual property rights fail to deliver minimally desired levels of protection, whether due to differences in rules, corrupt institutions, or conflicting policy

[107] See the discussion of selection into litigation in Chapter 2 for further elaboration.

[108] Goldstein (1994:33). One example is the decisions of "several federal courts" to extend the protections granted to public performances in 1(e) of the 1909 Copyright Act to radio broadcasts, even in the face of congressional inaction (Solberg 1930:189–190).

priorities, producers will rationally seek other avenues to protect their assets. If, in turn, these agents choose to ask U.S. courts to resolve transnational disputes, this gamble is premised on a belief that applicable law can be found (perhaps by interrogating unexamined ambiguities), and some expectation that any resulting judgment will yield benefits.

Enforcement capacity

The extraterritorial enforcement capacity of U.S. courts is far weaker in the intellectual property sphere than in other areas of comparable economic importance. Three factors work together to produce this weakness. The first is the existence of wholly non-U.S. markets for many unauthorized uses of U.S.-produced intellectual property.[109] When foreign entities perform an artistic work, affix a U.S. mark to counterfeit goods, or use U.S. patent-protected devices or processes, those outputs need not ever reach U.S. territory to be profitable. Consequently, the threat of exclusion matters little. This contrasts sharply with activities in more globally integrated markets for things like finance, securities, and banking.

Second, foreign entities accused of misappropriating American intellectual property often lack jurisdiction-conferring ties with the United States. This precludes extraterritorial enforcement on due process grounds, even in instances where U.S. law might, in theory, be found to reach the general category of conduct. (This factor alone largely excludes any possibility of a general strategy for unilateral extraterritorial intellectual property enforcement spearheaded by U.S. courts.)

Third, and relatedly, an absence of defendant contacts with U.S. territory also means an absence of assets for the satisfaction of adverse damage judgments, or to act bond for extraterritorial injunctions against further infringements. Few, if any, foreign courts are willing to enforce U.S. judgments applying American copyright, patent, or trademark law extraterritorially. It follows that even if U.S. courts were to relax the requirements for claiming personal jurisdiction, and also decide that U.S. laws apply extraterritorially, there would be little incentive for plaintiffs to bring such suits against wholly foreign defendants.

Who, or what, does this leave within the enforcement ambit of U.S. courts? One category encompasses U.S. citizens and others with substantial U.S. ties whose conduct outside U.S. territory leads to

[109] The commercial value of IP to non-owners comes from direct use (as opposed to restricting others' use).

infringement of U.S. copyrights or patents inside U.S. territory. U.S. jurisprudence labels this "contributory infringement". Another category encompasses those who engage in infringing activities inside the United States that are then used to generate revenue illicitly outside U.S. territory. This is known as "active inducement".[110] Finally, a pure effects theory of extraterritorial prescriptive jurisdiction may still operate where unauthorized extraterritorial use undermines the value of seeking intellectual property rights inside the United States, even in the absence of U.S. contacts. This last example presents a problem that cannot be addressed within a rigidly territorial legal framework.[111] Not coincidentally, these are precisely the areas of U.S. intellectual property law where extraterritorial litigation is most active.

*

U.S. federal courts have been, in general, roundly disinclined to apply U.S. copyright and patent law extraterritorially, though this has changed somewhat in recent decades. U.S. trademark law, however, has been interpreted more flexibly. Figuring out why this is so requires a theoretically informed tracing of how legal ambiguities developed, the emergence and objectives of key agents, along with attention to the shifting sands of enforcement capacity.

The ball got rolling on extraterritorial claims over intellectual property rights in 1952 with a U.S. Supreme Court case, *Steele v. Bulova Watch Company*. At issue was an alleged foreign infringement of a U.S. trademark by the American owner of a factory in Mexico City. The factory produced watches from Swiss- and American-made components and stamped them with the "Bulova" trademark.[112] The company brought a suit for injunction under the (then) newly minted Lanham Trademark Act after Bulova sales representatives in Texas began to receive complaints from retailers, who were being asked to provide warranty services

[110] Bradley (1997:522–526).

[111] Dinwoodie (2009:725). Another option that remains (in theory) open to U.S. courts involves expanding adjudicatory jurisdiction over extraterritorial claims by applying *foreign law* (Bradley 1997). U.S. courts have been reluctant to do this in line with longstanding reticence to apply foreign law in instances involving public policy (Dodge 2008:372). While this approach would widen the reach of U.S. courts, it also would not provide a full solution to the problem, given constraints on U.S. courts tied to personal jurisdiction.

[112] Note, Steele had been the registered holder of the Bulova mark in Mexico (which has a civil law system). This registration was valid under Mexican law when the federal circuit court heard the claim, but had been cancelled by the time it reached the U.S. Supreme Court.

on "defective" watches that turned out to be counterfeits.[113] In explaining why it was applying the Lanham Act to this situation, the Court majority emphasized the trans-boundary character of the harm:

> We do not deem material that petitioner affixed the mark BULOVA in Mexico City rather than here, or that his purchases in the United States when viewed in isolation do not violate any of our laws. [. . .] In sum, *we do not think that petitioner by so simple a device can evade the thrust of the laws of the United States in a privileged sanctuary beyond our borders.* (Emphasis added)[114]

The *Steele* Court thus sought to eliminate an easily followed – and therefore threatening – model for undercutting U.S. trademark rights inside U.S. territory.[115] It is worth underscoring that the injunction handed down in this case had teeth because of the defendant's U.S. citizenship and his continued ties to U.S. territory.

Markedly different patterns are evident in Figure 5.1 across the intellectual property categories in the data sample.[116] In trademark, (Figure 5.1(c)), for example, the 1952 *Bulova* decision was quickly followed by another (unsuccessful) case involving a request by an American underwear manufacturer for U.S. courts to enjoin a Canadian distributor-turned-manufacturer from using its trademark in Canada.[117] The next claim, commenced in 1971, succeeded. Here producers and global distributors of whiskey in Scotland sued an American distiller and marketer of alcoholic beverages alleging false designation of origin in violation of the Lanham Act.[118] At issue was a product called "blended scotch whiskey" that was made and bottled in Panama – not Scotland – using bottles and labels shipped from the United States. The whiskey was marketed in Panama, including in the Panama Canal Zone, which was then administered by the United States under U.S laws. An appellate court reversed the district court's dismissal for lack of extraterritorial jurisdiction and enjoined the American company from continuing the practice.

113 The factory owner had in 1933 registered the "Bulova" trademark in Mexico. The Mexican Supreme Court had, however, nullified that registration of the "Bulova" mark shortly before the U.S. Supreme Court considered the case.

114 344 U.S. 280, 287 (1952).

115 The decision was 6-2, with Justices Reed and Douglas dissenting. Justice Black did not take part in the decision.

116 For details on my sampling strategy, see Chapter 2.

117 *Vanity Fair Mills v. Eaton Co.* 234 F.2d 633 (2nd Cir. 1956) *cert.* denied 352 U.S. 871.

118 *Scotch Whisky Association v. Barton Distilling Co.*, 489 F.2d 809 (7th Cir. 1973).

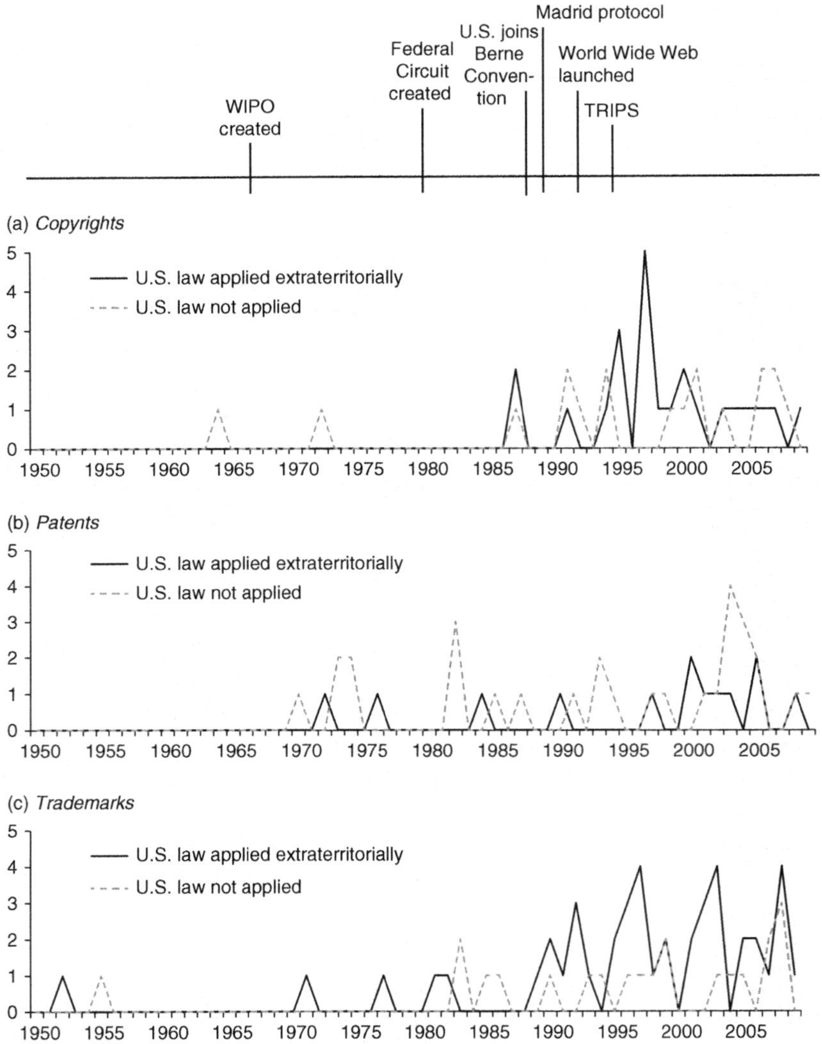

Figure 5.1 U.S. federal court cases involving extraterritorial claims (by subject)

The story with copyrights is quite different. No extraterritorial claims were attempted in the first part of this period, and none cleared the jurisdictional hurdle until the late 1980s. The first failed attempt involved a claim against a U.S. record manufacturer who had made copies of two Beatles songs from master recordings and sold them in the United States without permission from the British copyright owner, before the owner had marketed those songs in the United States.[119] (The *per curiam* panel found it necessary to explain "for posterity" that The Beatles are "four long-haired British 'rock and roll' performers currently enjoying a *succès fou*.") The U.S. court rejected the defendant's contention that a compulsory licensing provision of the U.S. Copyright Act had been triggered when the owners chose to manufacture recordings of the songs in England.[120]

Another attempt involved a lawsuit by the owners of the performance rights for the rock opera *Jesus Christ Superstar* against a group of Roman Catholic priests who staged unauthorized performances in the United States and Canada in violation of §101(b) of the U.S. Copyright Act. The court found the priests liable for the unauthorized U.S. performances, although they held that the statute did not reach the foreign performances, even though all preparations for those performances had occurred inside U.S. territory prior to traveling to Canada.[121]

Patent claims in which extraterritoriality was at issue had more mixed outcomes during the early part of this period. In the first such case in 1970, *Deepsouth Packing Co. v. Laitram Corp.*, U.S. courts resoundingly rejected the extraterritorial claim. At issue was whether the unauthorized U.S. manufacture and export of components for a shrimp deveining machine infringed the rights of the holder of the U.S. patent for the assembled machine where the exporter intended to assemble the components abroad. A bare majority of Supreme Court justices held there was no infringement on grounds that the patent covered only the assembled device, and U.S. patent law has no extraterritorial reach. Four dissenting justices argued, to the contrary, that allowing a non-patent holder to "reap the fruits of the American economy" in this way would "strip away a portion of the patentee's protection."[122]

Extending this logic, *John Mohr and Sons v. Vacudyne Corp.* similarly denied extraterritorial reach to U.S. patent law for the unauthorized use of process patents. Here, the U.S. patent holder for a steam process used to remoisten stored tobacco in the manufacture of cigarettes sued a domestic manufacturer that, without its authorization, had produced, assembled, and tested a machine using this method inside U.S. territory

[119] *Beechwood Music Corp. v. VeeJay Records, Inc.* 328 F.2d 728 (2nd Cir. 1964).

[120] The compulsory licensing clause, Copyright Act, 17 U.S.C. §1(e), was intended to prevent a single publishing outlet from monopolizing the distribution of works inside the United States by stipulating that once permission was granted to anyone in the United States, its further licensing could not be restricted without cause.

[121] *Robert Stigwood Group, Ltd. v. O'Reilly*, 530 F.2d 1096 (2nd Cir. 1976).

[122] Eventually, Congress was persuaded of this position, and overrode *Deepsouth* in 1988.

for foreign sales, which it also solicited from within the United States. Nonetheless, the court ruled no infringement occurred, since the actual process covered by the patent – moistening tobacco – was not among the acts the defendant performed in U.S. territory.

Other failed bids to persuade U.S. federal courts to apply U.S. patent law extraterritorially in this period involved the temporary presence of a U.S.-patented device in U.S. territory. In *Cali v. Japan Airlines*, for example, the U.S. patent holder of jet engine feature sued a foreign air carrier for infringement. The main issue was whether foreign aircraft were required to pay U.S. royalties when transporting passengers and freight to and from the United States. The court decided in favor of the foreign airline on grounds that use of patented devices on aircraft temporarily within another state's airspace is permitted under Article 27 of the 1944 Chicago Convention on International Civil Aviation (as codified domestically in 35 U.S.C. §272) and is also allowed by Article 5*ter* of the Paris Convention.[123] To find otherwise, it reasoned, would impermissibly interfere with the international treaty-making powers of the United States.[124]

However, other cases decided at roughly the same time allowed limited extraterritorial applications of U.S. patent law. In *Decca Ltd v. United States*, the U.S. Court of Claims found that the U.S. government infringed the plaintiff's patent for a tracking system for ships involving radio transmissions among geographically dispersed stations, one of which was located in Norway. That court held the foreign location of one component of the system could not be used to evade obligations under U.S. law, since, contra *Deepsouth*, the beneficial use of the completed device in this situation occurred in the United States, all of the foreign equipment had been purchased and installed by the U.S. government, and it continued to be controlled and maintained by the United States.[125]

The reach of U.S. law to foreign defendants in transnational infringement claims was tested and upheld in *Honeywell Inc. v. Metz Apparatewerke.*[126] In this case the U.S. patent holder for a photographic flash brought an

[123] In reaching this conclusion, the U.S. court relied on a case from 1857 involving patented elements of sails on foreign ships temporarily in U.S. harbors, *Brown v. Duchesne* 60 U.S. 183 (Poteet 2011:570).

[124] See also *Hughes Aircraft v. United States* 29 Fed Cl. 197 (1993) (but commenced in 1973), and Poteet (2011:577–579).

[125] *Decca Ltd. v. United States* 544 F.2d 1070 (Ct.Cl. 1976).

[126] 509 F.2d 1137 (7th Cir. 1975).

infringement suit against three American companies and a German company alleging unauthorized sales of German-produced devices in the United States in violation of §1 of the U.S. Patent Act. Metz filed for dismissal arguing that U.S. due process rules did not allow for personal jurisdiction. The U.S. district court agreed and dismissed the claim. Honeywell appealed, arguing that Metz had played an essential role in placing its products in the stream of U.S. commerce and in inducing its American agents to violate U.S. law. An appellate court reversed the lower court's holding, finding Metz's activities satisfied minimum contacts requirements for constitutional due process, and that jurisdiction was, therefore, appropriate.[127]

Overall, therefore, the record on extraterritorial patent litigation prior to the 1980s confirms the expectation that U.S. courts will resist applying U.S. patent law extraterritorially where the integrity of domestic rules (as distinct from the financial interests of domestic actors) is not at stake. The workhorse in maintaining this position was an inflexibly literalist approach to defining use of protected devices in U.S. territory – going so far as to require that each element of multi-stage actions occur domestically. Eventually, U.S. lawmakers, under pressure from powerful and highly coordinated private exported-oriented intellectual property owners, found this definition too restrictive. In 1988, Congress amended the Patent Act to extend the reach of U.S. law extraterritorially to contributory infringement of device patents, thereby overriding *Deepsouth*. Probing the limits of these changes, both on their own terms and in light of new developments, fueled, and continues to fuel, subsequent patterns of claims.

Another notable feature of Figure 5.1 is the explosion of claims involving novel extraterritorial applications of U.S. law beginning in the early 1980s. What explains this change? As previously, some of these claims involve litigants testing the boundaries of new legislation and/or court decisions on extraterritorial questions. This alone cannot explain the increase, or the dramatically different outcomes across intellectual property issue areas, however. For this, we need to look more broadly to structural and technological changes, and how they developed in each of these areas.

[127] In language echoing the *Bulova* decision, the *Honeywell* court held "in our view, it is not within the contemplation of the concepts of fairness and due process to allow a wrongdoing manufacturer to insulate himself from the long arm of the courts by using an intermediary or by professing ignorance of the ultimate destination of his products."

Among the more striking features of Figure 5.1 is the success of novel extraterritorial trademark claims relative to those in the other two categories. Why have U.S. federal courts been more willing to interpret U.S. trademark law permissively? This differentiation is intuitive under the theory of U.S. judicial extraterritoriality developed in this book, given the potential for trademark infringement anywhere to interfere with a mark's operation everywhere it is used by its owner. Where use of American trademarks includes U.S. territory, this essential element of the theory is therefore comparatively easy to satisfy. Nevertheless, accounting for the surge in extraterritorial litigation in the 1990s still requires looking to the sources and timing of structural and technological changes.

The trademark story has several dimensions. The first involves generalized concerns over foreign misappropriation of American-owned intellectual property.[128] Already in the Tokyo Round negotiations of the General Agreement for Tariffs and Trade in 1977, the U.S. Trade Representative (USTR) and European negotiators actively sought cooperation on an international agreement to limit trade in counterfeit goods.[129] These concerns were exacerbated by a second trend toward outsourcing low-skill, labor-intensive aspects of production to countries with lower labor costs, which began in the 1980s. For the textile and small electronics industries, for example, this entailed shifting consumer production to sites in Asia and Latin America. Because consumer goods produced for U.S. markets also have a high margin of brand-related profitability, the fact that governments in new sites of production often took a lax approach to intellectual property rights led to a spike in concern over counterfeiting.[130] Congress acknowledged this challenge by amending the Lanham Act to include the Anti-Counterfeiting Trademark Act of 1984, which U.S. courts subsequently applied to transnational claims.[131] A third influence reflected in post-1990

[128] For example, *Sterling Drug Inc. v. Bayer AG* 14 F.3d 733 (2nd Cir. 1994) (remanding global injunction against foreign marketing of jointly used trademark to limit it to products likely to make their way to U.S. territory); *Dunkin Donuts Inc. v. Mercantile Ventures. Inc.* 19 F.3d 14 (5th Cir. 1994) (applying Lanham Act to enjoin U.S. citizens, who were also franchisees of Dunkin Donuts in Texas, from operating "Donkin' Donas" stores in Mexico).

[129] Paradise (1999:36).

[130] See, for example, "GATT, Backing U.S. Votes to Prepare New Trade Round" *NYT*, November 29, 1985.

[131] *Levis Strauss & Co. v. Sunrise International Trading, Inc.* 51 F.3d 982 (11th Cir. 1995) (applying Lanham Act to enjoin foreign counterfeits, even if not intended for

intellectual property claims was the need to deal with new forms of branding, such as Internet domain names, and the extraterritorial threats to those new forms.[132]

To a far greater extent than for trademarks or copyrights, the increase in patent cases involving extraterritorial claims has been driven by legislative change, which was itself motivated by a mix of considerations. In the late 1960s, the United States entered what would prove to be a lengthy period of economic slowdown relative to postwar growth levels. This was reflected in declining rates of domestic labor productivity and corporate investment in research and development, and a decreasingly favorable balance of trade with America's main economic competitors. Of particular concern was the falling ratio of exports to imports of high-tech goods, which by the mid-1980s was at a rough parity.[133]

Among the explanations proffered for this decline, in Congressional hearings and elsewhere, was that the United States, though the world's main producer of basic science, was not able to commercialize its discoveries due to its outmoded U.S. patent system. Producers in Japan, Germany, and elsewhere were reaping those benefits by "stealing" U.S. ideas.[134] This narrative of U.S. economic woes during the 1970s and 1980s helped to incentivize extensive hearings, legislation, and, ultimately, a reworking of the international intellectual property regime.

For reasons largely unrelated to worries about the decline in U.S. economic competitiveness, in 1982 Congress created a specialized appellate court in the Federal Circuit for patent, customs, and government contract-related claims. Although the main purpose was to undercut forum-shopping and increase consistency in the judicial interpretation of U.S. law in these areas, following this development, patent use increased markedly.[135] Other federal legislative changes sought to address under-utilization of patents and patent rights by lowering required thresholds for novelty, and expanding the proprietary

U.S. markets); *Reebok Int'l Ltd. v. Sebelen* 930 F.Supp. 720 (D.P.R. 1996) (applying Lanham Act to a transnational scheme to produce counterfeit footwear for sale in the United States).

132 *CNN L.P. L.L.L.P. v. CNNews.com* 177 F.Supp.2d 506 (4th Cir. 2001) (issuing international transfer order re domain name in China on authority of ACPA), and Anti-Cyber-Squatting Consumer Protection Act of 1999, 15 U.S.C. § 1125(d).

133 Scherer (2009:177).

134 Drahos (1995:8); Scherer (2009:178). Note, Scherer is skeptical of this claim, arguing that "chains of causation were clearly more complex."

135 See also www.uspto.gov/web/offices/ac/ido/oeip/taf/h_counts.htm.

claims that government-funded researchers, in universities and elsewhere, could make on their inventions.[136]

On the transnational front as well, Congress began to tinker with the U.S. Patent Act. In 1984, it amended §271, which defines types of infringement, to provide a cause of action for "active inducement" of foreign misappropriation through acts undertaken inside U.S. territory. The change carved out an exception to the territorial limits of the statute.[137] Private litigants immediately tested this provision in a case involving the export and use in Venezuela of caliper pigs, a device for assessing the internal geometry of oil pipelines.[138] An Oklahoma district court found that the defendants had actively induced infringement in violation of U.S.C. §271(f) and were liable for damages, even though the harm was extraterritorial. Subsequent litigants have further probed the scope and meaning of this provision in cases involving hundreds of millions of dollars.[139] Amendments in 1988 added yet another basis for extraterritorial infringement. §271(g) prohibits unauthorized importation, use, sale, or offers to sell goods manufactured extraterritorially with U.S.-patented devices or processes, thus placing a §337-type mechanism in the hands of private plaintiffs.[140]

Figure 5.1 might suggest that U.S. courts were opposed to giving U.S. patent law extraterritorial reach in contested claims, including in the post-1980s period, despite statutory provisions providing for limited extraterritorial application of U.S. patent protections. Key to this story, however, are the selection and observation biases characteristic of federal litigation discussed in Chapter 2. That is to say, because only cases involving ambiguous points of law are likely to make it to litigation (as opposed to settling), litigated claims are unlikely to concern extraterritorial conduct that falls squarely within the statutory prohibition.[141]

[136] Scherer (2009:179–183).

[137] U.S.C. §271(f), Pub.L. 98-622, § 101, November 8, 1984. Note, §271(f) covers direct infringement, whereas §271(b) covers indirect infringement, which also may have an extraterritorial dimension.

[138] *T.D. Williamson Inc. v. Laymon* 723 F.Supp. 587 (N.D. Okl., 1989).

[139] See, for example, *Rotec Industries v. Mitsubishi Corp.* No. 99-1275 (Fed. Cir. 2000) (holding Mitsubishi not liable for infringement absent sufficient evidence of offer to sell inside U.S. territory); and *Microsoft Corporation v. AT&T* 550 U.S. 437 (2007) (Supreme Court held Microsoft not liable for infringement of AT&T-patented software that it caused to be installed abroad on foreign equipment, since installation involved copies not directly supplied from the United States).

[140] Pierson (2007:672).

[141] If private policing of intellectual property rights nevertheless reveals prohibited extraterritorial behavior, sound legal advice should produce settlements rather than litigation.

The claims in Figure 5.1, therefore, are those in which parties sought to push the legal envelope in some way – by seeking to bring new conduct, new persons, or new settings within the reach of U.S. laws (for plaintiffs) or by arguing for exceptions or exemptions to those laws (for defendants).[142]

The case pattern shows, therefore, that despite changes in the political winds in the 1970s and early 1980s, plaintiffs were not convinced that the courts' position on the extraterritoriality of the Patent Act was movable, given the Supreme Court precedent in *Deepsouth*. Thus it wasn't until Congress passed amendments to §271 to expressly incorporate extraterritorial acts that plaintiffs once again emerged to test the boundaries of that change. Interestingly, while U.S. courts have acknowledged, and in some cases expanded, the extraterritoriality of U.S. law, they have remained doggedly insistent that the jurisdiction involved is territorial.[143] This seemingly impossible feat has been achieved "not by broadly interpreting the Patent Act, but, rather, by broadening the concept of subject matter considered 'within the United States'."[144]

The situation with copyrights is, again, quite different. Figure 5.1 shows that the overhaul of the U.S. Copyright Act passed in 1976 did not serve as an immediate catalyst for extraterritorial litigation, despite inclusion of a provision banning the importation of infringing copies or phonorecords.[145] Instead, the post-1980 surge in extraterritorial copyright cases embodied efforts to analogize copyright threats to those addressed statutorily in the extraterritorial aspects of the Patent Act – specifically, inducement to infringe and contributory infringement.[146]

[142] For example, *Reebok v. McLaughlin* 49 F3d 1387 (9th Cir. 1997); *Freedom Wireless Inc. v. Boston Communications Group, Inc.* 198 F.Supp.2d 11 (D.Mass 2002); *BP Chemicals Inc. v. Formosa Chemical and Fibre Group* 229 F.3d 254 (3rd Cir. 2000); *Rotec Industries v. Mitsubishi Corp.* 215 F.3d 1246 (Fed. 2000); *Cardiac Pacemakers Inc. v. St. Jude Medical Inc.* 576 F.3d 1348 (7th Cir. 2009), *NTP v. Research in Motion* 392 F.3d 1336 (Fed. Cir. 2004).

[143] In this respect they are behaving similar to European courts in the antitrust sphere. See Chapter 4.

[144] Pierson (2007:654).

[145] 17 U.S.C. §602. One reason may be the statute's unusual negotiating history as a series of compromises hammered out among interested private actors and then subsequently adopted by Congress with little debate (Litman 1986).

[146] *Fantasy Inc. v. Fogerty* 984 F.2d 1524 (allowing a constructive trust to recover foreign profits derived from domestic infringement); *Danjaq S.A. v. MGM/UA Communications Co.* 773 F.Supp. 194 (C.D. Cal. 1991) (dismissed for failure to state a claim under the Copyright Act where the only act is a foreign offer to sell). Congress made several small additions to the Copyright Act beginning in 1989 "in light of the digital challenge" (Leaffer 2010:12–15).

As indicated by the black line in Figure 5.1(a), in a preponderance of cases these efforts were reasonably successful. By the late 1990s, efforts to manage the legal implications of new technologies that eased cross-border acquisition and distribution of protected works were gaining in relative importance, which reflects both the march of technology and the incorporation of earlier victories into settled rules that did not require further litigation.[147]

Finally, it is important to underscore that in each of these realms there has been no shortage of agents willing to seek extraterritorial applications of U.S. law in the post-1980 period. But who are the plaintiffs in these claims? With few exceptions, in the patent and copyright realms, they are all large export-oriented corporations at the cutting edge of their industries. The mix is more diverse for trademarks, though here too large corporations dominate. Most were U.S.-based entities, though a few were foreign entities seeking to use U.S. law to restrain U.S. competitors. Many in the first category were at the same time lobbying the U.S. government for more protection of intellectual property rights. On the opposing side, many defendants were also U.S. corporations, or multinational corporate entities with U.S.-based components. Among the foreign defendants, the early cases tended to involve German and Japanese companies, whereas companies based in new markets and sites of production are common in later claims.

To summarize, this survey of extraterritorial claims based on my sample of litigated cases suggests that although U.S. courts were active in transnational intellectual property claims with a clear U.S. nexus, they were often unwilling to maximize even their limited capacity to apply U.S. law to protect American intellectual property abroad. This is in tension with arguments that expect domestic courts to lean toward economic nationalism in close transnational cases, but fits with the expectation that U.S. courts will be overwhelmingly concerned with safeguarding the integrity and operation of U.S. law inside U.S. territory. This pattern of U.S. court responses forced U.S.-based enterprises to, once again, seek new legislation and new opportunities for

[147] *ITSI TV Productions Inc. v. California Authority of Racing Fairs* 785 F.Supp. 854 (ND Cal. 1991) (dismissing claim regarding unauthorized foreign broadcasts due to lack of U.S. nexus); *National Football League v. Prime Time 24 Joint Venture* 211 F.3 10 (C.A. 2, 2000) (affirming permanent injunction against foreign broadcast of material "uplinked" by satellite from U.S. territory); *Metro-Goldwyn-Mayer Studios Inc. v. Grokster* 243 F.Supp.2d 1073 (C.D. Cal. 2003) (upholding jurisdiction for extraterritorial inducement of a domestic copyright violation in music downloading).

international engagement, albeit this time with a critically important difference.

The real turn to bargaining

Intellectual property rights are today viewed as part of a larger fabric of international trade and competition concerns, though this was not always the case. This linkage resulted from a concerted effort among public officials and private sector agents in the early 1980s, which over the course of only a decade transformed the international intellectual property regime.[148] Seizing upon national economic angst, corporate executives serving on President Reagan's Advisory Committee on Trade Negotiations (ACTN) drew an explicit connection between the decline in U.S. trade and failures to adequately protect intellectual property rights internationally. Strengthening these rights, the ACTN argued, would help to restore American industrial productivity and increase exports. The ACTN formed an Intellectual Property Task Force to come up with proposals for addressing these issues.

The narrative linking trade and intellectual property issues resonated favorably in many parts of the Reagan administration. It also dovetailed with contemporaneous U.S. reassessments of long-dominant views on antitrust scrutiny that likewise aimed for more business-friendly policies.[149] Still more important, however, was aggressive lobbying of members of Congress by large private corporations and their trade associations. Through these efforts, intellectual property rights were redefined as business assets whose international protection was a matter of national urgency.[150]

Already in 1974, under pressure from export-oriented industries, Congress had amended §337 of the U.S. Tariff Act of 1930 to empower the International Trade Commission (ITC) to exclude imports that violated American intellectual property rights. A complementary amendment to §301 of the 1974 U.S. Trade Act granted the President direct authority to sanction states engaging in unfair practices.[151] Frustration on the part of private sector advocates of more robust intellectual

[148] Gadbaw (1989), Drahos (1995), Sell (2003), Scherer (2009).

[149] Abbott (1989:701–702). The ACTN was chaired by the CEO of Pfizer, Ed Pratt.

[150] Gadbaw (1989:227), Drahos (1995), Sell (2003).

[151] By the late 1970s, both statutes had been modified to allow private entities to petition for action on their behalf. These measures proved unsatisfactory, however, due to procedures that produced delays and uncertainties.

property protections with the inconsistent application of these measures fueled efforts to find other ways of incentivizing foreign governments to take those rights seriously.

The 1984 amendments to §301 of the U.S. Trade and Tariff Act required the President, acting through the United States Trade Representative (USTR), to condition preferential trade arrangements for developing countries (GSP benefits) on adequate protection of American intellectual property.[152] This succeeded in prompting a few states with large light manufacturing sectors (Taiwan, Korea, and Singapore) to tighten their rules.[153] However, a purely bilateral approach promised to be time-consuming and ineffective against states over which the United States had less trade leverage. Meanwhile, proposals for responding to "unfair" foreign trading practices, including those related to intellectual property, that were being debated in Congress began to include openly protectionist elements. This alarmed the ACTN, since raising U.S. tariffs and imposing quotas would have rebounded to harm the very export-oriented companies that were pressing for enhanced intellectual property protections.[154] In a bid to stay the course on free trade principles, the ACTN Task Force turned its attention to the Uruguay Round of GATT negotiations and to the possibilities it provided for multilateral bargaining.[155]

The American turn to multilateralism was not automatic, nor even particularly foreseeable. For starters, the United States often prefers unilateral or bilateral approaches to solving international policy problems, since this maximizes its flexibility and power over weaker states.[156] This, moreover, was a period in which many Americans feared that the United States was slipping in power as a result of over-provision of global public goods in prior decades. Also, there was little reason to believe in early 1986 that other economically highly developed states would support the effort to make intellectual property a trade issue.[157] At the time this strategy was coming together, it was barely mentioned in

[152] Gadbaw (1989:229). See §182 of the Trade Act of 1974, as amended by the Omnibus Trade and Competitiveness Act of 1988 and the Uruguay Round Agreements Act of 1994 (19 U.S.C. § 2242).

[153] Gadbaw (1989:229), Sell (2003:90).

[154] Sell (2003:87–90).

[155] Helfer (2004:20). The ACTN opted to bypass WIPO in these efforts due to WIPO's lack of enforcement leverage, and its stronger representation of developing country voices.

[156] Skidmore (2005).

[157] Drahos (1995:12). Sell (2003:104–105).

the GATT rules.[158] Finally, the U.S. position as a long-time outsider to key international intellectual property treaties made it still more unlikely. For any multilateral strategy to be credible, entrenched U.S. domestic interests, particularly in the copyright realm, had to openly concede that clinging to aspects of U.S. domestic law that had underwritten this isolation was becoming too costly.[159]

To tackle the problem of tepid international support in time for the launch of the Uruguay Round negotiations, the ACTN formed an Intellectual Property Committee (IPC) comprised of top U.S. corporations with strong multinational interests.[160] As Sell describes it, this involved a conscious shift in strategy from government-to-government contacts to American CEOs reaching out to similarly positioned foreign CEOs to convince them to support the intellectual property initiative and to intervene with their respective governments. Armed with a set of common talking points that included a sketch for what a GATT-based intellectual property code might look like, the IPC members, over the course of roughly seven months in 1986, convinced other company heads in Europe and Japan that this was an international trade problem that required multilateral trade-based solutions. Remarkably, this effort succeeded, and when the Uruguay Round began in Punta del Este in September 1986, a Negotiating Group on "Trade-Related Aspects of Intellectual Property Rights, Including Trade in Counterfeit Goods" was established as one of fourteen Groups within the Negotiation on Goods.[161]

Nearly eight years and numerous drafts later, the 1994 Trade Related Aspects of Intellectual Property (hereafter TRIPS) agreement was enacted. In its final form, TRIPS required signatories to recognize a common slate of intellectual property rights and to provide domestic institutions for their realization and protection.[162] On the substantive side, this involved directly incorporating core parts of the Paris and Berne Conventions, but also adding on to them. With regard to patents, for

[158] Abbott (1989:696). For it's part, the GATT organization was receptive to becoming a forum for coordination on intellectual property issues, since it promised to increase its relevance (Sell 2003:20).

[159] Drahos (1995:9).

[160] Corporate members of the IPC in 1986 were: Bristol-Meyers, DuPont, FMC Corporation, General Electric, General Motors, Hewlett Packard, IBM, Johnson & Johnson, Merck, Monsanto, Pfizer, Rockwell International, and Warner Communications.

[161] Gervais (2008:12).

[162] For a full negotiating history of the TRIPS Agreement, see Gervais (2008).

example, TRIPS formulated for the first time international-level definitions of patentable innovations and standardized minimum periods of protection. Several of the modifications included in TRIPS had been tried at WIPO, but had failed.

The most novel feature of TRIPS is its enforcement provisions. Much of the attention to TRIPS enforcement in international relations scholarship has focused on the addition of a state-to-state dispute resolution mechanism.[163] Nevertheless, the overall goal was to ensure this mechanism would be used only rarely. To this end, TRIPS included many obligatory procedural and institutional measures for ensuring effective protection of intellectual property rights. No longer, it was argued, would the mere existence of a formally enacted domestic law discharge a state's treaty obligations.[164] For example, TRIPS requires giving judicial authorities power to provide injunctive relief (i.e. court enforceable orders to cease infringement), and to order the destruction of infringing goods in their territories.[165] Also included are requirements for border and customs measures,[166] and even an obligation to establish criminal penalties.[167] Finally, these measures are required to be equitable, efficient, evidence-based, transparent, and not cost-prohibitive.

If the U.S. turn to multilateralism to manage intellectual property-related threats caught many states off guard, the range of options open to discussion at the international level was rather more predictable. Still, it is worth thinking about why U.S. negotiators sought the forms of protection they did, and not others. Specifically, at no time did the United States raise, or support, any proposal to centralize enforcement of intellectual property rights at the international level. (Even DSB decisions rely on national implementation.) Instead, the United States sought to extend and augment the most effective aspects of the existing system, while isolating those it considered unhelpful, or threatening.[168] This choice undoubtedly involved a heavy dose of path-dependence induced pragmatism with respect to how much, and in what directions, existing

[163] Smith (2000), Rosendorff (2005), Barton *et al.* (2008).

[164] Reichman (1996:338), TRIPS Articles 41–61.

[165] Article 44; Articles 59 and 61.

[166] Articles 51–60.

[167] Articles 41–50.

[168] The multilateral efforts of the United States in this period were not limited to GATT/WTO. They encompassed gap-filling efforts in WIPO and elsewhere, particularly around streamlining procedures for acquiring foreign rights. This produced, notably, the 1989 Madrid Protocol, 1994 Trademark Law Treaty, the 1996 WIPO Copyright Treaty.

institutions and preferences could be shifted.[169] The point here is that the international-level changes sought, and largely achieved, involved no attempt to undercut private means of transnational enforcement – though retaining territoriality as a central feature of the system also did little to enhance it.

Why did economically highly developed states ultimately support TRIPS, despite a weak initial commitment to the intellectual property–trade nexus? The story naturally involves more than intellectual property concerns, since the United States, European countries, and Japan were all heavily invested in the success of the Uruguay Round negotiations for a broad set of more traditional trade-related reasons.[170] Beyond this, TRIPS offered an opportunity to bring the United States more fully into the international intellectual property fold on terms that resonated with the preferences and concerns of many Europeans.

This was helped along when the United States finally agreed to join the Berne Convention in 1988. By the 1980s, the U.S. position in the UCC had grown complicated. In 1984, the United States withdrew from UNESCO, which houses the UCC, in protest over its support of restraints on press freedom in developing countries. Arrangements were worked out whereby the United States could continue to participate in and contribute funds to the UCC, but with a loss of influence and stature.[171] Perhaps predictably, the Berne Convention Implementation Act of 1988 took a "minimalist" line in amending the 1976 Copyright Act, making changes "only where there was a direct conflict" with Berne provisions. Still, this required eliminating several deeply entrenched formalities, including the (in)famous American notice and registration requirements. It also necessitated extending protection to new types of works, such as architectural plans, and modifying other U.S. rules, for example, on performance rights.[172]

The final TRIPS agreement required all economically developed state parties to make some adjustments. The United States substantially extended the period of its copyrights, even reinstating rights for numerous works that had already entered the public domain, and tightened its rules on sound and video recordings. In the trademark realm, the United States broadened protections for so-called famous marks, even where no likelihood of confusion is present, and bent to European insistence on

[169] Gervais (2008:141).
[170] Drahos (1995).
[171] Joyner and Lawson (1986).
[172] Leaffer (2010:11–12).

protection for geographic appellations.[173] Europeans agreed to extend copyright protections to computer programs and mask works and granted patent protections to microorganisms and micro non-biological processes – though they drew the line at patents for macro-biological organisms as contrary to public policy. Likewise, minor concessions in the realm of compulsory licenses, some of them temporary, were included in the agreement, albeit largely to ensure that developing countries had a fighting chance of reaching compliance.[174]

The changes TRIPS required of intellectual property producers, however, pale in comparison to what was demanded of developing states. Many of these states lacked basic substantive rules and procedural forms demanded by TRIPS. Why did developing states agree to these terms? Linking intellectual property rights to international trading privileges increased the bargaining leverage of intellectual property producers over reluctant developing states exponentially. A key moment early in the Uruguay Round, therefore, was the decision that the time was ripe to establish a permanent organization for coordinating international trade.[175] This meant TRIPS would be part of an all-or-nothing deal for membership in a new World Trade Organization (WTO) rather than a separate *a la carte* agreement.[176]

Even as the United States was hammering out the TRIPS agreement, Congress continued to augment U.S. unilateral and bilateral tools for incentivizing foreign protection of intellectual property rights. Amendments in 1988 to §271 of the Patent Act, formalizing its extraterritorial reach, were mentioned above. In addition, the Omnibus Trade and Competitiveness Act of 1988 introduced critically important changes to §301 of the Trade Act that required (instead of merely allowing) the USTR to actively monitor intellectual property protections of other countries. States on the USTR's Watch List and Priority Watch List were to receive "increased bilateral attention" in the form of specific requests for improvements and offers of technical assistance, backed by the threat of sanctions for failures to follow through which, under the statute, can include revocation of a state's most favored nation trading status.[177]

[173] Federal Trademark Dilution Act of 1995, Pub. L. No. 104-98, 109 Stat. 985 (January 16, 1996); Sell (2003:111–112).

[174] See TRIPS Article 31, and Ford (2000:958–959).

[175] The GATT was enacted as an interim measure in 1948 following a failed bid to create an International Trade Organization.

[176] Matsushita *et al.* (2006:6).

[177] Ford (2000:948).

Why did Congress take these steps? The U.S. decision to throw intellectual property in with an issue like international trade involved risks. Chief among them was the possibility that demands for stronger intellectual property rights might be sacrificed to other concerns of more central importance to the trade regime.[178] Moreover, at the moment changes to §301 were being passed in Congress, TRIPS negotiations were in deadlock over north–south issues, and it was unclear whether, or how, this would be resolved. Stated simply, advocates of more robust rights wanted additional assurances that their interests would be looked after – both in the near term and in the event multilateral mechanisms failed. In the end, having several options for credibly threatening extraterritorial enforcement of U.S. preferences allowed U.S. negotiators to wring concessions from other states. Indeed, avoiding U.S. §301 proceedings appears to have specifically contributed to the willingness of developing states to sign on to TRIPS.[179]

Still, TRIPS and its supporting array of bilateral mechanisms in no way rendered demand for U.S. judicial extraterritoriality obsolete. Figure 5.1 shows that, far from declining, the overall incidence of new extraterritorial claims involving U.S. intellectual property law rose after TRIPS was enacted. This can be explained by the fact that each had come to be understood as addressing a more or less distinct class of transactions. Neither TRIPS nor §301 procedures contain provisions for managing multi-jurisdictional complaints. Such claims, however, have become the "bread and butter" of U.S. extraterritoriality cases in the intellectual property sphere, due in no small part to the reticence of U.S. courts to interpret U.S. laws as having broader reach.

Moreover, to the extent foreign infringing activities have a causal U.S. nexus, it is debatable whether pressuring foreign governments over enforcement is worthwhile, or appropriate. Ambivalence over how to manage such claims persists in part due to the persistence of deep cross-national differences over the substance of intellectual property rights.[180] For those seeking greater protection of intellectual property rights, the harmonization of foreign laws and procedures at the heart of both TRIPS and §301 lays a more promising foundation not only for achieving more robust local protection but also – in theory – for domestic

178 Dam (1987:637).
179 Drahos (1995:11), Gervais (2008:23–24), Scherer (2009:205).
180 Basedow (2010), Goldstein and Hugenholtz (2012).

courts to begin applying *foreign* intellectual property laws in situations where other aspects of U.S. jurisdiction are satisfied.[181]

Why have private actors carried on seeking expansion of U.S. extraterritorial enforcement of U.S.-granted IP rights since the enactment of TRIPS? First, the implementation of TRIPS has not been as easy as some had hoped (or feared), even with the backing of WTO muscle. Developing states have proven resourceful at finding ways to exploit, or construct, loopholes and exceptions to this demanding set of requirements in order to further their development goals.[182] Second, USTRs have used §301 sanctions sparingly in the post-TRIPS era, despite acknowledged difficulties with TRIPS implementation – though the reporting mechanism and watch lists remain active.[183] This is due to the fact that unilaterally imposed §301 sanctions arguably violate GATT/WTO rules and also disrupt beneficial trade with target countries.[184]

In the meantime, the march of legal, technological, and structural change has continued, placing new questions about the scope of intellectual property rights before national courts and prompting additional treaty efforts.[185] Developed states have increasingly turned to "TRIPS-plus" arrangements – intellectual property clauses embedded in bilateral and regional free trade agreements (FTAs), bilateral investment treaties (BITs), and other treaty arrangements.[186] In this environment of high flux, opportunities to catch actors with U.S. ties in transnational misappropriations have remained valuable. In recognition of this, the U.S. Congress has continued to underwrite cautious expansions of judicial extraterritoriality – albeit largely through tacit endorsement of federal court decisions. This acquiescence is made easier by the fact that U.S. federal courts have likewise continued to resist the efforts of private seekers of U.S. extraterritoriality to extend U.S. law to conduct

[181] Namely, subject matter jurisdiction (which in cases involving foreign law may require only diversity jurisdiction) and personal jurisdiction over named defendants.

[182] Helfer (2004), Brewster (2012).

[183] Special 301 sanctions have been imposed just four times total, and only once (against Ukraine in 2001) since the enactment of TRIPS.

[184] In 1998, the legality of §301 itself was challenged at the World Trade Organization. A dispute settlement panel found the existence of the statute was not contrary to WTO rules, but that it could only be used with WTO approval. www.sice.oas.org/DISPUTE/wto/tract01e.asp.

[185] See, for example, Patent Law Treaty of 2000, and the Anti-Counterfeiting Trade Agreement of 2012.

[186] Helfer (2004).

that is unlikely to impair the integrity or operation of those rights in U.S. territory as my theory expects.

Discussion

This overview of private efforts to seek extraterritorial applications of U.S. law in the intellectual property realm using U.S. courts demonstrates several points relevant to theory building.

The first point is that U.S. extraterritoriality failed as a global strategy for protecting American intellectual property. How and why it failed is important. The problem was not that U.S. courts were handing down lots of extraterritorial decisions, only to see them ignored by foreign defendants and their governments. Instead, it was the refusal of U.S. courts to interpret ambiguous U.S. laws as having broad extraterritorial reach. This, combined with a deep reluctance to apply foreign intellectual property laws, cut off the jurisdictional competence of U.S. courts for the overwhelming bulk of foreign disputes involving American-owned intellectual property.

Throughout this period all relevant actors understood that U.S. courts lacked any real discretion to find and exercise jurisdiction over situations involving wholly extraterritorial acts of misappropriation – whether due to dominant interpretations of constitutional due process (personal jurisdiction) restrictions, or to the threat of legislative override. However, it is important to acknowledge that this apparent lack of discretion is itself constructed from prior ideas and practices about the scope and applicability of U.S. law in these areas. More specifically, it turns on conceptions of actionable harm from extraterritorial acts. This is highly relevant when it comes to the sub-class of disputes over transactions involving extraterritorial conduct *and also* acts inside U.S. territory. In these cases the jurisdictional competence of U.S. domestic courts was (or became) more thinkable.

It is within this range of thinkability without determinism in which court agency operates. Indeed, the closeness of decisions like those in *Deepsouth* and *Subafilms* suggests strongly that there are no convincing explanations for many of these outcomes ascertainable from within the law itself. Indeed, these disputes end up in federal litigation precisely because they lack ready answers in established sources. What, then, explains why U.S. courts would allow only a limited use of U.S. extraterritoriality in the intellectual property sphere, even as those very same courts were exercising extraterritorial jurisdiction more aggressively in other issue areas? Naïve conceptions of economic nationalism offer little insight. The theory elaborated and tested in prior chapters, however, provides an answer.

Most foreign misappropriations of intellectual property, while costing American owners a great deal in lost revenue, have little or no impact on the operation of intellectual property rights in U.S. territory. When changes in the U.S. position within the economic and political hierarchy of states increased international commercial opportunities for U.S. entities, this expansion at first affected the integrity of domestic rights only at the margins of trademark law. As a consequence, U.S. courts proved willing to apply U.S. patent law extraterritorially only when expressly directed to do so by Congress. Only once technological innovations appeared to radically alter the ability of actors around the world to gain unauthorized access to protected works – from within the United States, and from extraterritorial sources inside U.S. territory – have U.S. federal courts begun to change course.

A second point to underscore is that U.S. judicial reluctance to exercise extraterritorial jurisdiction over intellectual property disputes during much of the post-World War II era forced those claiming violations in foreign settings to look elsewhere for protection. In this way, U.S. courts helped to "select" the United States into international bargaining over international intellectual property rules. Had private efforts to convince U.S. courts to interpret U.S. laws as having extraterritorial reach been more successful, it is possible that the link between trade and intellectual property drawn by the ACTN, the IPC, and other key actors in the early the 1980s would not have been made, and efforts to restructure the international intellectual property regime (if they occurred at all) would have played out much differently.

Third, prior to TRIPS, those claiming harm from unauthorized foreign use of U.S. patents, copyrights, or trademarks could choose to (a) seek vindication through courts or other regulators in the foreign country;[187] (b) ask the U.S. government to pressure foreign governments to crack down on violations inside their territory;[188] or (c) do nothing.[189] TRIPS

[187] Importantly, this includes unauthorized use of foreign-registered marks inside the United States, see *Grupo Gigante* SA de CV *v. Dallo* & Co., Inc. 391 F.3d 1088 (9th Cir. 2004).

[188] This might entail, for example, threatening to impose so-called Super 301 sanctions, or, since 1996, to file a complaint at the WTO.

[189] I expect rights holders to attempt enforcement only where anticipated benefits outweigh expected costs.

did little to change this formula. Whether a role for territorially based private enforcement should be preserved was never questioned – even as developed states used their trade leverage to force a sweeping harmonization of the underlying rules. The continued embrace of territoriality as an organizing principle for intellectual property rights in the TRIPS/WTO regime, however, all but guaranteed that enforcement would continue to be a problem for the United States and other developed states.[190]

A fourth point is that even though U.S. judicial extraterritoriality did not offer a workable general strategy for international protection of American intellectual property, it has nevertheless proved useful for addressing transnational disputes with a substantial U.S. component. This has involved backing off a strictly territorial view of U.S. intellectual property rights, and the range of conduct that affects them. Still, at issue is no mere conduct test. More often than not, U.S. courts have veered from strict territoriality only when some actual infringement has occurred in U.S. territory, even in situations where private actors are cynically attempting to exploit international borders to defeat U.S. intellectual property rights.

Fifth, and finally, this case study underscores the joint necessity of all three elements of the analytic framework described in Chapter 3: legal ambiguity, private agency, and enforcement capacity. Although political contests over U.S. intellectual property rules are as old as the United States itself, it was not until perceived threats to American-produced intellectual property became transnational that agents emerged to demand transnational legal responses. Because courts in the United States provide the primary means for enforcing intellectual property rights domestically, rights holders naturally sought to extend the practice of judicial extraterritoriality operating in other areas of transnational concern, such as antitrust and securities regulation, into this area of law. These demands were, however, limited by perceived weaknesses in U.S. enforcement capacity due to a lack of jurisdiction-conferring ties to the United States on the part of alleged violators, their lack of U.S. assets, or both.

Conclusion

Intellectual property rights govern access to valuable resources. For this reason, their scope, content, and applicability are frequently contested,

190 Sell (2003:11).

both domestically and internationally. This chapter examines the origins and institutional path dependence of the territoriality principle in international intellectual property law, along with some of its consequences. Understanding why the United States embraced territoriality initially, and why it has remained wedded to this principle, despite the inefficiencies it generates, requires attention to political economies of incentives and opportunity structures.

A central theme of this volume is that states that assert legal control over transnational transactions not only select which rules apply but also decide scope and meaning of those rules. The analysis here demonstrates that whether U.S. courts are applying U.S. laws extraterritorially or declining to do so, their decisions affect the options and preferences of transnational actors seeking to protect claimed legal rights. In the intellectual property sphere, U.S. courts in most situations insisted on territorial limits to U.S.-granted patents and copyrights, despite clear economic losses to U.S. rights holders from unauthorized extraterritorial use. This is consistent with the theory of U.S. judicial extraterritoriality elaborated in Chapter 2 up to the point at which technological changes began to allow unauthorized copying and distribution of copyright-protected work on a scale that began to devalue these rights inside U.S. territory. At this point, however, U.S. courts became more open to applying U.S. law to extraterritorial infringement claims, albeit on a more modest scale than many rights holders would prefer.

The timing of U.S. efforts to engage with the international intellectual property regime beginning in the 1970s, together with its attempt to remake that regime in the 1980s and 1990s, can be traced in part to the frustrations of private actors with the refusal of U.S. courts to apply U.S. law extraterritorially to protect U.S. patents and copyrights. Indeed, forging the link between trade and intellectual property rights that proved so critical to U.S. efforts to remake the international regime may not have been possible, or necessary, if intellectual property rights had not evolved in such a rigidly territorial fashion.

If the failure of U.S. judicial extraterritoriality as a general strategy for protecting U.S. intellectual property rights influenced the U.S. government's willingness to bargain at the international level, U.S. preferences for specific modes of enforcement also limited the range of options the United States was willing to pursue. For example, at no point did the United States support internationalized intellectual property rights or the creation of robust centralized enforcement institutions. Instead, U.S. efforts sought to standardize substantive intellectual property rights at the national level on a multilateral scale. This preserved the ability of the U.S. government to "bilateralize" its discontent with foreign states' intellectual property rules and practices using §301 of the Trade Act or other provisions in U.S. free trade agreements and bilateral investment treaties. Also preserved was the ability of private rights holders to use domestic courts to police alleged transnational infringements where the conduct at issue threatened the integrity or operation of U.S. intellectual property rights inside U.S. territory.

6

U.S. extraterritoriality and human rights

Shaping a regime from within

The international struggle to promote human rights ideals and institutions globally has been a defining feature of the post-World War II era. Central to this project and its roots in Western liberalism is the notion that acts undertaken in violation of fundamental human rights demand justice in the form of legal accountability. The complexities of securing accountability have given rise to an international politics of human rights enforcement, which has drawn the focus of international relations (IR) scholars. Much of this attention has focused on the origins, mandates, and decisions of international courts and tribunals, or the activities of transnational activist networks.[1] A burgeoning literature also exists on transitional justice mechanisms, many of which involve courts or court-like proceedings.[2] Transnational human rights litigation in domestic courts, by contrast, has received relatively little consideration – and much of the attention it has garnered has been from legal scholars and political theorists.[3]

Turning to law and courts to vindicate individual rights is a long-standing American tradition, but extraterritoriality in this sphere has much shallower roots. Beginning in the 1980s, civil plaintiffs succeeded in prying open the doors of U.S. courts to complaints alleging egregious violations of human rights in other countries. Since then, U.S. courts have considered the appropriateness of exercising jurisdiction in more than 200 cases involving allegations of extraterritorial human rights abuses. This development was far from inevitable. Nor has it proven irreversible.

[1] See, for example, Keck and Sikkink (1998), Moravcsik (2000), Alter (2003 and 2014), Neumeyer (2005), Hafner-Burton (2008), Neuman (2008), Simmons (2009), Helfer and Voeten (2014).

[2] Mendez (2001), Putnam (2002), Snyder and Vinjamuri (2003), Hayner (2008), Sikkink (2011), Cronin-Furman (2013).

[3] Macedo (2004), Roht-Arriaza (2005), Sloss (2009), Whytock (2009), Langer (2011), but see also Putnam (2009) and Conant (2013).

This body of disputes provides a critical test of the second part of my theory of judicial extraterritoriality – that concerned with basic rights. Unlike in other issue areas discussed in detail thus far, in the human rights realm much of the substantive law that U.S. courts have applied has been international law – albeit as acknowledged and interpreted by U.S. judges. Consistent with my findings in prior chapters, the evidence here supports the hypothesis that where transnational actors observe domestic courts applying and enforcing legal rules extraterritorially, this shapes pragmatic understandings of what those rules require and affects the behavior of strategic actors within (or prospectively within) their reach.

After briefly describing the contours of international human rights law and discussing key challenges to its enforcement, I review my theory of U.S. court behavior as it applies to these types of claims. I then use the analytic framework from Chapter 3 to trace key developments in the rise, arc, and recent decline of extraterritorial human rights litigation in U.S. courts. I give specific attention to the precarious jurisdictional grounding of these suits, along with plaintiff efforts to expand the range of extraterritorial claims over which U.S. courts will exercise jurisdiction, and the range of defendants against whom violations may be alleged. Next I use original data to describe U.S. court actions when presented with claimed violations of human rights and draw some provisional conclusions about the effects of these interactions for developments in international human rights law.

Enforcing human rights in U.S. courts

Human rights law is international law, and international law has a complicated existence in U.S. domestic institutions. The substantive scope of international human rights law encompasses both civil and political rights, and economic, social, and cultural rights. Civil and political rights collectively embody the principle that there are limits to how states may legitimately treat their citizens and others under their physical control. This includes prohibitions on torture, extrajudicial killing, arbitrary detention, genocide or its attempt, disappearances, enslavement, politically motivated rape, and the infliction of cruel, inhuman, or degrading treatment. These offenses have articulations in civil law and in international criminal law as war crimes and crimes against humanity.[4] Economic, social, and cultural

[4] Crimes against humanity encompass extrajudicial killing, enslavement, forced deportations, violent intimidation, political and religious persecution, and other inhumane acts, such as torture or rape, practiced systematically, or on a wide scale. War crimes refer to all

rights encompass, for example, the right to work, the right to an education, and the right to ethnicity. These rights, however, have rarely been a focus of litigation in U.S. courts as matters of international law.

The main sources of international human rights law are international treaties and customary rules based in part (but only in part) on state practice.[5] These are supplemented by the judgments of international tribunals, the writings of legal scholars and jurists, and the domestic practices of individual states, which include the decisions of domestic courts.[6]

The corpus of international human rights treaty law has three distinctive features. The first is its incorporation of the individual as a subject. Most international law deals only with states and their obligations to one another. International human rights law, by contrast, obligates states to ensure respect for the rights of persons inside their territory, or under their control. This may involve restrictions on how the state exercises its power vis-à-vis individuals ("negative rights"), or it may encompass affirmative obligations to provide individuals with certain entitlements ("positive rights"). As with other areas of international law, however, the locus of obligation remains states and state officials.

A second distinctive feature is the quasi-aspirational character of the law articulated in international human rights treaties. That is to say, international human rights treaties do not simply codify existing state practices. Rather, they include a heavy dose of progressive rulemaking, whereby enacting states agree to create benchmarks for members to attain. The openly aspirational aspects of these treaties thus purposefully decouple substantive obligations from underlying state practice, thereby diminishing the legal impact of violations.[7] In a related point, international human rights law is also unusual in that treaty processes have been highly influential in the development of customary rules, rather than the reverse. This follows from the fact that these treaties are widely interpreted as creating obligations *erga omnes* (toward all states – not just other treaty members).[8] Eight multilateral treaties with a focus on civil

wanton or unnecessary damage to, or destruction of, persons (especially civilians) or property during wartime, the killing or abuse of prisoners in the course of armed conflict.

5 State practice in international law encompasses acts like domestic legislation, court decisions, official government position papers and statements in international fora, and condemnations of other states' practices.

6 See Article 38(1) of the Statute of the International Court of Justice, and the *Restatement (Third) of Foreign Relations Law of the United States* §103(2).

7 Goodman and Jinks (2008).

8 Shaw (2008).

and political rights have more than 140 state signatories each, and several other agreements have memberships encompassing 20 or more states.[9] The Americas, Europe, and Africa also have regional human rights treaties and structures, which operate in parallel to their global analogues.[10] Because the United States has joined relatively few of these treaties, or joins them with hefty reservations, or fails to adopt domestic legislation to implement those it joins, the ability of litigants in U.S. courts to draw upon progressive rules frequently turns on their status as customary law.

A third defining feature of human rights law is the wide empirical variation in whether and how governments fulfill their international human rights obligations.[11] The international system lacks institutions for the direct enforcement of these obligations.[12] Thus, for many people around the world, the *de facto* and *de jure* centrality of states in human rights enforcement is deeply unfortunate. Many governments are themselves large-scale violators of human rights. Others lack the political will, or the legal and administrative capacity to deal effectively with sources of abuse within their territory. Furthermore, whether by default or by design, many states in which grave rights violations occur have few (if any) institutions through which citizens can mobilize to secure respect for basic rights, or where victims can seek justice for violations that have already occurred.[13] Individuals and organizations seeking to improve respect for human rights, including through *ex post* accountability, are, therefore, often reliant to some degree on outside institutions and mechanisms.[14]

At the international level as well, under-enforcement in the face of known violations has been the historical norm.[15] The crux of the problem is that when governments commit human rights violations, the victims are generally their own citizens – not other states, or foreign citizens.

9 Office of the United Nations High Commissioner for Human Rights, www2.ohchr.org/english/law/.
10 The authority, competences, and levels of activity vary greatly among regional human rights systems, with the European system being by far the most robust (Alter 2014).
11 Hafner-Burton and Tsutsui (2007), Simmons (2009).
12 Koh (1998), Goodman and Jinks (2008), Simmons (2009). Even institutions, like U.N. monitors and international courts and tribunals, that are willing to call attention to violations rely upon states for punishment and efforts at prevention.
13 Joseph (2004), Simmons (2009). Grave violations of human rights are most common in non-democracies with weak accountability structures (Hafner Burton and Tsutsui 2007).
14 Keck and Sikkink (1998).
15 Simmons (2009).

Responding to these situations thus requires outside governments to balance their commitments to human rights with competing principles, such as respect for state sovereignty, particularly where the abuses show little sign of spilling beyond the offending state's borders. If the expected political costs of interceding appear high, this can tilt incentives further against taking action.

When, by contrast, the direct or indirect perpetrators of extraterritorial human rights violations are U.S. citizens, or others with ties to the United States, the political and legal menu of options for victims has, at least from the 1980s onward, tended to look quite different. That this should be so, however, was far from foreseeable and became a subject of intense contestation in U.S. courts. As with other legal issue areas examined in this volume, it is the transnational character of some human rights violations, and their connection – direct or indirect – to U.S. territory and citizens that creates the possibility of U.S. court involvement.

Whether and under what conditions U.S. courts might decide claims alleging extraterritorial human rights violations is an important question for individual victims and perpetrators. It has also been important to the United States and its authority in the international politics of human rights protection. The theory of U.S. court behavior elaborated in Chapter 2 encompasses two logics (or pathways) by which privately initiated extraterritorial claims have been able to find receptive U.S. judicial ears. The emergence and operation of the "regulatory logic" is examined in the prior two case chapters on antitrust and intellectual property rights. Here the focus is on the second logic – that involving judicial incentives to protect a narrow, but vitally important class of basic rights.

What does it mean to say that a right is "basic"? It requires, first, near-unconditional (as opposed to situational) respect when attached to U.S. citizens or other persons inside U.S. territory. Second, it means that the right features in the set of ideas and values from which U.S. national and political identity is constructed. It follows that violations of basic rights by, or against, members of the American polity, or entities with close U.S. ties, are harmful *per se* to that identity and to its external projection to wider political and legal audiences. As explained at greater length in Chapter 2, this encompasses any right to which a U.S. federal court must give strict scrutiny in constitutional review, and which most states consider a peremptory rule of international law. In substance, these two categories overlap in their prohibitions on deprivation of life and liberty without due process of law, freedom from discrimination based on race or national origin, as well as freedom from genocide torture, piracy, war crimes, and other crimes against humanity.[16]

The behavioral expectation that follows is that whenever a plaintiff properly alleges the violation of a basic right by a U.S. citizen, or others with close U.S. ties, U.S. courts will be inclined to exercise jurisdiction over that claim regardless of where the conduct occurred. Likewise, when a victim with U.S. ties properly alleges that a basic right has been violated, a U.S. court should be expected to exercise jurisdiction over the substance of the claim, provided that requiring the accused to answer to a U.S. civil court would not violate U.S. rules of constitutional due process.

As any American-trained lawyer will immediately recognize, there is a great deal packed into the notion of properly alleging a violation of U.S. law – some of it involving straightforward procedural formalities, and some of it involving murkier (in these types of claims especially) issues regarding the extraterritorial applicability of U.S. law and the effects of these determinations on the jurisdiction of U.S. courts.[17] The answers to these often highly technical questions control who may claim what rights under U.S. law and who (or what) is obligated to respect those rights.

Navigating these issues requires understanding how U.S. law interfaces with the international law of human rights, both of which are moving targets – in part due to the actions of judges and litigants.[18] Indeed, the roster of rights considered "basic," and the scope and content of rights previously acknowledged to be in the class, evolved, and continues to evolve, in response to iterative processes of legal contestation,[19] and through partially exogenous political and societal changes.

Why and how does judicial extraterritoriality affect broader transnational and international processes? U.S. court decisions to exercise jurisdiction over extraterritorial human rights claims have two separate but related types of influence. The first involves projecting information about the geographic reach of U.S. enforcement to private actors and foreign governments. Because U.S. court decisions favoring plaintiffs

[16] Gunther and Sullivan (1997:663–664), Shaw (2008:124–125).

[17] These two issues encompass questions of the adjudicatory and prescriptive jurisdiction of U.S. courts respectively.

[18] Zia-Zarifi (1999:90).

[19] Sandholtz and Stone Sweet (2004).

can be backed by sizeable penalties, the threat of being sued in the United States prompts other, similarly situated entities who are prospectively within the jurisdictional reach of U.S. courts to take steps to minimize that possibility. Conversely, when U.S. courts decide they lack jurisdiction, or they decline to exercise it, this highlights the limits of U.S. law and legal institutions in the same way, thus providing strategically inclined actors blueprints for avoiding U.S. legal liability.

Second, U.S. court decisions to exercise jurisdiction extraterritorially over human rights claims commit judges to issue rulings and assign liability (or not) based upon interpretations of the law at issue. These interpretations become part of the international jurisprudential domain, and the body of accompanying state practice. Because the United States is one of only a few countries whose domestic courts have agreed to decide extraterritorial human rights claims with any frequency – albeit in the civil, not the criminal realm – its actions matter, whether its courts are strengthening progressive views of applicable law or weakening them.

In general terms, U.S. extraterritoriality in human rights is less politically controversial internationally than in most other areas of law. This is because the international law of jurisdiction encompasses a doctrine of universal jurisdiction, which permits any state to try alleged perpetrators of grave human rights violations in their domestic courts regardless of where the violations occurred.[20] It is important to underscore, however, that U.S. courts have not relied upon this doctrine when asserting jurisdiction over foreign defendants in suits alleging human rights violations. Instead, U.S. courts have approached personal jurisdiction exclusively as an issue of U.S. constitutional law, as the structurally induced concern with the domestic operation of U.S. law discussed in Chapter 2 would expect.[21] Even so, U.S. litigants in human rights claims have on several occasions managed to steer U.S. courts into international political minefields.

[20] Amnesty International reports that 125 states have universal jurisdiction laws. See www.amnestyusa.org/our-work/issues/international-justice/universal-jurisdiction, accessed March 16, 2012. (The impetus behind many of these acts was to align domestic law with international treaty commitments, such as the Rome Statute of the ICC.) However, universal jurisdiction crimes are only weakly incorporated into U.S. criminal law (Cassel 2001).

[21] In short this presents an odd situation whereby international law is actually *more permissive* than U.S. law regarding the authority of domestic courts to decide extraterritorial claims.

With this situated overview of the theory in mind, I turn now to more detailed discussion of specific legal mechanisms, together with strategic and institutional constraints on their use.

Legal ambiguity, political agency, and enforcement

Understanding under what circumstances victims of human rights abuses may reasonably try to convince U.S. courts to exercise jurisdiction extraterritorially requires attention to several legal and political factors. To make the substantive and procedural complexities involved in transnational human rights litigation as practiced by U.S. federal courts more tractable, and more comparable to patterns of practice in other legal issue areas, I use the three-part framework developed in Chapter 3, and applied in the previous two chapters.

The framework elements are: (a) the ambiguity of legal rules and jurisdictional hooks, (b) the incentives of private actors in seeking to have those rules applied authoritatively, and (c) expectations regarding *ex post* enforcement. After discussing each of these elements separately, I consider how each interacts with the others, and with key features in the broader political-strategic context, to create, reinforce, or limit U.S. judicial extraterritoriality in the context of punishing grave violations of human rights.

Ambiguities of jurisdiction and substance

Pursuing extraterritorial human rights claims in U.S. courts has involved an especially complicated package of jurisdictional issues. Why is this so? In most situations where U.S. federal courts are asked to decide whether judicial extraterritoriality is appropriate, the statute in question will encompass both a basis for subject matter jurisdiction and the substantive law that plaintiffs are seeking to apply. The court's task at the jurisdictional phase is thus to decide whether the law has extraterritorial reach with regard to the facts alleged. It may surprise those unfamiliar with this topic that the U.S. statute under which most extraterritorial claims involving international human rights violations have been litigated in U.S. courts, the Alien Tort Statute (ATS), contains no reference to human rights.[22]

[22] Judiciary Act Ch. 20 §9, 1 Stat. 73, 77 (1789). The statute is also sometimes called the Alien Tort Claims Act (ATCA). Alternative bases for human right claims in U.S. civil courts at the federal level are 28 U.S.C. §1331 claims, which covers offenses "arising under" U.S. law, including federal common law), and the 1970 Racketeer Influenced and Corrupt

The text of the ATS reads in its entirety: "The district courts shall have original jurisdiction of [sic] any civil action by an alien for a tort only, committed in violation of the law of nations or a treaty of the United States." The statute is thus clear about who can sue – aliens, but not U.S. citizens.[23] The ATS is also clear that it allows only suits in tort (the law of civil wrongs). It is the third element – the requirement that tortious conduct must be in violation of international law or a U.S. treaty – that creates the complication. Because the bounds of these legal categories are undefined, they allow for several interpretations under U.S. constitutional and procedural law in ways that directly affect the scope of the statute, and its utility for extraterritorial human rights claims.

The ATS was enacted in 1789 as part of the First Judiciary Act, though it was rarely used in the first two centuries of its existence.[24] It was resurrected in 1980 from near-dormancy in a case against a high-ranking member of Paraguay's national police, Americo Peña-Irala, alleging the torture and extrajudicial killing of a Paraguayan citizen, Joelito Filartiga, in Paraguay in 1976.[25] In 1978, Dolly Filartiga, the sister of the victim, spotted Peña-Irala on the New York subway. After reporting Peña-Irala to U.S. immigration authorities, but prior to his deportation, she filed a civil action in U.S. federal court alleging violations of international human rights law. The U.S. district court dismissed the case on grounds that international law applies only between states. On appeal, however, a Second Circuit court reversed the dismissal. It held that the ATS provided a legitimate basis for individuals to bring such claims, and that customary international law prohibiting torture – as reflected in international treaties and "the renunciation of torture as an instrument of official policy by virtually all of the nations of the world" – satisfied the third prong of the ATS.[26] The extraterritorial nature of the conduct was

Organizations Act. At the state level, standard tort law also may apply. See Joseph (2004:65–80), and Stephens *et al.* (2008:104–127). For rights violations tied to international terrorism, additional causes of action may exist against foreign governments under the 1976 Foreign Sovereign Immunities Act, and against private entities under the 1992 Anti-Terrorism Act (Stephens *et al.* 2008:99–101 and 110–113).

23 This is unusual, since U.S. law normally applies to all persons inside U.S. territory, especially to U.S. citizens (Stephens *et al.* 2008:1).

24 The ATS was invoked in court in fewer than 25 cases between 1789 and 1989, and only twice successfully. Stephens *et al.* (2008:7, n.24). The two cases are: *Bolchos v. Darrell*, 3 F. Cas. 810 (D.S.C 1795) and *Adra v. Clift* 195 F.Supp. 857 (D.Md. 1961).

25 *Filartiga v. Peña-Irala* 630 F.2d 876 (2d Cir. 1980). An immense amount of scholarship discusses this case and its importance.

26 *Filartiga* at 880.

not a point of extended discussion.[27] In 1984, a default judgment against Peña-Irala awarded the plaintiffs US$10.4 million in damages.

In the decades since *Filartiga*, U.S. federal courts have wrestled with the details of finding ATS jurisdiction, along with the appropriateness of exercising it in more than 220 cases initiated by private claimants. U.S. courts dismissed the majority of these disputes for a variety of reasons examined below. Nevertheless, in a non-trivial number of instances, ATS plaintiffs succeeded in establishing U.S. court jurisdiction. In the process, they also pushed the boundaries of what ATS claims could encompass with respect to types of offenses, and who (or what) could be called to account. In many instances grappling with these issues raised fundamental questions about the place of international law in U.S. law and jurisprudence.

Demarcating boundaries of ATS jurisdiction

A key source of ATS-related ambiguity has been whether the statute itself includes substantive law through its reference to the law of nations and international treaties that can be leveraged to formulate claims ("causes of action"), or whether it is merely a jurisdiction-conferring statute. Under the second of these options, any rights applied using the ATS must be sourced elsewhere – namely, in international law as incorporated into U.S. law, or in the law of the country where alleged violations occurred.[28]

Under the first (unitary) approach, the range of possible claims that can support ATS jurisdiction is quite broad, encompassing all U.S. treaty obligations, whether or not incorporated into domestic law, and any international law with customary status. Thorny issues could still arise regarding the relationship between customary law and treaty law, and concerning whether any legal implications can (or should) be drawn from U.S. decisions *not* to ratify specific treaties.[29] But these issues are

[27] The opinion first classifies the plaintiff's claim as a transitory tort and explains that federal courts "regularly adjudicate" such claims between parties over whom they have jurisdiction. The second step, which grounds the decision firmly in basic rights logic, adds "[t]he prohibition [against torture] is clear and unambiguous, and admits of no distinction between treatment of aliens and citizens." *Filartiga* at 884.

[28] Judge Kaufman took the first position in *Filartiga*, which was likewise reflected in decisions the First and Ninth Circuits. Judge Bork adopted the second in *Tel-Oren v. Libyan Arab Republic*, 726 F.2d 774, 811 (D.C. Cir. 1984). The Fifth Circuit adopted this more restrictive position.

[29] A common U.S. practice when ratifying human rights treaties is to declare any obligations not already reflected in U.S. law to be non-self-executing, meaning they do not apply

minor compared to the complexities to which the second approach gives rise. These involve deciding whether courts should look only to federal statutory law as it incorporates international law, to federal common law (which includes customary international law and self-executing treaties of the United States), or to how applicable foreign law comprehends the rights and obligations at issue.[30]

At stake in these seemingly arcane and highly technical debates is nothing less than the ability of U.S. courts to recognize, and to give domestic effect to, international law independent of domestic legislative action.

In 2004, the U.S. Supreme Court addressed these questions in a case entitled *Sosa v. Alvarez-Machain*.[31] The plaintiff, Humberto Alvarez-Machain, was a Mexican doctor who was kidnapped and transported to the United States to stand trial for aiding in the torture and murder of an American Drug Enforcement Agency (DEA) agent in Mexico. Alvarez-Machain was acquitted of the murder. After returning to Mexico, he filed an ATS claim against his kidnappers, who were citizens of Mexico hired by the DEA.[32] The Supreme Court agreed to decide whether Alvarez-Machain's treatment at the hands of his kidnappers and the U.S. government constituted a violation of international law within the scope of ATS jurisdiction. The Court, which had never before decided an ATS claim, began by holding unanimously that the ATS is jurisdictional statute only. The Justices disagreed, however, on what this implied about the range of claims the ATS could support.

A three-justice minority took a strict view that the ATS should be, in the absence of further legislative action, interpreted to confer jurisdiction only for international law offenses recognized as such in 1789 for which individuals could claim harm.[33] The remaining six justices adopted a

domestically until Congress passes implementing legislation (Joseph 2004). However, many treaty obligations also have customary status. This prompts questions about whether and to what degree member states continue to be bound by parallel customary rules (Shaw 2008).

[30] Joseph (2004:55), Casto (2006:641). Looking to federal common law for causes of action is viewed by some judges and other legal experts as a judicial usurpation of legislative power. See Friendly (1964) and Bradley and Goldsmith (1997), c.f. Goodman and Jinks (1997) and P. Stephens (1997). This view insists U.S. statutory law is the only proper basis for ATS claims, thereby excluding CIL and even self-executing treaties as viable sources.

[31] 542 U.S. 692.

[32] Alvarez-Machain also sued the United States and DEA officials under Federal Tort Claims Act (FTCA) – an analogous statute for tort claims against the U.S. government. These claims were also dismissed by the Supreme Court on grounds that the FTCA does not apply to extraterritorial acts.

[33] The justices are Scalia, Rehnquist, and Thomas, *Sosa* 542 U.S. 692, 739.

more flexible view that emphasized the importance of common law in late-eighteenth-century legal thought, along with the (then) ubiquitous belief that international law was an integral part of common law.[34] On this basis, the majority insisted that the door to recognizing new offenses over which the ATS might plausibly confer jurisdiction was "still ajar," though it also underscored that it should be subject to "vigilant doorkeeping." Specifically, *Sosa* directs courts to "not recognize private claims under federal common law for violations of any international law norm with less definite content and acceptance among civilized nations than the historical paradigms familiar when §1350 was enacted."[35]

The *Sosa* decision thus provides mixed support for the ability to ground U.S. court jurisdiction over extraterritorial human rights claims in the ATS. The holding affirms the existence of a private right of action for ATS claims, and it also expressly acknowledges that international law itself has not remained static. However, the holding also stops well short of certifying an expansive view of ATS jurisdiction. Instead, it charts a cautious middle path that allows federal courts some agency to recognize new bases for ATS claims, but emphasizes the constitutional-structural restraints on its use.

Incorporating new offenses

Having found a basis for U.S. federal court jurisdiction in *Filartiga*, private plaintiffs subsequently sought to test the limits of that jurisdiction by asking U.S. courts to decide a range of tort claims beyond torture and extrajudicial killing, including genocide, crimes against humanity, war crimes, forced labor and displacement, human trafficking, property offenses, environmental offenses, administrative and due process violations, international terrorism, and product liability claims. Unsurprisingly, defendants in extraterritorial ATS cases have in most instances resisted these efforts and sought to keep the range of actionable claims as narrow as possible.[36] Managing competing claims in light of the many legal ambiguities surrounding the ATS prompted judges to formulate general criteria (or "tests") for recognizing new claims, and for defining the boundaries of recognized offenses.

[34] This claim is well documented by scholars. See, for example, Dickenson (1952:27) and Henkin (1984:1559–1560). See also *The Nerride* 13 U.S. (9 Cranch) 388, 423 (1815).

[35] *Sosa* at 725.

[36] Dodge (1996). Other common defenses include strategic use of procedural rules, immunity claims, and prudential arguments (Zia-Zarifi 1999).

Even prior to *Sosa*, many ATS claims failed due to judicial determinations that the offenses alleged by plaintiffs were not sufficiently grounded in broadly recognized rules of public international law.[37] In *Filartiga*, the appellate court anchored ATS jurisdiction in near-universal rejection of state torture as a legally permissible act. In justifying its decision, the court distinguished prior failed attempts to invoke the ATS by stating that the law at issue in those claims had not attained a similar level of international consensus. In oft-quote language, the court held "only where the nations of the world have demonstrated that the wrong is of mutual, and not merely several, concern, by means of express international accords, that a wrong generally recognized becomes an international law violation within the meaning of the statute."[38]

The *Filartiga* decision is, nevertheless, ambiguous about whether universal condemnation is necessary for ATS jurisdiction, or whether a lesser degree of consensus would suffice, provided, of course, it also reflects a U.S. treaty obligation or a rule of customary international law.[39] Subsequent federal court decisions opted for the narrower standard, effectively limiting ATS jurisdiction to claims involving violations of peremptory (*jus cogens*) norms. A key step along this path was a 1987 case, *Forti v. Suarez-Mason,* brought by citizens of Argentina against an Argentine general alleging responsibility for forced disappearances carried out in the context of that country's "Dirty War." The deciding court found that ATS jurisdiction did not exist on grounds that international legal prohibitions against forced disappearance were not recognized as "universal, definable, and obligatory."[40]

This basic formula was adopted five years later to uphold ATS jurisdiction in a case against the estate of former President of the Philippines, Ferdinand Marcos. The case alleged that Marcos, as President of the Republic of Philippines, had caused the torture, extrajudicial killing, or

[37] Early examples include *Pauling v. McElroy* 164 F.Supp. 390 (D.D.C. 1958) (no international law to enjoin nuclear weapons tests); *Lopes v. Reederei Richard Schroder*, 225 F. Supp. 292 (E.D.Pa.1963) (unseaworthiness doctrine not part of international law); *IIT v. Vencap, Ltd.*, 519 F.2d 1001 (2d Cir. 1975) (expressing doubt that fraud, conversion, and corporate waste are violations of international law); *Akbar v. New York Magazine Co.*, 490 F.Supp. 60 (D.D.C. 1980) (finding libel is not a violation of international law).

[38] *Filartiga*, 630 F.2d 876, 888 (C.A. 2, 1980). This language in *Filartiga* is quoted from a prior suit, *IIT v. Vencap* 519 F.2d 1001, 1015 (2d Cir. 1975), that tried, and failed, to invoke the ATS in a securities claim.

[39] Dodge (2001).

[40] *Forti v. Suarez-Mason*, 672 F.Supp. 1531–1539 (N.D. Cal. 1987). Dodge (2001) traces the origins of this formula to a 1981 law review article by Jeffrey Blum and Ralph Steinhardt.

disappearance of roughly 10,000 individuals between 1971 and 1982, during a period of martial law. In the course of finding that jurisdiction existed under the ATS for these claims, judges in Ninth Circuit Court of Appeals reworked the test slightly to require that international law be "specific, universal, and obligatory."[41] This version of the test was adopted verbatim in *Sosa* ten years later and has been recited in several dozen cases since.[42]

Overall, the range of offenses for which U.S. federal courts have held that a cause of action exists under the "specific, universal, and obligatory" test has been fairly uniform, and largely restricted to grave violations associated with political repression.[43] However, there have been disagreements at the margins. For example, ATS claims involving prohibitions against cruel, unusual, and degrading treatment have been dismissed by some U.S. federal courts on grounds that the alleged offense lacks requisite specificity, but allowed by others.[44] A similar discrepancy emerged in ATS claims arising out of incidents of international terrorism, which courts in some circuits dismissed on grounds that terrorism is not specifically defined, or universally condemned.[45]

Questions about the definitional boundaries of offenses under ATS jurisdiction raise similar issues, since ATS claims at times involve attempts at legal concept stretching.[46] Definitional boundaries figured heavily in the result in *Sosa v. Alvarez-Machain*, discussed above, where the primary claims involved allegations of torture and arbitrary detention tied to kidnapping. Here the Supreme Court held "a single illegal detention of less than a day, followed by the transfer of custody to lawful authorities and a prompt arraignment, violates no norm of customary international law so well defined as to support the creation of a federal

[41] *In re Estate of Ferdinand Marcos Litigation* 978 F.2d 493, 499 (1992), *cert.* denied 508 U.S. (1993).

[42] *Sosa v. Alvarez-Machain* 692, 732.

[43] See *Flores v. Southern Peru Copper Corp.* (2d Cir. 2003) (holding that negative health effects from foreign mining operations are not actionable under the ATS absent a clear "right to health" in international law).

[44] Goodman and Jinks (1997:506–508).

[45] Davis (2008:247). Contrast, for example, *Tel-Oren v. Libyan Arab Republic*, 726 F.2d 774 (D.C. Cir., 1984) and *Mwani v. Bin Laden*, 417 F.3d 1 (D.C. Cir., 2006) with *Almog v. Arab Bank, PLC*, 471 F.Supp.2d 257 (S.D.N.Y. 2007) and *Oveissi v. Islamic Republic of Iran*, 768 F.Supp.2d 1 (D.C. Cir., 2007).

[46] Sartori (1970). See Goodman and Jinks (1997:508), Joseph (2004:31). See also *Beanal v. Freeport-McMoran*, 197 F.3d 161 (1999) (holding that allegations of "cultural genocide" did not fall within international law definitions of genocide).

remedy."[47] As a result of this determination, Alvarez-Machain's ATS suit was dismissed.

One last category of offense in ATS jurisprudence that has generated an important stream of legal and political controversy has been the attempt to import aiding and abetting liability into ATS claims against private actors.[48] Here the idea is that a defendant need not directly carry out a human rights violation in order to share legal responsibility if it took some purposeful action directed at causing others to carry out the violation. Aiding abetting is thus a generic offense that ATS plaintiffs have tried to add on to a range of primary offenses – even when direct perpetrators are shielded from liability by sovereign immunity or otherwise not amenable to suit in U.S. courts. Because aiding and abetting liability is closely tied to efforts to bring private corporations within the reach of ATS jurisdiction, I discuss its use in specific ATS cases in that context below.

Expanding the range of ATS defendants

Efforts to expand the pool of potential ATS defendants have been equally important to the influence of U.S. judicial extraterritoriality in the human rights realm. As in other legal issue areas, deciding who, or what, may be forced to defend legal claims in U.S. courts involves both a prescriptive and a due process element. The prescriptive element asks whether the law at issue obligates a *general category* of actor of which the defendant is a member, and whether any exceptions exist in the form of status-based immunities. In ATS suits this typically involves deciding which actors may be liable for which violations of international human rights law. The second element concerns whether *specific defendants* within these categories have sufficient forum connections to satisfy U.S. due process requirements for personal jurisdiction. Such questions are tricky only where foreign defendants outside U.S. territory are concerned, since being a national of the United States, or an individual of any nationality present inside the United States, automatically satisfies this jurisdictional requirement. U.S. courts likewise have automatic jurisdiction over any claims against the U.S. government.

In the *Filartiga* case, for example, Peña-Irala, the foreign former Paraguayan police official, was served with process while he was visiting

[47] *Sosa v. Alvarez-Machain* 692, 738.

[48] Keitner (2008). "Vicarious" and "accomplice" liability are synonyms for the liability that attaches to aiding and abetting.

the United States. From this beginning, ATS plaintiffs have used presence inside U.S. territory to try to establish the existence of ATS-based personal jurisdiction over foreign private individuals, military commanders, and foreign officials, as well as over U.S. government officials, and, importantly, private corporations.

A landmark case in efforts to expand allowable categories of ATS defendants was a 1993 suit against Radovan Karadzic, the Bosnian Serb leader of the (mainly) internationally unrecognized Republika Srpska.[49] The plaintiffs in *Kadic v. Karadzic* – Muslims, Croats, and other minorities who resided in Bosnia Herzegovina in the early 1990s – alleged that Karadzic engaged in "genocide, war crimes, and crimes against humanity in his private capacity" and that he was responsible for additional international human rights violations as commander of the Bosnian Serb military.[50] A U.S. district court dismissed the claims for lack of jurisdiction on grounds that international law provides no redress for the acts of private individuals. A Second Circuit court of appeal reversed, stating "We do not agree that the law of nations, as understood in the modern era, confines its reach to state action. Instead, we hold that certain forms of conduct violate the law of nations *whether undertaken by those acting under the auspices of a state or only as private individuals*" (emphasis added).[51] A jury ultimately awarded the plaintiff class US$745 million in damages.[52]

ATS suits against foreign states and sitting high officials have been far less successful. A key reason is that suits against these types of defendants generally trigger well-established immunities that preclude domestic courts in the United States and elsewhere from exercising jurisdiction. There are, however, occasional exceptions to immunity rules, and these have been tested under the ATS. In U.S. law, the 1976 Foreign Sovereign Immunities Act (FSIA) enumerates exceptions to the immunity of states.

49 70 F.3d 232 (2d Cir. 1995). See Gibney and Emerick (1996).

50 *Kadic v. Karadzic* at 236. Karadzic was also served with process while on a trip to the United States.

51 *Kadic v. Karadzic* at 241. The court concluded further that genocide, war crimes, and crimes against humanity fall within this class and that private entities can be liable for other human rights offenses if they undertake the requisite acts under the color of law (i.e. with actual or apparent legal authority) – a concept borrowed from U.S. civil rights law (Paust 1992). The decision also reaffirmed the Nuremberg principle of command liability, which holds that those in positions of authority who fail to take appropriate measures to prevent the commission of atrocities are in violation of international law, *Kadic* at 242.

52 Plaintiffs in a companion case, *Doe v. Karadzic* 192 F.R.D. 133 (S.D.N.Y. 2000), were awarded $4.5 billion in damages.

Only one of these exceptions – a provision that allows jurisdiction over state sponsors of terrorism – has had any practical relevance in ATS claims.[53] In general, sitting heads of state and ambassadors also have traditionally enjoyed full legal immunity in domestic courts – though this norm has been challenged recently by activities at the International Criminal Court (ICC).[54] U.S. federal courts have toed the traditional line on this issue,[55] but they have been more open to ATS suits against former heads of state, as demonstrated by the Marcos case discussed above.

Other foreign officials operate under lesser packages of diplomatic and consular immunities, often limited to acts taken in an official capacity. This is an interesting area, since governments generally try to shield their officials from litigation in foreign courts, but likewise seek to avoid acknowledging abusive behavior as official policy. U.S. courts have demonstrated a willingness to engage in this kind of line drawing in the context of ATS suits. For example, an ATS suit against Liu Qi, Mayor of Beijing and President of the Beijing Organizing Committee of the 2008 Olympic Games, alleged responsibility for torture, arbitrary detention, and extrajudicial killing of Falun Gong practitioners by members of the Beijing police. The suit survived an immunity challenge on grounds that such activities were clearly outside the scope of official mayoral duties.[56]

The United States and U.S. officials are also in most instances shielded from suit by private citizens in U.S. courts under domestic sovereign immunity rules.[57] This protection continues indefinitely for acts undertaken in an official capacity.[58] ATS suits have tested the resilience of these immunities for alleged human rights violations, but without success. Some U.S. federal courts have even interpreted these immunities as extending to private entities, such as military contractors, where acts

53 This exception was not originally included in the FSIA, but was added in 1996.

54 The ICC Prosecutor has, as of May 2015, issued arrest warrants for four sitting heads of state: Omar al-Bashir of Sudan (2009), Uhuru Kenyatta of Kenya (2011), Muammar Gadaffi of Libya (2011), and Laurent Gbagbo of Cote d'Ivoire (2011).

55 *Tachiona v. Mugabe* 169 F.Supp.2d 259 (S.D.N.Y. 2001).

56 *Doe v. Liu Qi*, 349 F.Supp.2d 1258 (2004). Although the judge ultimately issued a default judgment against Qi, in a nod to political pragmatism, it encompassed only *declaratory* (not compensatory) relief.

57 Exceptions are sometimes allowed to cover the negligence or malfeasance of U.S. government employees under the 1946 Federal Tort Claims Act, currently 28 U.S.C. §1346(b).

58 For example, in *Sosa v. Alvarez-Machain* 542 U.S. 692, FTCA claims against the DEA were dismissed on grounds that no exceptions to U.S. sovereign immunity exists for acts undertaken outside the United States.

that form the focus of ATS claims were undertaken pursuant to U.S. security policy.[59]

These limitations against suing governments and sitting high officials notwithstanding, *Kadic* proved to be an important stepping-stone in extending ATS liability to another category of private entities: private corporations.[60] Corporate liability for human rights abuses is a thinly developed area of international law.[61] Many countries recognize corporate liability for human rights-related violations domestically,[62] but this liability generally has not extended extraterritorially. Corporate liability for human rights violations is also not formally codified in any international treaty. Consequently, most governments have been content to treat the extraterritorial human rights abuses of even their own enterprises as an acceptable (if unfortunate) externality of pursuing economic opportunities in repressive countries.

This hands-off approach to extraterritorial regulation was, however, tested in U.S. federal courts in more than 70 lawsuits with an ATS component. The first such suit concerned a class of Ecuadoran plaintiffs who in 1993 filed suit against the U.S. oil company Texaco (since 2001, ChevronTexaco) under the ATS and other U.S. statutes alleging harm from the company's extraction and pipeline operations in Ecuador from 1964 to 1990.[63] Although the main complaint in *Aguinda v. Texaco, Inc.* was conditionally dismissed from the U.S. federal courts in 2002 following a judicial determination that Ecuador had a greater interest in litigating the claims, the fact that the case was not dismissed for lack of jurisdiction at the outset pointed the way forward for other suits targeting corporations accused of directly engaging in international human rights violations.[64]

59 See, for example, *Al Shimari v. CACI Intern.*, Inc., 658 F.3d 413 (4th Cir., 2011).

60 Joseph (2004), Kaeb (2008). Note, Holocaust-era claims against foreign banks, railroads, and companies for the recovery of seized assets, or for forced labor fall under this category.

61 Paust (2002), Joseph (2004), Kinley and Tadaki (2004), Bernard (2010).

62 Australian law includes civil and criminal liability for corporations and corporate officers for severe human rights abuses, including "overseas." No civil claim brought under the *Trade Practices Act* (1974) has reached the jurisdiction phase of legal proceedings, however (Nicolson and Howie 2007:32). France and Belgium recognize limited extraterritorial criminal responsibility for corporations in the human rights realm, including indictment and prosecution of corporate officers (Kaeb 2008:328 fn5).

63 *Aguinda v. Texaco, Inc.*, No. 93 Civ 7527 (S.D.N.Y. November 3, 1993).

64 303 F.3d 470 (2d Cir 2002). Aspects of this suit are still pending in Ecuadoran and U.S. courts. The conditional aspect of the 2002 dismissal was that ChevronTexaco had to submit to the jurisdiction of courts in Ecuador. The company agreed and was eventually

Efforts to cast a still wider net for corporate ATS defendants in human rights claims prompted plaintiffs to reach for the concepts of indirect ("aiding and abetting") liability. In an ATS case filed in 1996, villagers in Myanmar (Burma) sued two international oil and gas companies, and a state-owed oil company that contracted with Myanmar's military junta to provide "security protection and rights of way and easements as may be requested" during construction of a gas pipeline in Myanmar's territory.[65] The villagers charged that the military units engaged in forced displacements, forced labor, torture, rape, and extrajudicial killings and other offenses in violation of international law. The claims against Myanmar Oil and Gas Enterprise were quickly dismissed on sovereign immunity grounds. The claims against Total S.A. of France were dismissed due to lack of personal jurisdiction, leaving Unocal as the lone defendant.[66]

It took nearly five years to litigate whether ATS jurisdiction existed over the claims against Unocal. A core issue of contestation was whether indirect liability could be considered a permissible cause of action. Unocal, a private corporation, did not directly carry out the alleged abuses. Nor was there any evidence that it specifically ordered their commission. Even so, the plaintiffs provided evidence that Unocal knew of the abuses, that it paid the Myanmar government for its actions, and that it derived commercial benefit from abuses carried out on its behalf.[67] A District Court granted Unocal's motion to dismiss in 2000 on grounds that international law lacks any basis for asserting liability on the basis of aid and abetting.[68] In 2002, a Ninth Circuit Court of Appeals reversed that decision citing international case law from the Nuremberg and Tokyo tribunals, along with more recent holdings by the International

slapped with a multi-billion-dollar judgment, which it is, at the time of writing, seeking to ensure remains unenforced in the United States and other countries where ChevronTexaco has assets.

65 Velazquez (2005). A federal district court in California agreed to hear the case in 1997, thus signaling the preliminary jurisdictional and substantive plausibility of the plaintiffs' ATS claims, *Doe v. Unocal* 963 F.Supp. 880 (C.D. Cal 1998).

66 The court found MOGE was a foreign government instrumentality, and therefore immune from U.S. jurisdiction, and that its conduct did not fall within any exception in the 1976 Foreign Sovereign Immunities Act. Note, the claims against Total S.A. were later pursued in both French and Belgian criminal courts (Kaeb 2008:328).

67 *Doe v. Unocal Corp.* 963 F.Supp. 880 (agreeing to hear the claim); and *Doe v. Unocal Corp* 248 F.3d 915 (9th Cir. 2001) (granting summary judgment to defendants). The 2001 dismissal of federal ATS claims shifted the litigation to state court, where the plaintiffs' allegations received sympathetic treatment under California state law.

68 110 F. Supp. 2d 1294, 1310 (C.D. Cal. 2000).

Criminal Tribunal for Yugoslavia, that incorporated theories of indirect liability.[69] With the jurisdictional question now decided against it, Unocal opted to settle the claim rather than risk a negative judgment on the merits.

Thereafter, private plaintiffs initiated several dozen ATS claims in U.S. federal courts alleging corporate complicity in human rights violations in settings as diverse as Colombia, Nigeria, Sudan, Indonesia, and Papua New Guinea. The companies targeted by this new wave of ATS litigation were mainly large multinationals. Several suits involved the labor practices of highly image-sensitive U.S.-based companies such as Coca-Cola, Levi-Strauss, and the Gap. A non-trivial number involved companies in the oil, gas, and mineral extraction sectors, which generally feature capital-intensive investments and limited mobility of operations. As with *Unocal*, many of these suits involved allegations of indirect liability for the abusive acts of foreign governments related to the provision of security services for commercial operations.[70] At this point, establishing the scope of aiding and abetting liability, and the degree of knowledge and intent required to trigger that liability under international law became critical issues of focus in corporate ATS litigation.

In 2009, a Second Circuit Court of Appeals tackled the knowledge and intent questions directly in *Presbyterian Church of Sudan v. Talisman Energy Inc.* This ATS case accused a Canadian oil and gas exploration company of complicity in acts of torture, genocide, war crimes, and crimes against humanity in Sudan against non-Muslim Sudanese in areas around the company's operations. The *Talisman* decision found that mere knowledge on the part of the company that assistance rendered to a foreign government might be used to carry out human right violations was insufficient to create indirect liability under international law. The court held, instead, that for aiding and abetting liability to stick, plaintiffs had to demonstrate corporations provided "substantial assistance" to a government with the purpose of aiding the government's unlawful conduct.[71] The *Talisman* decision thus clipped the wings of other similar ATS suits pending against corporations. However, a still larger threat to extraterritorial human rights claims in U.S. courts was

[69] *Doe I v. Unocal Corp.* 395 F.3d 932 (C.A.9, 2002); Joseph (2004:48–49).
[70] Watts (2005), Ballentine (2007).
[71] *Presbyterian Church of Sudan v. Talisman Energy, Inc.*, 582, F.3d 244.

already taking form in yet another aiding and abetting case against other foreign oil and gas companies.[72]

The plaintiffs in *Kiobel v. Royal Dutch Petroleum Co.* were members of the Ogoni ethnic group who alleged that between 1992 and 1995, Royal Dutch Petroleum and two subsidiary companies had actively encouraged the Nigerian government to use force in violation of international human rights laws to suppress protesters of the companies' operations in the Niger Delta.[73] In 2006, a Second Circuit District Court allowed ATS claims alleging torture, arbitrary detention, and crimes against humanity to proceed. In September 2010, the same appellate panel that issued the *Talisman* decision dismissed all claims against the defendants on grounds that international human rights law contains no clear rules creating corporate liability.[74] The *Kiobel* plaintiffs appealed the dismissal, and in October 2011, the Supreme Court agreed to hear the case to decide the question of whether international law recognizes a specific, universal, and obligatory norm of international human rights liability for corporations as required for suits under the Alien Tort Statute.[75]

Initial oral arguments took place in the Supreme Court on February 28, 2012. A few days later, however, the Court ordered the case to be rebriefed and reargued in the following term to include the question of whether and under what conditions 28 U.S.C. §1350 allows U.S. courts to recognize causes of action involving extraterritorial conduct.[76] Hanging in balance at this point was not only the issue of corporate liability under international law but also the broader viability of the ATS as a legal tool to reach extraterritorial violations of basic rights.

[72] The suit was filed in 2002 with *Wiwa v. Royal Dutch Petroleum Co.*, 226 F.3d 88 (2d Cir. 2002), which settled in 2009.

[73] The Court also dismissed ATS claims for destruction of property, forced exile, extrajudicial killing, and violation of rights to life, liberty, security, and association on grounds that the facts, as alleged, did not qualify as international law offenses, *Kiobel v. Royal Dutch Petroleum Co.*, 456 F.Supp.2d 457 (S.D.N.Y. 2006).

[74] *Kiobel v. Royal Dutch Petroleum Co.*, 621 F.3d 111 (2d Cir, 2010). Judge Leval filed an opinion concurring only in the judgment. Keitner (2012) notes that both *Talisman* and *Kiobel* were argued on the same day, on January 12, 2009.

[75] *Kiobel v. Royal Dutch Petroleum Co.*, 132 S.Ct. 472. It also agreed to decide whether ascribing tort liability under the ATS is an issue of jurisdiction, or of applying law to facts (i.e. the "merits"). See Transcript of Oral Argument No 10–1491, February 28, 2012, pp. 38–41. www.supremecourt.gov/oral_arguments/argument_transcripts/10–1491.pdf.

[76] The Court provided no justification for this decision. However, extraterritoriality questions (which were not briefed) came up frequently in the oral argument. A contemporaneous petition for *certiorari* in another ATS case raising similar issues, *Rio Tinto PLC et al. v. Sarei et al.* (No. 11–649), may also have been a factor (Keitner 2012).

The Supreme Court's 2013 decision in *Kiobel* largely gutted the ability of foreign human rights victims to use the ATS to bring extraterritorial claims against foreign corporations. The court decided unanimously that the ATS could not reach the claim against Royal Dutch Petroleum regarding its activities in the Niger Delta. A five-justice majority held that nothing in the text or the history of the ATS affirmatively suggests that Congress intended the statute to apply to conduct occurring in the territory of foreign sovereigns. The majority opinion anchored its reasoning in a judicially constructed presumption against the extraterritorial application of U.S. law. Even these five justices, however, differed on the strength of the presumption as it applies to the ATS.[77]

The remaining four justices, although concurring in the dismissal, rejected the majority's reasoning and, specifically, the use of the presumption against extraterritoriality. They argued, instead, that the ATS should be understood to apply to situations where a tort in violation of international law occurs on U.S. territory, where defendants are U.S. nationals, or where a tort "substantially and adversely affects an important American national interest." The opinion then goes on to define the third category as encompassing "a distinct interest in preventing the United States from becoming a safe harbor (free of civil as well as criminal liability) for a torturer or other common enemy of mankind."[78] These last two elements jointly echo the basic rights logic discussed above.

In Chapter 7, I return to the *Kiobel* decision to situate it within broader efforts to curtail U.S. judicial extraterritoriality in privately initiated claims across a range of issue areas. For the moment, however, it will suffice to note that the move to target corporations in ATS litigation beginning in the mid-1990s ultimately forced a direct contest between the regulatory logic of extraterritorial jurisdiction discussed in the prior two chapters, and the basic rights logic. Whereas the regulatory logic would favor eliminating extraterritorial jurisdiction except where the integrity of legal prohibitions operative inside U.S. territory is at stake, the basic rights logic would favor exercising jurisdiction over alleged violations of a short list of basic rights at the core of American civil and political

[77] Chief Justice Roberts wrote the majority opinion, joined by Justices Scalia, Alito, Thomas, and Kennedy. Alito and Thomas submitted a short concurring opinion stating domestic conduct meeting the *Sosa* standard for violations should be required for the ATS to apply. Justice Kennedy's concurrence underscored that the Court was leaving open "a number of significant questions" about the reach of the ATS.

[78] *Kiobel* slip op. p.7.

identity by entities with close U.S. ties. In this contest, at least, the regulatory logic prevailed.

Agency and opportunity structures

For any of the legal rules discussed above to matter in practical terms, private actors must have incentives to seek their observance and enforcement, and judges must have incentives (or lack disincentives) to allow claims based on those rules to proceed.[79] The second element of the analytic framework, thus, concerns the origins and limits of judicial and litigant agency. After first discussing each separately, I then consider how the preferences I ascribe to each may be influenced by expectations about the other's behavior, and how these strategic interactions influence the opportunity structures under examination.

Judges

Referring back to the discussion of judicial behavior in Chapter 2, my operative assumptions are that U.S. federal judges generally seek to carry out their tasks in accordance with acknowledged professional rules and norms and that they resolve cases and controversies under U.S. law with an eye to respect for the separation of powers as required by the U.S. Constitution. It follows that U.S. courts have few (if any) structural, political, or professional incentives to be at the vanguard of efforts to radically expand categories of actionable human rights violations beyond conduct that is broadly condemned domestically, and in international law. That U.S. judges respond pragmatically to these incentives is demonstrated by more than three decades of congressional acquiescence in court decisions under the Alien Tort Statute.

Since the contemporary resurrection of the ATS in the 1980s, the U.S. Congress has acted only to expand the scope of §1350 with the 1991 Torture Victim Protection Act (TVPA).[80] The TVPA allows private individuals (American or foreign) to bring civil claims against foreign officials for acts of torture and extrajudicial killing undertaken with foreign state authority.[81] Some domestic critics of transnational human rights

79 Putnam (2009).

80 Dodge (1996:224). In 1991, Congress amended §1350 to include the Torture Victim Protection Act, which allows U.S. citizens to sue in U.S. federal courts for acts of torture and extrajudicial killing, Pub.L. 102–256, H.R. 2092, 106 Stat. 73.

81 Since its enactment, the TVPA has been used primarily to support the tort claims of victims of international terrorism.

claims under the ATS have attempted to paint the TVPA's enactment as a limiting move, since it specifically enumerates only two offenses.[82] The majority view, however, which is well supported by the legislative record, is that the TVPA constitutes congressional endorsement of *Filartiga*, and with it the judiciary's cautious approach to identifying causes of action in international law under the ATS.[83]

To date, only one bill has been formally proposed in either chamber of Congress with the aim of checking use of the ATS in transnational human rights litigation. In 2005, Senator Diane Feinstein of California proposed a bill, dubbed the Alien Tort Statute Reform Act, to "clarify the jurisdiction" of U.S. federal courts.[84] The bill sought to replace the reference to the law of nations in the ATS with a list of enumerated offenses that excluded several causes of action that U.S. courts had held could support ATS jurisdiction, such as war crimes, crimes against and humanity, forced labor, and cruel, inhuman, and degrading treatment.[85] It likewise proposed to eliminate jurisdiction in situations where "a foreign state is responsible for committing the tort in question within its sovereign territory" and to limit ATS liability to "direct participants" in alleged torts acting with "specific intent" to violate human rights. It also would have required ATS plaintiffs to exhaust local remedies before suing in U.S. courts, while also setting a ten-year statute of limitations on ATS claims. It even sought to prohibit ATS plaintiffs from using protective pseudonyms. Finally, the bill would have given the President authority to withdraw ATS jurisdiction whenever necessary to safeguard U.S. foreign policy interests. The bill was warmly greeted by corporations and industry organizations,[86] but received immediate, sharp criticism from human rights and labor groups. One week

[82] Bradley and Goldsmith (1997).

[83] Goodman and Jinks (1997:514–516). In their respective Reports, both the House and the Senate underscore that torture and extrajudicial killing do not exhaust the possible claims under §1350, H.Rep. No. 102–367(I), (1991) at 86, S.Rep. No. 102–249 (1991) at 3, cf. Goodman and Jinks (1997:519, n.280). This opinion is also reflected in the statement of George H.W. Bush upon signing the TVPA into law on March 12, 1992, www.presidency.ucsb.edu/ws/index.php?pid=20715.

[84] www.govtrack.us/congress/bills/109/s1874.

[85] ERI (2005).

[86] Chevron, which is headquartered in Feinstein's Senate district, has been a significant election campaign contributor, and was a strong corporate supporter of the bill. Chevron has also been a defendant in two large extraterritorial ATS claims, *Bowoto v. Chevron*, and *Aguinda v. Texaco* (after Chevron purchased Texaco Inc. in 2000).

after introducing the bill, and prior to any Judiciary Committee hearing, Feinstein withdrew it.[87]

U.S. federal court judges likewise avoided any major friction with the executive branch over ATS claims for roughly two decades. Prior to 2003, executive branch officials and agencies occasionally intervened in pending ATS litigation, either as *amicus curiae* or to issue statements of interest – sometimes in opposition to exercising jurisdiction, and sometimes in support of it. Federal court judges also frequently, though not uniformly, responded deferentially to these interventions.[88] This pattern shifted dramatically during the presidency of George W. Bush. Although the rate of executive intervention in this period was no greater than in prior administrations, the absolute number of interventions was much higher, due to an increase in the number of ATS cases being filed. More notably, these interventions favored defendants' positions exclusively, and, for the first time, encompassed collateral attacks on the ATS and its extraterritorial application.[89]

Also during this period, extraterritorial ATS suits began to draw larger numbers of foreign government and corporate *amicus curiae* interveners. As discussed in Chapter 2, domestic courts are generally insulated from direct foreign government actions. However, discontent from these quarters does at times register with judges and can increase the likelihood of U.S. executive intervention. ATS suits against former political and military officials (including former heads of state) from countries that have undergone regime change have not been challenged either by the defendant's state of nationality or by third states. This is far different in suits against current officials and sitting heads of state, where the international law of immunities dominates. In these situations the U.S. State Department generally intervenes to support immunity claims, thereby

[87] Carter (2006:648, n.76), www.earthrights.org/campaigns/senator-feinstein-puts-brakes-anti-atca-bill-s-1874.

[88] At the request of the appellate court in *Filartiga*, the Carter administration, for example, submitted a brief strongly supporting recognition of IHR violations under the ATS (Stephens *et al.* 2008:9).

[89] Consistent with the results reported in Chapter 2, Davis (2008:153) finds that federal courts generally, including under the George W. Bush administration, deferred to executive preferences over the exercise of ATS jurisdiction where specific and immediate foreign affairs concerns were expressed. Where executive opposition to ATS claims was couched in general or speculative terms, however, federal judges accorded it far less weight. Davis attributes the Bush administration's approach to a broader strategy of maximizing executive power, coupled with an "ideological distaste for international law" (2008:128–137).

obviating the need for foreign governments to involve themselves directly in domestic court affairs.[90] The ATS suits that have prompted the greatest volume of foreign protest by far are those against multinational corporations.

In sum, the record suggests that U.S. judges have exercised their interpretative agency in extending U.S. jurisdiction to extraterritorial ATS claims comfortably within what Congress has been prepared to allow. The same can be said of judicial interactions with the Executive branch up until the George W. Bush administration. I examine this further below in the context of discussing the impacts of ATS litigation, and, specifically, how prospective defendants in these claims have responded strategically to heightened threats of legal liability.

Private litigants

Under what conditions might we expect plaintiffs to choose to sue in U.S. courts to seek redress for extraterritorial human rights abuses? As with judges, I assume that private plaintiffs in human rights claims are rational, and that they attempt to maximize private utility by weighing the expected benefits and costs of their actions against the strength of their preferences. As in other areas, this involves (in theory at least) individual assessments of the tradeoffs involved in choosing whether to pursue human rights grievances at all, and if so whether in the United States versus elsewhere. It also involves choices about the type of tactics to adopt. In short, whether or not victims choose to initiate litigation in U.S. federal courts concerns perceptions about the opportunity structures associated with different possible courses of action.[91]

The United States has been largely unique in allowing private individuals to initiate extraterritorial civil suits alleging human rights abuses.[92] As noted in other chapters, the U.S. legal system has several procedural features that make it attractive to private plaintiffs, including

[90] See, for example, *Tachiona v. Mugabe*, 169 F.Supp.2d 259 (S.D.N.Y. 2001) (dismissing ATS claims against President of Zimbabwe, Robert Mugabe), and *Ye v. Zemin* 383 F.3d 620 (7th Cir. 2004) (invalidating efforts to serve Chinese President Jiang Zemin with process in the United States).

[91] Hilson (2002).

[92] Joseph observes that while other common law countries allow civil claims for transitory torts in theory, in practice this mechanism remains "largely untested" (2004:122). See also Ward (2000). Some countries allow private parties to petition for *criminal* proceedings for universal jurisdiction offenses, but very few allow them to proceed without a state prosecutor, or equivalent. Langer (2011).

foreigners.[93] In addition to liberal rules for filing, discovery (the means by which litigants gather evidence for trial), and service of process, the U.S. system also recognizes class action suits, which permit large numbers of factually similar individual claims against the same defendant(s) to be aggregated into a single legal proceeding, including for ATS claims. The U.S. court system is internationally (in)famous for granting successful plaintiffs very high awards, due to copious use of punitive damages on top of compensatory damages. And, it generally does not require unsuccessful litigants to pay their opponents' legal fees, as is standard in many countries.[94]

Judicial extraterritoriality is part of a broader international human rights ecosystem encompassing many actors and approaches. In addition to states and individuals, relevant actors include, notably, international governmental organizations (IGOs) like the United Nations and its affiliated bodies, and non-governmental organizations (NGOs). Whereas IGOs have traditionally focused on the development and diffusion of international legal standards, they have begun to take on a more assertive role in monitoring, oversight, and, in rare cases, even in coordinating enforcement. NGOs support IGO activities indirectly (and sometimes also directly) through local and transnational rights education and capacity building, by documenting and publicizing violations, and by drafting legislative proposals and lobbying for their adoption within states. Some NGOs, on their own or with the support of *pro bono* sections of private law firms, also help individual victims of human rights violations to bring legal claims in domestic courts.[95]

Alleged victims of international human rights violations who lack legal or political options to pursue claims in the countries where their abuses occurred have been the main seekers of ATS litigation.[96] The material and emotional costs of litigating human rights claims against foreign governments and officials mean that only plaintiffs with an especially strong desire for justice, or retribution, are likely to choose this path. Indeed, in contrast to standard tort litigants, successful ATS plaintiffs often have little expectation of receiving monetary compensation.

93 Born (1996).

94 Merryman and Perez-Perdomo (2007).

95 Davis (2008:85–88).

96 These plaintiffs were also more likely to have their cases heard, as opposed to being dismissed on *forum non conveniens* grounds (Joseph 2004).

U.S.-based NGOs and law firms specializing in transnational human rights cases have been heavily involved in ATS litigation from *Filartiga* forward.[97] They are an example of what Galanter refers to as "repeat players" in litigation.[98] Consequently, their objectives may diverge at times from those of victim-plaintiffs. Whereas most NGOs and sponsoring firms in transnational human rights claims genuinely seek to help individual plaintiffs obtain redress, they are often simultaneously attempting to broaden the scope of U.S. jurisdiction or to facilitate elaboration of substantive law.[99] NGOs with a litigation focus, thus, may have incentives to bring comparatively risky suits, rather than focusing on maximizing victim recovery in safer claims.

Governments and corporate defendants in ATS cases likewise have had strong incentives to shape the transnational legal environment according to their interests and preferences, albeit in ways that are largely inimical to those of ATS plaintiffs. Corporations, especially, face non-trivial public relations costs and liability risks from contesting human rights litigation in which they are not certain to prevail. At the same time, gaining a reputation as an easy mark for predatory litigation by settling non-meritorious claims can itself be a substantial source of costs to private corporations, particularly those that frequently operate in countries with poor human rights records.[100] As in other legal issue areas, therefore, actual and potential defendants in transnational human rights litigation in U.S. courts have strong incentives to be close watchers of developments in U.S. law and to take steps to minimize their own liability in light of any changes.

ATS claims against corporations often attempt to equate corporate and natural "persons" when interpreting applicable international law. This has proven controversial internationally. Adding to the controversy is the fact that U.S. rules for establishing personal jurisdiction over foreign companies also have been quite permissive compared to those of many countries. For example, up until quite recently if a foreign corporation were sued under the ATS for human rights violations outside the United States, and that corporation had a U.S. subsidiary (or listed its shares on U.S. stock exchanges, or had financial or investment assets in the United States), this often would be enough to allow U.S. federal courts

[97] Davis (2008:84–85).
[98] Galanter (1974:97).
[99] Stephens (2002:37).
[100] Galanter (1974:99), Zia-Zarifi (1999), Joseph (2004:17).

to claim jurisdiction over the corporate parent, and perhaps even over other non-U.S. subsidiaries.[101]

As a result, ATS suits against foreign corporations have prompted a steady stream of *amicus curiae* briefs from transnational corporations and industry groups, such as the International Chamber of Commerce, urging U.S. federal courts to disallow these claims. Foreign governments have also occasionally intervened as *amici curiae* in ATS cases, arguing that extraterritorial regulation of foreign corporations is contrary to international legal norms of sovereignty.[102]

U.S. enforcement capacity

For much of the post-World War II era, no other state has had legal enforcement capacity as far-reaching as the United States. In Chapter 2, I describe extraterritorial enforcement capacity as deriving from the relative density of ties a state has with the universe of actors (both citizens and non-citizens) in a regulated issue area. A high density of such ties allows a state to obtain compliance with its regulatory preferences by exercising direct leverage over persons and assets inside its territory and by threatening to exclude non-complying entities from future transactions within its reach.[103]

Conservatively, U.S. federal courts have awarded upwards of US$7 billion in fully litigated ATS claims against foreign officials or their estates. Nevertheless, only a small fraction of this total has been recovered.[104] Most of these awards are default judgments – meaning the defendant was not present for, and did not formally contest, the court proceedings.[105] Often these defendants lack substantial U.S. assets. Although a few have had resources in banks and real property outside the United States, these assets

[101] But see *Daimler AG v. Bauman* No. 11-965, 134 S.Ct 746 (2014) discussed below.

[102] For example, the governments of South Africa, Canada, Germany, Switzerland, and the United Kingdom, along with the U.S. government, submitted briefs in an ATS claim alleging corporate complicity in sustaining the South African Apartheid regime arguing that the U.S. litigation exceeded permissible limits for the exercise of jurisdiction. See *In re South African Apartheid Litigation*, 617 F.Supp.2d 228 (S.D.N.Y. 2004).

[103] Putnam (2009:482).

[104] Amley (1998), Joseph (2004).

[105] Obtaining personal jurisdiction over individual defendants is often the main reason why entry into U.S. territory is crucial, since where such a non-U.S. national is formally served with notice of legal proceedings while inside U.S. territory, a substantial connection is presumed.

are generally beyond the reach of U.S. courts.[106] Calculated in this way, then, the unfortunate, but unavoidable, conclusion is that U.S. enforcement power is relatively weak for these types of claims.

At the same time, individuals with outstanding U.S. court judgments against them are effectively precluded from traveling to, or residing in, the United States, or any other country willing to recognize and enforce the U.S. judgment. For former victims of human rights abuses, this may provide at least some satisfaction – particularly since for former officials and collaborators of ousted regimes that engaged in human rights abuses against political opponents, or that carried out campaigns of indiscriminate violence and intimidation, life at home may be difficult. Among the individuals successfully targeted in this way under the ATS are a former Salvadoran Vice-Minister of Defense,[107] an assassin of Archbishop of El Salvador Oscar Romero,[108] and the former leader of a notorious Haitian death squad.[109]

The extraordinary enforcement capacity of the United States is far more evident in extraterritorial human rights claims against corporations. Having activities and assets in U.S. territory is often key to establishing personal jurisdiction over foreign corporate defendants. Beyond their use as a jurisdictional hook, U.S. assets also provide a basis for satisfying favorable judgments handed down by U.S. courts. Consequently, many of the same incentives that operate in the context of commercial and regulatory suits also have a direct role in this set of cases – for example, the economic costs and benefits of pursuing litigation, shareholder pressure, concerns over corporate reputation, and the like. As a direct result of this incentive structure, an important secondary mechanism for plaintiff recovery has emerged from ATS suits: proceeds from case settlements.[110] In most instances, when a corporation has faced the tangible threat of a successful ATS claim, it has opted to settle. To date all settled ATS cases but one have been against

[106] Amley (1998).

[107] *Chavez v. Carranza*, 413 F.Supp. 2d 891 (W.D. Tenn. 2005). The case involved command responsibility for crimes against humanity, torture, and extrajudicial killings, and resulted in a US$6 million award for the plaintiffs.

[108] *Doe v. Saravia*, 348 F.Supp. 2d 1112 (E.D. Cal. 2004).

[109] *Doe v. Constant*, 354 Fed. Appx. 543 (2009). In a default judgment, the court awarded plaintiffs US$19 million in damages for torture, crimes against humanity, and systematic rape and violence against women.

[110] The total amount recovered by plaintiffs in these settlements is unknown and difficult to estimate, since plaintiffs are often required as a condition of settlement not to reveal the amount or terms of the agreement reached.

corporations.[111] In addition, no U.S. federal court has yet handed down a decision against a corporate defendant, although two cases have been decided on their merits in favor of corporate defendants.[112] Under these conditions, U.S. enforcement power operates indirectly, but at the same time quite effectively.

*

Before moving to the data, a few observations are in order concerning interactive effects among the three parts of the analytic framework as applied to transnational human rights litigation. First, the task of identifying and interpreting legal rules is absolutely central to any court-based project of rights enforcement. Without disputes to resolve, courts in the United States cannot act – extraterritorially or otherwise. In the ATS context, this has required private victims of alleged human rights abuses, or their close relatives, to emerge with the intent of seeking legal redress, despite, in many instances, low expectations of monetary recovery.

At the same time, whatever agency private plaintiffs have had in choosing to bring human rights claims has been shaped to a non-trivial degree by opportunity structures and constraints created through judicial actions. Many examples were highlighted in which U.S. federal courts decisions expanded the scope of U.S. extraterritorial jurisdiction. Nevertheless, it is likewise important to understand that the recent and dramatic curtailment of the ability to bring extraterritorial ATS claims using the presumption against extraterritoriality was also the work of U.S. judges and determined corporate litigants.

Assessing patterns of ATS practice

In this section, I analyze the full universe of 222 ATS cases brought between 1970 and 2011 with the aid of professional legal counsel. Excluded from consideration are 68 ATS cases initiated by plaintiffs acting on their own behalf (*pro se*). Although occasionally meritorious, these cases often have obvious (and fatal) pleading defects along

[111] The exception is *Elmaghraby, et al. v. Ashcroft, et al.*, 04 Civ. 1809 (JG) (SMG), a case by an Egyptian plaintiff against the U.S. government for abusive treatment while in U.S. custody following the September 11, 2001, terrorist attacks. See www.clearinghouse.net/chDocs/public/IM-NY-0025-0001.pdf. The United States settled the claim for $300,000 (Davis 2008:97).

[112] *Romero v. Drummond Co*, 552 F.3d 1303 (11th Cir. 2008), and *Bowoto v. Chevron*, 621 F.3d 1116 (9th Cir. 2010).

dimensions of theoretical interest here.[113] More than half were initiated by individuals incarcerated in U.S. prisons at the time of filing, and most of these are against U.S government officials for acts undertaken wholly inside U.S. territory. Among the cases with extraterritorial aspects, several are frivolous on their face. Consequently, their inclusion in the data would inflate estimates of dismissal rates for well-pleaded claims, while adding nothing to the ability to track changes in the outer limits of what U.S. jurisdictional rules permit at any point in time.

In each of the figures that follow, the variable of interest is whether a U.S. federal court exercises jurisdiction over an extraterritorial ATS claim. A decision not to exercise jurisdiction can be based on several factors. The most basic is a determination that the court lacks jurisdiction due to an absence of applicable law. Federal courts sometimes also dismiss claims at the pre-trial phase for immunity, factual or procedural pleading flaws, for lack of personal jurisdiction over defendants, as well as for so-called prudential reasons, such as international comity or *forum non conveniens*. These will be discussed in more detailed in relation to Figure 6.5.

Note that several cases in this data contain legal claims other than those originating under 28 U.S.C. §1350. For example, an ATS case alleging extrajudicial killing might also include a conspiracy claim under the 1970 Racketeer Influenced and Corrupt Organizations statute, or a claim under the 2001 Anti-Terrorism Act. The statistics presented below track the fate of the ATS and TVPA aspects of the included cases only. Consequently, some cases coded here as dismissals with respect to §1350 claims continued to be litigated on other non-ATS and non-human rights grounds. Likewise, a few cases that are coded as positive exercises of jurisdiction involve §1350 dismissals with respect to specific plaintiffs.[114]

Figure 6.1 illustrates the annual count of new ATS claims filed in U.S. federal courts, together with the number for which a court decided to

[113] These claims rarely go beyond the pre-screening stage, and most would not be in the searchable record at all, but for the heightened standard of deference U.S. courts are obliged to give the claims of *pro se* litigants.

[114] For example, in *Saperstein v. Palestinian Authority*, 2008 WL 4467535, plaintiffs attempted to persuade a federal court to consider Federal Terrorism Act claims of U.S. citizens who perished with several foreign individuals in a terrorist attack in Israel together in a single case in which the foreign plaintiffs relied on the ATS. An 11th Circuit court severed the claims. See *Estate of Amergi ex rel. Amergi v. Palestinian Authority*, 611 F.3d 1350, 1353 (11th Cir. 2010).

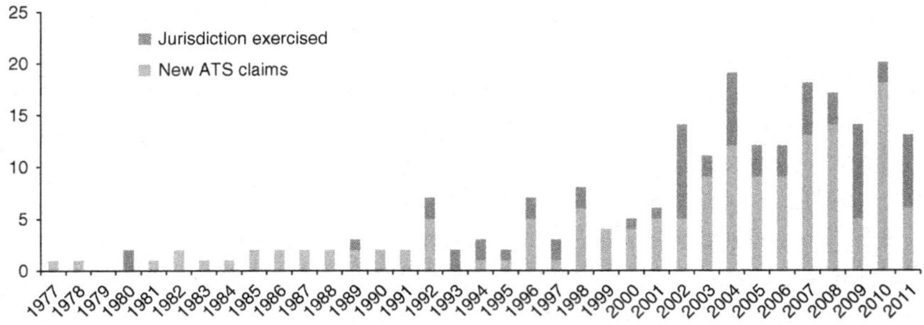

Figure 6.1 Alien Tort Statute claims by decision to exercise jurisdiction ($N = 222$)

exercise jurisdiction.[115] The figure shows that although *Filartiga* was a path-breaking case, it hardly triggered an immediate rush of ATS claims. Part of this is undoubtedly due to the unexpectedness of the *Filartiga* outcome itself, coupled with the fact that preparing transnational law suits often requires substantial effort even before filing. Because no international human rights NGOs specialized in these cases at the time, new ATS claims initially had to get in line behind existing NGO and *pro bono* firm projects.

A slight increase in the number of ATS claims is evident after the 1995 *Kadic* decision. This was fueled in part by private efforts to use the ATS for claims arising out of World War II-related atrocities.[116] It is also reflective of an overall rise in transnational litigation activities around human rights in international courts. The enactment of the TVPA in 1992 also served as a strong signal to plaintiffs' lawyers that this was stable ground for bringing suit.[117] By contrast, there is a noticeable increase in new extraterritorial ATS claims filed after the 2002 *Unocal* decision. However, not all of the latter increase is due to suits against corporations. Several post-2001 claims filed were against the U.S. government and U.S. government officials over actions taken against foreign detainees in the war on terror.

The overall trajectory of cases reflects the described judicial boundary-stretching enabled by experimentation on the part of plaintiffs. The post-2001 increase in the number (though not the rate) of claims clearing the

[115] Note, of the two ATS claims brought in 1980, only one, *Filartiga v. Pena-Irala,* involved extraterritorial conduct. The other, *Letelier v. Republic of Chile,* concerned the assassination of a Chilean dissident in Washington D.C. in 1976.

[116] Bilsky (2012).

[117] My thanks to Jacob Kopas for bringing this point to my attention.

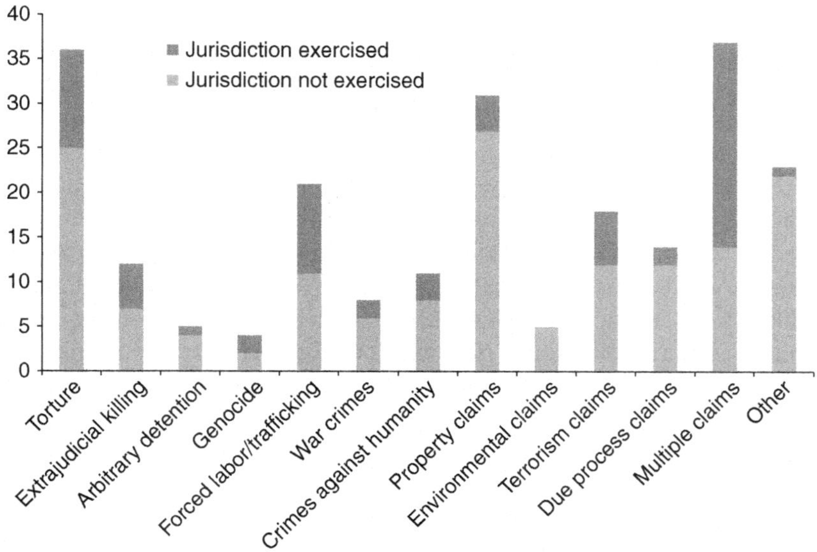

Figure 6.2 ATS claims 1980–2011 by core offense alleged ($N = 222$)

jurisdictional hurdle suggests ATS plaintiffs (or more accurately the NGOs and activist lawyers advising them) became more adept at formulating actionable claims. In addition, as U.S. federal courts opted to exercise jurisdiction in more claims, the notion of judicial extraterritoriality to enforce basic rights also became less exotic to plaintiffs and to federal judges. Fully 75 percent of the ATS suits that reached the litigation phase prior to 2011 occurred in just four judicial circuits; the Second Circuit alone accounts for 30 percent.[118]

These aggregate totals, although informative of broad patterns of litigation, nevertheless conceal a great deal of information key to understanding the evolving parameters of specific rules and practices. Below I therefore consider several additional aspects of the descriptive data in detail. Figure 6.2 shows the total number of ATS claims broken down according to the main violation at issue. Most of these categories have been discussed above, although a few have not. Among them are due process claims, which encompass issues of treatment while in U.S. or foreign government custody, or concerning denial of a desired U.S.

[118] Other circuits that have been active on ATS claims are the Ninth, Eleventh, and D.C. Circuits. These are areas of the country with both high non-U.S. born populations, and with high concentrations of multinational corporations.

immigration status.[119] I also include a column for cases involving "Multiple Claims," and a residual "Other" category.[120]

Several observations can be made from this figure. First, environmental claims, property claims, and due process claims very rarely result in U.S. courts exercising jurisdiction extraterritorially. The same is true of the "Other" category. A shared characteristic of these claims is that no authoritative source of international law currently considers them *jus cogens* offenses. By contrast, claims with the highest rates of jurisdictional acceptance fall almost exclusively within a narrow class of offenses codified in international treaties with broad memberships. These include torture, extrajudicial killing, genocide, and crimes against humanity. Interestingly, forced labor, which has a more marginal status as *jus cogens*, also has a comparatively high rate of success.[121]

Importantly, rates of jurisdictional success for claims concerning arbitrary detention, war crimes, crimes against humanity, and genocide may appear artificially low in this figure, since these offenses are often pled together with other human rights claims. The multiple claims category, which is the only bar to show a better-than-50-percent success rate, thus absorbs some of the persuasiveness (for jurisdictional purposes), of ATS pleadings on these grounds. At the same time, the high rate of success for cases encompassing multiple claims may be due in part to the fact that courts need only decide to exercise jurisdiction over one for the case to be coded positively.[122]

Figure 6.3 shows areas of geographic and thematic concentration among ATS cases. According to this figure, Latin America and the Caribbean far outstrip other geographic locations as sources of ATS claims. Significantly, the rate of U.S. federal courts exercising jurisdiction

119 Included in this category are claims related to alleged violations of the 1963 Vienna Convention on Consular Relations (VCCR) arising from the failure of local officials to notify alien arrestees of their right to consular services provided in Article 36 of the treaty. Most of these cases have been dismissed on grounds that the VCCR does not confer a private right of action, but see *Jogi v. Voges*, 480 F.3d 822 (7th Cir. 2007).

120 The residual category contains transnational child custody cases, free speech and libel claims, health care-related claims, and product liability claims.

121 Cleveland (1998:1569–1570). But see *Iwanowa v. Ford Motor Co.*, 67 F.Supp.2d 424, 440 n.18 (D.N.J.) (holding forced labor is actionable under the ATS, even if not a *jus cogens* offense).

122 Though this is far from an ideal category, the alternative of disaggregating the case data by claim is also not ideal, since it implicitly assigns equal weight to all parts of a set of claims, rather than permitting them to be considered in context. Practically speaking, in a realm where engaging in just a bit of very bad behavior is often insufficient to trigger enforcement, whether and how violations cluster can be important.

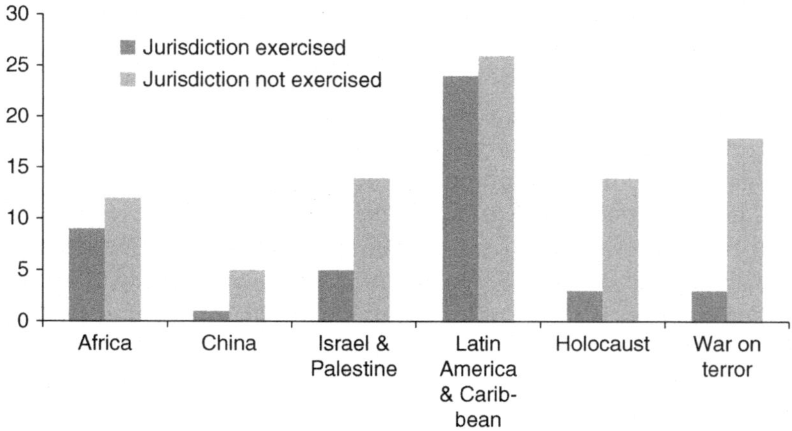

Figure 6.3 ATS claims by geographic and thematic focus ($N = 222$)

in these claims is also quite high, reaching almost 50 percent. While the large number of claims from this region is almost certainly tied to high intra-regional rates of immigration, the stronger than average rate of success in clearing jurisdictional hurdles could be a function of several factors.

First, it may be easier to gather witnesses and evidence for ATS claims arising in geographically proximate countries, and those with large communities of immigrants residing in the United States. Second, lawyers and judges may be more willing to take on claims for which there is some cultural familiarity. Third, the fact that there has been a high incidence of military dictatorships and civil conflicts in this region (though not necessarily higher than in other areas of the world with large numbers of developing states) undoubtedly also matters for these numbers. The fact that Africa appears to be close behind Latin America and the Caribbean Basin in the rate of jurisdictional success for ATS claims with a nexus in that region implies that the latter explanation is more persuasive.

The political situation in Israel and Palestine has likewise resulted in several ATS complaints, albeit with only moderate levels of jurisdictional success. Most of these claims involve either terrorist attacks in Israel or issues tied to the Israeli occupation of Palestine.[123] A sticking point in

[123] The Anti-Terrorism Act (ATA) of 2002 provides another statutory basis for seeking tort recovery from harms sustained in terrorist attacks. However, only U.S. citizens have standing to bring claims under the ATA.

claims arising from terrorist attacks concerns the difficulty of classifying Palestine and the Palestinian Authority within state action paradigms. Figure 6.3 also indicates that China has been a geographic source of ATS claims. Many of these cases were filed against Chinese officials by, or on behalf of, dissidents and asylum seekers. With few exceptions, these claims have failed due to immunity protections.

On the thematic front, Figure 6.3 includes bars for both Holocaust-related ATS claims (which have a geographic nexus with Europe) and claims arising out of the U.S. war on terror. This latter group of claims has three main sites of geographic focus: the Middle East, South-Central Asia, and the U.S. military base at Guantánamo Bay, Cuba. The jurisdictional success rate for Holocaust-related ATS claims is quite low for two reasons. First, many of these cases are centered on efforts to recover property (e.g. bank assets, fine art) seized by the Nazi regime and collaborating governments. As indicated in Figure 6.2, property offenses, in general, have a low rate of jurisdictional success. Second, several ATS claims against German corporate defendants were superseded by an agreement between the United States and Germany signed in 2000, which established a Foundation for the exclusive management of compensation for victims and survivors of the Holocaust.[124] ATS claims tied to the U.S. war on terror likewise have a low rate of success. The reason is that many of these claims target the U.S. government or U.S. officials as defendants, and U.S. officials are effectively immune from civil suit in U.S. courts, particularly when it comes to the conduct of foreign policy and national security.[125]

Figure 6.4 breaks down the data by defendant type. The categories are: foreign governments and officials (including heads of state), the U.S. government and U.S. officials, and corporations (including banks). The "Other" category includes primarily terrorist groups and their members, and also private citizens alleged to have engaged in trafficking of persons and forced labor. The figure shows that U.S. courts have been most likely to find and exercise jurisdiction in ATS suits against foreign officials or governments.[126] Even in this category, however, more claims have failed than have succeeded. It also confirms that ATS claims against the U.S. government and its officials have an extremely low rate of jurisdictional

[124] The settlement fund granted to the Foundation totals approximately $5 billion.

[125] Federal Tort Claims Act, 28 U.S.C. §1346(b).

[126] U.S. courts may exercise jurisdiction over a foreign government on where the case concerns one of the enumerated exceptions to the 1976 Foreign Sovereign Immunities Act (FSIA), 28 U.S.C. §1330.

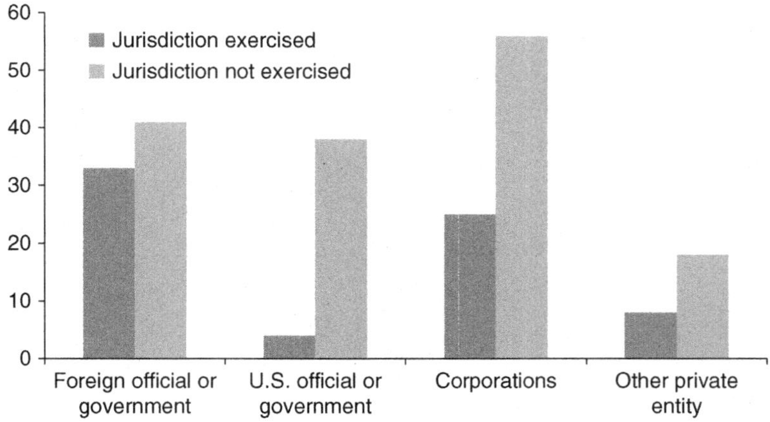

Figure 6.4 ATS claims by defendant type (N = 222)

success, for reasons noted. Next along the spectrum are cases against corporations. The low apparent rate of jurisdictional success here is due in part to high failure rates for Holocaust-related cases, and experimental failures in the pre- and early post-1980 era of ATS claims – that is, before non-state actor liability was established, and aiding and abetting theories were introduced in U.S. jurisprudence.

Bases of U.S. court dismissals of ATS claims are the focus of Figure 6.5. Because this figure includes data on ATS dismissals only, the N is 153 cases. The information is organized hierarchically for dismissals involving more than one basis. Failure to state a claim under international law is given first priority,[127] followed by the failure to plead facts sufficient to support a recognized cause of action, immunity, other pleading flaws,[128] lack of personal jurisdiction, and, finally, prudential dismissals.[129] The

127 For coding purposes I collapse dismissals based on Rule 12(b)(1) (lack of subject matter jurisdiction) and Rule 12(b)(6) (failure to state a claim) of the Federal Rules of Civil Procedure where absence of an international law violation as cognizable by U.S. courts is the basis. Rule 12(b)(1) motions to dismiss for lack of subject matter jurisdiction based on immunities are in a separate category. Rule 12(b)(6) dismissals based on factual pleadings insufficient to support a cause of action are likewise tracked separately.

128 In the ATS context, these "other flaws" may include, for example, not having alien status, not pleading a claim in tort, or the absence of a private right of action.

129 Prudential grounds for dismissing transnational claims include international comity, judicial determinations that a dispute primarily involves political questions, or that the claim would be more appropriately heard in another country (*forum non conveniens*) (Zia-Zarifi 1999, Stephens *et al.* 2008, Whytock and Robertson 2011). See also *Restatement (Third) of Foreign Relations Law of the United States* §403.

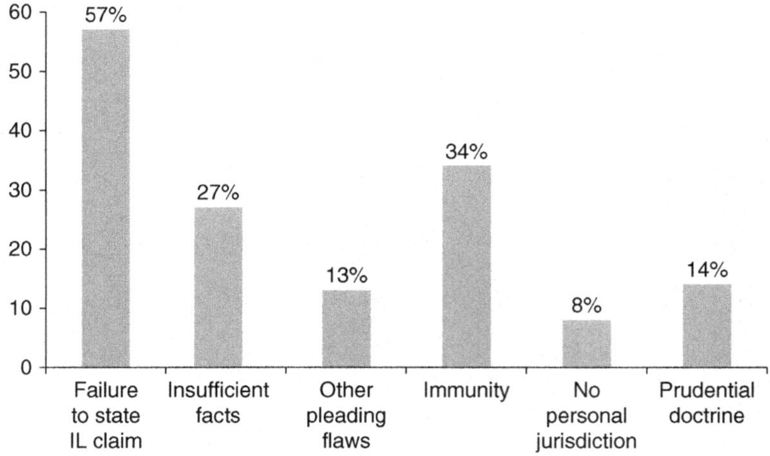

Figure 6.5 Bases of U.S. federal court dismissals for ATS cases ($N = 153$).

figure indicates that more than half of ATS dismissals involve a failure to state a claim under international law. This reflects a preference among federal judges to decide jurisdictional questions on clear-cut grounds where possible. It may also reflect the type of plaintiff experimentation with the scope of ATS jurisdiction discussed above, or incompetent lawyering.

Another frequent basis of dismissal in ATS claims is immunity. Once again, this type of dismissal is very common in ATS claims against the U.S. government and its officials, as well as against foreign states, and sitting foreign officials. The fact that roughly a fifth of ATS cases have foundered on this basis suggests strong plaintiff incentives to probe the relationship between classic principles of immunity under international law and emergent human rights principles that some contend are equally categorical, coupled with a measure of judicial openness to weighing these issues.

Figure 6.6 offers insight into the comparative influence of U.S. and foreign government preferences on U.S. court willingness to find and exercise jurisdiction in extraterritorial human rights claims. The data show, first, that government involvement in ATS claims is relatively high. In 48 percent of these cases, a government had either a structural interest in the outcome (meaning it or its officials were defendants) or an expressed preference over the outcome revealed using an *amicus curiae* ("friend of the court") intervention or statement of interest in the case

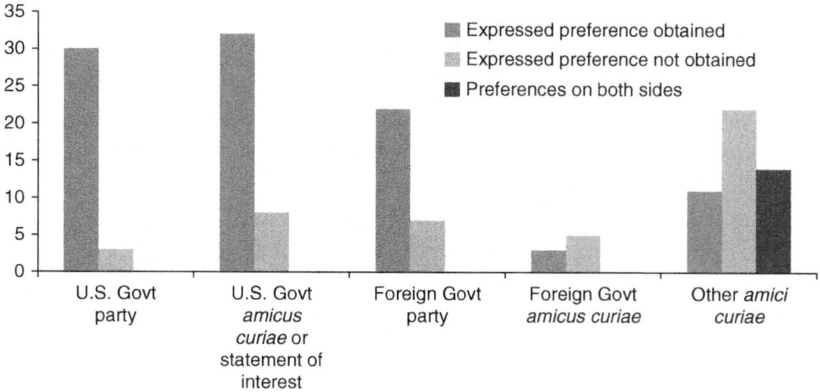

Figure 6.6 Expressed U.S. and foreign government preferences and outcomes

(U.S. government only).[130] Second, it shows that U.S. courts often make decisions on jurisdictional matters in line with what other branches of government prefer, whether those preferences are structural or expressed. Third, Figure 6.6 also shows the difficulty of obtaining U.S. court jurisdiction over U.S. and foreign governments and sitting officials in ATS claims where immunity rules are operative, as evidenced by the high success rates for structural determined preferences for the U.S. government and for foreign governments.

On a cautionary note, the fact that a case's outcome on jurisdiction accords with a structural or revealed preference of an intervening party is not definitive evidence that the preference was causally determinative. The possibility remains that outcomes are over-determined in at least some cases. In addition, in 13 cases the U.S. government intervened to support ATS claims in situations where a foreign government was either a defendant (and, therefore, structurally opposed to U.S. jurisdiction) or had intervened to oppose it. In two cases, the U.S. government intervened to take a position opposing that of a foreign government intervener.[131] Even so, the high correlation between U.S. government preferences and case outcomes far outstrips any other relationship indicated in the data, thus suggesting at least some judicial willingness to defer to the executive

[130] In no case has the U.S. government or a foreign government been a plaintiff in an ATS claim.

[131] These cases are: *Aguinda v. Texaco, Inc.*, 303 F.3d 470 (2d Cir., 2002), and *Kiobel v. Royal Dutch Petroleum Co.*, 642 F.3d 268 (2d. Cir., 2011).

branch on issues relating to foreign affairs even when basic rights are at issue.

These data show further that when foreign governments intervene as *amici curiae*, they are more likely than not to end up on the losing side of jurisdictional battles. This, combined with the very small number of cases in which foreign governments have intervened, suggests a shared understanding that the preferences of foreign governments carry little weight in U.S. domestic courts. For purposes of comparison, Figure 6.6 also includes data on the outcomes that followed non-governmental *amicus curiae* interventions by scholars, NGOs, corporations, and industry organizations. Although these interventions have been more frequent, their rates of success are comparably low.

These descriptive cuts are consistent with the incentives ascribed to judges and plaintiffs in the analytic framework. The data indicate that plaintiffs have sought to import a broad range of substantive claims into ATS jurisdiction and also that many of these attempts have failed. Likewise, ATS plaintiffs have sought to impose liability on a wide range of defendants. At the same time, this exercise offers no support to arguments that U.S. federal judges act recklessly in applying U.S. prohibitions against the violation of basic rights extraterritorially.[132] To the contrary, U.S. federal courts have been quite conservative when deciding to exercise jurisdiction in extraterritorial human rights claims. They have allowed only a narrow range of universally recognized offenses along with limiting rules and prudential doctrines to avoid direct clashes with the executive branch and foreign governments.

The data likewise indicate that the geographic coverage of extraterritorial ATS liability has been considerable, but focused primarily in areas of the world with a history of civil conflict and repressive governments. And finally, the willingness of plaintiff-sponsoring organizations to undertake claims calculated to push legal boundaries and the strong incentives for corporate actors to settle meritorious cases together have generated a lower overall rate of observable success in ATS claims than for other types of litigation.

Responses and impacts

For more than two decades ATS litigation in U.S. federal courts placed the United States at the vanguard of international human rights

[132] See, for example, Hufbauer and Mitrokostas (2003).

enforcement. Unfortunately, this says as much about the paucity of other options for pursuing these types of claims outside the United States as it does about the assertiveness – or the effectiveness – of U.S. judicial actions. That many victims of foreign human rights abuses were able to receive some official acknowledgment of the wrongfulness of their experiences is important. Beyond this, however, it is difficult to say with any certainty whether, or by how much, the threat of U.S. civil liability has deterred any human rights abuses that otherwise would have happened.

In an ideal world, establishing laws against egregious violations of human rights would be linked straightforwardly to decisions on the part of prospective abusers to avoid violations. The world of politics and law is, of course, far from ideal, or straightforward. Indeed, many factors intervene to thwart the ability of ATS liability (or, indeed, that of any law) to deter prospective rights abusers. Incomplete information, principal–agent problems, non-trivial amounts of reactive behavior on the part of dictators, military juntas, the leaders of rebel groups, and others with short time-horizons all confound the operation of legal deterrence, even among purportedly rational actors.

To be clear, the point here is emphatically *not* that complexity absolves rights abusers of legal or moral responsibility for the offenses they commit. It is, instead, to underscore the difficulty of deterring such behavior using the shadow of *ex post* legal liability. Others have pointed out that repressive governments often view the expected benefits of engaging in, or allowing, abusive behavior – such as staying in power – as outweighing the costs. This is particularly so when punishments for committing human rights violations are highly uncertain to materialize, or they are likely to be less costly (from the perspective of perpetrators) than what is expected to happen if no violations are committed.[133]

Questions about deterrence aside, the theory elaborated in Chapter 3 expects victims of foreign human rights violations who are seeking legal or political remedies to find litigation in U.S. courts attractive so long as it is easier to access, and provides a higher likelihood of prevailing, than other available options. For victims of human rights abuses and their advocates, pursuing legal action in the countries where alleged abuses occurred may be impossible, or likely to pose additional risks to them or their families. Mobilizing government-to-government efforts to address

[133] Snyder and Vinjamuri (2003), Ku and Nzelibe (2006).

abusive practices is also difficult, and may do little to address wrongs perpetrated against specific victims.

If one thing is clear, however, it is that transnational corporations that have been in the crosshairs of ATS suits, and others worried (whether justifiably or not) about this possibility have been far from indifferent to the threat of U.S. liability.

First, transnational corporations, unlike individuals, are present in multiple jurisdictions simultaneously. A clear marker of U.S. judicial involvement in the human rights-related extraterritoriality, as in other issue areas, has been the willingness of U.S. courts to assert personal jurisdiction over non-U.S. entities on the basis of substantial U.S. contacts. Up until quite recently, U.S. jurisprudence underlying assertions of general jurisdiction over foreign-based corporations was fairly permissive, allowing U.S. federal courts in some instances to assert general jurisdiction over entire corporations on the basis of the U.S. contacts of only one part of the corporation. Thus, having a U.S. subsidiary, a large U.S. customer base, or extensive financial and banking ties with U.S.-based institutions could, in some instances, expose a foreign corporate parent and its non-U.S. foreign subsidiaries to U.S. jurisdiction. This set of practices provides corporations with transnational operations strong incentives to try to avoid being called to task in U.S. courts for conduct alleged to violate international human rights laws.

Second, corporations over which U.S. courts may assert personal jurisdiction generally have substantial U.S. resources that can be seized to satisfy adverse legal judgments. It follows that ATS suits brought against corporations cannot be ignored, or left uncontested, as has frequently occurred in ATS claims against foreign individuals. Third, and relatedly, corporations plausibly within the jurisdictional reach of U.S. courts generally have U.S. market and financial ties that can be damaged by a court judgment labeling them as direct human rights violators, or aiders and abettors of foreign governments' violations.

Efforts to change opportunity structures

A key pathway by which corporations have sought to avoid liability for foreign human rights violations has been to attempt to alter the opportunity structures for plaintiffs to pursue such claims in U.S. courts and (for foreign corporations) those of their home countries. Specifically, they have sought to narrow, or eliminate, enabling domestic laws and procedures, and to expand due process limitations on the exercise of personal jurisdiction. In essence, therefore, this involves the inverse of the strategies pursued by victims and NGOs.

Changes in domestic law can be sought legislatively, or through judicial means. Where achieving desired changes is possible legislatively, this is often preferable, since legislative action directly guides a great deal of executive and judicial branch activity. However, it is also generally very difficult to accomplish, since mobilizing Congress to alter the *status quo* often requires a great deal of coordinated lobbying from expected beneficiaries, as well as efforts to neutralize, or marginalize, opponents. Seeking changes in legal rules through litigation is also far from simple. The costs and risks associated with litigating at the federal level are non-trivial, and victories – if they occur – may bring only incremental change. Litigation, however, generally requires far less in the way of outside coordination, although where large legal or financial stakes are involved, seeking third-party input is also increasingly an element of litigation strategy.

As described above, there are notable differences in how, and how vigorously, individuals, governments, and corporations have sought to defend themselves in ATS cases. Individuals who are sitting officials at the time of suit and foreign government defendants staunchly (and often successfully) insist on the priority of immunities to derail ATS claims. By contrast, many former officials have opted not even to formally contest ATS claims against them. The most common strategy to limit personal liability among this class of defendants is to flee the United States after being served with process, since in most instances this eliminates the enforcement power (though not the formal legal sanctioning power) of U.S. courts. By contrast, corporations have adopted both legislative and litigation-based approaches, often in parallel.

Litigation-based strategies

As discussed at length in Chapter 2, a number of factors influence the selection of claims for litigation. In the U.S. legal system, plaintiffs have primary discretion over which cases are ultimately pursued. In the civil realm, defendants have two choices. They can preempt claims through settlement, or respond with a vigorous defense. Corporations often have an interest is not appearing to be too quick to settle human rights cases, since this could be interpreted as an admission of fault. In addition, it could lead to a reputation as an easy mark, thereby encouraging additional suits from NGOs focused on rule development or from plaintiffs' law firms aiming to secure a cut on resulting settlements. Because defendants in litigated cases cannot choose their battles to nearly the same degree as plaintiffs, this limits their ability to use judicial mechanisms to shape legal rules.[134] Even so, they can attempt defenses that are calculated to have maximally far-reaching implications for the underlying law, or to insulate particular groups from future lawsuits.

Corporations targeted in extraterritorial ATS claims have defended against ATS suits using a range of strategies and tactics. These include challenging jurisdictional thresholds, plaintiff standing, statutes of limitations, and inconvenience of forum, along with collateral attacks on the ATS and the entire concept of private corporate liability under international law. Corporate defendants in ATS cases have encouraged the U.S. government and foreign governments to intercede in litigation in support of their positions. For example, Unocal, Exxon-Mobil, Talisman, Occidental, and Rio Tinto all repeatedly lobbied the State Department concerning ATS suits against them.[135] Large corporations defending ATS cases have also mobilized industry advocates and non-party multinational corporations to intervene as *amici curiae* on the public policy elements of ATS claims. As noted, the George W. Bush administration was particularly receptive to such pleas, intervening on behalf of corporations on ten different occasions in seven ATS cases.[136]

References in judicial opinions, supplemented by linked documents in Westlaw, likewise reveal a pattern of foreign government intervention in ATS cases.[137] In cases against individuals, foreign governments intervened on only five occasions. By contrast, as of May 2012, foreign governments had made fourteen interventions in six different ATS cases against corporations. Two interventions (by Liberia and Ecuador) favored a U.S. exercise of jurisdiction, and twelve opposed it. Third-party interveners (NGOs, legal scholars, historians, industry groups, other corporations) also have been active on both sides of ATS cases. Nearly 22 percent of the ATS cases in this period had non-governmental *amicus* interveners, with most (38 of 49) in cases filed in 2000 or later. Among

[134] In rare situations, prospective defendants can seek declaratory judgments, (although this tactic has not been used in the ATS context).

[135] Davis (2008:142–144).

[136] Key Bush administration staff openly supported robust executive legal privilege in foreign and security affairs (Henner 2009:8), a few of whom (Jack Goldsmith, Paul Clement, and John Yoo) were outspoken critics of the ATS as applied to human rights, or of judicial extraterritoriality more broadly. Under the Obama administration, the executive stance toward ATS litigation returned to pre-Bush patterns.

[137] Note, I count only primary interventions. Judicial references to foreign government interventions in other ATS and non-ATS cases are not included.

industry groups supporting corporate defendants in ATS claims, the U.S. Chamber of Commerce has been especially active, as have the National Foreign Trade Council, USA*Engage, the National Petroleum Institute, the Washington Legal Foundation, and the Business Roundtable. International and foreign industry groups, such as the International Chamber of Commerce, the Federation of German Industries, and the Confederation of Swedish Enterprise, also occasionally intervene. Third-party interventions by individual corporations have been less common, but the *Kiobel* case alone, for example, prompted several dozen to intervene as named *amici*.[138]

Lobbying-based strategies

Industry organizations and individual corporations also actively lobby members of Congress to build support for corporate positions concerning prospective legislation.[139] The U.S. Chamber of Commerce, which has been the largest lobbying client in the United States every year since 2001, has been especially active in these efforts.[140] Davis found, for example, that in the two-year period between 2003 and 2005, the U.S. Chamber of Commerce lobbied numerous executive bodies, including the State Department, the Justice Department, the National Security Council, and the U.S. Trade Representative on ATS-related matters.[141] A handful of industry organizations, including USA*Engage, and free-enterprise-focused NGOs, such as the Washington Legal Foundation, have also actively campaigned to eliminate corporate liability under the ATS.[142] The only direct evidence to date that these corporate and industry-level efforts have had an effect is the aborted Alien Tort Reform Act proposed by Senator Feinstein in 2005. It has not been an entirely one-sided game, however, since human rights NGOs, immigrant and labor organizations, and related groups likewise lobby members of Congress

138 They include corporate giants such as Caterpillar, ConocoPhillips, General Electric, Dow Chemical, Ford Motor, GlaxoSmithKline, Procter & Gamble, KBR, Inc., and Coca-Cola.

139 Collingsworth (2002). See, for example, Eric Lipton, Mike McIntire, and Don Van Natta, Jr., "Top Corporations Aid U.S. Chamber of Commerce Campaign," *New York Times*, October 10, 2010, www.nytimes.com/2010/10/22/us/politics/ 22chamber.html?pagewanted=all.

140 Center for Responsive Politics, www.opensecrets.org/lobby/top.php?indexType=s.

141 Davis (2008:143–144).

142 See http://usaengage.org/Issues/Litigation/Alien-Tort-Statute-/ and www.wlf.org/search_bing.asp?execsearch=Bing&offsetPage=1&searchText=%22alien+tort%22.

on pro-ATS grounds. The available resources on the corporate side are obviously far greater.

Nor have corporate efforts to stack the deck in ATS litigation been limited to the United States. Chesterman observes that Australian mining conglomerate BNP tried to eliminate potential liability for its activities in Papua New Guinea by prompting its legislature to pass a law making the filing of such a suit a criminal offense. BNP's actions subsequently became a subject of contempt proceedings in Australia.[143] In another example, advocates on the plaintiff side in *Aguinda v. Texaco* succeeded in persuading members of the Ecuadoran parliament to pass a law to formally close Ecuador's courts to lawsuits initiated outside Ecuador in order to preempt a *forum non conveniens* dismissal.[144] In 2002, however, Ecuador's Supreme Court proclaimed Interpretative Law 55 unconstitutional.

Limiting jurisdiction through corporate segmentation

Multinational corporations also may seek to limit U.S. court jurisdiction (and ultimately liability) through legal structuration and segmentation to make foreign corporate parents and affiliates more difficult to reach under U.S. law. Most large MNCs are complexes of geographic and sector-based subsidiaries, holding companies, and other entities that are wholly or partially owned by a parent corporation. Non-U.S. corporations may take steps to avoid the jurisdictional reach of U.S. law and U.S. courts by minimizing the contacts of core corporate components with U.S. forums and creating specialized local affiliates for various purposes. This can allow for access to U.S. markets, investment capital, and banking services, but stop short of giving U.S. courts general jurisdiction over the corporate parent.

For this reason, contesting personal jurisdiction has often been a first line of defense on the part of non-U.S. corporate defendants in extraterritorial ATS claims. Where the U.S. contacts of a foreign company (including foreign subsidiaries of U.S. parent corporations) implicated in extraterritorial human rights abuses are insufficient to support general

143 Chesterman (2004:323).

144 Interpretative Law 55 was hurriedly enacted in late 1998 after Texaco formally consented to jurisdiction in Ecuador. The "interpretative" character of the law concerned its status under Ecuador's Civil Procedure Code, thus allowing it to be applied retroactively to the *Aguinda* case, www.internationallawoffice.com/newsletters/detail.aspx?g=dcf7e15e-f706-407a-aea0-0b3810468427.

jurisdiction, plaintiffs must ground personal jurisdiction in acts specific to the suit, which has proven difficult in suits involving wholly extraterritorial claims. For example, in the *Unocal* case, the Ninth Circuit determined it had no jurisdiction over the French oil company Total S.A. – a result that one expert described as "a triumph of corporate formality over reality" in light of Total's (then) four-decade-long history of business activities in the United States.[145] By contrast, in *Kiobel*, the Second Circuit asserted jurisdiction over Royal Dutch Shell, a company headquartered in the Netherlands and Great Britain, through an Investor Relations Office in New York City tied to the company's New York Stock Exchange listing. The company insisted that its New York office was a minor part of its operations and had no relationship with its Nigerian subsidiaries. A Second Circuit court found this unpersuasive, thereby forcing Shell to defend the case.[146]

U.S. federal courts, however, have begun to narrow the bases for asserting personal jurisdiction over foreign corporations in extraterritorial tort claims. A 2014 U.S. Supreme Court decision in *Daimler AG v. Bauman* – a suit brought by victims of Argentina's "Dirty War" in the 1970s, alleging corporate complicity in the kidnapping, torture, and murder of regime opponents – held that the presence of a corporate subsidiary in a U.S. forum did not give U.S. courts general jurisdiction over the wholly foreign acts of a corporate parent or another foreign subsidiary.[147]

Other strategic uses of corporate formalities may be geared toward avoiding, or minimizing legal liability – the ability to reach the operations or assets of other parts of the corporate enterprise.[148] Each component of a corporation has a formal legal status ("personality") distinct from others within the corporate structure. In theory, therefore, suing one part of a corporation should have no legal effect on others. Exceptions sometimes exist, however, when a corporate parent and subsidiary share structural, financial, or operational links such that legally culpable behavior on the part of one can be reasonably attributed to the other.[149] To

[145] Zia-Zarifi (1999:128).
[146] Note, personal jurisdiction over Royal Dutch Shell in *Kiobel* actually carried over from a prior case arising out of related facts that Shell settled in 2009, *Wiwa v. Royal Dutch Shell Petroleum Company*, 226 F.3d 88 (2d Cir. 2000).
[147] No. 11-965, 134 S. Ct. 746 (2014).
[148] Corporate decentralization, or fragmentation, occurs for many reasons other than avoiding ATS liability (Hansmann and Kraakman 1991:1881).
[149] Kobrin (2009:350), Dearborn (2009:198), Ho *et al.* (1996:394), Marcks (2001), Nicolson and Howie (2007), Brilmeyar and Paisley (1986).

minimize liability exposure, therefore, companies might, for example, set up minimally capitalized subsidiaries to carry out risky projects, undertake reorganizations to split themselves into increasingly specialized entities, or adopt arms-length contracting practices. At the same time, corporate decentralization can also involve risks and downsides that may outweigh concerns over ATS or other forms of U.S. legal liability, thus limiting the utility of decentralization as a jurisdiction or liability-avoiding tactic.

Although the complex nature of ownership structures precludes precise estimates of how many foreign multinational corporations have U.S. subsidiaries, the number is non-trivial. The U.S. Commerce Department's Bureau of Economic Analysis estimates that in 2009, majority-owned U.S. affiliates of foreign multinationals employed 5.2 million workers in the United States, or 4.7 percent of the private workforce. From the other direction, multinational corporations with U.S.-based parent companies employed 23 million workers in the United States, and 11 million workers abroad, with a worldwide total capital expenditure of US$621 billion.[150]

Discussion

Three decades of ATS litigation in the international human rights realm have helped to change basic ideas about accountability for human rights violations – some conducive to incentivizing transnational actors to improve their human rights practices, and others not. This is most evident regarding large multinational corporations engaged in oil, gas, and other extractive industries where many of the ATS suits against corporations have concentrated. ATS cases against U.S. and foreign multinationals, in conjunction with other activist-based initiatives around corporate social responsibility, have contributed to forcing these entities to expend considerable legal, political, and public relations resources.[151] Unlike voluntary instruments, which allow some multinational corporations to pay lip service to human rights ideals while doing relatively little to change their behavior, the threat of ATS liability introduced the possibility of millions, or even billions, of

150 Matheson (2008); Bureau of Economic Analysis News Release, April 18, 2012, www.bea.gov/newsreleases/international/mnc/2012/mnc2010.htm.

151 Janey *et al.* (2009), Kaptein (2004).

dollars in adverse judgments. As a consequence, corporations took notice.[152]

If the most observable manifestation of the threat of corporate liability has been vigorous efforts to contest ATS proceedings, there is also evidence that multinational corporations are investing more in the communities where they operate.[153] Such investments may undercut the necessity for the types of harsh security practices that are the source of many ATS claims against private corporations that have succeeded in surviving federal jurisdictional review. Whether such changes can be attributed to the threat of ATS liability, however, is a question requiring additional research.[154]

Considered as a whole, the actions and inactions of U.S. courts in the international human rights sphere have had important implications for evolving transnational regulatory rules and structures. Although ATS litigation against foreign officials has rarely been successful in securing compensation for human rights victims, it has contributed to the development of international legal norms of direct and vicarious responsibility for human rights violations, as evidenced by references to U.S. litigation in international criminal tribunals, foreign courts, and international organizations.[155] ATS litigation in U.S. courts has also prompted international debate – though not acceptance – concerning the permissibility of holding private corporations liable for violations of international law, including under theories of aiding and abetting the violations of states.[156]

U.S. court jurisprudence under the ATS has also influenced developments in international human rights law at the level of specific offenses. For example, the willingness of U.S. courts to equate forced labor with slavery for the purpose of ATS jurisdiction has directly buttressed International Labor Organization arguments that it constitutes a *jus cogens* offense.[157] At times, however, U.S. courts have adopted cautious and even nationalistically self-serving definitions of other offenses. As noted, ATS claims involving cruel, inhuman, and degrading treatment

152 Ballentine (2007:127).
153 Spence (2011).
154 Aguinis and Glavas (2012).
155 Cleveland (2003–2004:975).
156 Muchlinski (2001), Shamir (2004), Kobrin (2009).
157 Cleveland (2004:978). Forced Labor Convention, 1930 (No. 29), ILO. The Convention currently has 175 state members, but the United States is not among them.

have been dismissed on grounds that the content of this international human rights prohibition is not well defined enough to support an ATS claim in all instances.

While U.S. judicial applications of international human rights law may not immediately alter legal definitions and discourse on an international scale – particularly when those applications clash with more progressive legal and normative understandings of the rights concerned – they nonetheless feed into ongoing legal and policy debates about the international politics of enforcement.[158] In addition, U.S. court decisions serve as important markers for private actors seeking to predict the likely future actions of U.S. courts. This holds both for those seeking vindication of international human rights and those seeking to avoid liability as may be imposed by U.S. courts.

Conclusion

The scope and meaning of international human rights law is a perpetual "work in progress." Because law develops over time through use, the fact that U.S. courts – not those of some other country, or countries – have been the most active in applying international human rights law transnationally has influenced how the law and associated expectations for its transnational and international enforcement have evolved. That U.S. domestic courts have had this role is attributable less to absolute numbers of cases decided, which have been quite modest relative to demand for human rights enforcement, and more to the paucity of other states and institutions playing a similar role.

That U.S. courts were able to operate at the vanguard of human rights enforcement for three decades is attributable to domestic legal opportunity structures in the United States and to the existence of NGOs, rights advocates, and private firms willing to help victims to pursue these claims. As a result, private plaintiffs suing under the Alien Tort Statute incrementally extended the extraterritorial reach of U.S. interpretations of human rights law to a wide range of geographical and political settings and contributed to expanding the categories of defendants who could be held accountable for human rights violations under international law more broadly.

[158] See, for example, *Medellin v. Texas* 552 U.S. 491 and reactions.

Still, international lawyers and those in the international human rights movement have had mixed views about human rights litigation in U.S. courts. On the plus side, ATS actions put much-needed enforcement teeth into international human rights standards – teeth capable of biting a range of otherwise untouchable actors.[159] At the same time, U.S. court pronouncements on international law, including on the boundaries of *jus cogens* offenses, have at times been out of step with those of more progressive institutions and actors. While U.S. courts are internationalist in the sense that they are willing to consider extraterritorial claims, they have been far from cosmopolitan in how they go about it. As a consequence, non-American international lawyers often see U.S. jurisprudence as "evolving within its closed community of ways which are not consistent with the authoritative interpretation of international law in the international community, and which are, in a word, *weird*" (emphasis in original).[160]

Ultimately, the success of ATS plaintiffs in creating extraterritorial liability threats for a wide range of human rights violators prompted efforts inside and outside the U.S. court system to rein in those threats. As ATS claims began to encompass theories of indirect liability for the human rights violations of foreign governments, large multinational corporations pushed back against the doctrinal foundations of the ATS mechanism, together with the expansive bases for asserting personal jurisdiction over foreign corporate entities that had underwritten numerous ATS claims. As a result of this backlash, which resulted in the U.S. Supreme Court sharply curtailing ATS litigation, the legal onus has now shifted to the home states of multinational and transnational corporations to hold their corporate citizens accountable – or not – for human rights violations perpetrated in the course of doing business abroad.

These developments are roughly in accordance with what the basic rights prong of my theory of U.S. judicial extraterritoriality would expect under conditions of waning U.S. hegemony. As will be discussed further in Chapter 7, the U.S. Supreme Court could have held that the ATS provided no basis for jurisdiction over extraterritorial claims whatsoever. Instead, the *Kiobel* decision, with its absence of a clear majority opinion on this issue, leaves open the possibility that where

159 Koebele (2009).
160 Anderson (2009:351).

some part of an international law violation "touches and concerns" U.S. territory, even if the harm is felt elsewhere, the presumption against extraterritoriality may be overcome for an ATS claim. Of course, this emphasis on U.S. territory and interests falls far short of a universalist approach to international human rights protection. However, U.S. domestic courts have never been in that business.

7

The waning of U.S. extraterritoriality?

Judicial extraterritoriality – the application and enforcement of law to conduct outside a country's borders by domestic courts – is a source of political and legal friction in a world of territorially structured rights. It is often in direct tension with a still core (if somewhat outmoded) default rule in international law that gives sovereigns exclusive legal authority within their own territory, and the corollary expectation that domestic law stops at the state's borders. When, however, conduct in one state affects actors or interests in others, as it does with growing frequency, questions about who regulates invariably arise. How states and sub-state institutions address these issues determines who wins or loses in legal battles, and with what consequences for the disputants. More broadly, the outcomes of jurisdictional contests also affect perceptions about the transnational regulatory capacity of the states involved among wider audiences of similarly situated private actors and their governments.

This book is centrally concerned with describing and explaining variation in the extraterritorial reach of U.S. law as it is applied and enforced by U.S. courts. To this end it engages two main questions. The first is under what conditions have U.S. federal courts agreed to find and exercise jurisdiction over persons and conduct outside U.S. territory. The second is how the extraterritorial practices of U.S. domestic courts have influenced broader transnational and international regulatory processes. In this final chapter, I summarize my arguments and key conclusions, and discuss how and why patterns of U.S. judicial extraterritoriality may be shifting as U.S. hegemony fades, and what this might mean for the future.

Extraterritoriality: a tool for the powerful

Although many states have some capacity to apply domestic law to the conduct of their own nationals temporarily outside their territory (i.e. by threatening enforcement upon return), far fewer have much capacity to enforce their own laws against non-nationals based outside their borders. Among those with such a capacity, still fewer have demonstrated any willingness to use it on a wide scale. The United States is exceptional in this respect. Understanding why and across what dimensions is important to explain how U.S courts have contributed, directly and indirectly, to the transnational diffusion of U.S. law and the policy preferences it embodies.

An important dimension of this exceptionalness is, not surprisingly, U.S. power. Shaping and constraining this power from the top down are broad macro conditions tied to the U.S. position in the international order. This is far from the whole story, however. From the bottom up, the practice of U.S. judicial extraterritoriality is guided by thoroughly American understandings of domestic and international law and legal process and accompanying notions of the proper role of courts and private litigants in ordering society.

How and why do the decisions of U.S. courts to take on extraterritorial disputes matter for wider processes of transnational and international regulation? States that assert regulatory authority over transnational claims help to shape, for better or for worse, the transnational regulatory landscape. Transnational actors who have, or desire, ties to U.S. territory, citizens, or markets have strong incentives to avoid running afoul of U.S. laws with a track record of extraterritorial enforcement even in their non-U.S. operations. Failing to do so may result in being called to account in U.S. courts with their liberal service of process and aggressive discovery rules, class actions, fee-shifting arrangements, and high damage awards.[1] This threat effectively transmits U.S. regulatory preferences abroad even when horizontal processes of regulatory diffusion are weak or non-existent.

The jurisdictional decisions of U.S. courts are important as authoritative, if inherently incomplete, statements of the reach of U.S. law and legal obligation at any given point in time. Nevertheless, legal contestation is an iterative process that at times generates its own endogenous momentum.[2] Although each court decision on the extraterritorial reach of U.S. law resolves some questions, it creates others. For example, decisions extending or affirming the extraterritorial reach of specific statutes can easily invite additional questions about whether the law

[1] Born (1996).
[2] Sandholtz and Stone Sweet (2004), Alter (2003).

also applies if the underlying conduct differs in minor (or major) ways, if the parties differ, or if the U.S. effect is slightly less. Conversely, negative decisions may also leave open the possibility that a different configuration of facts would support a different outcome, or even that highly similar facts may support extraterritorial application of U.S. law at a later point if relevant factors in the regulatory environment change. In short, legal rules are rarely if ever wholly settled.

Because U.S. law and legal processes affect who gets what, when, and how, and these tools are sometimes used outside the United States, it is important for IR scholars and international lawyers alike to understand what those processes encompass, when they may come into play, and how they affect the formal and informal diffusion of regulatory rules and standards internationally.

Picking transnational battles

The practice of U.S. judicial extraterritoriality encompasses variation over time and across issue areas. As the case studies in prior chapters demonstrate, U.S. federal courts have been relatively aggressive extraterritorially in the antitrust and human rights spheres, but not with respect to protecting intellectual property rights. The evidence also shows, however, that even in areas where U.S. courts have been assertive, they generally have not sought to exercise their authority to the limits of U.S. enforcement capacity.

This variation cannot be convincingly decoded with textual or doctrinal analysis alone. Nor can we attribute this variation to changing patterns of cross-border judicial communication, to efforts on the part of U.S. courts to safeguard the interests of American parties in foreign transactions, or to attempts to make the world safe for free enterprise. While litigated cases can be found that are consistent with each of these conjectures, none provides a compelling general explanation for the broad patterns of U.S. court behavior. My approach to sampling broadly across contested claims of extraterritorial jurisdiction involving both positive and negative outcomes thus provides a superior means of identifying correlates of new exercises of U.S. extraterritoriality.

To address these shortcomings, this book advances a novel theory of how U.S. federal courts have dealt with contentious questions regarding the extraterritorial reach of U.S. law. The theory encompasses two logics of judicial decision-making – one regulatory, and the other rights-based. The regulatory logic expects that where conduct outside U.S. borders threatens the integrity or operation of U.S. laws inside U.S. territory, domestic courts are most likely to find extraterritoriality appropriate. In other words, it is the threat of *public* harm inside the United States from extraterritorial acts that triggers the judicial willingness, or necessity, to interpret U.S. law as applying outside U.S. territory. That is to say, the fact of private harm alone is insufficient to support U.S. judicial extraterritoriality unless the conduct under dispute creates (or reveals) opportunities and incentives for others to evade U.S. law in ways that impair its operation inside the United States.

The second logic expects U.S. domestic courts to exercise jurisdiction over extraterritorial disputes that allege violations of a small set of basic rights. Here the impetus is not the protection of domestic sovereignty. Instead, it is to ensure respect for rights and values at the core of American political identity. This imperative is at its strongest when alleged violators (public or private) are members of the U.S. polity, though foreign entities with close ties to U.S. territory and institutions may also be implicated. The fact that these rights and values largely – but not perfectly – mirror fundamental precepts of international human rights law has, until recently, made the international politics-associated rights-based extraterritoriality quite different from extraterritoriality based on the regulatory logic. Here too, however, international political complications that arise in contemplated exercises of U.S. extraterritorial jurisdiction are often traceable to peculiarly American aspects of how these rights are understood, and how they are enforced.

As Chapter 2 demonstrates, applying these two logics explains a nontrivial proportion of the observable variation in U.S. extraterritorial judicial practice in the civil realm since 1945. U.S. federal courts are in general reluctant extraterritorial regulators, finding and exercising jurisdiction only where necessary to safeguard U.S. domestic sovereignty or to deal with alleged violations of basic rights. Where exceptions have emerged, for example, in international securities regulation, the stated reasons are generally a gloss on the rights-based logic. In a famously broad formulation handed down when the United States was still undisputedly an economic hegemon, a Second Circuit Court of Appeals held that federal securities laws applied extraterritorially to prevent the United States from serving as "a base for manufacturing fraudulent security devices for export, even when these are peddled only to foreigners." Even here, however, the court held that to support extraterritorial jurisdiction, fraudulent actions had to be "more than merely preparatory" and could not encompass only failures to prevent harmful acts performed abroad.[3]

On the whole, however, U.S. federal court practice concerning the extraterritorial application of U.S. law has been deeply inward-looking. Even so, the actions and inactions of U.S. courts affect the strategic behavior of a wide range of actors outside the United States. Understanding the consequences of U.S. judicial extraterritoriality for broader transnational and international political processes is therefore also important.

The inward-looking character of U.S. courts

U.S. courts are in many respects quintessentially domestic institutions. They exist primarily to interpret and apply forum law to disputes over conduct that takes place wholly inside U.S. borders. In this respect they are like the domestic courts of any other country. As is also true of courts in functioning judicial systems the world over, U.S. federal courts are constrained by constitutional structure, procedural rules, and judicial norms of practice when deciding the prescriptive reach of domestic law. U.S. domestic courts were far from the first to recognize a functional need to regulate disputes involving transnational elements. Indeed, entire areas of international law exist to deal with the allocation of jurisdiction among states and to sort out which laws should apply.

Three aspects of the U.S. approach to these issues set U.S. practice apart from the overwhelming majority of states. The first is related to determinations of proper venue – or where a dispute may be heard. The American (unilateralist) approach inquires only whether U.S. courts have jurisdiction over the substance of a dispute, along with the parties implicated.[4] This contrasts sharply with European (multilateralist) practice, which focuses, instead, on justifying assertions of adjudicatory jurisdiction to other states that might plausibly claim it.[5] In principle, unilateralism allows for many states to assert jurisdiction; multilateralism permits only one.[6] Whereas the theoretical roots of the American approach are centrally concerned with avoiding unreasonable restrictions of individual freedom by U.S. government power, the European

[3] *ITT v. Vencap* 519 F.2d (2d Cir. 1975) at 1017–1018.

[4] Increasingly, clauses pre-specifying applicable law and forum choice are part of transnational contractual arrangements. U.S. courts generally enforce these obligations.

[5] Michaels (2005:1045).

[6] Dodge (1998b:110).

approach is grounded in efforts to avoid intruding on foreign sovereigns.[7]

The second feature of U.S. extraterritorial practice that goes against the international grain is a strong preference among U.S. federal courts to apply U.S. law in deciding many categories of extraterritorial disputes. While U.S. courts are willing to apply foreign law in transnational disputes involving traditional categories of private law, including the law of contracts, torts (injury law), real property, and family law, they typically draw the line at anything smacking of public law. This includes, for example, disputes over market regulation, intellectual property, tax and customs, privacy rights, securities regulation, and even international human rights.[8] In these situations, U.S. federal courts either decide to apply U.S. federal law or they dismiss the claim – presumably to be heard in another forum.[9] Stated in more technical terms, although under the international law of jurisdiction and conflict of laws there is no necessary correspondence between the legislative source of legal rules and the jurisdiction of domestic courts to adjudicate disputes, jurisdiction to prescribe and jurisdiction to adjudicate are often inextricably linked in U.S. extraterritorial practice. Although domestic courts in Europe are, in principle, more willing to apply foreign public law when deciding transnational disputes, they also hear fewer such disputes than American courts. Why this is so is connected to another distinguishing feature of U.S. judicial extraterritoriality.

This third feature is the decentralized character of regulatory enforcement in the U.S. legal system tied to the wide availability of, and reliance upon, private rights of action.[10] Private entities in the U.S. legal system have an uncommon degree of delegated agency to initiate litigation over the enforcement of public law. In the context of extraterritorial disputes, this gives private actors willing to gamble on litigation an ability to decide whether, when, and against whom to set the regulatory enforcement machinery of the United States into motion. As a consequence, American law and enforcement power is applied in numerous foreign

[7] Michaels (2005:1027–1029), Von Mehren (1983), Brilmayer (1987).

[8] Dodge (1998b). U.S. courts will apply foreign law in solidly private law disputes, such as contracts, family law, and standard torts, although these types of disputes are increasingly managed through mediation and arbitration.

[9] McConnaughay (1999). Mixed questions of public and private law, such as transnational contracts claims with antitrust implications, or tort claims involving human rights violations, are likewise swept into this approach.

[10] Maier (1984), Buxbaum (2001).

situations and against foreign actors that U.S. officials would be unlikely to target. Moreover, plaintiffs are not required to take the broader public interest, including the foreign policy preferences of the U.S. government, into account when choosing targets or the timing of their actions. It thus falls to domestic courts to juggle these competing interests in the face of incomplete, or ambiguous, legislative guidance.

In sum, permissive U.S. forum rules, coupled with judicial biases for applying U.S. law, and the mixing of public and private enforcement, all come together in a distinctly American cocktail of extraterritorial jurisdictional entitlement. When U.S. courts assert legal authority over conduct that takes place wholly or partially outside U.S. territory, they are, in effect, taking international action. These practices effectively prioritize U.S. domestic sovereignty over other, often competing, principles and objectives, such as respect for sovereign equality and legal predictability. It is thus unsurprising that many foreign governments have been unhappy with U.S. judicial extraterritoriality, among them, at various times, most of the United States' closest economic partners.

Extraterritoriality and legal diffusion

Although institutional and capacity-based constraints on U.S. judicial extraterritoriality appear as structural features in the regulatory environment as viewed from the perspective of individual disputes, each new effort to prompt a U.S. federal court to regulate extraterritorially either reinforces existing constraints or brings adjustments.[11] There is never "no effect" in Bayesian terms. Achieving these effects may be a large part of a plaintiff's motive for engaging in transnational litigation. Or, they may simply be artifacts of efforts on the part of one private actor to change the behavior of another, or to secure compensation for past harm. However, because U.S. courts are embedded in an exceptionally powerful state, their actions and inactions influence what larger audiences understand to be the transnational rules of the game. This, in turn, contributes to the international diffusion of legal and regulatory ideas.

International regulatory diffusion is a dynamic concept. It can be uncoordinated or coordinated, purposeful or incidental. It can lead to convergence around a single regime, or to consolidation of rules in multiple competing regimes.[12] Where efforts at formal coordination

[11] Sell (2003), Sandholtz and Stone Sweet (2004).
[12] Drezner (2007), Simmons *et al.* (2007).

occur, they are generally preceded by uncoordinated, or minimally coordinated, actions in which behavior nevertheless resolves into stable patterns (or equilibria). Judicial unilateralism on the part of the United States and other countries can be a factor in the uncoordinated spread of law and legal ideas, either in the absence of formal international rules or in response to them. As such, it can be a precursor to, or a substitute for, more formalized efforts at international regulatory cooperation.

Efforts to promulgate, diffuse, and enforce regulatory rules often encompass state efforts to limit, or direct, the behavior of private entities. Even where the domestic legal rules of powerful states lack global reach or perfect enforcement, their existence and operation in some areas alters the nature of strategic action in the system as a whole. This occurs through the shadow of enforcement along with shared expectations regarding potential for its expansion or contraction. However, private entities are rarely passive recipients of legal constraint. Instead, they respond strategically, anticipating the costs and benefits of complying with various rules, together with the likelihood and magnitude of punishment for non-compliance.

In situations characterized by rival regulatory standards, transnational private actors may face difficult choices about which states' rules to follow.[13] The difficulty of their situation may vary depending on whether U.S. law is simply less permissive, or whether it contains obligations that are actually incompatible with the law that is displaced by U.S. judicial extraterritoriality. Many aspects of international antitrust fall into the first category. Legal rules surrounding the privacy of personal and commercial information and the regulation of certain types of speech are examples of the second. Thus, private entities with close ties to the United States may opt to follow U.S. rules where they are more restrictive so as to eliminate threats of future U.S. court-imposed liability. By the same token, when a U.S. court that might plausibly claim jurisdiction over a class of disputes decides *not* to do so, this likewise imparts strategically important information to private actors and foreign governments about the limits of U.S. power, or the willingness of U.S. courts to exercise it.

In the case study chapters, I trace the emergence and development of U.S. judicial extraterritoriality in three legal issue areas – antitrust, intellectual property rights, and human rights – and highlight some of its consequences for transnational legal diffusion. Understanding the behavior of courts and litigants requires situating them within the

[13] Drezner (2007:53), Simmons and Elkins (2004).

political and institutional environments in which they operate. I draw attention to three elements I argue are jointly necessary for U.S. judicial extraterritoriality to emerge as a viable strategy for transnational actors: legal ambiguity, the emergence of litigants, and U.S. enforcement capacity.

Changes in macro- and micro-level conditions increase the potential for ambiguity in the law, and for existing ambiguities to become politically salient. Whether legal ambiguities, in turn, prompt the emergence of litigants willing to bring, and contest, legal claims is, in turn, a function of the stakes for private actors, and, where efforts to shape legal rules and regimes are at issue, the absence of legislative options for achieving those goals. Actors who lose under one set of rules often seek opportunities to circumvent them, or to remake the rules to their own advantage. Those who benefit from the legal *status quo* generally resist both types of efforts unless they too expect to gain.[14]

As theorized in Chapter 3, private agents will seek to extend the geographic reach of domestic legal rules where they are subject to domestic laws that are more onerous than those of their foreign competitors, and they are unable to achieve favorable (to them) adjustments of those rules using political or administrative means. This is the case, for example, with anti-cartel rules under U.S. antitrust law as examined in Chapter 4. Alternatively, where domestic rules favor U.S.-based actors in some way, private actors also may seek to have them applied as widely as possible. This may be because those rules are more protective than available foreign law, as is the case with many human rights claims. Or it may be that U.S. law is differently protective – encompassing different legal categories, or involving idiosyncratic, but nonetheless deeply embedded, procedures and formalities – as is the case with U.S. trademark laws.

Litigation is often not the first choice of those seeking broader legal change. It is an incremental strategy, and one with high barriers to use in the form of various jurisdictional and procedural hurdles.[15] Private rights of action are neither universally available nor are they unlimited where they are recognized to exist.[16] Likewise, the enforcement capacity of

[14] Krasner (1991).

[15] Stephan (2011).

[16] Many federal statutes, including several with explicit extraterritorial reach, do not encompass private rights of action. This is one reason why, for example, there have been relatively few litigated cases under the 1977 Foreign Corrupt Practices Act. Likewise, the U.S. government retains a tight hold on policing compliance with U.S. export

U.S. courts is often tightly bound to traditional territorial factors: control over persons, assets, and future rights of access.

Nevertheless, where domestic law reflects the preferences of entities without substantial transnational concerns, foreign states are resistant to adopting U.S. laws and practices, and foreign sources of harm are identifiable and reachable, extraterritorial litigation, or its credible threat, may be an appealing course of action.

U.S. judicial extraterritoriality, as discussed in Chapter 1, is a hybrid of state-based and private modes of diffusion. Whether used by private actors against other private actors, by the U.S. government against private actors, or by private actors against foreign governments or their officials, the litigation examined here contributes to the development of law and legal regimes. Faced with the fact (or threat) of assertive extraterritorial regulation, governments may opt to adjust their domestic rules to reflect – or at least not directly contradict – those of more powerful states. But this outcome is far from guaranteed. Indeed, judicial extraterritoriality can also generate backlash and resistance.

In situations where judicial extraterritoriality constitutes at least a moderately effective means of protecting the interests of transnational actors with U.S. ties, it can reduce the need for the U.S. executive to strong-arm foreign governments over legal obstacles on behalf of private interests. It also can undercut political pressure for the U.S. government to negotiate with other governments over rules and enforcement. This is demonstrated in Chapter 4 in the context of international antitrust. By the same token, where judicial extraterritoriality is (or becomes) less efficacious, the United States may seek to bargain internationally. Even so, resulting agreements will preserve existing options for unilateral public and private enforcement of embodied rights, rules, or standards. This dynamic is illustrated in the intellectual property case study in Chapter 5.

U.S. extraterritoriality in decline?

Although the United States is still a dominant power in the international system, its era of undisputed economic hegemony is fading. The consolidation of Europe under the auspices of the European Union has created an economic entity on par with the United States in terms of

controls, and with sanctions against Cuba, Iran, and other states. This occurs through penalties imposed by the Office of Foreign Assets Control in the U.S. Treasury Department, which may employ civil or criminal penalties, depending on the extent and willfulness of violations.

its productive capacity. Simultaneously, several large developing states, among them China, India, and Brazil, have experienced steep upward trajectories in economic growth accompanied by rapid integration into global product and investment markets. As a result, the U.S. capacity to guide global economic developments is diminishing – and with it, arguably, the resolve to try to do so.

The U.S. position as the undisputed leader of the international capitalist juggernaut that resulted in unprecedented levels of global economic growth from the 1950s to the early 1970s provided immense opportunities for American commercial expansion. It also gave U.S. regulators leeway to impose unwelcome policies on America's strategic partners without risking serious political rifts.[17] At the same time, the U.S. commitment to maintain the post-World War II liberal-democratic order, coupled with the uncertainties of Cold War balancing, also gave foreign states some ability to demand U.S. restraint.[18] However, the rising costs of maintaining the postwar international trading and monetary system, coupled with the economic resurgence of several European states and Japan, eventually began to erode the relative economic position of the United States, and with it the political willingness to shoulder that burden.[19] This was the point at which U.S. judicial extraterritoriality driven by private plaintiffs began to occur with some frequency. By then, however, the United States, with its large internal market and it deep engagement in global finance and investment, was a critical hub of international commercial activity.

In the meantime, the conditions that enabled broad-ranging U.S. extraterritorial practices are disappearing. U.S. enforcement capacity is experiencing a long, slow decline tied to the decreasing centrality of the United States in the global economy. This has helped to underwrite a growing trend toward U.S. judicial minimalism in U.S. extraterritorial practice, as illustrated by two recent U.S. Supreme Court decisions on two very different legal issues.

Morrison *and* Kiobel: *The end of an era?*

In 1998, the National Australia Bank ("NAB"), Australia's largest financial institution, acquired HomeSide Lending ("HomeSide"), a Florida-

[17] Frieden (2006), Raustiala (2009).
[18] Ikenberry (2009).
[19] Frieden (2006).

based mortgage company, which at the time was the sixth-largest mortgage servicer in the United States.[20] After the purchase, the Bank learned that American officers of HomeSide had manipulated, and were continuing to manipulate, its financial models, in violation of internationally accepted accounting standards, to inflate the value of its mortgage servicing rights.[21] National Australia Bank reproduced this fraudulent financial information in its annual reports to investors.[22] Following exposure of the fraud in 2001, HomeSide's value was written down by more than 3 billion Australian dollars.[23] In 2002, Robert Morrison and three Australian holders of NAB securities purchased on Australian exchanges filed suit against the Bank, HomeSide, and four individual defendants in a U.S. federal district court in New York.[24] They sought compensation for financial harm from what they alleged was a fraudulent scheme carried out in Florida and New York in violation of Rule 10b-5 of the U.S. Securities Exchange Act (SEA) of 1934.

At roughly the same time, a different set of plaintiffs filed suit in the same federal district court against Royal Dutch Shell, an Anglo-Dutch multinational corporation, and its wholly owned subsidiary Shell Petroleum Development Company of Nigeria Ltd ("SPDC"), under another U.S. law – the Alien Tort Statute. Surviving family members of Dr. Barinem Kiobel and eleven other individuals from the Ogoni ethnic group alleged that the companies had aided and abetted Nigerian police in carrying out extrajudicial killings, arbitrary detention, torture, and other crimes against humanity in 1994 and 1995 in an effort to halt Ogoni activism, and the threat it posed to Shell's petroleum operations in the region, in violation of international human rights law. During the period of the alleged violations, Royal Dutch Shell maintained a business office in New York, and its stock traded on the New York Stock Exchange.

20 Brief for Petitioners, No. 08–1191, page 4.

21 Specifically, plaintiffs claimed HomeSide officers misrepresented the company's value by intentionally using higher than projected interest rates in prepayment estimation models. This generated "over-inflated earnings targets." They also alleged the Bank had specific notice of the fraud no later than 1999. Brief for Petitioners, No. 08–1191, pages 6–10.

22 NAB's American depository receipts were traded on the New York Stock Exchange, and it filed its financial statements with the U.S. Securities Exchange Commission. See www.law.cornell.edu/supct/cert/08-1191.

23 www.nytimes.com/2001/09/08/business/international-business-oops-bank-will-write-off-1.75-billion.html.

24 Note, the district court dropped Morrison – the only American on the plaintiff side – from the suit for failure to adequately allege harm from the alleged fraud. The case, however, continued under his name.

By 2002, when the suit was filed, Esther Kiobel, the lead plaintiff and surviving wife of Dr. Kiobel, had become a permanent resident of the United States.

Despite obvious differences in the substance of these cases, both *Morrison* and *Kiobel* share several features of interest to this study. First, each involves an important extraterritorial component. In the securities fraud case, the Australian plaintiffs purchased overvalued Australian securities on Australian exchanges. In the human rights case, all of the claimed violations were carried out in Nigeria. Second, plaintiffs in each case anchored their respective claims in statutory provisions that U.S. courts had previously applied extraterritorially. Each also sought to justify U.S. jurisdiction to hear and decide their claims by analogy to these prior cases. Third, in each case defendants chose to contest the extraterritorial reach of U.S. law – and with it, U.S. court jurisdiction – rather than settling the claim. Fourth, each case also involved high stakes for the parties, and ambiguity regarding the extraterritorial reach of the law in question. Fifth, the U.S. Supreme Court held unanimously in both cases that U.S. law did *not* provide a basis for extraterritorial jurisdiction on the facts alleged, thereby setting broadly observable limits on the reach of U.S. law.[25] Sixth, also in both cases the deciding justices disagreed sharply on the scope and rationale of the holding. A particular point of judicial contention concerns the role of a judicially crafted doctrine, the "presumption against extraterritoriality."

The presumption against extraterritoriality holds that where there is ambiguity regarding the extraterritorial reach of a statute, courts should begin from the presumption that Congress intended the law to apply only within the territory of the United States and then search for disconfirming evidence. The U.S. Supreme Court revived a robust version of this presumption in the early 1990s after decades of relative disuse.[26] As several scholars have observed, the presumption against extraterritoriality has been applied inconsistently over time and across issues – both in its early manifestations and in more recent ones.[27]

In *Morrison*, the Court held that U.S. federal securities law, which exists primarily to protect the integrity and operation of U.S. exchanges,

[25] *Kiobel v. Royal Dutch Petroleum Co.*, 569 U.S. – (2013), *Morrison et al. v. National Australia Bank Ltd. et al.*, 561 U.S. 247 (2010). In both cases the Court split, with the more conservative justices (in both instances the majority) insisting on a robust presumption against extraterritoriality to determine the scope of the law.

[26] Dodge (1998a:85–86). See also Chapter 1.

[27] Gibney and Emerick (1996), Estey (1997), Dodge (1998a), Ward (2001), Knox (2010).

and secondarily to shield U.S. investors, did not apply to the alleged losses of the Australian plaintiffs. Key to this decision was the factual determination that the harm to Australian stockholders was most directly caused by NAB having falsely represented the value of HomeSide Lending to Australian investors after discovering the U.S. fraud. The Court declared that, without clear legislative guidance, it could not conclude that Rule 10b-5 of the Securities Exchange Act was intended to reach foreign acts of that nature.[28] The Court thus drew a new bright line on the prescriptive reach of U.S. securities law over outward-directed malfeasance.[29] Its decision overturned decades of precedent supporting a U.S. cause of action allowing U.S. federal courts to hear extraterritorial securities fraud claims in which conduct inside U.S. territory is used to defraud foreign investors.[30]

A majority of Supreme Court Justices in *Kiobel* also (and for the first time in an ATS claim) applied the presumption against extraterritoriality to set far more restrictive limits on the ability of foreign plaintiffs to sue non-U.S. entities for extraterritorial violations of international human rights law. As described in Chapter 6, prior to the *Kiobel* ruling, lower federal courts had incrementally extended jurisdiction over extraterritorial conduct over an expanding range of actors (many of them foreign) and offenses in violation of core principles of international human rights law where the alleged offenders or the victims had close U.S. ties with no interference from Congress.

Much of the early attention to the *Kiobel* and *Morrison* holdings focused on what changed. Nevertheless, both arguably leave at least some prior extraterritorial jurisprudence intact. Both are examples of "foreign cubed" suits – with foreign plaintiffs, foreign conduct, and foreign defendants. As such, these suits are by definition at the outer reaches of how U.S. extraterritorial jurisdiction has been used. *Morrison* does not, however, prohibit suits involving extraterritorial conduct where U.S. exchanges and U.S. investors are allegedly harmed. Therefore, even

[28] Justice Scalia (writing), joined by Chief Justice Roberts, and Justices Kennedy, Thomas, and Alito. Justice Breyer filed a partially concurring opinion, and Justice Stevens provided a concurring opinion joined by Justice Ginsburg. Justice Sotomayor did not take part.

[29] In *Schoenbaum v. Firstbrook*, 68 F.2d 1326 (2d Cir. 1972). Interestingly, the court in this case considered, but rejected, the presumption against the extraterritorial application of Rule 10(b) and found jurisdiction over a malfeasance claim involving a transaction in Canada involving Canadian stock where that stock was also traded on U.S. exchanges.

[30] The now-discredited line of cases begins with *Schoenbaum v. Firstbrook*, 405 F.2d 200, 2d Cir. (1968) and *Leasco Data Processing Equip. Corp. v. Maxwell*, 468 F.2d 1326, 2d Cir. (1972).

post-*Morrison*, the prescriptive shadow of Rule 10(b) will continue to stretch well beyond U.S. borders. Likewise, the Supreme Court's main holding in *Kiobel* leaves open the possibility that the ATS may support extraterritorial claims in which U.S.-based actors are the primary agents of alleged harm, and where the conduct at issue is held to "touch and concern" the United States.[31]

If these cases represent the "new normal" in U.S. extraterritorial practice, how, then, should political scientists and legal scholars make sense of them? Legal analysts and scholars of judicial behavior might look to the increasingly conservative composition of the Supreme Court.[32] Although the juridical and ideological leanings of individual judges may matter to particular case outcomes, especially at the appellate level, this explanation is unsatisfying on its own, since it fails to consider how deeper structural, institutional, and political factors combine to influence ideological preferences and to create opportunities for the enactment of those preferences.[33] This, in turn, leaves important questions unasked and unanswered.

Hegemonic decline and judicial presumptions

The argument advanced in this book looks to political and structural causes and enabling conditions to account for variation in U.S. extraterritorial practice over time and across issue areas. When U.S. hegemony was on the rise or holding steady, U.S. federal courts had a generous amount of leeway to interpret U.S. legal rules broadly, although in many instances they opted not do so. This is evident in issue areas ranging from labor rights to environmental law to intellectual property rights. Even in issue areas where U.S. courts have applied U.S. law extraterritorially, this was often a reluctant step taken in situations where the integrity or operation of domestic rules would have been compromised by a failure to act, or where American adherence to basic rights was at issue.

As noted above, in a few areas – notably in extraterritorial securities fraud – U.S. extraterritoriality was more extensively practiced than my theory would expect.[34] The era in which such outcomes were possible is,

31 Hathaway (2013), Chander (2013).
32 See, for example, Kontorovich (2014), Knox (2010).
33 Lax (2011), Clark and Lauderdale (2010).
34 Note, in the coding of the data for the statistical analysis in Chapter 2, all foreign-cubed cases are coded as *not* posing a threat to U.S. domestic sovereignty or political identity.

by all appearances, ending. As the United States slips into becoming one of several economic great powers, its government and institutions are becoming less concerned with self-image and system maintenance, and more concerned with countering threats to its own internal order.[35] A harbinger of this change is the widening judicial embrace, issue area by issue area, of the presumption against extraterritoriality.

An important issue in debates over the reinvigoration of the presumption against extraterritoriality concerns justifications for judicial line-drawing in the absence of legislative guidance. Indeed, the legal literature offers no explanation for why certain statutes have been exempted from the presumption, nor for why the presumption fell into disuse in the post-1945 era, only to be revived following the end of the Cold War. The macro- and micro-elements of my argument together provide such a theory.

An additional feature of the recent high judicial preoccupation with extraterritoriality that buttresses the macro-claim concerning hegemonic decline is its overt concern with the foreign affairs implications of judicial actions. The potential for U.S. judicial extraterritoriality to create foreign policy complications has never been entirely absent from judicial concern throughout the post-1945 era.[36] Efforts to avoid these clashes led some scholars and judges to attempt to craft "balancing tests" by applying the tools of private international choice-of-law analysis to extraterritorial disputes initiated by private plaintiffs that involved, to varying degrees, public law questions.[37] Due to the doggedly unilateralist orientation of the U.S. jurisdictional approach, these tests were not well received among many judges and scholars, and they wreaked havoc on the internal coherence of U.S. legal doctrine.

The main problem was, and remains, that transnational disputes that begin as nominally private can become sources of foreign policy friction in situations where U.S. extraterritoriality is viewed as jurisdictionally or procedurally intrusive, which is especially likely when U.S. law is incompatible with the territorial sovereign's own laws and policies. Foreign governments have at times chosen to protest, or even intervene in, extraterritorial (from a U.S. perspective) disputes to protect their nationals, and to prevent U.S. courts from overriding how their own laws operate within their respective territories. Whereas foreign

[35] Layne (2012).
[36] Franck (1992), *Baker v. Carr* 369 U.S. 186 (1962).
[37] McConnaughay (1999), Lowenfeld (1979).

governments generally frame arguments against U.S. judicial extraterritoriality in terms of international law, in the United States the dominant discourse in recent years has been mainly constitutional and is becoming more so.[38]

A fundamental tension that courts everywhere continuously negotiate is between the rule-elaborating consequences of their actions (or inactions), on one side, and the idea that courts are properly restricted to applying existing law on the other.[39] One prominent view in the domestic extraterritoriality debate holds that judicial power is dangerous in constitutional terms if not constantly forced to hew to the strict textual meaning of legislative acts.[40] In *Morrison*, for example, Justice Scalia railed against the role of "judicial-speculation-made-law" in extending the reach of SEA 10b(5) to "foreign cubed" cases. A competing view, holds, however, that there are inherent limits to the existence and expression of legislative intent, and that, therefore, it is only reasonable to assume legislatures grant courts a degree of agency, subject to oversight, to fill gaps in the law through interpretation and application.[41]

At the political heart of this debate is whether and how the deck should be stacked when courts are resolving questions of statutory and constitutional ambiguity. Even in situations where judges have not traditionally invoked the presumption against extraterritoriality, effects and conduct tests have similar functions for determining the prescriptive reach of U.S. law. But, as noted repeatedly throughout this book, some effects matter more than others from the perspective of fulfilling judicial functions and mandates. Federal court judges have done a fairly good job of intuiting this, even in the absence of articulated rules. Consequently, this book offers support to those who view heavy-handed versions of the presumption against extraterritoriality as unnecessary, and potentially damaging to U.S. legal influence globally.

Occasionally Congress has agreed that the U.S. Supreme Court has gone too far in limiting judicial extraterritoriality. For example, following the Supreme Court's decision in *Equal Employment Opportunity Commission v. Aramco*, Congress amended Title VII to clarify its intent to allow precisely the type of claim that the Supreme Court had rejected.[42] Similarly, a mere six weeks after the *Morrison* decision, a partial override

[38] Michaels (2011).
[39] Merryman and Pérez-Perdomo (2007), Kmiec (2004).
[40] Bradley (2000), Bradley and Goldsmith (1997).
[41] Brilmayer (1987), Dodge (1998b:146), Ferejohn and Kramer (2002).
[42] 499 U.S. 244.

was passed as part of the 2010 Dodd-Frank Wall Street Reform and Consumer Protection Act. The provisions in question expressly provided the Securities Exchange Commission (SEC) authority to initiate extraterritorial fraud claims, and also required the SEC to study whether private rights of action should be reinstated also.[43]

Even as U.S. federal courts have made it harder for private entities to bring several types of extraterritorial claims, during this same period, use of extraterritorial regulatory tools on the part of the U.S. executive branch has increased. Some of this counter-trend can be attributed to the U.S. war on terror and its accompanying sanctions and restrictions on dealings with blacklisted individuals, organizations, and states.[44] Other aspects of the increase represent stepped up enforcement. As noted in Chapter 5, in the antitrust sphere, this is attributable to criminal proceedings undertaken by the Justice Department that are often followed by private suits. Likewise, the Treasury Department has recently increased enforcement of the Foreign Corrupt Practices Act. Also, in an exceptionally aggressive move against a foreign sovereign, a U.S. Second Circuit Appeals Court ordered the government of Argentina to repay defaulted debts to private lenders in the United States that had refused to participate in Argentina's restructuring on the same schedule as holders of restructured debts. The court then issued an order permitting post-judgment discovery of Argentina's foreign assets worldwide, which the U.S. Supreme Court allowed to stand by refusing review.[45]

A key difference with these areas of practice is that, because the U.S. executive branch is the initiator, courts need not trouble themselves over any foreign affairs implications – though they may still have to wrestle at times with constitutional questions regarding the balance between executive and legislative power. What appears to be happening, then, is less of a dismantling of the U.S. extraterritoriality than its *de-privatization* – that is, the piecemeal foreclosure of opportunities for private actors to use domestically recognized private rights of action for extraterritorial claims.

Is more U.S. jurisdictional restraint a good thing?

In this book, I have approached the development and testing of the arguments largely as a descriptive and explanatory exercise. U.S.

[43] Dodd-Frank Wall Street Reform and Consumer Protection Act §929Y(b).

[44] See, for example, www.treasury.gov/press-center/press-releases/Pages/jl2447.aspx.

[45] *NML Capital, Ltd. v. Republic of Argentina*, 727 F.3d 230 (2d Cir. 2013); *Exchange Bondholder Group v. NML Capital Ltd.*, 134 S. Ct. 2819 (2014).

extraterritoriality, however, also raises important normative and policy questions. Indeed, it is natural to ask whether U.S. extraterritorial practices were and are, on balance, a good or a bad thing for both the United States, for other states, and the international system as a whole.

Many international lawyers, and many non-Americans, are likely to view contractions of U.S. judicial extraterritoriality positively.[46] This is because U.S. extraterritoriality as a governance mechanism is anti-democratic and anti-pluralistic. Transnational legal claims decided in U.S. courts frequently impact not only Americans but also private entities and foreign governments who have little opportunity to weigh in on domestic acts of legislation. One might counter that the openness of the U.S. court system to nationals and non-nationals alike still gives foreign entities some ability to influence the development of U.S. rules, and the conditions of their enforcement. For many foreign transnational actors, however, this idea provides little comfort.

Arguing from the other side, U.S. extraterritoriality is, in theory, capable of supplying public goods in the form of legal enforcement – although only to the extent there is rough international agreement on what the applicable rules and standards are (or should be). In some issue areas – especially human rights – U.S. extraterritoriality is often protective of liberal values, and thus may contribute to the maintenance of a pluralistic international system.[47] But this holds only to the extent U.S. extraterritoriality is not overriding, or substituting for, local enforcement that would otherwise occur. In these situations, states and governments care a great deal about who regulates. For example, concern that a U.S. federal court might claim jurisdiction over Royal Dutch Shell in the *Kiobel* was the focus of multiple *amicus curiae* briefs from foreign governments arguing against it on international law grounds. And, even before *Kiobel* was dismissed from the U.S. federal courts, legal proceedings were underway in the Netherlands to hold the company accountable for the same violations.[48]

Of course, there are those who will be less pleased with the structurally induced contraction of U.S. regulatory power. As underscored in Chapter 3 and in the case studies, many private entities have benefitted, directly and indirectly, from the assertive extraterritorial application and enforcement of U.S. law. Even so, the outcomes described here generally

[46] Parrish (2011), Anderson (2009).
[47] Cohen (2012).
[48] Jägers *et al.* (2013:e-37–38).

provide far from optimal solutions to transnational regulatory problems – whether considered from an individual or a social perspective. To the extent private actors have fewer options for pursuing their interests through U.S. domestic courts, it may prompt them to consider other more cooperative options for addressing transnational legal and regulatory issues.

Taken together, these observations suggest a need for more theoretical and empirical attention to the rule-generating character of private strategic behavior and its normative implications.

Questions for the future

National courts are often theorized as "takers" of law from the international level in the form of customary rules, international treaties, and, increasingly also the decisions of international courts and tribunals.[49] As contributors to state practice, and as sources of general principles of law, domestic courts are also makers of law inside and outside their own states. This book provides several theoretically and empirically grounded conjectures about the conditions under which domestic courts may be instrumental in projecting the shadow of domestic law extraterritorially.

For much of the past seventy years, the United States has been exceptional in the degree to which its courts have been willing to decide extraterritorial claims. This observation, couched in the preceding analysis, suggests two counterfactual hypotheses. The first is that U.S. domestic courts would not have had the same degree of international influence absent U.S. hegemony. The second is that U.S. hegemony would not have had the same degree of transnational legal impact without U.S. extraterritorial jurisdiction. Together these hypotheses raise the question of whether a comparably powerful state with a domestic regulatory system not centrally structured around courts and private litigation would behave similarly.

Arguing inductively from observations of U.S. behavior since World War II, and of Britain and Spain in earlier eras, Krisch finds hegemons often seek to update international rules by applying their own domestic law externally. Aid conditionality, certification mechanisms such as human rights reporting, §301 reviews in international trade, and mechanisms designed to prevent terrorist activities are all contemporary

[49] Alter (2014).

examples. Court-based extraterritoriality involving private actors is another.[50]

As noted above, it is increasingly evident that the macro-structural and political conditions that enabled the rise and persistence of U.S. judicial extraterritoriality in its most familiar forms are changing. Other states are changing as well. European states, in particular, appear increasingly ready to test the relationship between power, domestic institutions, and extraterritorial assertiveness.[51]

The economic and regulatory centralization of Europe under the auspices of the European Union has given its institutions an enforcement capacity that now rivals that of the United States in several issue areas.[52] If the U.S. experience is a guide, this may create both opportunities for extraterritorial assertiveness on the part of European courts at both the national and supranational level, and internal pressure to use it. Indeed, European institutions have begun to experiment with conferring private rights of action in a few areas of public law, among them competition policy, albeit with tighter controls over their use.[53]

At the same time, there are several reasons to expect that similarly assertive patterns of judicial extraterritoriality will not be replicated elsewhere. The first concerns configurations of relative power. Uncoordinated judicial extraterritoriality exercised in the context of multipolarity is more likely to prompt short-term political strife in the international sphere than in situations characterized by hegemonic control. Where such strife undercuts the benefits of extraterritoriality to private actors, they will look elsewhere for solutions to their problems. Second, as the statistical analysis in Chapter 2 and the evidence in the case studies indicate, even in the United States the capacity for extraterritorial regulatory enforcement may exist without states choosing to use it – or to use it to its full potential.[54] The long tradition of state-directed regulation in Europe suggests that these states are unlikely to cut the leash of government oversight on private rights of action anytime soon.

[50] Krisch (2005:400–405).

[51] Layne (2012), Quintanilla and Whytock (2011), Watt (2002).

[52] Bradford (2012), Kelemen (2011).

[53] As explained in Chapter 4, in Europe private actors are permitted to bring private damage suits for violations of competition law only *after* a public regulator has undertaken enforcement.

[54] Even within issue areas where courts and other regulators have sought to apply rules extraterritorially, defining and reevaluating the limits of such applications is a constant task.

In addition to this set of very broad questions, several smaller, but interesting issues related to extraterritoriality and the boundaries of state jurisdiction warrant further exploration. Among them are questions related to transnational actors and their ties to multiple polities. Such ties may be formal (as with dual-citizenship regimes) or behaviorally determined, as when corporations undertake actions, or maintain a presence in multiple jurisdictions simultaneously. Fragmented ownership, intra-firm trade, and complex licensing practices have all contributed to a blurring of jurisdictional lines.[55] Indeed, ambiguities around the character and extent of U.S. ties needed to trigger the personal jurisdiction of U.S. courts may (at times intentionally) defeat U.S. jurisdiction.

Whether U.S. ties among one or more nodes in a complex corporate structure, or set of contractual relationships, should serve to extend the reach of U.S. rules to actors and transactions that would otherwise be outside a state's jurisdiction is an increasingly salient question.[56] As discussed in Chapter 6, another key debate involving corporations concerns their status as subjects of international law. This issue was not extinguished for American courts by the Supreme Court's decision in *Kiobel* and it remains important both to the law and the politics of corporate accountability for human rights violations.

Yet another important, though sometimes difficult question is what counts as U.S. territory. Classic variants on this issue involve ships, planes, embassy grounds, military bases, and trust territories.[57] This has a been a central issue with respect to whether U.S. constitutional rights, such as the right of *habeas corpus*, are due to "enemy noncombatants" detained in U.S. military facilities in Guantanamo Bay, Cuba. Similar questions have also arisen with regard to U.S. insular and trust territories – for example, with regard to U.S. environmental legislation requiring impact assessments for federal agency actions. The need to provide governance for the Internet and cyber issues has introduced new complications with respect to theorizing the jurisdictional consequences of these networks.[58]

55 Note, in *Kiobel*, the U.S. corporate presence of Royal Dutch Petroleum subsidiary, and the trading of its shares on the NYSE proved sufficient to ground personal jurisdiction under the ATS in part because it was grandfathered in under a prior related case.

56 See, for example, *Goodyear Dunlop Tires Operations, S.A. v. Brown* 131 S.Ct. 2846 (2011) (holding U.S. courts had no jurisdiction over the foreign subsidiaries of a U.S. corporation in a suit seeking compensation for the deaths of two 13-year-old residents of North Carolina in a bus accident near Paris, France).

57 Raustiala (2009).

58 Goldsmith (1998).

Still other issues have emerged in extraterritorial practice of the United States, and increasingly also other countries, concerning the scope and applicability of rules that grant states and high officials immunity from suit in domestic courts. U.S. legal suspensions, or curtailments, of immunities for designated state sponsors of terrorism are one controversial example. U.S. government efforts to regulate the dealings of foreign entities with a U.S. presence with such states and individuals are another. In the human rights realm, debates over whether absolute immunities granted to heads of state, and lesser immunities tied to official acts for lower-level officials, should be interpreted to continue after individuals leave office is a further critical area.[59] Finally, in the security sphere, questions about whether private military contractors should be accorded the same legal rights as members of states' military forces when it comes to issues of immunity from suit for official acts have also been a growing focus of debate in U.S. law and elsewhere.

Questions about whether and under what conditions domestic laws apply extraterritorially, and to whom, are increasing both in frequency and in importance in contexts beyond the United States.[60] This is unsurprising. Indeed, as long as the international system remains economically integrated and territorially fragmented, extraterritoriality – active or latent – will continue to be an important issue in international politics and international law.

[59] *Yousef v. Samantar* 699 F.3d 763 (4th Cir. 2012).
[60] Quintanilla and Whytock (2011).

BIBLIOGRAPHY

Abbott, Frederick M. 1989. "Protecting First World Assets in the Third World: Intellectual Property Negotiations in the GATT Multilateral Framework." *Vanderbilt Journal of Transnational Law* 22, 689–746.

Abbott, Kenneth and Duncan Snidal. 2000. "Hard Law and Soft Law in International Governance." *International Organization* 54:3, 421–456.

Agnew, John H. 1985. *Competition Law.* Taylor & Francis.

Aguinis, Herman and Ante Glavas. 2012. "What We Know and Don't Know about Corporate Social Responsibility a Review and Research Agenda." *Journal of Management* 38:4, 932–968.

Ahn, Yong Soek and Yu Jin Kim. 2005. "Recent Developments in Korean Antitrust Law." *Global Competition Review*, available at http://leeko.com/Data/Publication/Article_YSA_2.pdf.

Alford, Roger P. 1992–1993. "The Extraterritorial Application of Antitrust Laws: The United States and European Community Approaches." *Virginia Journal of International Law* 33, 1–50.

Alter, Karen J. 1998. "Who Are the Masters of the Treaty? European Governments and the European Court of Justice." *International Organization* 52, 121–147.

Alter, Karen J. 2000. "The European Union's Legal System and Domestic Policy: Spillover or Backlash?" *International Organization* 54, 489–518.

Alter, Karen J. 2003. "Do International Courts Enhance Compliance with International Law?" *Review of Asian and Pacific Studies* 25, 51–78.

Alter, Karen J. 2008. "Agent or Trustee: International Courts in Their Political Context." *European Journal of International Relations* 14, 33–63.

Alter, Karen J. 2014. *The New Terrain of International Law: Courts, Politics, Rights.* Princeton University Press.

Amley Jr., Edward A. 1998. "Sue and Be Recognized: Collecting §1350 Judgments Abroad." *Yale Law Journal* 107, 2177-2210.

Anderson, Kenneth. 2009. "The Rise of International Criminal Law: Intended and Unintended Consequences." *European Journal of International Law* 20:2, 331–358.

Andreas, Peter. 2013. *Smuggler Nation: How Illicit Trade Made America.* Oxford University Press.

Anghie, Antony. 2004. *Imperialism, Sovereignty, and the Making of International Law*. Cambridge University Press.

Aronofsky, David. 1985. "Piercing the Transnational Corporate Veil: Trends, Developments, and the Need for Widespread Adoption of Enterprise Analysis." *North Carolina Journal of International Law and Commercial Regulation* 10, 31–86.

Ashcroft, John and John Ratcliff. 2012. "Recent and Unusual Evolution of an Expanding FCPA." *Notre Dame Journal of Law, Ethics, and Public Policy* 1, 25–38.

Bach, David and Abraham L. Newman. 2007. "The European Regulatory State and Global Public Policy: Micro-Institutions, Macro-Influence." *Journal of European Public Policy* 14:6, 827–846.

Baldwin, David Allen. 1985. *Economic Statecraft*. Princeton University Press.

Ballance, Michael W. 1994. "Third Party Innocence: Domestic Authorization of Foreign Copyright Infringement and *Subafilms v. MGM-Pathe Communications, Co.*" *North Carolina Journal of International Law and Commercial Regulation* 20, 435–456.

Ballentine, Karen. 2007. "Promoting Conflict-Sensitive Business in Fragile States: Redressing Skewed Incentives" in *Trade, Aid, and Security: An Agenda for Peace and Development* (Oli Brown, Mark Halle, Sona Pena Moreno, and Sebastian Winkler, eds.). Sterling, VA: Earthscan, 126–157.

Bar-Hillel, Maya. 1973. "On the Subjective Probability of Compared Events." *Organizational Behavior and Human Performance* 9, 396.

Bardach, Eugene and Robert A. Kagan. 2002. *Going by the Book: The Problem of Regulatory Unreasonableness*. Transaction Publishers.

Barnett, Michael and Raymond Duvall. 2005. "Power in International Politics." *International Organization* 59:1, 39–75.

Baroncelli, Eugenia, Carsten Fink, and Beata Smarzynska Javorcik. 2005. "The Global Distribution of Trademarks: Some Stylized Facts." 3270, http://papers.ssrn.com/sol3/papers.cfm?abstract_id=610311.

Barton, John L., Judith L. Goldstein, Timothy E. Josling, and Richard H. Steinberg. 2008. *The Evolution of the Trade Regime: Politics, Law, and Economics of the GATT and the WTO*. Princeton University Press.

Basedow, Jurgen. 2000. "International Antitrust: From Extraterritorial Application to Harmonization." *Louisiana Law Review* 60, 1037–1052.

Basedow, Jurgen. 2010. "Foundations of Private International Law in Intellectual Property" in *Intellectual Property in the Global Arena: Jurisdiction, Applicable Law, and the Recognition of Judgments in Europe, Japan and the US* (Jurgen Basedow, Toshiyuki Kono, and Axel Metzger, eds.). Tubingen, Germany: Mohr Siebeck, 3–29.

Bassiouni, M. Cherif. 1996. "International Crimes: 'Jus Cogens' and 'Obligatio Erga Omnes'." *Law and Contemporary Problems* 59:4, 63–74.

Baum, Lawrence. 2006. *Judges and Their Audiences: A Perspective on Judicial Behavior*. Princeton University Press.

Baum, Lawrence. 2011. *Specializing the Courts*. University of Chicago Press.

Ben-Atar, Doron. 2004. *Trade Secrets: Intellectual Piracy and the Origins of American Industrial Power*. Yale University Press.

Benvenisti, Eyal. 2008. "Reclaiming Democracy: Strategic Uses of Foreign and International Law by National Courts." *American Journal of International Law* 102:2, 241–274.

Berman, Paul Schiff. 2002. "The Globalization of Jurisdiction." *University of Pennsylvania Law Review* 151, 311–545.

Bernard, Anthony. 2010. "Holding Corporations Liable in the United States for Aiding and Abetting Human Rights Violations Abroad: A Statutory Solution." *The George Washington Law Review* 78, 615–635.

Bernstein, David E. 2003. "Lochner's Legacy's Legacy." *Texas Law Review* 82, 1–64.

Bhagwati, Jagdeesh N. 2004. *In Defense of Globalization*. Oxford University Press.

Bilsky, Leora. 2012. "Transnational Human Rights Litigation." *European Journal of International Law* 23:2, 349–374.

Blakeney, Michael. 2004. "The International Protection of Industrial Property: From the Paris Convention to the Agreement on Trade-Related Aspect of Intellectual Property Rights," available at WIPO/IP/UNI/DUB/04/01.

Blum, Jeffrey M. and Ralph G. Steinhardt. 1981. "Federal Jurisdiction over International Human Rights Claims: The Alien Tort Claims Act after *Filartiga v.* Peña-Irala." *Harvard International Law Journal* 22, 53–114.

Blumberg, Phillip I. 1990. "The Corporate Entity in an Era of Multinational Corporations." *Delaware Journal of Corporate Law* 15:2, 285–375.

Borchers, Patrick J. 2001. "The Problem with General Jurisdiction." *University of Chicago Legal Forum* 2001, 119–140.

Bodenhausen, G.H.C. 1969 (reprinted in 1991). *Guide to the Application of the Paris Convention for the Protection of Industrial Property, as Revised at Stockholm in 1967*. Geneva: WIPO.

Bork, Robert H. 1979. "The Antitrust Paradox (1978)." *Harvard Law Review* 92, 1376–1390.

Born, Gary B. 1992. "A Reappraisal of the Extraterritorial Reach of U.S. Law." *Law & Policy in International Business* 24:3, 1–100.

Born, Gary B. 1996. *International Civil Litigation in United States Courts*. Kluwer Law International.

Boyle, James. 1997. "A Politics of Intellectual Property: Environmentalism for the Net?" *Duke Law Journal* 47:1, 87–116.

Bradford, Anu. 2007. "International Antitrust Negotiations and the False Hope of the WTO." *Harvard International Law Journal* 48:2 (Summer), 383–439.

Bradford, Anu. 2012. "The Brussels Effect." *Northwest University Law Review* 107:1, 1–68.

Bradley, Curtis A. 1997. "Territorial Intellectual Property Rights in an Age of Globalism." *Virginia Journal of Intellectual Property Law* 37, 505–586.

Bradley, Curtis A. 1998. "The Charming Betsy Canon and Separation of Powers: Rethinking the Interpretive Role of International Law." *Georgetown Law Journal* 86:3, 479–538.

Bradley, Curtis A. 2000. "Chevron Deference and Foreign Affairs." *Virginia Law Review* 86, 649–726.

Bradley, Curtis A. and Jack L. Goldsmith III. 1997. "The Current Illegitimacy of International Human Rights Litigation." *Fordham Law Review* 66, 319–369.

Brand, Ronald A. and Scott R. Jablonski. 2007. *Forum Non Conveniens: History, Global Practice, and Future under the Hague Convention on Choice of Court Agreements*. Oxford University Press.

Brewster, Rachel. 2012. "The Surprising Benefits to Developing Countries of Linking International Trade and Intellectual Property." *Chicago Journal of International Law* 12, 1–54.

Brilmayer, Leah. 1987. "The Extraterritorial Application of American Law: A Methodological and Constitutional Appraisal." *Law and Contemporary Problems* 66, 11–38.

Brilmayer, Leah and Kathleen Paisley. 1986. "Personal Jurisdiction and Substantive Legal Relations: Corporations, Conspiracies, and Agency." *California Law Review* 74, 1–40.

Brodley, Joseph F. 1987. "The Economic Goals of Antitrust: Efficiency, Consumer Welfare, and Technological Progress." *New York University Law Review* 62, 1020–1053.

Brougham, Henry. 1841. *Speeches of Henry Lord Brougham upon Questions Relating to Public Rights: With Historical Introductions*. Lea and Blanchard Publishers.

Brunell, Thomas L. and Alec Stone Sweet. 2008. "Litigating the Treaty of Rome: The European Court of Justice and Articles 226, 230, and 234." New Modes of Governance Project, www.eu-newgov.org/datalists/deliverables_detail.asp?Project_ID=26.

Busch, Mark L. 2007. "Overlapping Institutions, Forum Shopping, and Dispute Settlement in International Trade." *International Organization* 61:4, 735–761.

Büthe, Tim and Walter Mattli. 2011. *The New Global Rulers: Privatization of Regulation in the Global Economy*. Princeton University Press.

Büthe, Tim and Gabriel Swank. 2007. "The Politics of Antitrust and Merger Review in the European Union: Institutional Change and Decisions from Messina to 2004." CES Working Paper, no. 142.

Buxbaum, Hannah L. 2001. "The Private Attorney General in a Global Age: Public Interests in Private International Antitrust Litigation." *Yale Journal of International Law* 26, 219–263.

Buxbaum, Hannah L. 2005. "German Legal Culture and the Globalization of Competition Law: A Historical Perspective on the Expansion of Private Antitrust Enforcement." *Berkeley Journal of International Law* 23, 474–495.

Cameron David. 1978. "The Expansion of the Public Economy." *American Political Science Review* 72, 1243–1261.

Carruba, Clifford J. 2005. "Courts and Compliance in International Regulatory Regimes." *Journal of Politics* 67:3, 669–689.

Carter, Kevin R. 2006. "Amending the Alien Tort Claims Act: Protecting Human Rights of Closing Off Corporate Accountability?" *Case Western Reserve Journal of International Law* 38, 629–652.

Cassel, Douglass. 2001. "Empowering United States Courts to Hear Crimes Within the Jurisdiction of the International Criminal Court." *New England Law Journal* 35:2, 421–445.

Casto, William R. 2006. "The New Federal Common Law of Tort Remedies for Violations of International Law." *Rutgers Law Journal* 37, 635–670.

Cavanagh, Edward D. 2003. "The FTAIA and Subject Matter Jurisdiction over Foreign Transactions under the Antitrust Laws: The New Frontier in Antitrust Legislation." *SMU Law Review* 56, 2151–2190.

Chander, Anupam. 2013. "Unshackling Foreign Corporations: *Kiobel's* Unexpected Legacy." *American Journal of International Law* 107, 829–834.

Chemerinsky, Erwin. 2007. *Federal Jurisdiction* (Fifth Edition). Aspen Publishers.

Chesterman, Simon. 2004. "Oil and Water: Regulating the Behavior of Multinational Corporations through Law." *International Law and Politics* 36,307–329.

Choi, Stephen J. and Andrew T. Guzman. 1998. "Portable Reciprocity: Rethinking the International Reach of Securities Regulation." *Southern California Law Review* 71, 903, 914–915.

Cini, Michelle and McGowan Lee. 1998. *Competition Policy in the European Union*. New York: St. Martin's Press.

Clark, Aubert J. 1960. *The Movement for International Copyright in Nineteenth Century America*. Catholic University of America Press.

Clark, Harry S. 1999. "Dealing With U.S. Extraterritorial Sanctions and Foreign Countermeasures." *University of Pennsylvania Journal of International Economic Law* 20, 61–96.

Clark, Tom S. and Benjamin Lauderdale. 2010. "Locating Supreme Court Opinions in Doctrine Space." *American Journal of Political Science* 54:4, 871–890.

Clarke, Julian L. and Simon Evenett. 2003. "The Deterrent Effects of National Anticartel Laws: Evidence from the International Vitamins Cartel." *The Antitrust Bulletin Fall* 2003, 689–726.

Cleveland, Sarah. 1998. "Global Labor Rights and the Alien Tort Claims Act" (Book Review). *Texas Law Review* 76, 533–579.

Cleveland, Sarah. 2003–2004. "The Alien Tort Statute, Civil Society, and Corporate Responsibility." *Rutgers Law Review* 56, 971–988.

Cohen, Jean L. 2012. *Globalization and Sovereignty: Rethinking Legality, Legitimacy, and Constitutionalism.* Cambridge University Press.

Colangelo, Anthony J. 2011. "A Unified Approach to Extraterritoriality." *Virginia Law Journal* 97, 1019.

Colino, Richard R. 1962. "Copyright Protection Abroad for U.S. Cultural Exports." *Duke Law Journal* 1962:2, 219–248.

Collingsworth, Terry. 2002. "The Key Human Rights Challenge: Developing Enforcement Mechanisms." *Harvard Human Rights Journal* 15, 183–204.

Conant, Lisa. 2013. "Whose Agents? The Interpretation of International Law in National Courts" in *Interdisciplinary Perspectives on International Law and International Relations: The State of the Art* (Jeffrey Dunoff and Mark Pollack, eds.). Cambridge University Press, 394–420.

Connor, John M. 2007. "Effectiveness of Antitrust Sanctions on Modern International Cartels" in *The Political Economy of Antitrust* (Vivek Ghosal and Johan Stennek, eds.). New York: Elsevier, 176–215.

Connor, John M., Albert A. Foer, and Simcha Udwin. 2010. "Criminalizing Cartels: An American Perspective." *New Journal of Criminal Law* 1:2, 199–217.

Coppola, Maria. 2014. "International Competition Network." *Global Competition Review*, section 1, http://globalcompetitionreview.com/reviews/54/sections/181/chapters/2135/international-competition-network/.

Coyle, Anne. 2003. "Modest Reform: The New Rule 32.1 Permitting Citation to Unpublished Opinions in the Federal Courts of Appeals, A." *Fordham Law Review* 72, 2471–2502.

Cross, Frank B. 2009. *Theory and Practice of Statutory Interpretation.* Palo Alto: Stanford University Press.

Cross, Frank B. and Blake J. Nelson. 2001. "Strategic Institutional Effects on Supreme Court Decision Making." *Northwestern University Law Review* 95: 3,1437–1494.

Crowley, Michael T. 1996. "Raise the Yellow Submarine – *Subafilms* and Extraterritorial Application of the Copyright Act." *Federal Communications Law Journal* 48, 133–162.

Cutler, A. Claire. 2003. *Private Power and Global Authority: Transnational Merchant Law in the Global Political Economy.* Cambridge University Press.

Cutler, A. Claire, Virginia Haufler, and Tony Porter, eds. 2001. *Private Authority and International Affairs.* S.U.N.Y. Press.

Dam, Kenneth W. 1983. "Extraterritoriality and Conflicts of Jurisdiction." *Proceedings of the American Society of International Law* 77, 370–377.

Dam, Kenneth W. 1987. "The Growing Importance of International Protection of Intellectual Property." *Intellectual Lawyer* 21, 627–638.

Davidow, Joel. 1997. "Some Reflections on the OECD Competition Guidelines." *Antitrust Bulliten* 22, 441–458.

Davis, Jeffrey. 2008. *Justice Across Borders: The Stuggle for Human Rights in U.S. Courts*. New York: Cambridge University Press.

Daynard, Richard A. 1972. "Test Case Litigation as a Source of Significant Social Change." *Catholic Lawyer* 18, 37–42.

Dearborn, Meredith. 2009. "Enterprise Liability: Reviewing and Revitalizing Liability for Corporate Groups." *California Law Review* 97, 195–261.

Deere-Birkbeck, Carolyn. 2010. "Developing Countries in the Global IP System before TRIPS: The Political Context for the TRIPS Negotiations" in *Research Handbook On the Protection of Intellectual Property Under WTO Rules* (Carlos R. Correa, ed.). Edward Elgar Publishing.

Dickenson, Edwin D. 1952. "The Law of Nations as Part of the National Law of the United States." *University of Pennsylvania Law Review* 101, 27–56.

Dinwoodie, Graeme B. 2004. "Trademarks and Territory: Detaching Trademark Law from the Nation-State." *Houston Law Review* 41:3, 886.

Dinwoodie, Graeme. B. 2009. "Developing a Private International Intellectual Property Law: The Demise of Territoriality." *William and Mary Law Review* 51, 711–800.

Dinwoodie, Graeme B., William O. Hennessey, and Shira Perlmutter. 2001. *International Intellectual Property Law and Policy*. LexisNexis Casebook Series.

Djelic, Marie-Laure. 2011. "International Competition Network" in *Handbook of Transnational Governance: New Institutions and Innovations*. Cambridge: Polity, 80–88.

Dodge, William S. 1996. "Historical Origins of the ATS Statue: A Response to the 'Originalists'." *Hastings International and Comparative Law Review* 19, 221–258.

Dodge, William. S. 1998a. "Understanding the Presumption against Extraterritoriality." *Berkeley Journal of International Law* 16, 85–125.

Dodge, William S. 1998b. "Extraterritoriality and Conflicts of Laws Theory: An Argument for Judicial Unilateralism." *Harvard International Law Journal* 39:1, 101–169.

Dodge, William S. 2001. "Antitrust and the Draft Hague Judgments Convention." *Law and Policy in International Business* 32, 363–390.

Dodge, William S. 2008. "The Public-Private Distinction in the Conflict of Laws." *Duke Journal of Comparative and International Law* 18, 371–394.

Dodge, William S. 2011. "The Presumption against Extraterritoriality after Morrison" in *Proceedings of the 105th Annual Meeting*. Vol. 105. American Society for International Law, 396–399.

Drahos, Michaela. 2001. *Convergence of Competition Laws and Policies in the European Union: Germany, Austria, and the Netherlands*. Kluwer Law International.

Drahos, Peter. 1995. "Global Property Rights in Information: The Story of TRIPS at the GATT." *Prometheus* 13:1, 6–19.

Drezner, Daniel W. 2000. "Bottom Feeders." *Foreign Policy* 121, 64–70.

Drezner, Daniel W. 2007. *All Politics is Global: Explaining International Regulatory Regimes.* Princeton University Press.

Dubin, Joseph S. 1954. "The Universal Copyright Convention." *California Law Review* 42:1, 89–119.

EarthRights International. "Senator Feinstein Introduces Bill to Protect Perpetrators of Human Rights Abuses." October 20, 2005, www.earthrights.org/campaigns/senator-feinstein-introduces-bill-protect-perpetrators-human-rights-abuses.

Edwards, C.D. 1944. "International Cartels as Obstacles to International Trade." *The American Economic Review* 34, 330–339.

Edwards, Corwin D. 1965. "Cartelization in Western Europe." *Antitrust Bull* 10, 253–278.

Edwards, Corwin D. 1967. *Control of Cartels and Monopolies: An International Comparison.* Oceana Publications.

Efrat, Assaf and Abraham Newman. 2015. "Deciding to Defer: The Importance of Fairness in Resolving Transnational Jurisdictional Conflicts." *International Organization* 70:2, 409–441.

Eskridge, William N. 1987. "Dynamic Statutory Interpretation." *University of Pennsylvania Law Review* 135:6, 1479–1555.

Estey, Wade. 1997. "The Five Bases of Extraterritorial Jurisdiction and the Failure of the Presumption against Extraterritoriality." *Hastings International and Comparative Law Review* 21, 177–208.

Fairbank, John King. 1953. *Trade and Diplomacy on the China Coast.* Vol. 1. Harvard University Press.

Falk, Richard A. 1958. "International Jurisdiction: Horizontal and Vertical Conceptions of Legal Order." *Temple Law Quarterly*32:3, 295–321.

Farhang, Sean. 2008. "Public Regulation and Private Lawsuits in the American Separation of Powers System." *American Journal of Political Science* 52:4, 821–839.

Fearon, James D. 1998. "Bargaining, Enforcement, and International Cooperation." *International Organization* 52, 269–305.

Federico, P.J. 1936 (reprinted 2003). "Operation of the Patent Act of 1790." *Journal of the Patent and Trademark Office Society* 85, 33–45.

Federico, P.J. 1954 (reprinted 1993). "Commentary on the New Patent Act." *Journal of the Patent and Trademark Office Society* 75, 161–231.

Feinberg, Kenneth R. 1980–1981. "Economic Coercion and Economic Sanctions: The Expansion of U.S. Extraterritorial Jurisdiction." *American University Law Review* 30, 323–348.

Ferejohn, John A. and Larry D. Kramer. 2002. "Independent Judges, Dependent Judiciary: Institutionalizing Judicial Restraint." *New York University Law Review* 77 962–1039.

Ferejohn, John A. and Barry R. Weingast. 1992. "A Positive Theory of Statutory Interpretation." *International Review of Law and Economics* 12:2, 263–277.

Fidler, David P. 1992. "Competition Law and International Relations." *International and Comparative Law Quarterly* 41, 563–589.

Fiebig, Andre. 2005. "Modernization of European Competition Law as a Form of Convergence." *Temple International and Comparative Law Journal* 19, 63–86.

Fioretos, Orfeo. 2001. "The Domestic Sources of Multilateral Preferences: Varieties of Capitalism in the European Community" in *Varieties of Capitalism* (Peter A. Hall and David Soskice, eds.). Oxford University Press, 213–235.

Fishel, Wesley R. 1952. *The End of Extraterritoriality in China.* University of California Press.

Fisher, William W. III. 1999. "A History of the Ownership of Ideas in the United States" in *Eigentumskulturen im Vergleich.* Vandenhoeck & Ruprecht.

Fligstein, Neil and Mara-Drita Iona. 1996. "How to Make a Market: Reflections on the Attempt to Create a Single Market in the European Union." *American Journal of Sociology* 102:1, 1–33.

Ford, Sara M. 2000. "Compulsory Licensing under the TRIPS Agreement: Balancing Pills and Patents." *American University International Law Review* 15:4, 941–974.

Forrester, Ian. 2011. "A Challenge for Europe's Judges: The Review of Fines in Competition Cases." *European Law Review* 2, 185–207.

Fox, Eleanor M. 2002–2003. "International Antitrust and the Doha Dome." *Virginia Journal of International Law* 43, 911–932.

Fox, Eleanor M. 2009. "Linked-In: Antitrust and the Virtues of a Virtual Network." *International Lawyer* 43:1, 151–174.

Fox, William T.R. 1941. "Competence of Courts in Regard to 'Non-Sovereign' Acts of Foreign States." *American Journal of International Law* 35:4, 632–640.

Franck, Thomas M. 1992. *Political Questions, Judicial Answers: Does the Rule of Law Apply in Foreign Affairs?* Princeton University Press.

Frank, Isaiah. 1994. "Whither U.S. Trade Policy Beyond the Uruguay?" *SAIS Review* 14:2, 29–46.

Freeman, Harriet R. 1995. "Reshaping Trademark Protection in Today's Global Village: Looking Beyond GATT's Uruguay Round Toward Global Trademark Harmonization and Centralization." *ILSA Journal of International and Comparative Law* 1, 67–102.

Frey, Linda and Marsha Frey. 1999. *The History of Diplomatic Immunity.* Ohio State University Press.

Freyer, Tony A. 2006. *Antitrust and Global Capitalism, 1930–2004.* Cambridge University Press.

Fried, Barbara H. 2009. *The Progressive Assault on Laissez Faire: Robert Hale and the First Law and Economics Movement.* Harvard University Press.

Frieden, Jeffry A. 2006. *Global Capitalism: Its Fall and Rise in the Twentieth Century.* W.W. Norton and Company.

Friedman, Lawrence M. 2002. *American Law in the 20th Century.* Yale University Press.

Friedmann, Wolfgang G. and Verloren van Themaat. 1956. "International Cartels and Combines" in *Antitrust Laws: A Comparative Symposium.* Vol. 3 (Wolfgang G. Friedmann, ed.). Stevens.

Friendly, Henry J. 1964. "In Praise of *Erie* – And of the New Federal Common Law." *New York University Law Review* 36, 383–422.

Furman, Cronin and Kathleen Renee. 2013. "Managing Expectations: International Criminal Trials and the Prospects for Deterrence of Mass Atrocity." *International Journal of Transitional Justice* 7:3, 434–454.

Furse, Mark. 2008. *Competition Law of the EC and UK* (Sixth Edition). Oxford University Press.

Gadbaw, R. Michael. 1989. "Intellectual Property and International Trade: Merger or Marriage of Convenience?" *Vanderbilt Journal of Transnational Law* 22:2, 223–242.

Galanter, Marc. 1974. "Why the 'Haves' Come out Ahead: Speculations on the Limits of Legal Change." *Law and Society Review* 9:1, 95–160.

Garth, Bryant, Ilene H. Nagel, and S. Jay Plager. 1987. "The Institution of the Private Attorney General: Perspectives from an Empirical Study of Class Action Litigation." *Southern California Law Review* 61, 353–398.

Gauer, Celine, Dorothe Dalheimer, Lars Kjolbye, and Eddy de Smijter, Directorate-General Competition, unit A-2. 2003. "Regulation 1/2003: A Modernised Application of EC Competition Rules." *Competition Policy Newsletter* (Spring), http://ec.europa.eu/competition/publications/cpn/2003_1_3.pdf.

Geradin, Damien. 2009. "The Perils of Antitrust Proliferation – The Process of 'Decentralized Globalization' and the Risks of Over-Regulation of Competitive Behavior." *Chicago Journal of International Law* 10, 189–212.

Gerber, David J. 1983. "The Extraterritorial Application of German Antitrust Laws." *American Journal of International Law* 77:4, 756–783.

Gerber, David J. 1984. "Beyond Balancing: International Law Constraints on the Reach of International Law." *Yale Journal of International Law* 10, 185–221.

Gerber, David J. 1994. "Constitutionalizing the Economy: German Neo-Liberalism, Competition Law and the 'New' Europe." *The American Journal of Comparative Law* 42, 25–84.

Gerber, David J. 2005. "International Antitrust Convergence: The Real and Imagined Role of U.S. Antitrust Law." ABA Spring Antitrust Meeting, March 30, 2005.

Gerber, David J. 2010. *Global Competition: Law, Markets, and Globalization.* Oxford University Press.

Gervais, Daniel. 2008. *The TRIPS Agreement: Drafting History and Analysis* (Third Edition). Sweet and Maxwell.

Ghosal, Vivek. 2008. "The Genesis of Cartel Investigations: Some Insights from Examining the Dynamic Interrelationships between US Civil and Criminal Antitrust Investigations." *Journal of Competition Law and Economics* 4:1, 61–88.

Gibney, Mark. and R. David Emerick. 1996. "Extraterritorial Application of United States Law and the Protection of Human Rights: Holding Multinational Corporations to Domestic and International Standards." *Temple International and Comparative Law Journal* 10, 123–146.

Goldman, Abe A. 1955. "History of U.S.A. Copyright Law Revision 1901–1954" Prepared for Subcommittee on Patents, Trademarks, and Copyrights, Pursuant to Senate Res. 53. Washington, DC: G.P.O.

Goldsmith, Jack L. 1998. "Against Cyberanarchy." *University of Chicago Law Review* 65:4, 1199.

Goldstein, Judith. 1986. "The Political Economy of Trade: Institutions of Protection." *American Political Science Review* 80:01, 161–184.

Goldstein, Paul. 1994. *Copyright's Highway: From Gutenberg to the Celestial Jukebox.* Hill & Wang.

Goldstein, Paul and Bernt Hugenholtz. 2012. *International Copyright: Principles, Law, and Practice.* Oxford University Press.

Goodman, Ryan and Derek Jinks. 1997. "Filartiga's Firm Footing: International Human Rights and Federal Common Law." *Fordham Law Review* 66:2, 463–529.

Goodman, Ryan and Derek Jinks. 2008. "Incomplete Internationalization and Compliance with International Human Rights Law." *European Journal of International Law* 19:4, 725–748.

Greely, Arthur P. 1902. "Pending Trademark Legislation." *American Lawyer* 10, 386–391.

Greely, Arthur P. 1905. *Registration of Trademarks under the New Trademark Act of the United States: With Notes on the Act.* Washington, DC: John Byrne & Co.

Greve, Michael S. 1989. "Public Law and Judicial Review." *Journal of Law and Politics* 6, 559–572.

Griffin, Joseph P. 1993. "EC and US Extraterritoriality: Activism and Cooperation." *Fordham International Law Journal* 17, 353–388.

Griffin, Joseph P. 1999. "Extraterritoriality in U.S. and EU Antitrust Enforcement." *Antitrust Law Journal* 65:1, 159–199.

Grossman, Gene M. and Elhanan Helpman. 2002. *Special Interest Politics*. The MIT Press.

Gunther, Gerald and Kathleen M. Sullivan. 1997. *Constitutional Law* (Thirteenth Edition). Foundation Press.

Guzman, Andrew T. 1998. "Is International Antitrust Possible?" *New York University Law Review* 73, 1501–1548.

Guzman, Andrew T. 2002. "Choice of Law: New Foundations." *Georgetown Law Journal* 90, 883–940.

Hacking, D.L. 1979. "Increasing Extraterritorial Impact of US Laws: A Cause for Concern amongst Friends of America." *Northwestern Journal of International Law and Business* 1, 1–10.

Hafner-Burton, Emilie. 2008. "Sticks and Stones: Naming and Shaming the Human Rights Enforcement Problem." *International Organization* 62:4, 689–716.

Hafner-Burton, Emilie and Kiyoteru Tsutsui. 2007. "Justice Lost! The Failure of Human Rights Law to Matter Where Needed Most." *Journal of Peace Research* 44, 407–425.

Haight, James T. 1960. "The Restrictive Business Practices Clause in United States Treaties: An Antitrust Tranquilizer for International Trade." *The Yale Law Journal* 70, 240–257.

Hall, Peter A. 1999. "The Political Economy of Europe in an Era of Interdependence" in *Continuity and Change in Contemporary Capitalism* (Herbert Kitschelt, Peter Lange, Gary Marks, and John D. Stephens, eds.). Cambridge: Cambridge University Press.

Hall, Peter A. and David Soskice. 2001. *Varieties of Capitalism*. Oxford University Press.

Hammes, D. and D. Wills. 2005. "Black Gold: The End of Bretton Woods and the Oil-Price Shocks of the 1970s." *Independent Review* 9:4, 501–511.

Hanney, William M. 2011. "The Air Cargo Antitrust Conspiracy: A Report on the Criminal and Civil Cases in the U.S." Schiff Hardin LLP, Chicago.

Hansmann, Henry and Reinier Kraakman. 1991. "Toward Unlimited Shareholder Liability for Corporate Torts." *Yale Law Journal* 100, 1879–1934.

Harding, Christopher and Julian Joshua. 2003. *Regulating Cartels in Europe: A Study of Legal Control of Corporate Delinquency*. Oxford University Press.

Hathaway, Oona A. 2002. "Do Human Rights Treaties Make a Difference?" *Yale Law Journal* 111, 1935–2042.

Hathaway, Oona A. 2013. "Kiobel Commentary: The Door Remains Open to "Foreign Squared" Cases." *scotusblog* (April 18, 2013, 4:27 PM), www.scotusblog.com/2013/04/kiobel-commentary-the-door-remains-open-to-foreign-squared-cases/.

Hayner, Priscilla B. 2008. *Unspeakable Truths: Transitional Justice and the Challenge of Truth Commissions*. Routlege.

Heckscher, E.F. and B.G. Ohlin. 1991. *Heckscher-Ohlin Trade Theory*. The MIT Press.

Heenan, John C. 2004. "Graceful Maneuvering: Corporate Avoidance of Liability Through Bankruptcy and Corporate Law." *Montana Law Review* 65, 99–134.

Helfer, Laurence R. 1999. "Forum Shopping for Human Rights." *University of Pennsylvania Law Review* 148:2, 285–400.

Helfer, Laurence R. 2004. "Regime Shifting: The TRIPS Agreement and New Dynamics of International Intellectual Property Lawmaking." *Yale International Law Journal* 29, 1–84.

Helfer, Laurence R. and Erik Voeten. (2014). "International Courts as Agents of Legal Change: Evidence from LGBT Rights in Europe." *International Organization* 68:01, 77–110.

Henkin, Louis. 1984. "International Law as Law in the United States." *Michigan Law Review* 82:1555–1569.

Henner, Peter. 2009. *Human Rights and the Alien Tort Statute: Law, History, and Analysis*. ABA Publishing.

Herb, Guntram H. 1999. "Nationality Identity and Territory" in *Nested Identities: Nationalism, Territory, and Scale* (Guntram H. Herb and David H. Kaplan, eds.). Rowman and Littlefield, 9–30.

Hillman, Arye L. 1982. "Declining Industries and Political-Support Protectionist Motives." *American Economic Review* 72, 1180–1187.

Hilson, Chris. 2002. "New Social Movements: The Role of Legal Opportunity." *Journal of European Public Policy* 9:2, 238–255.

Hirst, Paul and Grahame Thompson. 2002. "The Future of Globalization." *Cooperation and Conflict* 37:3, 247–265.

Hiscox, Michael J. 2001. "Class versus Cleavages: Inter-Industry Factor Mobility and the Politics of Trade." *International Organization* 55, 1–46.

Ho, Laura, Catherine Powell, and Leti Volpp. 1996. "(Dis)assembling Rights of Women Workers Along the Global Assembly Line: Human Rights and the Garment Industry." *Harvard Civil Rights and Civil Liberties Law Review* 31, 383–414.

Hofstadter, Richard. 1964. "What Happened to the Antitrust Movement? Notes on the Evolution of an American Creed," in *The Business Establishment* (Earl F. Cheit, ed.), 113–151.

Holdsworth, W.S. 1914. "Rules of Venue and the Beginnings of the Commercial Jurisdiction of Common Law Courts." *Columbia Law Review XIV* 7, 551–562.

Hopkins, James Love. 1917. *The Law of Trademarks, Trade Names, and Unfair Competition*. Cincinnati: W.H. Anderson.

Hopmann, P. Terrence. 1995. "Two Paradigms of Negotiation: Bargaining and Problem Solving." *Annals of the American Academy of Political and Social Science* 542:1, 24–47.

Hornbeck, Sean K. 1995. "Transnational Litigation and Personal Jurisdiction over Foreign Defendants." *Alabama Law Review* 59, 1389–1448.

Hovencamp, Herbert. 2005. *The Antitrust Enterprise: Principle and Execution.* Cambridge, MA: Harvard University Press.

Hudec, R.E. 2003. "Private Anticompetitive Behavior in World Markets: A WTO Perspective." *Antitrust Bulletin* 48, 1045.

Hufbauer, Gary Clyde and Nicholas K. Mitrokostas. 2003. *Awakening Monster: The Alien Tort Statute of 1789.* Peterson Institute.

Huffman, Max. 2007. "A Retrospective on Twenty-Five Years of the Foreign Trade Antitrust Improvements Act." *Houston Law Review* 44:2, 285–347.

Hughes, Justin. 2006. "Copyright and Incomplete Historiographies: Of Piracy, Propertization, and Thomas Jefferson." *Southern California Law Review* 79, 993–1084.

Ikenberry, G. John. 2009. *After Victory: Institutions, Strategic Restraint, and the Rebuilding of Order after Major Wars.* Princeton University Press.

Iselin, J.F. 1898. "The Protection of Intellectual Property." *Journal of the Society of the Arts* 46, 293–304.

Jacquemin, Alexis. 1993. "The International Dimension of European Competition Policy." *Journal of Common Market Studies* 31:1, 91–101.

Jägers, Nicola, Katinka Jesse, and Jonathan Verschuuren. 2013. "The Future of Corporate Liability for Extraterritorial Human Rights Abuses: The Dutch Case against Shell." *American Journal of International Law* 107, E36–E41.

Janey, Jay J., Greg Dess, and Victor Forlani. 2009. "Glass Houses? Market Reactions to Firms Joining the UN Global Compact." *Journal of Business Ethics* 90:3, 407–423.

Jennings, Robert Y. 1957. "Extraterritorial Jurisdiction and the United States Antitrust Laws." *British Yearbook of International Law* 33, 146–175.

Johns, Adrian. 2009. *Piracy: The Intellectual Property Wars from Gutenberg to Gates.* University of Chicago Press.

Jones, Clifford A. 1999. *Private Enforcement of Antitrust Law in the EU, UK, and USA.* Oxford University Press.

Jones, Clifford A. 2004. "Exporting Antitrust Courtrooms to the World: Private Enforcement in a Global Market." *Loyola Consumer Law Review* 16, 409–429.

Joseph, Sarah. 2004. *Corporations and Transnational Human Rights Litigation.* Hart Publishing Company.

Joyner, Christopher C. and Scott A. Lawson. 1985/1986. "The United States and UNESCO: Rethinking the Decision to Withdraw." *International Journal* 41:1, 37–71.

Juenger, Friedrich K. 1988. "Forum Shopping, Domestic and International." *Tulane Law Review* 63, 553, 606.

Juenger, Friedrich K. 1992. *Choice of Law and Multistate Justice.* Springer Netherlands.

Julian, Ku and Jide Nzelibe. 2006. "Do International Criminal Tribunals Deter or Exacerbate Humanitarian Atrocities." *Washington University Law Review* 84:4, 777–833.

Kaczmarek, Sarah and Abraham Newman. 2011. "The Long Arm of the Law: Extraterritoriality and the National Implementation of Foreign Bribery Legislation." *International Organization* 65, 745–770.

Kaeb, Caroline. 2008. "Emerging Issues of Human Rights Responsibility in the Extractive and Manufacturing Industries: Patterns and Liability Risks." *Northwestern Journal of International Human Rights* 6:2, 327–353.

Kahneman, Daniel and Amos Tversky. 1972. "Subjective Probability: A Judgment of Representativeness." *Cognitive Psychology* 3, 430.

Kaptein Muel. 2004. "Business Codes of Multinational Firms: What Do They Say?" *Journal of Business Ethics* 50, 15–31.

Kastellec, John and Jeffrey Lax. 2008. "Case Selection and the Study of Judicial Politics." *Journal of Empirical Legal Studies* 5:3, 407–446.

Kastellec, Johnathan P. 2010. "Panel Composition and Voting on the US Courts of Appeals Over Time." *Political Research Quarterly* 42:2, 226–256.

Katzenstein, Peter J. 1985. *Small States in World Markets.* Cornell University Press.

Keck, Margaret E. and Kathryn A. Sikkink. 1998. *Activists Beyond Borders: Advocacy Networks in International Politics.* Cornell University Press.

Keitner, Chimene I. 2008. "Conceptualizing Complicity in Alien Tort Cases." *Hastings Law Journal* 60, 61–104.

Keitner, Chimene I. 2012. "The Reargument Order in *Kiobel v. Royal Dutch Petroleum* and Its Potential Implications for Transnational Human Rights Cases." *ASIL Insights* 16, 10.

Kelemen, R. Daniel. 2011. *Eurolegalism: The Transformation of Law and Regulation in the European Union.* Harvard University Press.

Kelemen, R. Daniel and Eric Sibbitt. 2004. "The Globalization of American Law." *International Organization* 58:1, 103–136.

Keohane, Robert O. and Joseph S. Nye Jr. 1977. *Power and Interdependence: World Politics in Transition.* Little, Brown.

Kestenbaum, Lionel. 1982. "Antitrust's 'Extraterritorial' Jurisdiction: A Progress Report on the Balancing of Interests Test." *Stanford Journal of International Law* 18, 311–346.

Khan, B. Zorina. 2005. *The Democratization of Invention: Patents and Copyrights in American Economic Development 170–1920.* New York: Cambridge University Press.

Khan, B. Zorina and Kenneth L. Sokoloff. 2001. "History Lessons: The Early Development of Intellectual Property Institutions in the United States." *Journal of Economic Perspectives* 15:3, 233–246.

Kim, Won-Ki. 2003. "The Extraterritorial Application of U.S. Antitrust Law and Its Adoption in Korea." *Singapore Journal of International and Comparative Law* 7, 386–411.

Kinley, David and Junko Tadaki. 2004. "From Talk to Walk: The Emergence of Human Rights Responsibilities for Corporations at International Law." *Virginia Journal of International Law* 44, 931–1023.

Klein, Joel. 1999. "The War against International Cartels: Lessons from the Battlefront." US Department of Justice, available at www.justice.gov/atr/speech/war-against-international-cartels-lessons-battlefront.

Kmiec, Keenan D. 2004. "The Origin and Current Meanings of 'Judicial Activism'." *California Law Review* 92, 1441–1477.

Knox, John H. 2010. "A Presumption Against Extrajurisdictionality." *American Journal of International Law* 104, 351–396.

Knox, John H. 2011. "The Unpredictable Presumption Against Extraterritoriality." *Southwestern Law Review* 40, 635–653.

Kobrin, Stephen J. 2009. "Private Political Authority and Public Responsibility: Transnational Politics, Transnational Firms, and Human Rights." *Business Ethics Quarterly* 19:3, 349–374.

Koebele, Michael. 2009. *Corporate Responsibility under the Alien Tort Statute: Enforcement of International Law through U.S. Torts Law*. Martinus Nijhoff Publishers.

Koh, Harold Hongju. 1998. "How Is International Human Rights Law Enforced?" *Indiana Law Journal* 74, 1397–1417.

Koh, Harold Hongju. 2004. "Separating Myth from Reality about Corporate Responsibility Litigation." *Journal of International Economic Law* 7:2, 263–274.

Kolko, Gabriel. 1962. "American Business and Germany, 1930–1941." *The Western Political Quarterly* 15:4, 713–728.

Kontorovich, Eugene. 2014. "Kiobel Surprise: Unexpected by Scholars but Consistent with International Trends." *Notre Dame Law Review* 89, 1671–1694.

Kovacic, William E. 2006. "The Role of Non-Litigation Strategies: Advocacy, Reports, and Studies as Instruments of Competition Policy" in *Handbook of Research in Trans-Atlantic Antitrust* (Philip Marsden, ed.). Edward Elgar Publishers, 541–551.

Kovacic, William E. and Carl Shapiro. 2000. "Antitrust Policy: A Century of Legal and Policy Thinking." *Journal of Economic Perspectives* 14, 43–60.

Kozlowski, Mark. 2003. *The Myth of the Imperial Judiciary: Why the Right is Wrong About the Courts*. N.Y.U. University Press.

Kramer, Larry. 1991. "Vestiges of Beale: Extraterritorial Application of American Law." *The Supreme Court Review* 1991, 179–224.

Kramer, Larry. 1995. "Extraterritorial Application of American Law after the Insurance Antitrust Case: A Reply to Professors Lowenfeld and Trimble." *American Journal of International Law* 89:4, 750–758.

Krasner, Stephen D. 1976. "State Power and the Structure of International Trade." *World Politics* 28:3, 317–347.

Krasner, Stephen D. 1991. "Global Communications and National Power: Life on the Pareto Frontier." *World Politics* 43:3, 336–366.

Krasner, Stephen D. 1999. *Sovereignty: Organized Hypocrisy*. Princeton University Press.

Krisch, Nico. 2005. "International Law in Times of Hegemony: Unequal Power and the Shaping of the International Legal Order." *European Journal of International Law* 16:3, 369–408.

Ladas, Stephen P. 1949. "The Lanham Act and International Trade." *Law and Contemporary Problems* 14:2, 269–287.

Lamoreaux, Naomi R. and Kenneth L. Sokoloff. 2001. "Market Trade in Patents and the Rise of a Class of Specialized Inventors in the 19th Century United States." *American Economic Review* 91:2, 31–44.

Lande, Robert H. and Joshua P. Davis. 2008. "Benefits from Private Antitrust Enforcement: An Analysis of Forty Cases." *University of San Francisco Law Review* 42, 879.

Landers, Amy L. 2012. *Understanding Patent Law* (Second Edition). LexisNexis.

Langer, Maximo. 2011. "The Diplomacy of Universal Jurisdiction: The Political Branches and the Transnational Prosecution of International Crimes." *American Journal of International Law* 105:1, 1–50.

Lasserre, B. 2009. "The New French Competition Law Enforcement Regime." *Competition Law International* 5, 15–20.

Lasswell, Harold D. 1936. *Politics: Who Gets What, When, How*. Meridian Books.

Lauderdale, Benjamin E. and Tom S. Clark. 2012. "The Supreme Court's Many Median Justices." *American Political Science Review* 106:4, 847–866.

Laura, Ho, Catherine Powell, and Leti Volpp. 1996. "(Dis)assembling the Rights of Women Workers Along the Global Assembly Line." *Harvard Civil Rights and Civil Liberties Law Review* 31, 383–414.

Lax, Jeffrey R. 2011. "The New Judicial Politics of Legal Doctrine." *Annual Review of Political Science* 14, 131–157.

Layne, Christopher. 2012. "This Time It's Real: The End of Unipolarity and the *Pax Americana*." *International Studies Quarterly* 56:1, 203–213.

Leaffer, Marshall A. 1991. "Protecting United States Intellectual Property Abroad: Toward a New Multilateralism." *Iowa Law Review* 76, 273–308.

Leaffer, Marshall A. 2010. *Understanding Copyright Law* (Fifth Edition). Lexis Nexis.

Legro, Jeffrey W. 1996. "Culture and Preferences in the International Cooperation Two-Step." *American Political Science Review* 90:1, 118–137.

Letwin, William. 1981. *Law and Economic Policy in America: The Evolution of the Sherman Antitrust Act.* University of Chicago Press.

Leveque, Francois. 2007. "Merger Control: More Stringent in Europe than in the United States?" CERNA Working Paper.

Levy, David L. and Aseem Prakash. 2003. "Bargains Old and New: Multinational Corporations in Global Governance." *Business and Politics* 5:2, 131–150.

Lin, Li-Wen. 2009. "Legal Transplants Through Private Contracting: Codes of Vendor Conduct in Global Supply Chains as an Example." *American Journal of Comparative Law* 57, 711–744.

Litman, Jessica D. 1986. "Copyright, Compromise, and Legislative History." *Cornell Law Review* 72, 857–905.

Loevinger, Lee. 1964. "The Rule of Reason in Antitrust Law." *Virginia Law Review* 50, 23–35.

Lowenfeld, Andreas. 1979. "Public Law in the International Arena: Conflicts of Laws, International Law, and Some Suggestions for Their Interaction" in *II Recuiel des Cours.* Martinus Nijhoff, 311.

Lowenfeld, Andreas. 1997. "Forum Shopping, Antisuit Injunctions, Negative Declarations, and Related Tools of International Litigation." *American Journal of International Law* 91:2, 314–324.

Macedo, Stephen. 2004. *Universal Jurisdiction: National Courts and the Prosecution of Serious Crimes under International Law.* University of Pennsylvania Press.

Macey, Jonathan R. 2003. "Regulatory Globalization as a Response to Regulatory Competition." *Emory Law Journal* 52, 1353–1380.

Maier, Harold G. 1982. "Extraterritorial Jurisdiction at a Crossroads: An Intersection Between Public and Private International Law." *American Journal of International Law* 76, 280–320.

Maier, Harold G. 1983. "Interest Balancing and Extraterritorial Jurisdiction." *American Journal of Comparative Law* 31:4, 579–597.

March, James G. and Herbert A. Simon. 1958. *Organizations.* Wiley (USA).

Marcks, Eric. 2001. "Avoiding Liability for Human Rights Violations in Project Finance." *Energy Law Journal* 22, 301–333.

Mark, Gideon. 2012. "Private FCPA Enforcement." *American Business Law Journal* 49:3, 419–506.

Matheson, John H. 2008. "The Modern Law of Corporate Groups: An Empirical Study of Piercing the Corporate Veil in the Parent-Subsidiary Context." *North Carolina Law Review* 87, 1091–1155.

Matsushita, Mitsuo, Thomas J. Schoenbaum, and Petros C. Mavrodis. 2006. *The World Trade Organization: Law, Practice, and Policy* (Second Edition). Oxford University Press.

Mattei, Ugo and Jeffrey Lena. 2001. "U.S. Jurisdiction over Conflicts Arising Outside of the United States: Some Hegemonic Implications." *Hastings International and Comparative Law Review* 24, 381–400.

Mattli, Walter and Tim Büthe. 2005. "Global Private Governance: Lessons from a National Model of Setting Standards in Accounting." *Law and Contemporary Problems* 68, 225–262.

May, Christopher and Susan K. Sell. 2006. *Intellectual Property Rights: A Critical History*. Lynne Rienner.

McClellan, William Smith. 1912. *Smuggling in the Colonies at the Outbreak of the American Revolution: With Special Reference to the West Indies Trade*. (Monograph) Williams College.

McConnaughay, Philip J. 1999. "Reviving the Public Law Taboo in International Conflict of Laws." *Stanford Journal of International Law* 35, 255–312.

McDougal, Myres S. 1956. "Law as a Process of Decision: A Policy-Oriented Approach to Legal Study." *National Law Forum* 1, 53–72.

McGinnis, John O. 2003. "The Political Economy of Antitrust Harmonization." *William and Mary Law Review* 45:2, 549–594.

McGowan, Lee. 2010. *The Antitrust Revolution in Europe: Exploring the European Commission's Cartel Policy*. Edward Elgar Publishers.

Meessen, Karl M. 1989. "Competition of Competition Laws." *Northwestern Journal of International Law and Business* 10, 17–30.

Meessen, Karl M. 1996. *Extraterritorial Jurisdiction in Theory and Practice*. Martinus Nijhoff Publishers.

Mehra, Salil K. 2002–2003. "'A' Is for Anachronism: The FTAIA Meets the World Trading System." *Dickinson Law Review* 107:4, 763–774.

Mehra, Salil K. 2004. "More Is Less: A Law and Economics Approach to the International Scope of Antitrust Enforcement." *Temple Law Review* 77, 47–70.

Melitz, Marc J. and Giancarlo I.P. Ottaviano. 2008. "Market Size, Trade, and Productivity." *Review of Economic Studies* 75:1, 295–316.

Mendez, Juan E. 2001. "National Reconciliation, Transnational Justice, and the International Criminal Court." *Ethics and International Affairs* 15:1, 25–44.

Merges, Robert P. 2000. "One Hundred Years of Solicitude: Intellectual Property Law, 1900-2000." *California Law Review* 88, 2187–2240.

Merryman, John H. and Rogelio Pérez-Perdomo. 2007. *The Civil Law Tradition: An Introduction to the Legal Systems of Europe and Latin America*. Stanford University Press.

Michaels, Ralf. 2005. "Two Paradigms of Jurisdiction." *Michigan Journal of International Law* 27:4, 1003–1069.

Michaels, Ralf. 2011. "Empagran's Empire: International Law and Statutory Interpretation in the U.S. Supreme Court in the Twenty-First Century," available at http://scholarship.law.duke.edu/cgi/viewcontent.cgi?article=2942&context=faculty_scholarship.

Miller, Sidney T. 1910. "The Reasons for Some Legal Fictions." *Michigan Law Review* 8:8, 623–636.

Milner, Helen V. 1988. *Resisting Protectionism: Global Industries and the Politics of International Trade*. Princeton University Press.

Milner, Helen V. 1997. *Interests, Institutions, and Information*. Princeton University Press.

Mnookin, Robert H. and Louis Kornhauser. 1979. "Bargaining in the Shadow of the Law: The Case of Divorce." *The Yale Law Journal* 88:5, 950–997.

Moravcsik, Andrew T. 1991. "Negotiating the Single European Act: National Interests and Conventional Statecraft in the European Community." *International Organization* 45:1, 19–56.

Moravcsik, Andrew T. 1993. "Preferences and Power in the European Community: A Liberal Intergovernmentalist Approach." *Journal of Common Market Studies* 31:4, 473–524.

Moravscik, Andrew T. 1998. *The Choice for Europe: Social Purpose and State Power from Messina to Maastricht*. Ithaca, NY: Cornell University Press.

Moravcsik, Andrew T. 2000. "The Origins of Human Rights Regimes." *International Organization* 54: 217–252.

Muchilinksi, Peter T. 2001. "Human Rights and Multinationals: Is there a Problem?" *International Affairs* 77L1, 31–47.

Mwaura, Kiarie. 2012. "Internalization of Costs to Corporate Groups: Part-Whole Relationships, Human Rights Norms and the Futility of the Corporate Veil." *Journal of International Business and Law* 11, 85–110.

Neuman, Gerald L. 2008. "Import, Export, and Regional Consent in the Inter-American Court of Human Rights." *European Journal of International Law* 19:1, 101–123.

Neumeyer, Eric. 2005. "Do International Human Rights Treaties Improve Respect for Human Rights?" *Journal of Conflict Resolution* 49:6, 925–953.

Newman, Abraham. 2008. *Protectors of Privacy: Regulating Personal Data in the Global Economy*. Cornell University Press.

Nicolson, Rachel and Emily Howie. 2007. "The Impact of the Corporate Form on Corporate Liability for International Crimes: Separate Legal Personality, Limited Liability, and the Corporate Veil – An Australian Law Perspective." Paper for ICJ Expert Legal Panel on Corporate Complicity in International Crimes. Available at http://www.hrlrc.org.au/files/icj-paper-e-howie-and-r-nicolson-final-0207.pdf.

Nimmer, Melville B. 1967. "Implications of the Prospective Revisions of the Berne Convention and the United States Copyright Law." *Stanford Law Review* 19, 499–554.

Nollkaemper, Andre. 2007. "Internationally Wrongful Acts in Domestic Courts." *American Journal of International Law* 101:4, 760–799.

Noonan, C. 2008. *The Emerging Principles of International Competition Law*. Oxford University Press.

Norton, Joseph Jude. 1979. "Extraterritorial Jurisdiction of U.S. Antitrust and Securities Laws." *International and Comparative Law Quarterly* 28, 575–597.

Nye, Joseph. 1974. "Multinational Corporations in World Politics." *Foreign Affairs* 53, 153–175.

Ortblad, Vanessa. 2008. "Criminal Prosecution in Sheep's Clothing: The Punitive Effect of OFAC Freezing Sanction." *The Journal of Criminal Law and Criminology* 98:4, 1439–1465.

Paradise, Paul R. 1999. *Trademark Counterfeiting, Product Piracy, and the Dollar Threat to the U.S. Economy*. Quorum Books.

Parrish, Austen L. 2008. "The Effects Test: Extraterritoriality's Fifth Business." *Vanderbilt Law Review* 61, 1455–1505.

Parrish, Austen L. 2011. "*Morrison*, the Effects Test, and the Presumption against Extraterritoriality: A Reply to Professor Dodge." *Proceedings of the 105th Annual Meeting of the American Society of International Law* 105, 399–402.

Paust, Jordan J. 1992. "The Other Side of Right: Private Duties under International Law." *Harvard Human Rights Journal* 5, 51–64.

Paust, Jordan J. 1999. "Non-Extraterritoriality of Special Territorial Jurisdiction of the United States: Forgotten History and the Errors of Erdos." *Yale Journal of International Law* 24, 305–328.

Paust, Jordan J. 2002. "Human Rights Responsibilities of Private Corporations." *Vanderbilt Journal of Transnational Law* 35, 801–825.

Pelc, Krzyzstof. 2014. "The Politics of Precedent in International Law: A Social Network Analysis." *American Political Science Review* 108:3, 547–564.

Pelzman, Sam. 1976. "Toward a More General Theory of Regulation." *Journal of Law and Economics* 19, 211–240.

Peritz, Rudolph A. 1990. "A Counter-History of Antitrust Law." *Duke Law Journal* 2, 263–320.

Pettit, P.C.F. and C.J.D. Styles. 1982. "The International Response to the Extraterritorial Application of United States Antitrust Laws." *The Business Lawyer* 37:2, 697–715.

Pierson, Paul. 2000. "Increasing Returns, Path Dependence, and the Study of Politics." *American Political Science Review* 94:2, 251–267.

Pierson Jr., Robert W. 2007. "Extraterritorial Reach of U.S. Patent Law: Has the Federal Circuit Gone Too Far." *Fordham Intellectual Property Media and Entertainment Law Journal* 17, 651–692.

Pogge, Thomas. 2008. *World Poverty and Human Rights* (Second Edition). Polity Press.

Polinsky, Mitchell A. and Steven Shavell. 1998. "Punitive Damages: An Economic Analysis." *Harvard Law Review* 111:4, 869–962.

Ponsoldt, J.F. and C.D. David. 2006. "Comparison between US and EU Antitrust Treatment of Tying Claims against Microsoft: When Should the Bundling of Computer Software be Permitted." *Northwestern Journal of International Law and Business* 27, 421–452.

Posner, Richard A. 1970. "A Statistical Study of Antitrust Enforcement." *Journal of Law and Economics* 13:2, 365–419.

Posner, Richard. A. 1979. "The Chicago School of Antitrust Analysis." *University of Pennsylvania Law Review* 127:4, 925–948.

Posner, Richard A. 1981. "The Present Situation in Legal Scholarship." *The Yale Law Journal* 90, 1113–1130.

Poteet, Scott. 2011. "The Temporary Presence Defense to Patent Infringement and Its Applicability to Airline Security Patents." *Journal of Air Law and Commerce* 76, 559–593.

Priest, George and Benjamin Klein. 1984. "The Selection of Legal Disputes for Litigation." *Journal of Legal Studies* 13, 1–55.

Putnam, Tonya L. 2002. "Human Rights and Sustainable Peace" in *Ending Civil Wars: The Implementation of Peace Agreements* (Stephen J. Stedman, Donald Rothchild, and Elizabeth Cousens, eds.). Lynne Rienner, 237–272.

Putnam, Tonya L. 2009. "Courts Without Borders: Domestic Sources of U.S. Extraterritoriality in the Regulatory Sphere." *International Organization* 63, 459–490.

Quintanilla, Marcus S. and Christopher A. Whytock. 2011. "The New Multipolarity in International Judgments: Transnational Litigation, Foreign Courts, Foreign Judgments, and Foreign Law." *Southwestern Journal of International Law* 18, 31–52.

Rahl, James A. 1974. "American Antitrust and Foreign Operations: What Is Covered?" *Cornell International Law Journal* 8:1, 1–15.

Raustiala, Kal. 2002. "The Architecture of International Cooperation: Transgovernmental Networks and the Future of International Law." *Virginia Journal of International Law* 43, 1–92.

Raustiala, Kal. 2006. "The Evolution of Territoriality: International Relations & American Law" in *Territoriality and Conflict in an Era of Globalization* (Miles Kahler and Barbara Walter, eds.). Cambridge University Press.

Raustiala, Kal. 2009. *Does the Constitution Follow the Flag? The Evolution of Territoriality in U.S. Law*. Oxford University Press.

Raustiala, Kal and Christopher Sprigman. 2009. "The Piracy Paradox Revisited." *Stanford Law Review* 61:5, 1201–1225.

Reichman, Jerome H. 1996. "Enforcing the Enforcement Procedures of the TRIPS Agreement." *Virginia Journal of International Law* 37, 335–356.

Rich, Giles S. 1953. "Infringement Under Section 271 of the Patent Act of 1952." *Journal of the Patent Office Society* 35, 476–500.

Riesenfeld, Stefan A. 1954. "The New U.S. Patent Act in the Light of Comparative Law I." *University of Pennsylvania Law Review* 102:3, 291–322.

Rill, James F. 1988. "Antitrust: Where We Stand Today." *Antitrust Law Journal* 57:3, 3–11.

Ringer, Barbara A. 1966–1967. "The Stockholm Intellectual Property Conference of 1967." *Bulletin of the Copyright Society, USA* 14, 417–434.

Ringer, Barbara A. 1968. "The Role of the United States in International Copyright – Past, Present, and Future." *Georgetown Law Journal* 56, 1050–1079.

Risse, Thomas, Stephen C. Ropp, and Kathryn Sikkink. 1999. *The Power of Human Rights: International Norms and Domestic Change.* Cambridge University Press.

Roberts, Anthea. 2011. "Comparative International Law? The Role of National Courts in Creating and Enforcing International Law." *International and Comparative Law Quarterly* 60:1, 57–92.

Rodman, Kenneth A. 1998. "'Think Globally, Punish Locally': Non-State Actors, Multinational Corporations, and Human Rights Sanctions." *Ethics and International Affairs* 12, 19–41.

Rodman, Kenneth A. 2001. *Sanctions Beyond Borders: Multinational Corporations and US Economic Statecraft.* Rowman and Littlefield.

Rodrik, Dani. 2000. "How Far Will International Economic Integration Go?" *The Journal of Economic Perspectives* 14:1, 177–186.

Rogowski, Ronald. 1987. "Political Cleavages and Changing Exposure to Trade." *American Political Science Review* 81:4, 1121–1137.

Roht-Arriaza, Naomi. 2005. *The Pinochet Effect: Transnational Justice in the Age of Human Rights.* University of Pennsylvania Press.

Rosamond, Ben. 2005. "The Uniting of Europe and the Foundations of EU Studies: Revisiting the Neofunctionalism of Enrst B. Haas." *Journal of European Public Policy* 12:2, 237–254.

Rosendorff, B. Peter. 2005. "Stability and Rigidity: Politics and Design of the WTO's Dispute Settlement Procedure." *American Political Science Review* 99:3, 389–400.

Rosenthal, Douglas E. and William M. Knighton. 1982. *National Laws and International Commerce – The Problem of Extraterritoriality.* Routledge.

Ruggie, John G. 2008. *Embedding Global Markets.* Ashgate Publishing.

Ruggie, John G. 2013. *Just Business: Multinational Corporations and Human Rights.* WW Norton and Company.

Ryngaert, Cedric. 2008. *Jurisdiction in International Law.* Oxford University Press.

Saks, Michael J. and Robert F. Kidd. 1980–1981. "Human Information Processing and Adjudication: Trial by Heuristics." *Law & Society Review* 15:1, 123–160.

Salop, Steven C. and Lawrence J. White. 1986. "Economic Analysis of Private Antitrust Litigation." *Georgetown Law Journal* 74, 11–76.

Sandholtz, Wayne and Alec Stone Sweet (eds.). 1998. "Integration, Supranational Governance, and the Institutionalization of the European Polity" in *European Integration and Supranational Governance*. Oxford University Press.

Sandholtz, Wayne and Alec Stone Sweet. 2004. "Law, Politics, and International Governance" in *The Politics of International Law* (Christian Reus-Smit, ed.). Cambridge University Press, 238–271.

Sartori, Giovanni. 1970. "Concept Misformation in Comparative Politics." *American Political Science Review* 64, 1033–1053.

Scafuri, Allison L. 1965. "United States Antitrust Laws in Relation to American Businesses Operating in the Common Market." *Boston College Industrial and Commercial Law Review* 6:3, 561–567.

Scherer, F.M. 2009. "The Political Economy of Patent Policy Reform in the United States." *Journal of Telecommunications and High Technology Law* 7, 167–216.

Scheuerman, William E. 1999. "Free Market Anti-Formalism: The Case of Richard Posner." *Ratio Juris* 12:1, 80–95.

Schuman, Robert. 1950. "The Schuman Declaration," www.schuman.info/.

Scully, Eileen P. 2001. *Bargaining with the State from Afar: American Citizenship in Treaty Port China, 1844-1942*. Columbia University Press.

Segal, Jeffrey A. 1997. "Separation-of-Powers Games in the Positive Theory of Congress and Courts." *American Political Science Review* 91, 28–44.

Segal, Jeffrey. A. and Harold. J. Spaeth. 2002. *The Supreme Court and the Attitudinal Model Revisited*. Cambridge University Press.

Sell, Susan K. 2003. *Private Power, Public Law: The Globalization of Intellectual Property Rights*. New York: Cambridge University Press.

Shamir, Ronen. 2004. "Between Self-Regulation and the Alien Tort Claims Act: On the Contested Concept of Corporate Social Responsibility." *Law and Society Review* 38:4, 635–664.

Shavell, Steven. 1996. "Any Frequency of Plaintiff Victory is Possible." *Journal of Legal Studies* 25, 493–502.

Shaw, Jo. 1996. *Law of the European Union*. Palgrave MacMillan.

Shaw, Malcom. 2008. *International Law* (Sixth Edition). Cambridge University Press.

Shughart Jr., W.F. 1990. "Private Antitrust Enforcement: Compensation, Deterrence, or Extortion." *Regulation* 13, 53–61.

Sikkink, Kathryn A. 2011. *The Justice Cascade: How Human Rights Prosecutions are Changing World Politics*. W.W. Norton and Company.

Simmons Beth A. 1994. *Who Adjusts?* Princeton, NJ: Princeton University Press.

Simmons, Beth A. 2001. "The International Politics of Harmonization: The Case of Capital Market Regulation." *International Organization* 55:3, 589–620.

Simmons, Beth A. 2009. *Mobilizing for Human Rights: International Law in Domestic Politics*. Cambridge University Press.

Simmons, Beth A., Frank Dobbin, and Geoffrey Garrett. 2007. "The Global Diffusion of Public Policies: Social Construction, Coercion, Competition or Learning?" *Annual Review of Sociology* 33, 449–472.

Simmons, Beth A. and Zachary Elkins. 2004. "The Globalization of Liberalization: Policy Diffusion in the International Political Economy." *American Political Science Review* 98, 171–189.

Singer, David A. 2007. *Regulating Capital: Setting Standards for the International Financial System*. Cornell University Press.

Skidmore, David. 2005. "Understanding the Unilateralist Turn in U.S. Foreign Policy." *Foreign Policy Analysis* 1:2, 207–228.

Skowronek, Stephen. 1982. *Building a New American State: The Expansion of National Administrative Capacities 1877–1920*. Cambridge University Press.

Slaughter, Anne-Marie. 2003. "A Global Community of Courts." *Harvard International Law Journal* 44, 191–220.

Slaughter, Anne-Marie. 2004. "Sovereignty & Power in a Networked World Order." *Stanford Journal of International Law*. 40, 283–328.

Slaughter, Anne-Marie. 2009. *A New World Order*. Princeton University Press.

Sloss, David (ed.). 2009. *The Role of Domestic Courts in Treaty Enforcement: A Comparative Study*. Cambridge University Press.

Sloss, David L. "Kiobel and Extraterritoriality: A Rule without a Rationale." *Maryland Journal of International Law* 28, 241–255.

Small, David H. 1987. "Managing Extraterritorial Jurisdiction Problems: The United States Government Approach." *Law and Contemporary Problems* 50:3, 283–302.

Smith, James McCall. 2000. "The Politics of Dispute Settlement Design: Explaining Legalism in Regional Trade Pacts." *International Organization* 54:1, 137–180.

Snyder, Jack S. and Leslie Vinjamuri. 2003. "Trials and Errors: Principle and Pragmatism in Strategies of International Justice." *International Security* 28:3, 5–44.

Sokol, Daniel D. 2009. "The Future of International Antitrust and Improving Antitrust Agency Capacity." *Northwestern University Law Review* 103, 1081–1096.

Solberg, Thorvald. 1925. "Copyright Law Reform." *Yale Law Journal* 35:1, 48–75.

Solberg, Thorvald. 1930. "The Present Copyright Situation." *Yale Law Journal* 40:2, 184–214.

Spence, David B. 2011. "Corporate Social Responsibility in the Oil and Gas Industry: The Importance of Reputational Risk. *Chicago-Kent Law Review* 86, 59–86.

Sprigman, Christopher. 2005. "Fix Prices Globally, Get Sued Locally? U.S. Jurisdiction over International Cartels." *The University of Chicago Law Review* 72:1, 265–287.

Standford, J.S. 1978. "The Application of the Sherman Act to Conduct Outside the United States: A View from Abroad." *Cornell International Law Journal* 11,195–214.

Stanford, J.S. 1979. "Extraterritorial Application of United States Antitrust Law: A Canadian Comment." *Canada-United States Law Journal* 2, 176–178.

Stephen, Harris, H. 2001. *Competition Law Outside the United States.* American Bar Association.

Stephan, Paul B. 2005. "Global Governance, Antitrust, and the Limits of International Cooperation." *Cornell International Law Journal* 38, 173–218.

Stephan, Paul B. 2011. "Privatizing International Law." *Virginia Law Review* 97, 1573–1664.

Stephens, Beth, Judith Chomsky, Jennifer Green, Paul Hoffman, and Michael Ratner. 2008. *International Human Rights Litigation in U.S. Courts* (Second Edition). Martinus Nijhoff Publishers.

Stephens, Beth S. 2002. "Translating *Filartiga*: A Comparative International Law Analysis of Domestic Remedies for International Human Rights Violations." *Yale Journal of International Law* 27, 1–57.

Stephens, Pamela. 2007. "Spinning *Sosa*: Federal Common Law, the Alien Tort Statute, and Judicial Restraint." *Boston University International Law Journal* 25, 1–36.

Steuer, Richard M. 1999. "Executive Summary of the Antitrust Laws." Meyer Brown, LLP, http://library.findlaw.com/1999/Jan/1/241454.html.

Stigler, George. 1971. "The Theory of Economic Regulation." *Bell Journal of Economics and Management Science* 2, 3–21.

Stiglitz, Joseph E. 2011. "Brief of *Amicus Curiae* in Support of Petitioners Ester Kiobel *et al.*" Supreme Court of the United States, Nos. 11–88 and 10–1491.

Stolper, W.F. and P.A. Samuelson 1941. "Protection and Real Wages." *The Review of Economic Studies* 9:1, 58–73.

Stone Sweet, Alec and Thomas L. Brunell. 1998. "Constructing a Supranational Constitution: Dispute Resolution and Governance in the European Community." *American Political Science Review* 92:1, 63–81.

Swaine, Edward. 2001–2002. "The Local Law of Global Antitrust." *William and Mary Law Review* 43, 627–786.

Tamura, Jiro, J. Mark Gidley, and Douglas M. Jasinski. 2005. "Japan Cartels." *Global Competition Review*, available at jp.whitecase.com/files/Publication/19aa418a-df00-4956-b42b-0a5329a27367/Presentation/PublicationAttachment/04fb4494-c715-4d1a-9be1-132cb1512a86/article_Japan_Cartels.pdf.

Taylor, Graham R. 1979. "The Extraterritoriality of the Australian Antitrust Law." *Journal of International Law and Economics* 13, 273–310.

Thelen, Kathleen. 1999. "Historical Institutionalism in Comparative Politics." *Annual Review of Political Science* 2:1, 369–404.

Timberg, Sigmund. 1953. "Restrictive Business Practices: Comparative Legislation and the Problems that Lie Ahead." *American Journal of Comparative Law* 2:4, 445–473.

Timberg, Sigmund. 1957. *Remarks During the Discussion Period on the Subject "Extraterritorial Effects of the U.S. Antitrust Laws"*. Section of Antitrust Law, 105–110.

Timberg, Sigmund. 1973. "An International Antitrust Convention: A Proposal to Harmonize Conflicting National Policies towards the Multi-National Corporation." *Journal of International Law and Economics* 8, 157.

Townsend, James B. 1980. *Extraterritorial Antitrust: The Sherman Antitrust Act and U.S. Business Abroad*. Westview Press.

Trachtman, Joel P. 1993. "International Regulatory Competition, Externalization, and Jurisdiction." *Harvard International Law Journal* 34:1, 48–104.

Triggs, Gillian. 1979. "Extraterritorial Reach of United States Anti-Trust Legislation: The International Law Implications of the Westinghouse Allegations of a Uranium Procedures Cartel." *Melbourne University Law Review* 12, 250–283.

Tritell, Randolph and Elizabeth Kraus. 2015. *The Federal Trade Commission's International Antitrust Program* (May), www.ftc.gov/system/files/attachments/international-competition/the_ftcs_international_antitrust_program_may_2015.pdf.

Turk, Alexander J. 2009. *Judicial Review in EU Law*. Edward Elgar Publishing.

Turley, Jonathan. 1990. "When in Rome: Multinational Misconduct and the Presumption against Extraterritoriality." *Northwestern University Law Review* 84, 598–664.

Tversky, Amos and Daniel Kahneman. 1973. "Availability: A Heuristic for Judging Frequency and Probability." *Cognitive Psychology* 5, 207–232.

Tversky, Amos and Daniel Kahneman. 1974. "Judgment Under Uncertainty: Heuristics and Biases." *Science* 185, 1124–1131.

Twitchell, Mary. 1988. "The Myth of General Jurisdiction." *Harvard Law Review* 101, 610–681.

Van Schaak, Beth. "With All Deliberate Speed: Civil Human Rights Litigation as a Tool for Social Change." *Vanderbilt Law Review* 57, 2305–2348.

Van Waarden, Frans V. and Michaela Drahos. 2002. "Courts and (Epistemic) Communities in the Convergence of Competition Policies." *Journal of European Public Policy* 9:6, 913–934.

Varney, Christine. 2010. "The Capper-Volstead Act, Agricultural Cooperatives, and Antitrust Immunity." *The Antitrust Source.com* (December), www.jwhmlaw.com/pub/bjs/968756/Varney,%20Capper-Volstead%20article.pdf.

Velazquez, Manuel. 2005. "UNOCAL in Burma," www.scu.edu/ethics/practicing/focusareas/business/Unocal-in-Burma.html.

Verzijl, J.H.W. 1961. "The Controversy Regarding the So-Called Extraterritorial Effect of the American Antitrust Laws." *Netherlands International Law Review* 8, 3–30.

Viscusci, Kip, Joseph E. Harrington, and John M. Vernon. 2005. *Economics of Regulation and Antitrust.* Vol. 1 (Fourth Edition). The MIT Press.

Vogel, David. 1997. "Trading Up and Governing Across: Transnational Governance and Environmental Protection." *Journal of European Public Policy* 4:4, 556–571.

Von Mehren, Arthur T. 1983. "Adjudicatory Jurisdiction: General Theories Compared and Evaluated." *Tel Aviv Universities Studies in Law* 6, 50–122.

Wai, Robert. 2001. "Transnational Liftoff and Juridical Touchdown: The Regulatory Function of Private International Law in an Era of Globalization." *Columbia Journal of Transnational Law*, 40, 209–274.

Waller, Spencer Weber. 1990. "The Ambivalence of United States Antitrust Policy Towards Single Country Export Cartels." *Northwestern Journal of Law and Business* 10, 98–113.

Waller, Spencer Weber. 2002. "The United States as Antitrust Courtroom to the World: Jurisdiction and Standing Issues in Transnational Litigation." *Loyola Consumer Law Review* 14, 523–536.

Ward, Halina. 2000. "Securing Transnational Corporate Accountability through National Courts: Implications and Policy Questions." *Hastings International and Comparative Law Review* 24, 451–474.

Ward, James E. 2001. "Is That Your Final Answer – The Patchwork Jurisprudence Surrounding the Presumption against Extraterritoriality." *University of Cincinnati Law Review* 70, 715–750.

Wasserman, Howard M. 2011. "The Demise of 'Drive-By Jurisdictional Rulings'." *Northwestern University Law Review Colloquy* 105, 947–968.

Wasserman, Melissa F. 2007. "Divided Infringement: Expanding the Extraterritorial Scope of Patent Law." *New York University Law Review* 82:1, 281–309.

Watt, Horatia Muir. 2002. "Yahoo Cyber-Collision of Cultures: Who Regulates?" *Michigan Journal of International Law* 24, 673–698.

Watts, Michael J. 2005. "Righteous Oil? Human Rights, the Oil Complex and Corporate Social Responsibility." *Annual Review of Environmental Resources* 30, 373–407.

Wells, Wyatt. 2002. *Antitrust and the Formation of the Postwar World.* Columbia University Press.

Westin, David. 1987. "Enforcing Foreign Commercial Judgments and Arbitral Awards in the United States, West Germany, and England." *Law and Policy in International Business* 19, 325–360.

Wharton, Francis. 1905. *A Treastise on the Conflict of Laws, or Private International Law.* Vol. 1. The Lawyers' Cooperative Publishing Co.

White, Peter J. 2010. "International Judicial Assistance in Antitrust Enforcement: The Shortcomings of Current Practices and Legislation, and the Roles of International Organizations." *Administrative Law Review* 62, 263–278.

Whytock, Christopher A. 2009. "Domestic Courts and Global Governance." *Tulane Law Review* 84, 67–124.

Whytock, Christopher A. and Cassandra B. Robertson. 2011. "Forum Non Conveniens and the Enforcement of Foreign Judgments." *Columbia Law Review* 111:7, 1444–1521.

Wigger, Angela and Andreas Nolke. 2007. "Enhanced Roles of Private Actors in EU Business Regulation and the Erosion of the Rhenish Model of Capitalism." *Journal of Common Market Studies* 45, 487–513.

Wilks, Stephen. 2005. "Agency Escape: Decentralization or Dominance of the European Commission in the Modernization of Competition Policy?" *Governance* 18:3, 431–452.

Willison, Paige Keenan. 2000. Europe and Overseas Commodities Traders v. Banque Paribas London: Zero Steps Forward and Two Steps Back." *Vanderbilt Journal of Transnational Law* 33, 469–502.

Wils, Wouter P.J. 2003. "Should Private Antitrust Enforcement Be Encouraged in Europe?" *World Competition* 26:3, 473–488.

Wils, Wouter P.J. 2010. "The Increased Level of EU Antitrust Fines, Judicial Review and the ECHR." *World Competition* 33:1, 5–29.

Windsor, Duane. 2001. "The Future of Corporate Social Responsibility." *International Journal of Organizational Analysis* 9:3, 225–256.

Winston, Morton. 2002. "NGO Strategies for Promoting Corporate Social Responsibility." *Ethics and International Affairs* 16:1, 71–87.

Wood, Diane P. 1992. "The Impossible Dream: Real International Antitrust." *University of Chicago Legal Forum* 1992, 277–314.

Wood, Diane P. 1995. "The Internationalization of Antitrust Law: Options for the Future," remarks at the DePaul Law Review Symposium Cultural Conceptions of Competition: Antitrust in the 1990's, www.justice.gov/atr/public/speeches/0099.htm.

Wood, Diane P. 2004. "Cooperation and Convergence in International Antitrust: Why the Light is Still Yellow" in *Competition Laws in Conflict: Antitrust Jurisdiction in the Global Economy* (Richard A. Epstein and Michael S. Greve, eds.). AEI Press, 177–188.

Woods, Donnacadh. 2004. "Private Enforcement of Antitrust Rules – Modernization of the EU Rules and the Road Ahead." *Loyola Consumer Law Review* 16, 431–461.

Wuerth, Ingrid B. 2013. "The Supreme Court and the Alien Tort Statute: *Kiobel v. Royal Dutch Petroleum Co.*" *American Journal of International Law* 107, 601–621.

Wurmnest, Wolfgang. 2005. "A New Era for Private Antitrust Litigation in Germany? A Critical Appraisal of the Modernized Law against Restraints of Competition." *German Law Journal* 6:8, 1173–1189.

Yuan, Arthur Anyuan. 2004. "Enforcing and Collecting U.S. Money Judgments in China from a U.S. Judgment Creditor's Perspective." *George Washington International Law Review* 36, 757–782.

Zanettin, Bruno. 2002. *Cooperation between Antitrust Agencies at the International Level*. Hart Publishing.

Zia-Zarifi, Saman. 1999. "Suing Multinational Corporations in the U.S. for Violating International Law." *UCLA Journal of International Law and Foreign Affairs* 4, 81–147.

Zimmerman, James Michael. 1992. *Extraterritorial Employment Standards of the United States: The Regulation of the Overseas Workplace*. Quorum Books.

INDEX

Lightning Source UK Ltd.
Milton Keynes UK
UKOW05n1806010217
293406UK00003B/58/P

9 781107 137097